Advanced Studies in the Old Testament
Volume 2

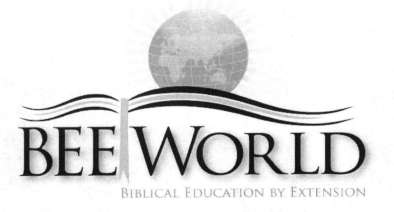

BEE WORLD

BIBLICAL EDUCATION BY EXTENSION

ADVANCED STUDIES IN THE OLD TESTAMENT, VOLUME 2

For information regarding permissions or special orders, please contact:

BEE World
International Headquarters
990 Pinon Ranch View, Ste. 100
Colorado Springs, CO 80907

ISBN: 978-1-937324-19-3

First Edition

Printed in the United States of America

1 2 3 4 5 6 7 8 9 10

10252012

Contents

Advanced Studies in the Old Testament, Vol.2

Introducing Advanced Studies in the Old Testament, Vol.2

This course is a continuation of *Advanced Studies in the Old Testament, Vol.1*. You should study the first course before taking *Advanced Studies in the Old Testament, Vol.2*. The entire course of study comprises eight units divided into twenty-four lessons. These twenty-four lessons tackle the Old Testament (OT) in chronological order to give you an overview of the history of God's workings with Israel.

Advanced Studies in the Old Testament, Vol.1 covered the Pentateuch, the pre-exilic historical books, and the wisdom literature. *Advanced Studies in the Old Testament, Vol.2* will cover the prophetic and postexilic historical books. The first course traced Israel's history from its birth and growing pains to its national glory and zenith in David's and Solomon's reigns. It went on to study the loss of its temple and its land to the Assyrians and the Babylonians.

This course never sees Israel at its peak strength. In fact, we see God's chosen nation divided, splitting into two separate nations. We then see these two nations consistently losing strength through disobedience to the covenant, despite God's faithful warnings and His call for repentance in order to return to covenant blessings. Eventually, both nations lose their land, and Judah loses the temple as it is carried off into captivity for seventy years. However, God remains faithful, enabling a remnant to return and rebuild the temple, though it is never as great as Solomon's was in its glory. The last book we study leaves the nation with a warning about the coming day of the Lord, the advent of the Messiah:

> Look, I will send you Elijah the prophet before the great and terrible day of the Lord arrives. He will encourage fathers and their children to return to me, so that I will not come and strike the earth with judgment. (Mal 4:5-6)

Course Objectives

By the end of this course you will be able to do the following:

- Discuss the general content of the thirty-nine OT books, including a key word for each book, and show how the books compare and contrast with one another
- Discuss how the background of each book helps you understand its message
- Apply the teachings of each book to your culture and ministry
- Discuss how a biblical theology of the OT helps us understand each book in light of the kingdom theme of Scripture
- Discuss a general chronology of Israel's history and the dates of key events, demonstrating how the time period relates to the message of each book
- Discuss the geography and peoples of the Old Testament world in order to appreciate cultural practices during those times
- Understand God's covenants with His people and how they applied to them
- Apply those covenants to us as well

Units of Study

The Old Testament can be studied in at least three different ways:

- *Sequential* (Scriptural): This method studies the books in the order in which they appear in the Old Testament.
- *Biographical* (Author): This method addresses all the books by one author together, for example, all books by Moses, then by Joshua, etc.
- *Chronological* (Time): This method studies the OT books in their historical context by placing the various prophetic and poetic writings with the corresponding historical books. We will follow this method in this two-part course.

The following list serves as our overall reference diagram for *Advanced Studies in the Old Testament Volume 2*:

Unit 1: Later Pre-Exilic Prophets

Lesson 1: Prophetic Literature and Obadiah

Lesson 2: Jonah and Amos

Lesson 3: Hosea and Micah

Unit 2: Early Prophetic Books

Lesson 4: Isaiah

Lesson 5: Nahum and Habakkuk

Lesson 6: Joel and Zephaniah

Unit 3: Exilic Prophets

Lesson 7: Jeremiah and Lamentations

Lesson 8: Daniel

Lesson 9: Ezekiel

Unit 4: Post-Exilic Books

Lesson 10: Ezra 1–6, Haggai and Zechariah

Lesson 11: Esther and Ezra 7–10

Lesson 12: Nehemiah and Malachi

As you plan your study schedule, set a goal date for finishing each unit. You can then divide this time into study periods for each lesson. We suggest that you try to do a lesson a week, or three lessons per month. You can do this if you study about one hour each day.

Lesson Organization

Please give careful attention to every part of the lesson:

- Title
- Introduction
- Outline
- Objectives

- Assignments
- Development
- Illustrations

The title, introduction, outline, and objectives provide a preview of the lesson that will help your mind to be more alert, receptive, and ready to learn. The lesson assignments clarify how to complete the lesson. Lessons follow the lesson outline, helping you reach the lesson objectives through comments, suggestions, and questions. Check your answers to each question with the ones the course gives, which will focus your attention again on the lesson's main points and make your learning more effective and long-lasting. Make special note of the maps, charts, and other illustrations because they will help you to identify with life in the Old Testament era, gripping your heart with the day-to-day issues and tremendous truths these Scriptures reveal. These illustrations are also useful for preaching and teaching.

Bibliography

Achtemeier, Elizabeth. *Preaching from the Old Testament*. Louisville: John Knox, 1989.

Arnold, Bill T. and Bryan E. Beyer. *Encountering the Old Testament: A Christian Survey*. Grand Rapids: Baker, 1999.

Baxter, J. Sidlow. *Baxter's Explore the Book*. Grand Rapids: Zondervan, 1960.

Fee, Gordon D. and Douglas Stuart. *How to Read the Bible for All Its Worth*. Grand Rapids: Zondervan, 1993.

Gleason L. Archer, *Encyclopedia of Bible Difficulties*.

Goldsworthy, Graeme. *Gospel and Kingdom*. Great Britain: Paternoster, 1981.

Hall, Terry. "How We Got Our Old Testament." *Moody*, January 1987, 32-34.

Hamington, Daniel J. "Introduction to the Canon," in *The New Interpreter*, vol. 1, ed. Lender E. Keck. Nashville: Abingdon, 1994.

La Sor, William, David A. Hubbard and Frederic W. Bush. *The Old Testament Survey: The Message, Form and Background*. Grand Rapids: Eerdmans, 1982, 1996.

Merrill, Eugene H. *Kingdom of Priests: A History of Old Testament Israel*. Grand Rapids: Baker, 1987.

Osborne, Grant R. "Biblical Theology," in *Baker Encyclopedia of the Bible*, vol. 1, ed. Walter A. Elwell. Grand Rapids: Baker Book, 1988.

Schultz, Samuel J. *The Old Testament Speaks*, 5th ed. San Francisco: Harper, 2000.

Smith, William. *Smith's Bible Dictionary*. Smith's, 1884. Public domain.

Walvoord, John F. and Roy B. Zuck. *Bible Knowledge Commentary*. Wheaton: SP Pub, Victor, 1983.

Wilkinson, Bruce and Kenneth Boa. *Talk Thru the Old Testament*. Nashville: Thomas Nelson, 1983.

Zuck, Roy B., ed. *A Biblical Theology of the Old Testament*. Chicago: Moody, 1991.

Unit 1: Later Pre-Exilic Prophets

Unit Introduction

Tragically, for many people the prophetic books of the Old Testament are the unknown territory of Scripture whose message lies hidden among the shadows of ignorance and neglect. But because these books comprise one fourth of the Bible, they present us with an indispensable portrait of God through the words of prophets who delivered God's message.

These men were not identical. Their lives and messages were stamped by individuality and diversity.

HISTORICAL	POETIC	PROPHETIC
Genesis Exodus Leviticus Numbers Deuteronomy	Job Psalms Proverbs Ecclesiastes Song of Solomon	Isaiah Jeremiah Lamentations Ezekiel Daniel
Joshua Judges Ruth 1 Samuel 2 Samuel 1 Kings 2 Kings 1 Chronicles 2 Chronicles		Hosea Joel Amos Obadiah Jonah Micah Nahum Habakkuk Zephaniah
Ezra Nehemiah Esther		Haggai Zechariah Malachi

- Isaiah would have been well known in his day, but Amos would not have had the opportunity to read Isaiah's book of prophecies.

- Haggai delivered his rebuke without being concerned about how he was understood, while Zechariah gave his balms of encouragement straight from the heart.

- Hosea sobbed his way through a message of divine love for the sinner, while Amos stomped his way through a message of divine wrath for sins.

- Isaiah felt at home in the royal palaces, while Micah felt at home in the rural places.

Some of the prophets were verbal geniuses; others were literary mediocrities. But through all of this uniqueness wove common threads of courage, conviction, and commitment. These men of varying personalities, backgrounds, interests, and styles shared a common mission: to represent, without a stutter, the God of heaven to the people of earth.

The scope of the prophets is great in many ways. Historically, their lives spanned over four hundred years, from the ninth century BC to the late fifth century BC. Many of them lived prior to the Babylonian exile in 586 BC, some of them lived through the exile, and others lived after it. Geographically, their messages extended over the known world of their day. Eighteen different nations become the targets of their verbal missiles. Chronologically, their messages could be labeled "from here to eternity," for they were just that—messages that applied to today and prophesied the future into eternity. Learning from the past, living in the present, and looking to the future, these preachers had a grip on the entire immovable plan of God. They saw the time when time would be no more.

These books may be neglected, but they cannot be negated. "The word of the Lord endures forever" (1 Pet 1:25, which references Isa 40:8). That word from the prophets will find its way to the core of life and godliness today as cleanly as it did when spoken over 2,500 years ago.

Unit Outline

Lesson 1: Prophetic Literature and Obadiah

Lesson 2: Jonah and Amos

Lesson 3: Hosea and Micah

Unit Objectives

By the end of this unit you will be able to do the following:

- Give the key word for each book and tell how it relates to the kingdom theme
- Discuss the historical background, timeline, and characteristics of the books in this unit
- Discuss how God's program and promises are advanced through a disobedient people and external opposition
- Discuss the books' purpose to encourage the Jewish people that God remembers His covenant with them
- Discuss the increasing danger to both Israel and Judah of exile for disobedience, according to the Palestinian covenant in Deuteronomy 28

Lesson 1: Prophetic Literature and Obadiah

Lesson Introduction

Chart of Prophetic Books

	BOOK	MEANING OF NAME	DATE	SCRIPTURE	KINGS*	THEME
Pre-Exilic	OBADIAH	"Worshipper of Jehovah"	840-830	2 Kings 8–12	Jehoram, Ahaziah, Athaliah, Joash (S)	Retribution
	JOEL	"Jehovah is God"	830-820	2 Kings 12	Joash (S)	Visitation
	JONAH	"Dove"	780-760	2 Kings 14	Jeroboam II (N)	Commission
	AMOS	"Burden bearer"	755-750	2 Kings 14	Jeroboam II (N)	Threatened
	HOSEA	"Salvation"	760-710	2 Kings 4–17	Jeroboam II, Zechariah, Shallum, Menahem, Pekahiah, Pekah, Hoshea (N)	Estrangement
	ISAIAH	"Jehovah is salvation"	740-690	2 Kings 15–21	Jotham, Ahaz, Hezekiah, Manasseh (S)	Salvation
	MICAH	"Who is like Jehovah"	735-700	2 Kings 15–20	Jotham, Ahaz, Hezekiah (S)	Arraignment
	NAHUM	"Compassionate" (Counselor, Comforter)	650-620	2 Kings 21–23	Manasseh, Amon, Josiah (S)	Doom
	ZEPHANIAH	"Hidden by Jehovah" (Protected)	630-620	2 Kings 22–23	Josiah (S)	Vindication
	HABAKKUK	"Embraced"	620-605	2 Kings 22–24	Josiah, Jehoahaz, Jehoiakim (S)	Justice
	JEREMIAH	"Established by Jehovah"	625-585	2 Kings 22–25	Josiah, Jehoahaz, Jehoiakim, Jehoiachin, Zedekiah (S), Nebuchadnezzar	Warning
EXILE	LAMENTATIONS	"Grieving"	585-580	2 Kings 25	Nebuchadnezzar	Disconsolate
	EZEKIEL	"Strength of God"	593-570	2 Kings 24–25	Zedekiah (S)	Glory
	DANIEL	"God is my Judge"	606-530	2 Kings 23–25; Ezra 1–4	Jehoiakim (S), Nebuchadezzar, Belshazzar, Darius, Cyrus	Dominion
POST-EXILE	HAGGAI	"Festal"	520	Ezra 5–6	Zerubbabel, Darius I (Persian)	Consider
	ZECHARIAH	"Remembered by Jehovah"	520-480	Ezra 5–6	Zerubbabel, Darius I, Xerxes	Consummation
	MALACHI	"My messenger"	430-420	Nehemiah 13	Artaxerxes, Darius II	Apostasy

*N = Northern kingdom   S = Southern kingdom

Prophets served as covenant *preachers* to get the covenant *people* to show covenant *behavior* based in the Law. Israel's responsibility was to show faith in God by obeying the Mosaic covenant, while God was responsible to uphold His promises in the Abrahamic covenant.

The prophets of the Old Testament were unique men. Called by God to an exciting, but at times unenviable task, these tender men of steel told the people what they needed to hear and brushed aside the temptation to say what they wanted to hear.

Refusing their lips the luxury of uttering palatable verbal tidbits, these mouthpieces of God sounded forth stinging condemnations of sin. Seldom did they hesitate; rarely did they flinch; never did they fail. They clothed God's words with humanness, but never confined them to the temporal sphere. Those words were destined by heaven to be spoken, not stored—so speak the prophets did!

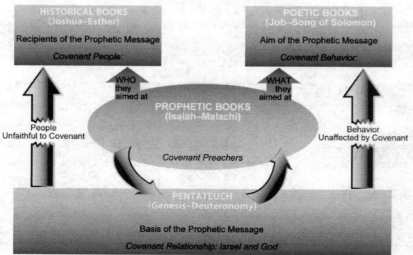

Purpose of the Prophetic Books

Lesson Outline

Topic 1: Biblical vs. Pagan Prophecy

Topic 2: Interpreting Prophetic Literature

Topic 3: Israel and the Church

Topic 4: Guidelines for Interpreting and Teaching

Topic 5: The Minor Prophets

Topic 6: Introduction to Obadiah

Topic 7: Obadiah

Topic 8: Knowing, Being, Doing

Lesson Objectives

By the end of this lesson you will be able to do the following:

- Discuss how to discern between true and false prophets
- Explore the difference between the different functions of prophecy
- Explain the various literary forms that prophets used
- Discuss the importance of distinguishing between Israel and the church
- Discover the distinctive characteristics of the Minor Prophets
- Discuss God's accusations against Edom and blessings on His people
- Evaluate the judgments and blessings of the day of the Lord

Topic 1: Biblical vs. Pagan Prophecy

Christians today need to apply biblical standards to modern prophets in the church. Sometimes we act as though the Old Testament is the only place prophetic guidelines are found. In 1 Corinthians 12–14, while speaking of spiritual gifts, the apostle Paul discusses how the Corinthians had been led into speaking pagan prophecy. In 1 Corinthians 12:2-3 Paul says,

> You know that when you were pagans you were often led astray by speechless idols, however you were led. So I want you to understand that no one speaking by the Spirit of God says, "Jesus is cursed," and no one can say, "Jesus is Lord," except by the Holy Spirit.

Just because someone claims to be a Christian or attends a Christian church and claims to speak for God, it does not relieve the believer of his or her responsibility to apply the biblical prophetic tests to his message.

What should the church do today with a person who claims to be a true prophet of God but fails to fulfill the Old Testament prophetic tests? For example, how should the church respond if one makes a prediction which proves false, or the prophet falls into moral sin?

Assignment

- Please read 1 Corinthians 12–14 on the proper use of the spiritual gifts.
- Please read "Biblical vs. Pagan Prophecy."

Biblical vs. Pagan Prophecy

Definitions:

- The Hebrew word for prophet, *nabi*, carries the idea of one who is a mouthpiece for Yahweh, chosen to proclaim God's direct words to man. However, the same word is used for false prophets.

- The Greek word for "prophet" refers to "one who speaks for God, proclaiming what God wants to make known…" (*Friberg Lexicon*).

Why Should We Have Requirements for Accepting a Prophet as True?

- Accuracy in what God says is one of the most important things about Him. Since God is truth, it is vital that we know accurately what He is saying to us.

- Even if knowing God's words is not important to us, it was to those who wrote Scripture. The OT prescribes death for false prophecies (Deut 18:20)!

- Many today claim to speak prophetic messages from God. Therefore, since we must know how to distinguish true from false prophets, this study compares and contrasts them.

Common Elements of True and False Prophecy

Call: Both prophets of Yahweh and pagan prophets saw themselves as representatives individually appointed by a deity to speak to man. Both contain the same formula: "I send you." The prophecies to King Zimri-Lim (a king of Mari who lived in the 1700s BC) and to David (2 Sam 7:8-16) both appear in the first person as they seek to report the direct words of a deity, and both have punishments for disobedience and blessings for obedience.

Signs: Both may have received their prophecy with accompanying signs (Ex 4:29-31), purification of the mouth (Isa 6), or from dreams (Jer 23:25, 27) and visions (Isa 1:1).

Content: Both included promises of protection in battles.

Style: Both prophets used similar literary forms (e.g., lawsuit and suzerain-vassal treaty).

Modern Pagan Prophecy

Temple mediums in Buddhist temples of Singapore claim to know the future (e.g., successful lottery numbers) through being controlled by a spirit. Supposed auspicious days are "prophetically" pre-determined as days where wealth can be gained during festivals such as marriages on these days. Since these predictions lack a 100-percent accuracy rate, they are false prophecies to be avoided.

Many who claim the name of Christ today predict things which do not come true. Due to the mandate for 100-percent accuracy in Deuteronomy 18:18-20, these persons must be deemed false prophets.

Conclusion

There's no single right way to determine the validity of a prophet's testimony. However, the character of a true godly prophet would be consistent with the holy and righteous nature of God. The high moral quality and spiritual content of the message itself would separate it from false prophets' man-pleasing words. Finally the truth in the believer's own heart would confirm the truth of the prophet's word.

QUESTION 1

The Hebrew word for "prophet" is used only for true prophets. *True or False?*

QUESTION 2

Those who claim the name of Christ today and predict things that do not come true can be properly classified as false prophets. *True or False?*

QUESTION 3

Which of the following are distinctive signs of a true prophet? *(Select all that apply.)*

    A. Seeing oneself as called by a deity to speak with man

    B. The truth in the believer's heart that confirms the prophet's word

    C. Giving prophecy accompanied by signs and wonders

    D. The distinctive form in which a prophecy is given

    E. Giving prophecy in the name of the Lord (Yahweh)

    F. The character of the prophet is consistent with God's holy nature

QUESTION 4

Please read through the following three questions and choose one to answer in your Life Notebook:

- In light of this study, what do you think of the following definition of prophecy by Wayne Grudem: "Prophecy is telling something that God has spontaneously brought to mind." Is it true prophecy even if it is erroneous? Why or why not?

- Do you think the teaching that all believers can prophesy has biblical support (1 Cor 12:29 vs. 1 Cor. 14:1)? Support your answer with Scripture.

- What would you say to someone who claimed that his prophecy is inspired but not equal in authority to Scripture? (In other words, they argued for different levels of inspiration or inerrancy.) Support your answer with Scripture.

Topic 1 Key Points

- The Hebrew word for prophet (*nabi*) carries the idea of one who is a mouthpiece for Yahweh; however, the same word is used for false prophets.

- Those in the church today who predict things that do not come true can be properly classified as false prophets.

- No single test is sufficient to authenticate a prophet, but his character should be consistent with God's holy nature

Topic 2: Interpreting Prophetic Literature

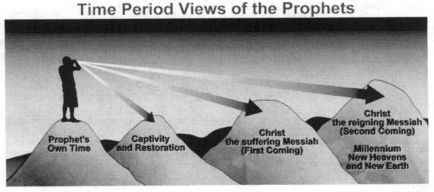

One problem Christians commonly have with prophecy is their ignorance of eschatology, or the study of the end times. Most Christians cannot state a biblical view of future things and therefore find it difficult to fit the prophetic eschatology into a larger framework. To understand these writings fully, one must know something about the biblical covenants and eschatological events in succession. Though prophecy does not always foretell (predict), significant amounts of biblical prophecy at the time did foretell. It is helpful to have a basic biblical timeframe to put prophetic events into. For example, what would you do with the following verses if you did not understand that they apply to different periods of time?

- "Proclaim this among the nations: Prepare for a holy war! Call out the warriors! Let all these fighting men approach and attack! **Beat your plowshares into swords, and your pruning hooks into spears!** Let the weak say, 'I too am a warrior!'" (Joel 3:9-10, emphasis added).

- "**They will beat their swords into plowshares, and their spears into pruning hooks.** Nations will not take up the sword against other nations, and they will no longer train for war" (Isa 2:4, emphasis added).

Assignment

- Please read "Interpreting Prophetic Literature."

Interpreting Prophetic Literature

Problems and Tips in Interpreting Prophecy (Fee, 149f.)

Inaccurate Presuppositions: We tend to think that prophecy always concerns predictions about the future, but that is actually only part of the story. Prophecies actually have themes of repentance and judgment. These two elements appear in the following distinction of the two types of prophecies.

1. *Ethical*: The prophets relate to the *present moral* life of the hearers. All prophetic books contain ethical teaching that demands repentance from the hearers. The foundation of their preaching was the Mosaic covenant. Often they referred to the blessings and curses of obeying or disobeying the Law (Lev 26; Deut 28).

2. *Predictive*: The prophets also relate to *future eschatological* events about the Messiah, Israel, Judah, and other nations (but never the church, which is not mentioned in the OT; see Eph 3:2-11). Here the reference is to the Abrahamic covenant. In broad terms, the predictive prophecies can be categorized into two types:

Fulfilled

Concerning *Israel, Judah, and other nations*

Concerning *Jesus' first advent*

Unfulfilled

Concerning *Israel, Judah, and other nations* (mostly relating to the judgment preceding the kingdom and especially about the kingdom age itself).

Concerning *Jesus' Second Advent*, specifically His return to earth after the tribulation to set up His Millennial Kingdom.

Hearer Orientation: The Hebrew word for "prophet" is related to the word for "mouth" since prophets spoke for God. This means the writings actually served better as oral sermons than written literature. Thus, structural markers in the text itself, such as new paragraphs and subjects, should carry more weight than chapter and verse divisions that were added much later.

Incomplete Background Data with Non-Chronological Orientation: The longer books (Major Prophets) are essentially "collections of spoken oracles, not always presented in their original chronological sequence, often without hints as to where one oracle ends and another begins, and often without hints as to their historical setting. And most of the oracles were spoken in poetry!" (Fee, 150-51). Prophets wrote to people familiar with the Law, so they alluded to events, practices, words, etc. without explanation. Examples include:

1. Isaiah's use of an exodus motif (see Isa 4:5; 10:24-26; 11:16; 43:14-21; 48:20-21; 51:9-10).

2. Amos' ironic use of traditions related to Israel's election (Amos 3:2), the day of the Lord (Amos 5:18-20), and the Passover (Amos 5:17).

3. The secular "suzerain-vassal" treaty relationship model. In this model, God acts as the "Great King" (suzerain) towards His people (who represent the vassal) according to the (conditional) Mosaic covenant. In this relationship, prophets serve as messengers of Yahweh who have stood in His council and speak by His authority. They accuse Israel (Yahweh's disobedient vassal) of breaching the covenant, and threaten the covenant's curses. Compare the prophets' accusations with the covenant *stipulations* (see Hos 4:2 with Ex 20:7, 13-16), and their warnings with the covenant *curses* (see Isa 1:7-8 with Deut 28:33, 51–52 and Isa 1:9 with Deut 28:62; 29:23).

4. The *promise* or salvation oracle of the prophets also pictures God's restoration of His people after judgment. This is based on God's covenant promise to grant the Promised Land to Abraham's descendants. This covenant was originally made with Abraham, extended to David, and was even foreseen by Moses (Deut 30:1-10). Prophets also anticipate the ultimate fulfillment of the Abrahamic promises (see Hos 1:10) and the establishment of the Davidic throne (see Isa 11). There are three common elements: reference to the future, mention of radical change, and mention of blessing (Amos 9:11-15; Hos 2:16-22; 2:21-23; Isa 45:1-7; Jer 31:1-9).

5. The *covenant lawsuit* (Isa 3:13-26; Hos 3:3-17; 4:1-19, etc.) is still another form of prophecy, depicting God "imaginatively as the plaintiff, prosecuting attorney, judge, and bailiff in a court case against the defendant, Israel" (Fee, 150-51).

6. The *woe oracle* (Mic 2:1-5; Hab 2:6-8; Zeph 2:5-7) makes use of the common word "woe" (NASB), which Israelites cried out when experiencing disaster, death, or funeral mourning. "Woe oracles contain three unique elements: They announce distress or woe, give the reason for it, and predict doom.

Historical Distance: Even if we know the historical setting, it is very much different than we are used to today. Therefore, it is important for us to be familiar with the date, audience, and circumstances of the prophetic passages we read. In general terms, the sixteen prophets wrote in a relatively small time period of only four centuries from Obadiah (845 BC) to Malachi (425 BC). This period was characterized by three factors (adapted from Fee, 157):

1. *Unprecedented upheaval* in the political, military, economic, and social realms

2. *Religious unfaithfulness* on Israel's part to the Mosaic covenant

3. *Shifts* in populations and national boundaries

Lack of appreciation for poetry because people do not read poetry as often as they do prose.

Unfamiliarity with prophetic books since they are rarely preached and taught. They constitute 17 writings to six different audiences in three time periods, with many geographical and situation changes.

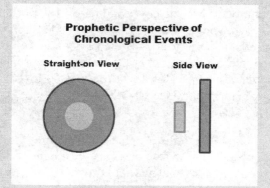

Dual Eschatological Viewpoint: The prophets themselves often blur chronological distinctions. They often depict as a single event two or more events which we now know to be separate. In this scheme, the fulfillment of the nearer event is like a "down payment" guaranteeing that the entire vision will be eventually fulfilled. This has been diagrammed as different perspectives on two disks. From a front view, the smaller one appears to be immediately in front of a larger one. But "from the perspective of subsequent history [we can] see them from a side view and thus see how much distance there is between them" (Fee and Stuart, 164).

QUESTION 5

Ethical prophecy refers to future eschatological events. *True or False?*

QUESTION 6

Please match the form or practice the prophets used to communicate with the corresponding explanation of it.

Form	Explanation
The suzerain-vassal treaty	Pictures God restoring His people after judgment
The promise or salvation oracle	Pictures God imaginatively in a court case against Israel
The covenant lawsuit	Contain a distress, its reason, and the predicted doom
The woe oracle	God acts as the Great King toward His people

QUESTION 7

Which of the following is a characteristic of prophecy that can lead to misinterpreting it?

    A. A lack of appreciation for poetry

    B. Religious unfaithfulness on Israel's part

    C. Depicting as a single event several things that we now know to be separate

    D. Unprecedented upheaval in political, military, economic, and social realms

Topic 2 Key Points

- **Ethical prophecy** refers to how the teaching relates to the *present moral* life of the hearers, while **predictive prophecy** relates *future eschatological* events about the Messiah, Israel, Judah, and other nations (but never the church).

- Prophets used many literary forms to communicate their message:

  In the suzerain-vassal treaty, God acts as the Great King.

  In the salvation oracle, God restores His people after judgment.

  In the covenant lawsuit, God is pictured in a court case against Israel.

  The woe oracle contains a distress, its reason, and the prediction of doom.

- Most difficulties with prophetic interpretation lie with the reader, but one problem is that the prophets themselves often saw separate events as a single event.

Topic 3: Israel and the Church

The *Law* can refer to several things in Scripture. However, in this study, the Law refers to the five books of Moses. The Law as a code of conduct no longer has direct bearing on Christians, since it was given only to Israel.

Israel refers to the physical descendants of Abraham through Isaac and Jacob. This includes anyone from the twelve tribes that came from Jacob, his wives, and their handmaidens. It also includes both believing and unbelieving descendants of Jacob. A good synonym is the word "Jew."

The *church* refers to the universal family of persons trusting Christ by faith for salvation. It began on the day of Pentecost and includes both Jews and Gentiles (Acts 11:15 looks to Acts 1:5; 2:1 as "the beginning").

Your view on Israel and the church is one of the most important interpretive foundations to decide when studying the prophetic genre.

Assignment

- Please read "Israel and the Church."

Israel and the Church

Why must we discern between Israel and the church?

Interpreting the Prophets:

The issue concerns whether one will use the normal, grammatical-historical method of interpreting the prophets. When one does so, "Israel" will always refer to the literal descendants of Abraham (rather than to the church).

The prophets often prophesy events concerning Israel that have not been fulfilled, e.g., Ezekiel's temple and land (Ezk 37; 40–48). With apparently unfulfilled prophecies, the interpreter has but a few options:

1. Consider the prophecy an error and ignore it (not an option for the evangelical believer).

2. Pick a past event and try to make the prophecy apply to it, making it appear as if it were fulfilled.

3. Spiritualize the prophecy so that it finds fulfillment only in the church (abandon normal use of language).

4. Look for future fulfillment of the prophecy with a literal nation of Israel (i.e., take the prophecy at face value).

Applying the Prophets

"All Scripture is profitable for teaching, rebuking, correction, and training in righteousness" (2 Tim 3:16); this includes the prophetic books. As obsolete elements of the Law can still be applied in principle, so the prophetic literature applies today.

QUESTION 8

If you believe the promises to Israel in the Old Testament are now fulfilled by the church, it is likely you use the normal, grammatical-historical method of interpreting the prophets. *True or False?*

QUESTION 9

Generally speaking, the teachings in the prophets apply to Christians in principle the same way that obsolete elements of the Law still apply. *True or False?*

QUESTION 10

Read the following statements and decide whether you agree or disagree with the teaching. Open your Life Notebook and record your thoughts on these vital subjects.

- The church is the new Israel because it has replaced national or ethnic Israel due to that nation's rejection of Christ.
- A prophetic future for a believing remnant of national Israel still exists on God's timetable.
- The term "Israel" in the Bible always applies to ethnic descendants of Abraham.
- The abolishment of the Mosaic covenant with Israel means that the nation no longer exists as God's people.
- The metaphor of God divorcing Israel (Isa 50:1; Jer 3:1) meant that Jews would never again be the people of God.

Topic 3 Key Points

- When a person uses the normal, grammatical-historical method of interpreting the prophets, Israel will always refer to the literal descendants of Abraham, rather than to the church.
- Contrary to the opinions of some Christians who believe prophetic books are unimportant, these books contain principles that can be applied in principle to the believer today.
- Your view on Israel and the church is one of the most important interpretive matters to decide when studying the prophetic genre.

Topic 4: Guidelines for Interpreting and Teaching

Three Periods of the Prophets

Before Babylonian Exile (930-586 BC)	Babylonian Exile (586-516 BC)	After Babylonian Exile (516-424 BC)
DIVIDED KINGDOM PERIOD (930-722 BC) **OBADIAH** (848-41 to Edom) **JOEL** (835-796 to Judah) **JONAH** (782-750 to Assyria) **AMOS** (782-739 to Israel) **HOSEA** (755-715 to Israel) **MICAH** (740-690 to Judah) **ISAIAH** (740-680 to Judah)	**DANIEL** (606 to Babylon) **EZEKIEL** (593-571 to Babylon) **LAMENTATIONS** (586 to Judah)	**HAGGAI** (520 to Judah) **ZECHARIAH** (520-518 to Judah) **MALACHI** (435-424 to Judah)
SURVIVING KINGDOM PERIOD (722-586 BC) **NAHUM** (661-612 to Assyria) **ZEPHANIAH** (630 to Judah) **JEREMIAH** (627-586 to Judah) **HABAKKUK** (610-599 to Judah)	*(Dates refer to years of their ministries.)*	

Observations:

- Most prophets ministered before the exile; God gave plenty of warning before judgment.
- Most prophets preached to Judah; God made special effort to protect the Davidic line.
- All Major Prophets preached to Judah.

- There were no major post-exilic prophets.

- God's faithfulness to communicate with His people extended even into judgment (via Ezekiel and Daniel); we also should never give up seeking to restore errant believers.

- Prophets made predictions concerning four nations as a major concern—Judah, Israel, Assyria, and Edom. One could also add Babylon and other nations noted in parts of various prophetic writings (e.g., Isa 13–23; Jer 46–51, etc.).

All of these observations help us to understand, interpret, and apply the various prophetic messages. The more you know about the distinctive characteristics of prophecy in general, the better you'll understand the message the prophet intended.

Assignment

- Please read "Guidelines for Interpreting and Teaching."

Guidelines for Interpreting and Teaching

Understanding the big picture is often a good place to start. Make the effort to develop a consistent eschatological framework for yourself. Systematize the biblical revelation about the future. It might be helpful for you to chart or outline a whole book before trying to study just a part of it.

Identify the historical context of OT prophecy and then make efforts to help others understand it. In particular, you need to understand the history surrounding the two major exiles (in 722 BC and 586 BC), since the prophets are primarily grouped around them.

Keep in mind that the prophets spoke to a people "under the Law" who were accountable to the Law—believers today are not under the Law. Hence, we must ask this question: Are the sins pointed out by the prophets also sins under the new covenant?

Also, remember to not confuse God's plan for national Israel with His plan for the church. Don't make vain efforts to make the church fit into the Old Testament.

Relate the prophets to the governing principles of Deuteronomy 28–30. The prophets frequently call attention to the curses, which result from disobedience to the Law, and to the possibility of blessings, which are based on repentance.

Learn to look for the various types of "oracles" within a prophetic book. They often alternate between judgment oracles and salvation oracles. The salvation oracles look to the future, when God's discipline has run its course, and He fulfills His ultimate intention to bring blessing (Gen 12; Deut 30). Since this is most often linked to Israel's future under her Messiah when He establishes His kingdom, this is where we often find "prophecies" related to the *Messianic era,* or the second coming.

One must understand the developing motif within the Old Testament of God's intention to fulfill the New Covenant. Learn the terminology of this emerging motif in order to heighten your sensitivity to New Covenant prophetic expectations. Recognize that the New Covenant was inaugurated at the cross and is now operational, though it is not totally fulfilled yet.

Use teaching aids to help your audience. Not all the material in the prophetic books is eschatological, but a great deal is. When teaching or preaching about these sections, see if charts or pictures can help people see the overall plan and how the details fit into it.

QUESTION 11

On what two events of history are the prophets primarily centered?

    A. The two advents of the Messiah

    B. The two major exiles of Israel and Judah

    C. The exodus and crossing the Jordan

    D. David's reign and Messiah's reign

QUESTION 12

Which of the following statements is true?

    A. Most prophets ministered after the exile

    B. More prophets preached to Israel than Judah

    C. God stopped communicating with His people when they went into judgment

    D. All Major Prophets preached to Judah.

Topic 4 Key Points

- The prophets center on the two major exiles—722 BC and 586 BC—so understanding the history surrounding these events is important.
- God's faithfulness to communicate with His people extended even into judgment (via Ezekiel and Daniel); we also should never give up seeking to restore errant believers.

Topic 5: The Minor Prophets

The twelve short books that make up the Minor Prophets—so called because of their length, not lesser importance—were originally grouped together on one scroll in the Hebrew Bible, and were called the Twelve. Together, they cover a time span of about four hundred years (800-400 BC). Theologically, the Minor Prophets focus on warnings of impending judgment, teachings on righteous living, encouragement to the faithful and oppressed, and predictions of God's future plans.

Nonwriting Prophets					Major Prophets				Minor Prophets											
Samuel	Nathan	Elijah	Micaiah	Elisha	Isaiah	Jeremiah	Ezekiel	Daniel	Hosea	Amos	Joel	Micah	Habakkuk	Zephaniah	Obadiah	Jonah	Nahum	Haggai	Zechariah	Malachi
United Kingdom	Divided Kingdom						Babylon		Israel	Judah						Nineveh		Judah		
Monarchy							Exile		Pre-Exile									Post-Exile		

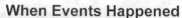

When Events Happened

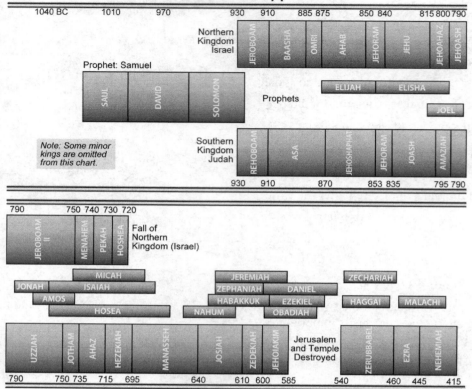

Assignment

- Please read "The Minor Prophets."

The Minor Prophets

The Minor Prophets are considered to be a parallel unit to Isaiah, Jeremiah, and Ezekiel and were written together on one scroll. Early church fathers called this grouping the Minor Prophets, referring to the small size of these books in comparison with the longer prophetic books, and not at all suggesting that they are of minor importance.

In both the traditional Jewish canon and in more modern Bibles, these works are arranged in what was thought to be their chronological order: (1) the books that came from the period of Assyrian power (Hosea, Joel, Amos, Obadiah, Jonah, Micah), (2) those written about the time of the decline of Assyria (Nahum, Habakkuk, Zephaniah), and (3) those dating from the post-exilic era (Haggai, Zechariah, Malachi). On the other hand, their order in the Septuagint—the earliest Greek translation of the OT—is slightly different: Hosea, Amos, Micah, Joel, Obadiah, Jonah, Nahum, Habakkuk, Zephaniah, Haggai, Zechariah, Malachi. The order of the first six was probably determined by their length, except for Jonah which is placed last among them because of its different nature.

It appears that within a century after the composition of Malachi, the Jews had put the twelve shorter prophecies together in a book of prophetic writings that was received as canonical and paralleled the three major prophetic books of Isaiah, Jeremiah, and Ezekiel. The twelve Minor Prophets appear after the Major Prophets in Bibles today.

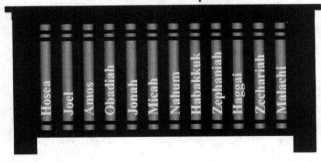

The Minor Prophets

Hosea • Joel • Amos • Obadiah • Jonah • Micah • Nahum • Habakkuk • Zephaniah • Haggai • Zechariah • Malachi

QUESTION 13

Please match the chronological grouping of the books in the traditional Jewish canon with the political situation of the time.

Chronological Order	*Political Situation*
First	Those dating from the post-exilic era
Second	The books that came from the period of Assyrian power
Third	Those written about the time of the decline of Assyria

QUESTION 14

These books are called the Minor Prophets because their content is less important than that of the Major Prophets. *True or False?*

Topic 5 Key Points

- The books of the Minor Prophets cover about four hundred years and were written during the time of Assyrian power, the Assyrian decline, and the post-exilic era.
- These books are called the Minor Prophets because of their size and not because of their lack of importance.

Topic 6: Introduction to Obadiah

Obadiah				
Edom's Destruction for Opposing Judah				
Edom's Destruction			Day of the Lord	
Verses 1-14			Verses 15-21	
Judgment on Edom			Blessing on Judah	
Proud Esau Defeats Defenseless Jacob			Powerful Jacob defeats humbled Esau	
Edom's contempt & crimes			Edom's condemnation & Calamities	
Past			Future	
Author	Judgment	Reasons	Destruction	Possession
Inspired Title 1a	Humbling Prophesied 1b-9	Judgment for Injustices 10-14	Judgment on Modern Enemies 15-16	Blessing on Modern Israel 17-21
c. 845 BC				

Obadiah prophesied a message of judgment upon Edom to comfort the people of Judah who saw Edom gloat over the recent devastation of Jerusalem by the Philistines and Assyrians. In fact, Edom didn't stop at gloating, but instead participated with Judah's invaders in their plunder and slaughter (Ob 11-14). God takes it personally when His people are threatened or attacked and was outraged at Edom for treating Him this way especially since Edom (Esau) was Jacob's brother (Ob 10)!

God truly expects other countries to treat His chosen people with respect. That's another reason we can rest in His promise and not try to take vengeance ourselves: "Do not avenge yourselves, dear friends, but give place to God's wrath, for it is written, 'Vengeance is mine, I will repay,' says the Lord" (Rom 12:19, emphasis added). Next time you seek vengeance, remember that God is for us and is aware of how we're treated.

- **Key Word:** Edom
- **Key Verses:**

  Judgment on Edom: (God to Edom) "Because you violently slaughtered your relatives, the people of Jacob, shame will cover you, and you will be destroyed forever" (Obad 10).

  Blessing on Israel: "Those who have been delivered will go up on Mount Zion in order to rule over Esau's mountain. Then the Lord will reign as King!" (Obad 21).

- **Summary Statement:** Destruction, of Edom in the near future and of all nations in the day of the Lord, will come as God's judgment for opposing Judah. But Judah can be comforted with a promise of blessing due to God's promise of protection in the land covenant.

- **Application:** God judges the prideful who try to destroy His people. God "does unto you" as you have "done unto others" (Obad 15). We should strive to treat those around us in a way that we would want to be treated not only by others, but also by God.

Assignment

- Please read "Introduction to Obadiah."

Introduction to Obadiah

Title

The name Obadiah means "servant of Yahweh" and is derived from a Hebrew word for "servant." Significantly, Obadiah's name refers to Yahweh, while his prophecy concerns

Edom, which worshipped other gods.

Authorship

External Evidence: Obadiah was a common name, shared by at least twelve Old Testament men. Some of the likeliest candidates for this prophecy include:

1. Ahab's servant who hid the prophets of God in a cave (1 Kgs 18:3 in 845 BC)

2. Jehoshaphat's official who was sent out by the king to teach the law in the cities of Judah (2 Chr 17:7 in 860 BC)

3. Josiah's Levite temple repair overseer (2 Chr 34:12 in 620 BC)

4. Ezra's leader who returned from the exile (Ezr 8:9 in 458 BC)

5. A priest involved in the revival of Nehemiah's time (Neh 10:6 in 445 BC).

Based on our reading, we believe the evidence supports the first Obadiah mentioned.

Internal Evidence: The superscription of the book does not help to identify the author. It simply reads, "The vision of Obadiah" (1:1) and does not mention his father's name, his home region, or the reign of a king. Obadiah remains an obscure prophet who probably lived in the southern kingdom and did not come from a royal or priestly line.

Circumstances

Date: The book itself gives little help in determining its date, which is why the candidates for Obadiah listed above range from the ninth to fifth century BC. The only indication of date is the recent invasion mentioned in verses 10-14, which is explained below under "Occasion." It seems that the best evidence suggests a date of around 845 BC.

Recipients: While Obadiah prophesies of the destruction of Edom, the mention of Jerusalem (Ob 11, 20) and Judah (Ob 12) indicate that the prophecy was originally delivered to the southern kingdom, not to Edom itself.

Occasion: The Edomites, descendants of Jacob's brother Esau, rejoiced over a major foreign invasion of Judah (Ob 12-13). They even took advantage of the situation by standing nearby without helping, looking down on Judah in arrogance (Obad 11, 12, 13), taking some of the spoil for themselves (Ob 13), and ambushing survivors to give to the enemy (Ob 14). The difficult issue is determining which *specific* calamity had overcome Judah. Four possibilities exist (*Wilkinson*, 251-52):

1. In 926 BC, Egypt plundered Jerusalem's temple and palace during Rehoboam's reign (1 Kgs 14:25-26). This view is unlikely, though, since Edom was subject to Judah at this time, whereas verses 10-14 indicate that Edom was independent.

2. In 848-841 BC, under Jehoram, the Philistines and Arabs looted the palace (2 Chr 21:16-17) and Edom revolted, becoming a bitter enemy (2 Kgs 8:20-22; 2 Chr 21:8-20) fitting Obadiah's description (Ob 10-14).

3. In 790 BC, King Jehoash of Israel invaded Judah (2 Kgs 14; 2 Chr 25). This cannot be the invasion spoken of by Obadiah since verse 11 refers to *foreign* invaders.

4. In 586 BC, Nebuchadnezzar of Babylon completely destroyed Jerusalem's city and temple (2 Kings 24–25), which was encouraged by the Edomites (Ps 137:7). However, this late date does not seem likely since: (a) Obadiah does not indicate complete destruction, (b) Nebuchadnezzar, in his arrogant despotism, would not have "cast lots for Jerusalem" with anyone (Ob 11), (c) Obadiah does not mention Nebuchadnezzar or Babylon by name as other prophets do, (d) Nebuchadnezzar left no fugitives such as those mentioned in verse 14 (except Zedekiah and his party, who were soon captured), (e) Joel 2:32 (in 590 BC) quotes Obadiah 17, so it must have been written earlier, and (f) the Hebrew verb forms translated "You should not…" (Ob 12-14) warn Edom against repeating *again* what she had already done, which would have been impossible following Jerusalem's complete destruction by Nebuchadnezzar.

In our opinion, the second view seems to marshal the best evidence, especially since the oldest known Jewish tradition identifies the Obadiah of this prophecy with the Obadiah of Ahab's reign (Talmud *Sanh.* 39b). It also seems very possible that the Philistines, Arabs, and Edomites would have cast lots to designate the parts of the city for each to plunder (Walvoord 1:1454). This early date would make the author a contemporary of Elisha and the earliest of the writing prophets.

Characteristics

- Obadiah is the shortest book of the Old Testament.

- Obadiah is the earliest of the prophetic writings.

- Although not quoted in the New Testament, three other Old Testament prophets quote from this short prophecy. Dependence is hard to determine, but one statement in Joel 2:32 refers to Obadiah 17 as what "the LORD has said," thus showing Obadiah's order chronologically. Other prophets' quotations or allusions are as follows:

    1. Amos wrote in 755 BC; he refers to Obadiah in Amos 1:6, 11-12 and Amos 9:12.

    2. Jeremiah wrote in 604 BC; he refers to Obadiah in Jeremiah 49:7, 9-10, 12, 14-16, 22.

    3. Joel wrote in 590 BC; he refers to Obadiah in Joel 1:15; 2:1, 32 and Joel 3:3-4, 14, 17, 19.

- Judgment against Edom appears in more OT books than judgment against any other nation (see Isa 11:14; 34:5-17; 63:1-6; Jer 9:25-26; 25:17-26; 49:7-22; Lam 4:21-22; Ezk 25:12-14; 35; Joel 3:19; Amos 1:11-12; 9:11-12; Mal 1:4), but Obadiah is the *only entire book* devoted to Edom's destruction.

Summary Statement for the Book

Destruction of Edom in the near future and of all nations in the day of the Lord will come as God's judgment for their opposing Judah. But Judah can be comforted with a promise of blessing due to God's promise of protection in the Land Covenant.

The Lord, through Obadiah, extends His comforting, protective hand toward Judah, describing Edom's future destruction for committing injustices against Judah (Obad 1-14).

Obadiah declares that his vision concerning Edom is from the Lord (Ob 1), encouraging Judah that God will sovereignly and irrevocably protect His people by destroying Edom.

The Lord describes how Edom will be destroyed by deceptive allies through a humiliating slaughter and plundering (Fulfillment: The Nabateans, around 500 BC, were invited to an Edomite banquet, but they used the invitation instead to slaughter and plunder) (Ob 1–9). God invites the nations to come and judge Edom [which occurred as the Nabateans, Jews under John Hyrcanus, and Romans under Titus all contributed to the annihilation of the Edomites] (Ob 1). The Edomites, God says, will be brought low and humiliated, like an eagle whose nest is in space (Ob 1–4). Invaders will plunder her wealth (Ob 5–6), and she will be totally deceived and overpowered by her allies (Ob 7), her people slaughtered—the wise, the warriors, and the common people alike (Ob 8–9).

The Lord prophesies the ultimate shame and destruction of Edom as a nation for its injustices done to Judah (Ob 10). He lists the specific ways Edom wronged Judah to justify His judgment upon it and to comfort Judah by His protective hand (Ob 11–14).

Rather than helping Judah when the Philistines and Arabs attacked, Edom participated in dividing the plunder of Jerusalem (Ob 11). Edom looked down on Judah in arrogance and took some of the spoil for itself (Ob 12–13). The Edomites even handed survivors over to the enemy (Ob 14).

The day of the Lord will be God's judgment upon all nations who have opposed Judah. That judgment will accomplish God's law of retribution (Ob 15–16).

The day of the Lord will be God's blessing upon the future nation of Israel because of God's commitment to His people and their land (Ob 17–21). Future Israel will be characterized by holiness in its own land (Ob 17). She will triumph over Edom like fire consumes wood, leaving only stubble (Ob 18), and her boundaries will encompass Edom, Philistia, Samaria, Gilead, Zarephath, and the Negev (Ob 19–20). The Lord, through modern Israel, will govern the area formerly occupied by Edom (Ob 21).

Note: Since Judah has yet to possess these enlarged boundaries, this prophecy must still await fulfillment at the return of Messiah, when the modern nation of Israel will trust in Christ. Also, blessings will come to individuals in modern Israel's neighboring nations as they trust in Him.

QUESTION 15

The key word for Obadiah is _____.

QUESTION 16

Which of the following is the most likely invasion that Obadiah refers to in his prophecy?

   A. In 926 BC, Shishak of Egypt plundered both Jerusalem's temple and palace during Rehoboam's reign (1 Kgs 14:25-26).

   B. In 848-841 BC, under Jehoram, the Philistines and Arabs looted the palace (2 Chr 21:16-17) and Edom revolted, becoming a bitter enemy (2 Kgs 8:20-22; 2 Chr 21:8-20).

   C. In 790 BC, King Jehoash of Israel invaded Judah (2 Kgs 14; 2 Chr 25).

   D. In 586 BC, Nebuchadnezzar of Babylon completely destroyed Jerusalem's city and temple (2 Kgs 24–25), which was encouraged by the Edomites (Ps 137:7).

QUESTION 17

Which of the following are true of the book of Obadiah? *(Select all that apply.)*

   A. It is the shortest book in the Bible.

   B. It is most likely the earliest of the prophetic writings.

   C. It is quoted in the New Testament.

   D. It is the only entire book devoted to Edom's destruction.

Topic 6 Key Points

- The key word for Obadiah is "Edom." God's judgment of Edom comforted Judah that God would fulfill His promise of blessing through the Palestinian covenant.

- Obadiah most likely describes the events when Edom joined in the invasion of Judah by the Philistines and Arabs in the 840s BC.

- Obadiah is the shortest book in the Old Testament, the earliest prophetic writing, and the only book devoted entirely to Edom's destruction.

Topic 7: Obadiah

The first part of the prophecy (Ob 1-14) describes Edom's downfall for committing injustices toward Judah, so that Judah might be comforted with Yahweh's vengeance upon its behalf. The Lord invites the nations to judge Edom (Obad 1), describes the fall of the nation from its pride (Ob 1-9), and delineates the reasons for Edom's judgment (Ob 10-14).

In the second division of the vision (Ob 15-21), Obadiah states that *all* nations who opposed Judah will be judged, because of God's commitment to His people (Ob 15-16). However, Judah will experience His blessings of holiness, enlarged territories, and victory over Edom (Ob 17-21). Edom is probably used as a symbol of all nations who oppose God by opposing His people.

Jesus carried forward this thought—of God's sensitivity to how His chosen people are treated—in His teaching on the judgment of the sheep and goats (Mt 25:31-46). Jesus explains that He will judge the people based on how they treated His brothers and sisters; He views it as how they treated Him personally (Mt 25:39-40, 45-46). It was not only Israel in the Old Testament that He felt this way about, for when Saul was persecuting the church on earth, Jesus saw it as Saul persecuting Him (Acts 9: 1-5). God must be against those who are the enemy of His people. If God is for us, who can be against us (Rom 8:31-39)? He prepares us a table in the presence of our enemies (Ps 23:5). We can rest in that truth in this world that is at enmity with us (Jas 4:4).

QUESTION 18

In Obadiah 4, the fall of Edom is compared to the fall of an _____ from soaring on high.

QUESTION 19

Please match the reference with God's corresponding accusation against Edom.

Reference	Accusation
Obadiah 10	You entered the city of my people when they suffered distress.
Obadiah 11	You captured and slaughtered the escaping refugees.
Obadiah 12	You gloated when your relatives suffered calamity.
Obadiah 13	You violently slaughtered your relatives, the people of Jacob.
Obadiah 14	You stood aloof while strangers took Jacob's army captive.

QUESTION 20

Please match the reference with the characteristics of Israel in the day of the Lord.

Reference	Characteristics
Obadiah 17	Israel will triumph over Edom like fire consumes wood, leaving only stubble.
Obadiah 18	Israel will be characterized by holiness in its own land.
Obadiah 19-20	The LORD, through modern Israel, will govern the area formerly occupied by Edom.
Obadiah 21	Israel will have enlarged boundaries encompassing surrounding nations.

Topic 7 Key Points

- Obadiah describes the arrogance of Edom that God promises to bring low.
- God accuses Edom of taking advantage of Judah while it was besieged by its enemies.
- In the day of the Lord, Edom, representing all the enemy nations of Israel, will be judged and Israel will rule over her neighbors through God's blessing.
- We can trust God to defend us from our enemies and learn to not seek vengeance ourselves but rather rest in His care.

Topic 8: Knowing, Being, and Doing

QUESTION 21
Match the event with the chapter of Obadiah in which it occurs.

Events in Obadiah

	Obadiah 1:1-2	Obadiah 1:3-9	Obadiah 1:10-14	Obadiah 1:15-21
Edom's Violence against Judah				
The Day of the Lord				
Edom's Mountains will be Destroyed				
God Promises Edom's Coming Destruction				

Instructions

QUESTION 22

Please open your Life Notebook and record anything new you have learned from this lesson, including any applications you should make to your life.

Lesson 1 Self Check

QUESTION 1

Those who claim the name of Christ today and predict things that don't come true can be properly classified as true prophets. *True or False?*

QUESTION 2

Which one of the following is the most distinctive sign of a true prophet?

    A. The character of the prophet is consistent with God's holy nature.

    B. Seeing oneself as called by a deity to speak with man

    C. Giving prophecy accompanied by signs and wonders

    D. Giving prophecy in the name of the Lord (Yahweh)

QUESTION 3

Predictive prophecy refers to future eschatological events. *True or False?*

QUESTION 4

Which of the following is a characteristic of prophecy that can lead to misinterpreting it?

    A. Religious unfaithfulness on Israel's part

    B. Depicting as a single event several things that we now know to be separate

    C. A lack of appreciation for poetry

    D. Unprecedented upheaval in the political, military, economic, and social realms

QUESTION 5

Generally speaking, the teachings in the prophets apply to Christians in principle the same way that obsolete elements of the Law still apply. *True or False?*

QUESTION 6

What two events of history are the prophets mainly grouped around?

    A. The two advents of the Messiah

    B. David's reign and Messiah's reign

    C. The exodus and crossing the Jordan

    D. The two major exiles of Israel and Judah

QUESTION 7

The first prophetic books to be written came from the period of the Babylonian exile. *True or False?*

QUESTION 8

Which of the following is true of Obadiah?

    A. It is the shortest book in the entire Bible.

    B. It is quoted in the New Testament.

    C. It is most likely the earliest of the prophetic writings.

    D. It is the only prophetic book that mentions Edom.

QUESTION 9

The key word for Obadiah is:

- A. Judgment
- B. Edom
- C. Prophecy
- D. Esau

QUESTION 10

God takes it personally when His people are threatened and attacked. *True or False?*

Lesson 1 Answers to Questions

QUESTION 1: False [The Hebrew word for "prophet" (nabi) carries the idea of one who is a mouthpiece for Yahweh, chosen to proclaim God's direct words to man. However, the same word is used for false prophets.]

QUESTION 2: True [Due to the mandate for 100-percent accuracy in Deuteronomy 18:18-20, these persons must be deemed false prophets.]

QUESTION 3

B. The truth in the believer's heart that confirms the prophet's word

F. The character of the prophet is consistent with God's holy nature

[No single test was sufficient to authenticate the claims of a prophet. Both the true and the false prophets could prophesy in the name of Yahweh.]

QUESTION 4: *Your answer*

QUESTION 5: False [Ethical prophecy relates to the present moral life of the hearers. All prophetic books contain ethical teaching that demands repentance from the hearers.]

QUESTION 6

Form	Explanation
The suzerain-vassal treaty	God acts as the Great King toward His people
The promise or salvation oracle	Pictures God restoring His people after judgment
The covenant lawsuit	Pictures God imaginatively in a court case against Israel
The woe oracle	Contain a distress, its reason, and the predicted doom

QUESTION 7

C. Depicting as a single event several things that we now know to be separate

QUESTION 8: False [When one uses the normal, grammatical-historical method of interpreting the prophets, Israel always refers to the literal descendants of Abraham (rather than to the church).]

QUESTION 9: True ["All Scripture is profitable for teaching, rebuking, correction, and training in righteousness" (2 Tim 3:16); this includes the prophetic books. As obsolete elements of the Law can still be applied in principle, so the prophetic literature applies today.]

QUESTION 10: *Your answer*

QUESTION 11

B. The two major exiles of Israel and Judah [In particular, the prophets center on the two major exiles—722 BC and 586 BC. Understanding the history surrounding these events would be very helpful.]

QUESTION 12

D. All Major Prophets preached to Judah. [God's faithfulness to communicate with His people extended even into judgment (via Ezekiel and Daniel), so we also should never give up seeking to restore errant believers.]

QUESTION 13

Chronological Order	Political Situation
First	The books that came from the period of Assyrian power
Second	Those written about the time of the decline of Assyria
Third	Those dating from the post-exilic era

QUESTION 14: False [The twelve short books which make up the Minor Prophets are called that because of their length, not their unimportance.]

QUESTION 15: Edom

QUESTION 16

B. In 848-841 BC, under Jehoram, the Philistines and Arabs looted the palace (2 Chr 21:16-17) and Edom revolted, becoming a bitter enemy (2 Kgs 8:20-22; 2 Chr 21:8-20). [This early date would make the author a contemporary of Elisha and the earliest of the writing prophets. Although one cannot be dogmatic, this view seems to marshal the best evidence, especially since the oldest known Jewish tradition identifies the Obadiah of this prophecy with the Obadiah of Ahab's reign.]

QUESTION 17

A. It is the shortest book in the Bible.

B. It is most likely the earliest of the prophetic writings.

D. It is the only entire book devoted to Edom's destruction.

QUESTION 18: Eagle [God describes Edom's destruction as being brought low in humiliation from her arrogant dwellings high in the rocks, and as an eagle fallen from the sky (Ob 1-4)]

QUESTION 19

Reference	Accusation
Obadiah 10	You violently slaughtered your relatives, the people of Jacob.
Obadiah 11	You stood aloof while strangers took Jacob's army captive.
Obadiah 12	You gloated when your relatives suffered calamity.
Obadiah 13	You entered the city of my people when they suffered distress.
Obadiah 14	You captured and slaughtered the escaping refugees.

QUESTION 20

Reference	Characteristics
Obadiah 17	Israel will be characterized by holiness in its own land.
Obadiah 18	Israel will triumph over Edom like fire consumes wood, leaving only stubble.
Obadiah 19-20	Israel will have enlarged boundaries encompassing surrounding nations.
Obadiah 21	The LORD, through modern Israel, will govern the area formerly occupied by Edom.

QUESTION 21:

Events in Obadiah

Instructions

God Promises Edom's Coming Destruction	Edom's Mountains will be Destroyed	Edom's Violence against Judah	The Day of the Lord
Obadiah 1:1-2	Obadiah 1:3-9	Obadiah 1:10-14	Obadiah 1:15-21

QUESTION 22: *Your answer*

Lesson 1 Self Check Answers

QUESTION 1: False

QUESTION 2

    A. The character of the prophet is consistent with God's holy nature.

QUESTION 3: True

QUESTION 4

    B. Depicting as a single event several things that we now know to be separate

QUESTION 5: True

QUESTION 6

    D. The two major exiles of Israel and Judah

QUESTION 7: False

QUESTION 8

    C. It is most likely the earliest of the prophetic writings.

QUESTION 9

    B. Edom

QUESTION 10: True

Lesson 2: Jonah and Amos

Lesson Introduction

Some prophets ministered during times of poverty, but others faithfully preached during Israel's prosperous times. Jonah and Amos belonged to the latter group, ministering during the reign of Jeroboam II while Israel was at its economic height. Just as Jesus would later observe, it was difficult even then for the rich to enter the kingdom of God (Mk 10:23). This lesson explores Jonah's role in putting Israel's focus on other nations and Amos's concern for internal issues during these prosperous times.

What was Israel's role in testifying of Yahweh? It was a nation separate and distinct from the evil practices of other nations (Ex 33:16; Lev 20:24). But is that the entirety of Israel's call? Merely to administer condemnation to other nations? Jonah's reluctance to minister to Nineveh clearly indicates the role God's people saw for themselves in representing Him. This attitude is seen even in Jesus' answer to the Syrophoenician woman in Mark 7:24-30, when He says that He was sent to the lost sheep of Israel and therefore her needs are secondary. However, He responded immediately to her answer of faith.

Meanwhile, Amos was sent to Israel with God's report card. This report contains only eight positive verses out of nine chapters. Even those eight verses do not refer to anything that Israel was doing positively, but instead give God's promise of restoration for the nation in the future (Amos 9:8-15). That restoration is based on God's covenant promises from the past; if not for those promises, the nation would have been destroyed for its wickedness (Amos 7:4-6).

Israel's Privileges & Responsibilities

Lesson Outline

Topic 1: Introduction to Jonah

Topic 2: Disobedience to the Missionary Mandate

Topic 3: Obedience to the Missionary Mandate

Topic 4: Introduction to Amos

Topic 5: Eight Judgments and Three Sermons

Topic 6: Five Visions and Future Restoration

Topic 7: Knowing, Being, and Doing

Lesson Objectives

By the end of this lesson you will be able to do the following:

- Discuss the links in Jonah and Amos between prosperity and spiritual laxness
- Discuss why we believe Jonah is a historical document
- Discuss Israel's missionary mandate as a chosen people
- Discuss God's compassion for wicked people who repent
- Look at the unusual calls and roles of Jonah and Amos
- Explore Israel's responsibilities before God and the reasons for God's judgment
- Discuss the basis of Israel's future restoration

Topic 1: Introduction to Jonah

All prophetic writings record what God said through the *words* of a prophet, but Jonah is unique in that it records what God intended to communicate through the *experiences* of a prophet. The story of what happens to Jonah is the message of the book and Jonah is the only prophetic writing that is in the form of a narrative. However, God has the first (Jon 1:1-2) and the last word (Jon 4:11), and Jonah is not the principal person in the book—God is.

Jonah					
God's Compassion on Gentiles					
Disobeys Missionary Mandate			Obeys Missionary Mandate		
Chapters 1-2			Chapters 3-4		
God's Mercy on Jonah			God's Mercy on Nineveh		
The Great Sea			The Great City		
Commissioning 1:1-2	Disobedience 1:3	Consequences 1:4-2:10	Re-commissioning 3:1-2	Obedience 3:3-4	Consequences 4:5-4:10
"Go!"	"No!"	"So Row!" Jonah Overboard	"Go!"	To Nineveh	Forgiveness And Regret
Jonah's Perversity Chapter 1	Jonah's Prayer Chapter 2		Jonah's Preaching Chapter 3		Jonah's Pouting Chapter 4
c. 760 BC					

If we read just this book, we might think Jonah was unique among the prophets because he was disobedient to God. But Jonah is mentioned as a prophet and described as "God's servant" who gave a successful prophecy in 2 Kings 14:25. Therefore, he probably represents more of a typical, rather than unusual, attitude of God's prophets and people at this time.

- **Key Word:** Compassion
- **Key Verse:** "He prayed to the Lord and said, 'Oh, Lord, isn't this just what I said when I was in my own country. This is what I took the initiative to run off to Tarshish, because I knew that you are gracious and compassionate, slow to wrath and abounding in loyal love, and one who relents concerning disaster.'" (Jon 4:2)
- **Summary Statement:** Jonah's disobedience and indifference toward Nineveh reflect the same sins in Israel. The book depicts God's sovereignty and compassion for responsive Gentiles in order to remind Israel of its missionary purpose to the nations.
- **Application:** Responding to God's heart means catching His heart for the lost.

Assignment

- Please read "Introduction to Jonah."

Introduction to Jonah

Title

The name Jonah means "dove." The metaphor of a dove is used to describe Israel in the Old Testament (see Hos 7:11; 11:11; Ps 74:19), indicating that the experience of Jonah represents the experience of the entire nation of Israel.

Authorship

The only verse in the Old Testament outside the book of Jonah that mentions the prophet is 2 Kings 14:25. It states that Jonah had correctly prophesied that during the reign of Jeroboam II, Israel's borders would once again expand from Hamath in the north to the Sea of Arabah (Dead Sea) in the south. It also reveals Gath Hepher, a small town three miles north of Nazareth, as Jonah's hometown.

The book nowhere states that Jonah is the author, and some have supposed that he could not have penned the writing since he is referred to in the third person (Jon 1:3, 5, 9, 12; 2:1; 3:4; 4:1, 5, 8-9). This argument ignores the fact that third-person autobiographies were common in ancient times. This writing style was used by Moses for entire books in which he is included (e.g., Exodus, Numbers, Deuteronomy), and by Daniel and Isaiah in portions of their prophecies (e.g., Isa 37:21; 38:1; 39:3-5; Dan 1:1–7:1). As the book contains little about the admirable qualities of the prophet, Jonah should be commended for recording such a faithful autobiographical work.

Circumstances

Date: Jonah prophesied during the reign of Jeroboam II of Israel (2 Kgs 14:25; 782-753 BC), making him a contemporary of Amos. Christ Himself supported the historical accuracy of the book (see Mt 12:39-41). Jonah probably wrote during the end of Jeroboam's reign (ca. 760 BC) when his popularity was high from his fulfilled prophecy about Israel's expansion (2 Kgs 14:25).

Recipients: Jonah recorded his autobiographical account for the benefit of the self-sufficient northern kingdom, where he himself lived. However, this message for Israel had strong implications for the southern kingdom as well.

Occasion: The time of Jeroboam II was characterized by great expansion to reclaim Israel's former borders, since Assyria, the ruling power, was in temporary decline due to internal dissension. These factors resulted in a narrow, nationalistic focus in Israel, which enjoyed its prosperity. Unfortunately, Israelite nationalism contributed to its religious decline and blinded God's covenant people from seeing beyond their own borders to other peoples who needed to know the God of Israel. Among those whom Israel cared about the least were the ruthless Assyrians, whose capital city was Nineveh and whose cruelty had become legendary. Through Jonah, the people of God learned that God remained the God of all nations as well as of Israel. Inclusion of the Gentiles in God's program was not a new concept to Israel at this time (see Gen 9:27; 12:3; Lev 19:33-34; 1 Sam 2:10; Isa 2:2; Joel 2:28-32), but the short-sightedness of the nation nevertheless needed a sharper focus on God's compassion for all.

Characteristics

Jonah is the only prophet in Scripture who attempted to run from God. In fact, the book is unique among writings in Scripture in that of all people and things in the book—the storm, the lots, the sailors, the fish, the Ninevites, the plant, the worm, and the east wind—only Jonah himself failed to obey.

Jonah is the only whole book that emphasizes Israel's response to the Gentile nations.

The historical authenticity of Jonah has been denied by many scholars who have difficulty believing a story about a man actually living for three days in a great fish (Jon 1:17). It is also hard for some to believe that Nineveh was so large it had 120,000 inhabitants (Jon 4:11). There exists no tangible evidence that all of Nineveh really repented (Jon 3:5). That it took three days to walk through Nineveh (Jon 3:3) is also questioned. However, this can also be explained in one of two ways:

1. "The great city of Nineveh" (Jon 1:2; 3:2; see also Jon 4:11) almost surely included three other towns in the vicinity as well. Four cities (Nineveh, Rehoboth Ir, Calah, and Resen) are mentioned in Genesis 10:11-12 as "the great city".

2. If one remains unconvinced about the four-city theory, then he can also realize that since Jonah stopped along the way as he preached through the city (Jonah 3:3-4), it is not unreasonable that such a trip would take three days.

The historical authenticity of Jonah's experience is supported by other factors:

- Jesus Himself confirmed the fact that Nineveh did indeed repent as the book of Jonah records (Mt 12:40-41). Those who deny that this was possible contend with the Lord, who affirmed that Jonah was indeed a historical figure.

- Jonah served as a type of Christ, and "if the antitype was historical, then the type must also have been historical" (Gleason, 302).

- Known cities are mentioned in the book: Nineveh (Jon 1:2; 3:2-4, 6-7; 4:11), Tarshish (Jon 1:3; 4:2), and Joppa (Jon 1:3). Jonah is viewed as a literal person from Gath Hepher (2 Kgs 14:25) who lived during the reign of another historical figure, Jeroboam II.

- Considering Jonah to be figurative places its literary form out of character in comparison with the other prophetic books, which all record literal, historical prophets.

QUESTION 1

The key word for Jonah is _____.

QUESTION 2

Please match the reference with the corresponding teaching on God's inclusion of Gentiles in His plan.

Reference	Teaching
Genesis 9:27	The foreigner who resides with you must be to you like a native citizen among you.
Genesis 12:3	All the nations will stream to the Lord's mountain.
Leviticus 19:33-34	After all of this I will pour out my Spirit on all kinds of people.
1 Samuel 2:10	The Lord executes judgment to the ends of the earth.
Isaiah 2:2	To Abraham: all the families of the earth will be blessed through you.
Joel 2:28-32	May God enlarge Japheth's territory and numbers! May he live in the tents of Shem.

QUESTION 3

Since other prophetic books are written as parable, allegory, or fiction, it is reasonable that Jonah can also be interpreted this way. *True or False?*

Topic 1 Key Points

- The key word for Jonah is "compassion" to remind Israel of its purpose to reach out to other nations.
- God included the Gentiles in His plan throughout the Old Testament.
- Considering Jonah as figurative places its literary form out of character with the other prophetic books, which all record literal, historical prophets.

Topic 2: Disobedience to the Missionary Mandate (Jon 1-2)

The actions of Jonah depicted the actions of the entire nation of Israel. In much the same way that Jonah disobeyed God in his lack of concern for the nations, so had Israel been disobedient (Jon 1–2). Further, just as Jonah brought the message of God to Nineveh and learned that God's compassion extends toward Gentiles, so must Israel extend compassion (Jon 3–4). Throughout the book, God demonstrates His sovereign means of accomplishing His purposes in order to remind Israel of its missionary purpose to the nations.

Assignment

- Please read Jonah 1 and Jonah 2.
- Please read "Disobedience to the Missionary Mandate."

Disobedience to the Missionary Mandate

Summary Statement for the Book

Jonah's disobedience to God and indifference toward Nineveh reflect the sins of Israel. The book depicts God's sovereignty and compassion for responsive Gentiles in order to remind Israel of its missionary purpose to the nations.

Jonah's disobedience to God's commission to preach to Nineveh and his subsequent deliverance by the fish depict Israel's neglect of its missionary mandate and God's compassion toward Israel even in its disobedient state (Jon 1—2).

God commissioned Jonah to preach against Nineveh to illustrate His mandate for Israel to share His compassionate love with the nations (Jon 1:1-2). But Jonah disobeyed that commission—a picture of Israel's failure to carry out its mandate (Jon 1:3).

The consequences of Jonah's disobedience demonstrated both the difficulties Israel would undergo for spurning God's call and God's compassion toward His wayward people (Jon 1:4–2:10). God sent a great wind and storm to discipline Jonah, and symbolically Israel, for rejecting His call (Jon 1:4-16). But symbolic of Israel's apathy toward their own disobedience, Jonah complacently slept through the travail until the desperate sailors awakened him (Jon 1:5-6). Searching for a cause for the maelstrom, the sailors correctly determined that Jonah was the at the root of this wrath (Jon 1:7-9). Similarly, even Israel's Gentile neighbors saw the divine discipline on the nation, while Israel remained apathetic. The sailors' lives were spared when they threw Jonah overboard, depicting God's mercy on Gentiles despite the unfaithfulness of His people (Jon 1:10-16).

Chiastic Structure of Jonah 1

A. The sailors are afraid; the sea rages (1:4-5)
  B. The sailors cried to their gods (1:5)
    C. Attempts to save the ship (1:5-6)
      D. Jonah is exhorted to help (1:6)
        E. The sailors ask the cause of their plight (1:7)
          F. The lot fell upon Jonah (1:7)
            G. Jonah is asked to explain (1:8)
              H. I fear Yahweh, the creator (1:9-10)
            G. Jonah is asked to explain (1:10)
          F. They knew Jonah was fleeing from Yahweh (1:10)
        E. The sailors ask Jonah the remedy to their plight (1:11)
      D. Jonah gives instructions that will help (1:12)
    C. Attempts to save the ship are in vain (1:13)
  B. The sailors cry to Yahweh (1:14)
A. The sea ceased from its raging; the sailors feared Yahweh (1:15-16)

The above graphic demonstrates how the chiastic structure and parallel literary elements of the first chapter of Jonah converge on the central statement "I fear Yahweh, the Creator." God, who was by no means finished with Jonah yet, was drawing attention to Himself even in Jonah's retelling (R. Pesch in Talbert, Charles H. *Literary Patterns, Theological Themes, and the Literary Genre of Luke–Acts*. Missoula, MT: Scholars Press, 1974. 71-72).

And so the Lord provided a great fish as His merciful means of deliverance for His wayward prophet, even as He was merciful toward His chosen nation while they were indifferent to their calling (Jon 1:17). Jonah's psalm of thanksgiving for being delivered by the fish is an example of how Israel should also thank God for the mercy He had shown in sparing the nation despite its disobedience (Jon 2:1-9). The fish vomited Jonah by God's command, illustrating how God sovereignly uses even nature to motivate His people to fulfill their missionary mandate (Jon 2:10).

QUESTION 4

What is the central point of the chiastic literary form of Jonah 1:4-16?

    A. The lot fell on Jonah (Jon 1:7)

    B. "I fear Yahweh the creator" (Jon 1:9-10)

    C. The sailors asked Jonah to remedy their plight (Jon 1:11)

    D. The sailors cried to Yahweh (Jon 1:14)

QUESTION 5

Even though the story of Jonah is a narrative, Jonah can be understood as representing the nation of Israel. *True or False?*

Topic 2 Key Points

- Jonah 1:4-16 is written in a literary form that emphasizes the central point, "I fear Yahweh the creator" (Jon 1:9-10).

- Jonah depicts Israel disobeying their missionary mandate of sharing God's compassionate love with the nations.

Topic 3: Obedience to the Missionary Mandate (Jon 3–4)

As can be seen in this table, God did a lot to prepare the hearts of the Ninevites to receive His message. As a prophet, Jonah likely delivered messages to which people either responded well or did not respond at all. Given his experience, he may have sensed that God had prepared the hearts of the Ninevites. Most teachers of God's Word would love being sent to a receptive audience. But Jonah despised the Ninevites. In order to truly be God's servant, Jonah needed to understand God's heart of compassion, as well as that the wickedness in his own heart needed to be corrected. God illustrated both for him through the rapid life cycle of a plant.

> **Events leading to Nineveh's Repentance in 758 BC**
>
> Pagan peoples see bad omens in political and natural phenomena (e.g., plagues, eclipses). These calamities, along with recent worship of only one God, would have made Nineveh very receptive to Jonah's message of judgment!
>
> 787 – Monotheistic worship of a pagan god started
> 765 – Plague throughout Assyria
> 763 – Revolt in the city of Assur
> 763 – Eclipse of the sun
> 762-760 – Revolts in the cities of Assur and Arrapha
> 759 – Another plague
> 758 – "Peace in the land" (repentance under Jonah?)

Would proper self-examination reveal a lack of God's attitude in your own life? Is there ever anyone for whom you don't wish the best?

Assignment

- Please read Jonah 3 and Jonah 4.

- Please read "Obedience to the Missionary Mandate."

Obedience to the Missionary Mandate

Jonah's obedience to God's repeated commission and Nineveh's subsequent belief demonstrate God's compassion on all people, who do not deserve it but can receive it by faith. This should motivate Israel to share His love with the lost nations (Jon 3—4).

God again commissioned Jonah to preach against Nineveh, illustrating again the opportunity for Israel to share His compassionate love with the nations (Jon 3:1-2). This time, Jonah obeyed God's directive (Jon 3:3-4).

Nineveh was spared from destruction because the people and the king believed and repented. This demonstrates God's great compassion on all people who trust Him (Jon 3:5-10). The people repented, immediately believing, fasting, and wearing sackcloth. Gentiles can turn to God if given the opportunity by Israel as His mediating instrument (Jon 3:5). The repentance of the king went even further than that of the people: He extended the fast to include drinking and declared that even animals should participate. This showed the great extent of belief that can happen if the nation of Israel was faithful to its missionary mandate (Jon 3:6-9). In response to the obvious belief of Nineveh, God relented. This demonstrated to Israel His great compassion on all peoples who trust Him (Jon 3:10).

Jonah was angry about God's compassion for Nineveh, but God answered that all deliverance comes through His mercy. This should motivate Israel to share His compassion with the nations since it can be claimed by faith (Jon 4). Jonah's unjustified anger over God delivering Nineveh symbolizes how Israel, having experienced God's compassion, should allow Him to extend it to Gentiles (Jon 4:1-5). God answers by providing a vine to shelter Jonah, reaffirming His sovereign, merciful actions toward the disobedient prophet. Just as Jonah did not deserve the vine, neither did all nations deserve God's mercy, even though God still gave them opportunity to receive it by faith (Jon 4:6-10).

QUESTION 6

After Jonah repented, God re-commissioned him and sent him to preach repentance to Nineveh. *True or False?*

The Parable of Jonah's Plant

If you care (get angry) about even the plant that sheltered you (Jonah 4:9-10)

Shouldn't I care about a city with many animals (Jonah 4:11b)?

Shouldn't I care about a city with many animals (Jonah 4:11b)?

QUESTION 7

Please describe the signs of repentance the king of Nineveh and his people showed after hearing Jonah's message.

QUESTION 8

The main lesson that Jonah was supposed to learn from the plant that grew up and then withered was that he was being selfish and concerned only for himself. *True or False?*

QUESTION 9

How would you respond if someone questioned how you could possibly believe the Bible, and used the story of Jonah being swallowed by a big fish as an example of an unbelievable story? Please open your Life Notebook and record your answer.

Topic 3 Key Points

- After rescuing Jonah with a great fish, God gave him a second chance by again commissioning him to take God's message to the Ninevites.

- After hearing Jonah's message, the Ninevites immediately believed and visibly repented in sackcloth and fasting, while the king extended the fast to include drinking and declared that even animals should participate.

- The lesson from the plant in Jonah 4 was that if Jonah became angry about a plant that grew and died quickly, shouldn't God be concerned about the souls of 120,000 people in Nineveh?

Topic 4: Introduction to Amos

Amos prophesied during a pre-exilic time of tremendous optimism. Due to Assyria's pressure on Syria and the battle between Damascus and Hamath over control of their area, Israel's borders had increased to the original dominion enjoyed under the reigns of David and Solomon (2 Kgs 14:25). Judah had also conquered the Philistines, Arabians, and Ammonites. During these years, Assyria, Babylon, Syria, and Egypt all had weak influence. Israel's prosperity, even though it had not resulted from their own godliness, made it difficult for the hearers of Amos' message to envision disaster from

Amos Judgment for Social Injustice			
Eight Judgments	Three Sermons	Five Visions	Promise of Restoration
Chapters 1-2	Chapters 3-6	7:1-9:7	9:8-15
"This is what the Lord says…" (1:3, 6,9, 11, 13; 2:1, 4)	"Hear this word…" (3:1; 4:1; 5:1)	"This is what the Sovereign Lord showed me…" (7:1, 4, 7; 8:1)	"In that day…" and "The days are coming…" (9:11, 13)
God's Impartiality	God's Justice	God's Judgments	God's Grace
Pronouncements of Judgment	Provocations of Judgment	Future of Judgment	Promises after Judgment
Judgment			Renewal
Horror			Hope
Neighbor Nations	Northern Nation		
767-753 BC (before the fall of Samaria)			

enemies in the near future. Israel may have had a good king, humanly speaking, in Jeroboam II, but his heart was not right before God. All this contributed to an attitude of self-sufficiency and its accompanying problems.

HAMATH

(*Smith's Bible Dictionary*)

(*Fortress*), the principal city of upper Syria, was situated in the valley of the Orontes, which it commanded from the low screen of hills which forms the water-shed between the source of the Orontes and Antioch. The Hamathites were a Hamitic race, and are included among the descendants of Canaan (Gen 10:18). Nothing appears of the power of Hamath until the time of David (2 Sam 8:9). Hamath seems clearly to have been included in the dominions of Solomon (1 Kgs 4:21-24). The "store-cities" which Solomon "built in Hamath," (2 Chr 8:4) were perhaps staples for trade. In the Assyrian inscriptions of the time of Ahab (B.C. 900) Hamath appears as a separate power, in alliance with the Syrians of Damascus, the Hittites and the Phoenicians. About three-quarters of a century later Jeroboam the Second "recovered Hamath" (2 Kgs 14:28). Soon afterwards the Assyrians took it (2 Kgs 18:34; 19:13) etc., and from this time it ceased to be a place of much importance.

Do you recognize the spiritual effects of worldly prosperity? As a church leader, you may have to deal with this problem often.

- **Key Word:** Injustice

- **Key Verse:** "Justice must flow like torrents of water, righteous actions like a stream that never dries up" (Amos 5:24).

- **Summary Statement:** Amos proclaims a message of judgment on the social injustices of Israel and the surrounding nations. He warns of the coming exile, urges the nation to repent, and declares God's promise to restore a remnant in faithfulness to the Abrahamic covenant.

- **Application:** Prosperous Christians must not ignore social injustice.

    1. What social injustices do you see in your country today?

    2. What responsibility does the church have to correct these wrongs?

    3. What is God telling *you* to do about a social inequity?

Assignment

- Please read Amos 1–3.

- Please read "Introduction to Amos."

Introduction to Amos

Title

The name Amos is derived from the Hebrew verb *'amas*, which means "to load," and thus means "burden." The significance of such a name is seen in the largely heavy nature of the prophecy. Of the nine chapters, only eight verses refer to anything positive: the restoration of the nation (see Amos 9:8-15).

Authorship

Internal Evidence: Amos describes himself as a shepherd (Amos 1:1), a herdsman (Amos 7:14), and a grower of sycamore figs (Amos 7:14). He came from the rural area of Tekoa, nineteen kilometers south of Jerusalem. While this description makes him sound like a poor man, the Hebrew may suggest otherwise (Walvoord, 1:1425):

The word used for "shepherd" in Amos 1:1 is not the usual word *ro'eh*, but the unusual word *noqed*, which refers to one who raises, deals, or sells sheep. The only other occurrence of this word in Scripture is in 2 Kings 3:4 where it describes Mesha, king of Moab, who raised a hundred thousand sheep and a hundred thousand rams. Therefore, Amos probably owned a large quantity of sheep. Similarly, the word for "herdsman" (Amos 7:14) appears only here in the Old Testament and properly refers to a herdsman who oversaw livestock operations. Finally, since sycamore figs did not grow in Tekoa, but only in the warmer lowlands in western Judah (1 Kgs 10:27), it is possible that Amos supervised the care of these trees as a seasonal sideline.

Regardless, Amos himself admitted that he was not a prophet by occupation (Amos 7:14-15).

Circumstances

Date: Two powerful and long-lived kings were ruling the divided kingdom during the short time that Amos prophesied (Amos 1:1). Jeroboam II, king of Israel, ruled forty-one years in the north (coregent with Jehoash 793-782 BC, sole king 782-753 BC) and Uzziah (Azariah) ruled Judah fifty-two years in the south (790-739 BC). The overlapping reigns of these kings leaves us with a date of composition between 767-753 BC—only about forty years before the northern tribes were taken into captivity by Assyria (LaSor, 320). Astronomical calculations note that a solar eclipse occurred in Israel on June 15, 763 BC—an event perhaps fresh in the minds of Amos' audience (Amos 8:9; *Talk Thru The Bible, 245*).

Characteristics

Most of the book is negative, with all but the last eight verses pronouncing judgment. This gives it the highest ratio of judgments to blessings of any prophetic book.

Amos is also characterized by blunt, direct sermons and language that made imagery of everyday objects.

The Use of Amos 9 in Acts 15

Amos 9:11-12	Acts 15:16-18
"In that day I will rebuild the collapsing hut of David. I will seal its gaps, repair its ruins, and restore it to what it was like in days gone by. As a result they will conquer those left in Edom, and all the nations subject to my rule." The Lord, who is about to do this, is speaking.	"After this I will return, and I will rebuild the fallen tent of David; I will rebuild its ruins and restore it, so that the rest of humanity may seek the Lord, namely, all the Gentiles I have called to be my own,' says the Lord, who makes these things known from long ago."

QUESTION 10

The key word for Amos is _____.

QUESTION 11

Please explain why the meaning of Amos' name is especially appropriate for this prophecy.

QUESTION 12

Which of the following was **not** a self-described occupation of Amos?

    A. Sycamore fig grower

    B. Herdsman

    C. Prophet

    D. Shepherd

Topic 4 Key Points

- The key word for Amos is "injustice"; Amos proclaims a message of judgment for injustice in Israel and the surrounding nations, looks for repentance, and warns of exile before promising eventual restoration.

- Amos means "burden-bearer," and the significance of such a name is seen in the largely heavy nature of the prophecy, as only eight verses referring to anything positive.

- Amos himself admitted that he was not a prophet by occupation; nor had he been trained as a "son of a prophet" in the ministry schools (Amos 7:14-15).

Topic 5: Eight Judgments & Three Sermons (Amos 1–6)

The book of Amos begins with judgments on Israel and seven nations that surrounded it (Amos 1–2), followed by three sermons against Israel's injustices (Amos 3–6). These are illustrated through five visions of judgment (Amos 7:1–9:7), and the book concludes with eight verses of hope for restoration (Amos 9:8-15). Amos's purpose for declaring judgment on Israel for its social injustices is to motivate the nation to repent, since God is committed to the Abrahamic covenant.

How much warning did God give Israel of approaching judgment, and what was the eventual outcome? As a church leader, you will have to deal with sin and God's eventual judgment on it, both in your life and in the lives of other Christians. Do you have your own house in order? Do you know how to advise others trapped by sin and facing God's judgment? What can you learn from Amos?

Assignment

- Please read Amos 4–6.
- Please read "Eight Judgments and Three Sermons."

Eight Judgments & Three Sermons

Summary Statement for the Book

Amos proclaims judgment on social injustices of Israel and the surrounding nations. He warns of the coming exile, urges the nation to repent, and declares God's promise to restore a remnant as He remains faithful to the Abrahamic covenant.

Amos composed the message of judgment on Israel several decades before its actual accomplishment, giving the nation plenty of time to repent (Amos 1:1-2).

Amos noted that he was a shepherd from Tekoa; this strengthened his message by showing that God chose him specifically, even though he was not a professional prophet (Amos 1:1). He prophesied two years before a great earthquake (possibly in 760 BC; Zech 14:5) during the reigns of Jeroboam II and Uzziah (767-753 BC) (Amos 1:1), so Israel had nearly forty years to repent before judgment took place in the form of the Assyrian invasion of 722 BC. The theme of the prophecy is that God, like a roaring lion and thunder, will devastate Israel as judgment for its sins (Amos 1:2).

Amos declared God's judgment on seven surrounding nations and on Israel itself so that Israel might realize that God will punish each nation for its sin (Amos 1:3–2:16).

God indicts the nations surrounding Israel for sins against Israel, starting with the farthest nations but moving progressively closer to Israel with each indictment so that Israel might realize its greater responsibility before God (Amos 1:3–2:5).

Structural Marker: "This is what the Lord says" (Amos 1:3, 6, 9, 11, 13; 2:1, 4).

God indicts:

- Aram, Israel's bitter enemy, for its opposition to Transjordan Israel (Amos 1:3-5).

- Philistia, Israel's bitter enemy, for selling Israel into slavery (Amos 1:6-8).

- Tyre, a former ally of Israel (1 Kgs 5), for selling Israel into slavery and breaking its covenant of brotherhood (Amos 1:9-10).

- Edom, blood relatives through Esau yet enemies of Israel, for persistent hostility toward its brother nation Israel (Amos 1:11-12).

- Ammon, blood relatives through Lot yet enemies of Israel, for taking Transjordan Israel's land by bloodshed of pregnant women (Amos 1:13-15).

- Moab, blood relatives through Lot yet enemies of Israel, for mistreating Edom (Amos 2:1-3).

- The Southern Kingdom of Judah, for rejecting the Law of God even in its privileged position, so that Israel might know that God's judgment is just (Amos 2:4-7).

God's longest indictment is against Israel itself for sins committed against its own people, even though it had much revelation (Amos 2:6-16). Israel broke the Mosaic covenant and became involved in injustice, materialism, oppression of the poor, sexual immorality, and ritualistic worship (Amos 2:6-8). They rejected God's grace, which He had revealed by removing the Amorites from among them, delivering them from Egypt and sending prophets and Nazirites to them (Amos 2:9-12). Because God keeps His word, Israel would be punished (Amos 2:13-16).

Amos delivers three sermons of judgment to Israel to show God's righteous reasons for judging the nation (Amos 3–6).

Structural Marker: "Hear this word" (Amos 3:1; 4:1; 5:1).

Israel's deserved its judgment (Amos 3:1-10), which would be stricter than the judgment other nations received. God had redeemed the people from Egypt and given them their status as a chosen nation (Amos 3:1-2). As certain events in ordinary life are always associated, so Israel's judgment was inevitable and must be spoken by God's prophets (Amos 3:3-8). God summoned pagans to witness Israel's destruction for its unrighteousness (Amos 3:9-10).

God would use an enemy to destroy the strongholds and fortresses (Amos 3:11). Only a remnant would be saved to fulfill the Abrahamic covenant (Amos 3:12). God would destroy Israel's pagan altars and beautiful homes because of the nation's idolatry and materialism (Amos 3:13-15).

Judgment would also come on the rich women of the region of Bashan because they exploited the poor to satisfy their expensive tastes (Amos 4:1-3). God mockingly invited these women to heap up more sins of religious ritualism without proper deeds (Amos 4:4-5).

God had already sent a series of righteous judgments to motivate the nation to repent:

- Through famine (Amos 4:6).

- Through drought (Amos 4:7-8).

- Through crop failure (Amos 4:9).

- Through plagues (Amos 4:10).

- Through the devastation of some cities (Amos 4:11).

But the people had persisted in their sin, unwilling to repent. The coming chastening of God would be completely justified (Amos 4:12-13).

Exile and death would come to Israel for its sins (Amos 5–6). Amos sings God's funeral song about Israel's exile, which would come with a ninety percent mortality rate in war, to warn the people that soon most of them would be dead (Amos 5:1-3). God tells the people:

- To turn from cult centers in order to seek Him as the sovereign Creator God (Amos 5:4-9).

- To turn from their legal injustices in order to seek Him as the Lord God Almighty (Amos 5:10-15).

- The impending judgment and exile would be a time of mourning for the secure and prideful nation (Amos 5:16–6:14).

- The deliverance associated with the day of the Lord would be accompanied by mourning, darkness, and judgment (Amos 5:16-20).

- God would exile the nation and turn a deaf ear towards its religious ritual accompanied by idolatry (Amos 5:21-27).

- The cities of Calneh, Hamath, and Gaza had all been defeated, even though they were larger and better defended than Samaria, so Israel's wealthy men should not feel secure and arrogant (Amos 6:1-7).

- God would so utterly destroy the nation for its arrogance that even those who survived would fear mentioning God's name lest He hear and strike them too (Amos 6:8-11).

- Because the nation had done the unthinkable by pridefully perverting justice, God promised to raise up another nation (Assyria) to oppress them (Amos 6:12-14).

QUESTION 13

According to Amos 1:1-2, how long did God give Israel to repent after Amos prophesied?

   A. Nearly ten years

   B. Nearly twenty years

   C. Nearly thirty years

   D. Nearly forty years

QUESTION 14

Please match the reference with the corresponding reason that God indicted each of Israel's surrounding nations.

Reference	Reason
Amos 1:3-5	God indicted Aram for its opposition to Transjordan Israel.
Amos 1:6-8	God indicted Judah for rejecting the Law of God.
Amos 1:9-10	God indicted Tyre for selling Israel into slavery and breaking its covenant of brotherhood.
Amos 1:11-12	God indicted Edom, the descendants of Esau, for persistent hostility toward Israel, the descendants of Jacob, with whom there should have been kinship.
Amos 1:13-15	God indicted Ammon for taking Transjordan Israel's land by bloodshed of pregnant women.
Amos 2:1-3	God indicted Moab for mistreating Edom.
Amos 2:4-7	God indicted Philistia for selling Israel into slavery.

QUESTION 15

According to Amos 3:1-2, Israel will be judged more strictly because God redeemed it out of Egypt. *True or False?*

Topic 5 Key Points

- From the time Amos started prophesying, Israel had nearly forty years to repent before the predicted judgment took place.

- God indicted Israel's surrounding nations in an ever-tightening circle before addressing Israel's offenses.

- God explained that Israel would be judged more strictly because He redeemed them out of Egypt and chose them as His people.

Topic 6: Five Visions & Restoration (Amos 7–9)

Amos had the missionary challenge of leaving Judah to prophesy in Israel. His message was unpopular, his nationality was foreign, and his credentials considered suspect since he was a common man who became a prophet (Amos 7:14). Do you think this lessened his authority? Amos certainly had to face this issue when challenged by the priest, Amaziah (Amos 7:10-17). Have you settled the issue of God's call in your life so you are able to face opposition to your authority and role as God's servant?

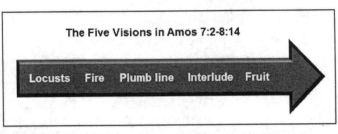

The political peace during Amos' time brought about false, religious worship (Amos 3:14; 5:4-5, 21-23; 7:9; 9:1-4), great material prosperity (Amos 3:15; 4:1; 6:1, 4-6), and increased international trade. All of these in turn resulted in greed, injustice, neglect of the poor, and finally persecution of the poor (Amos 5:10, 15; 6:4; see LaSor, 321). Thus God raised up Amos to speak out against the religious and moral evils of his day in the northern kingdom, so that justice could "roll on like a river, righteousness like a never-failing stream" (Amos 5:24). Again Amos shows a connection between prosperity and sinful behavior.

Assignment

- Please read Amos 7–9.
- Please read "Five Visions and Restoration."

Five Visions & Restoration

Amos illustrates the nature of the coming judgment to the nation through five visions to show Israel that the terrible judgment can be avoided by repentance (Amos 7:1–9:7).

Structural Marker: "This is what the Sovereign LORD showed me" (Amos 7:1, 4, 7; Amos 8:1)

In a vision, God showed Amos His preparations to strip the land bare with locusts (Amos 7:1). But because Israel would die from famine if the locusts completely consumed the crops, God relented in order to uphold the Abrahamic covenant (Amos 7:2-3).

In the vision of the fire, God showed His plans to burn the entire nation, but again, He did not actually do it because of His covenant (Amos 7:4-6).

In another vision, God showed Amos a plumb line on a correctly built house (Amos 7:7-8). The plumb line illustrated how the nation was morally crooked compared to God's absolute standards, so He would destroy the people and the altars (Amos 7:8-9).

Amos then records a historical interlude in which the priest, Amaziah, sought to stop him from prophesying. Even the religious establishment in Israel refused to hear his message (Amos 7:10-17). Amaziah accused Amos of disturbing the peace before King Jeroboam II (Amos 7:10-13). Amos told Amaziah he prophesied only because God told him to do it—not because he was a professional prophet (Amos 7:14-15). Amos then prophesied judgment against Amaziah's wife, children, land, life, and nation (Amos 7:16-17).

In the vision of the ripe fruit, God related that the nation's end would soon come (Amos 8:1-3) because of their disregard for the poor, the New Moon festival, the Sabbath, and fair business practices (Amos 8:4-6). The nation would be severely judged in its land, sky, and religious feasts. Furthermore, God would be silent to them prophetically (Amos 8:7-14).

God declared that He would destroy the pagan religious system so that His name would no longer be profaned (Amos 9:1-4). The Almighty God would judge Israel as He would any disobedient foreign power (Amos 9:5-7).

But God declared that He would not totally destroy Israel, but would leave a remnant to demonstrate His loyalty to the Davidic covenant (Amos 9:8-10). He would restore the Davidic line, which promised that David's descendants would never be wiped out but would rule forever (Amos 9:11; see 2 Sam 7:12-16). Israel would be restored to its original evangelistic purpose as a light to the Gentile nations (Amos 9:12), as well as being restored materially and geographically in accordance with the Palestinian covenant (Amos 9:13-15) during the kingdom era.

QUESTION 16

Please match the vision with the corresponding result.

Vision	Result
Locusts	Famine
Fire	Judgments in nature and God's silence
Plumb Line	Moral crookedness
Historical Interlude	Judgment on Amaziah
Ripe Fruit	Destruction

QUESTION 17

God relented from the first two visions, which would have caused Israel's complete destruction, because Israel temporarily repented. *True or False?*

QUESTION 18

Which of the following covenants will be fulfilled when Israel is restored, according to Amos 9:8-15? *(Select all that apply.)*

A. The Abrahamic covenant

B. The Davidic covenant

C. The Mosaic covenant

D. The Palestinian covenant

QUESTION 19

Please open your Life Notebook and explain, from Jonah and Amos, the association between prosperity and spiritual laxness and how this applies to your ministry.

Topic 6 Key Points

- In Amos's five visions, God graciously gave Israel almost forty years to repent and illustrated the coming judgment.
- In the first two visions, God relented from His severe judgments because of the Abrahamic covenant, because either one would have destroyed Israel completely as a nation.
- Amos's promise of restoration in Amos 9:11-15 is based on the Abrahamic, Davidic, and Palestinian covenants.
- In both Jonah and Amos, there is a link between prosperity and spiritual laxness.

Topic 7: Knowing, Being, and Doing
QUESTION 20

Sections of Jonah

			Instructions
Jonah's Preaching			
Jonah's Perversity			
Jonah's Prayer			
Jonah's Pouting			
Jonah 1	Jonah 2	Jonah 3	Jonah 4

(Merrill, 271)

QUESTION 21

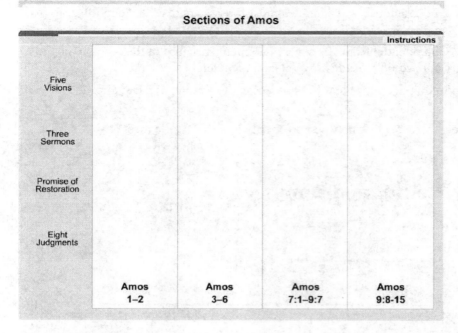

QUESTION 22

Please open your Life Notebook and record anything new you have learned from this lesson, including any applications you should make to your life.

Lesson 2 Self Check

QUESTION 1

The key word for Jonah is _____.

   A. Compassion

   B. Disobedience

   C. Injustice

   D. Repentance

QUESTION 2

Jonah can legitimately be interpreted as fiction since other prophetic Bible books also fall into that category. *True or False?*

QUESTION 3

What is the central point of the literary form of Jonah 1:4-16?

   A. The lot fell on Jonah (Jon 7)

   B. I fear Yahweh the creator (Jon 1:9-10)

   C. The sailors asked Jonah to remedy their plight (Jon 1:11)

   D. The sailors cried to Yahweh (Jon 1:14)

QUESTION 4

Which of the following was NOT a sign of repentance shown by the Ninevites?

   A. Immediate belief

   B. Sitting in dust and ashes

   C. Fasting and wearing sackcloth

   D. Making the animals fast

QUESTION 5

What was the main lesson Jonah was supposed to learn from the plant that shaded him and then died?

   A. That life is temporary

   B. That God is concerned about even animals and plants

   C. That God should be concerned about wicked people

   D. That Jonah has no right to be angry

QUESTION 6

The meaning of Amos's name is especially suited to his prophecy because it means "restorer." *True or False?*

QUESTION 7

Which of the following was NOT a self-described occupation of Amos?

   A. Shepherd

   B. Prophet

   C. Herdsman

   D. Sycamore fig grower

QUESTION 8

According to Amos 3:2, why will Israel receive a stricter judgment from God than the neighboring nations?

- A. Because of His covenant with Abraham
- B. Because of His covenant with David
- C. Because He has given them His laws
- D. Because they are His chosen people

QUESTION 9

Which of the five visions in Amos 7:1–9:7 resulted in God's silence?

- A. Locusts
- B. Fire
- C. Plumb line
- D. Ripe fruit

QUESTION 10

Amos describes Israel's promised future restoration according to the Mosaic covenant. *True or False?*

Lesson 2 Answers to Questions

QUESTION 1: Compassion [Jonah's disobedience and indifference toward Nineveh reflect the same sins in Israel. The book depicts God's sovereignty and compassion for responsive Gentiles in order to remind Israel of its missionary purpose to the nations.]

QUESTION 2

Reference	Teaching
Genesis 9:27	May God enlarge Japheth's territory and numbers! May he live in the tents of Shem.
Genesis 12:3	To Abraham: all the families of the earth will be blessed through you.
Leviticus 19:33-34	The foreigner who resides with you must be to you like a native citizen among you.
1 Samuel 2:10	The Lord executes judgment to the ends of the earth.
Isaiah 2:2	All the nations will stream to the Lord's mountain.
Joel 2:28-32	After all of this I will pour out my Spirit on all kinds of people.

QUESTION 3: False [Considering Jonah as figurative places its literary form out of character in comparison with the other prophetic books, which all record literal, historical prophets.]

QUESTION 4
  B. "I fear Yahweh the creator" (Jon 1:9-10).

QUESTION 5: True [God commissions Jonah to preach against Nineveh to illustrate His missionary mandate for Israel to share His compassionate love with the nations (Jon 1:1-2). But Jonah disobeys that commission, as a picture of Israel's failure to carry out its missionary mandate (Jon 1:3).]

QUESTION 6: True [God re-commissioned Jonah to preach against Nineveh, and this time Jonah obeyed, illustrating again the opportunity and responsibility Israel had to share the Lord's compassionate love with the nations (Jon 3:1-4).]

QUESTION 7: *Your answer should be similar to the following:*
The repentance of the people was shown by their immediate belief, fasting, and wearing sackcloth, while the repentance of the king went even further: He expanded the fast to include drinking and declared that even animals should participate.

QUESTION 8: False [The lesson was that if Jonah could feel righteously angry about a plant that grew and died quickly, shouldn't God be concerned about the souls of 120,000 people in Nineveh?]

QUESTION 9: *Your answer*

QUESTION 10: Injustice [God judges the injustices of Israel and the surrounding nations with a request for repentance and warning of exile before promising eventual restoration according to the Abrahamic covenant.]

QUESTION 11: *Your answer should be similar to the following:*
Amos means "to load" or "to carry a load," and thus indicates a burden or burden-bearer. The significance of such a name is seen in the largely heavy nature of the prophecy: Only eight verses refer to anything positive.

QUESTION 12
  C. Prophet [Amos himself admitted that he was not a prophet by occupation (Amos 7:14-15).]

QUESTION 13
  D. Nearly forty years [Amos prophesied two years before a great earthquake (possibly in 760 BC; Zech 14:5) during the reigns of Jeroboam II and Uzziah (767-753 BC), so Israel had nearly forty years to repent before judgment took place in the form of the Assyrian invasion of 722 BC.]

QUESTION 14

Reference	Reason
Amos 1:3-5	God indicted Aram for its opposition to Transjordan Israel.
Amos 1:6-8	God indicted Philistia for selling Israel into slavery.
Amos 1:9-10	God indicted Tyre for selling Israel into slavery and breaking its covenant of brotherhood.
Amos 1:11-12	God indicted Edom, the descendants of Esau, for persistent hostility toward Israel, the descendants of Jacob, with whom there should have been kinship.
Amos 1:13-15	God indicted Ammon for taking Transjordan Israel's land by bloodshed of pregnant women.
Amos 2:1-3	God indicted Moab for mistreating Edom.
Amos 2:4-7	God indicted Judah for rejecting the Law of God.

QUESTION 15: True [Israel's judgment is deserved; Israel will receive a stricter judgment than the other nations because God chose the people and redeemed them from Egypt (Amos 3:1-2).]

QUESTION 16

Vision	Result
Locusts	Famine
Fire	Destruction
Plumb Line	Moral crookedness
Historical Interlude	Judgment on Amaziah
Ripe Fruit	Judgments in nature and God's silence

QUESTION 17: False [Israel would have died from the famine caused by the locusts, and the fire would have destroyed the entire nation; therefore, God relented from these acts because of the Abrahamic covenant.]

QUESTION 18

A. The Abrahamic covenant
B. The Davidic covenant
D. The Palestinian covenant

[God leaves a remnant to demonstrate His loyalty to the Abrahamic covenant (Amos 9:8-10). He promises to restore the Davidic line in fulfillment of the Davidic covenant (Amos 9:11). He promises to restore Israel materially and geographically in accordance with the Palestinian covenant (Amos 9:13-15); this will be fulfilled in the kingdom era.]

QUESTION 19: *Your answer*

QUESTION 20:

Sections of Jonah

Instructions

Jonah's Perversity	Jonah's Prayer	Jonah's Preaching	Jonah's Pouting
Jonah 1	Jonah 2	Jonah 3	Jonah 4

QUESTION 21:

Sections of Amos

Instructions

Eight Judgments	Three Sermons	Five Visions	Promise of Restoration
Amos 1–2	**Amos 3–6**	**Amos 7:1–9:7**	**Amos 9:8-15**

QUESTION 22: *Your answer*

Lesson 2 Self Check Answers

QUESTION 1
   A. Compassion

QUESTION 2: False

QUESTION 3
   B. I fear Yahweh the creator (Jon 1:9-10)

QUESTION 4
   B. Sitting in dust and ashes

QUESTION 5
   C. That God should be concerned about wicked people

QUESTION 6: False

QUESTION 7
   B. Prophet

QUESTION 8
   D. Because they are His chosen people

QUESTION 9
   D. Ripe fruit

QUESTION 10: False

Lesson 3: Hosea and Micah

Lesson Introduction

This lesson continues God's warnings to Israel during her time of prosperity under Jeroboam II. The Lord's attributes of loyalty (Hosea) and justice (Micah) should have been evident in Israel, just as they should be seen in believers today. Unfortunately, the nation neglected to respond properly to these prophets' accurate, articulate portrayals of these attributes of God.

God desires His people to reflect His character. God is always loyal, as He was to Joshua (Josh 1:5). He is always true, as described in Hebrews 6:18-20:

> So that we who have found refuge in him may find strong encouragement to hold fast to the hope set before us through two unchangeable things, since it is impossible for God to lie. We have this hope as an anchor for the soul, sure and steadfast, which reaches inside behind the curtain, where Jesus our forerunner entered on our behalf.

The challenge for us is to learn to reflect God's character—not superficially, not ritualistically, but in reality and straight from the heart.

Lesson Outline

Topic 1: Introduction to Hosea

Topic 2: Marriage of Hosea

Topic 3: Message of Hosea

Topic 4: Introduction to Micah

Topic 5: Exploitation in Israel

Topic 6: The Leaders' Exploitation of Israel

Topic 7: Wicked Ritualism

Topic 8: Knowing, Being, Doing

Lesson Objectives

By the end of this lesson you will be able to do the following:

- Discuss God's loyal covenant love (*hesed*) and His people's corresponding responsibilities.
- Discuss God's use of Hosea's marriage to illustrate His relationship with His people.
- Discuss God's indictment of His people.
- Lay out the basic timeframe of major events surrounding the exiles.
- Examine Micah's teachings on the Messiah.
- Explain what God really expects from His people.

Topic 1: Introduction to Hosea

Hosea God's Loyalty to Repentant Israel							
Unfaithful Gomer			Unfaithful Israel				
Faithful Hosea			Faithful Lord				
Marriage of Hosea			Message of Hosea				
Personal			National				
Chapters 1-3			Chapters 4-14				
Personal marital tragedy 1:1-2:1	Judgments/ restoration 2:2-23	Gomer received back 3	Lawsuit summary 4:1-3	Spiritual knowledge 4:4-6:3	Loyal love 6:3-11:11	Faithfulness 11:12-13:16	Repentance yields fruitfulness 14
Northern nation of Israel							
755-710 BC (before, during, and after Israel's exile in 722 BC)							

The book of Hosea flows in two broad sweeps. In Hosea 1–3, Hosea's personal marital tragedy unfolds. It parallels Hosea 4–14, where Israel's unfaithfulness is contrasted with God's faithfulness.

God summarizes an official lawsuit against Israel in Hosea 4:1-3, which provides the outline for the remainder of the book (except chapter 14). This lawsuit marshals evidence against Israel, the defendant, who is guilty of failing in three covenantal requirements: knowledge of God (Hos 4:4–6:3); loving loyalty (Hos 6:4–11:11); and faithfulness (Hos 11:12–13:16). Finally, God calls for the wise and righteous in the nation to repent and turn to Him (Hos 14).

All humanity is guilty before God (Rom 3:23). What specifically was the guilt of His people in Hosea?

- **Key Word:** Loyalty
- **Key Verse:** (God about Israel: "Then I will plant 'God-Plants' (Jezre'el) as my own in the land. I will have compassion on 'No-Compassion' (Lo-Ruhamah). I will say to 'Not-My-People' (Lo-Ammi) 'You are my people!' And he will say, 'You are my God!'" (Hos 2:23).
- **Summary Statement:** Hosea experiences a personal marital tragedy that illustrates God's faithful pursuit of His unfaithful people Israel, who lack knowledge of God, reject His loyal love, and are unfaithful to His covenant.
- **Application:** God's loyal love is tough love, so He'll do whatever it takes to bring us back to Him. How loyal are you in return (Mt 10:33; 2 Tim 2:12-13)? Loyalty is expected from His people, and those who are disloyal will see loss.

Assignment

- Please read Hosea 1:1–2:1 on Hosea's personal marriage tragedy.
- Please read "Introduction to Hosea."

Introduction to Hosea

Title

The name Hosea (*hoshea*) means "salvation." In Hebrew, it is exactly the same name as that of Hoshea, the last king of Israel, and is also the original name of Joshua (Moses changed it from Hoshea to Joshua; Num 13:8, 16). The names Joshua and Jesus both come from the same root as Hoshea, but carry the additional concept of Yahweh being salvation.

Authorship

Hosea is not mentioned in Scripture outside of this prophecy, but critics rarely debate Hosea's authorship on those grounds.

The first verse of the prophecy notes that Hosea ministered during the reigns of kings in both Israel and Judah. Therefore, Hosea's message, though primarily given to Israel, included all the people of God. The book alludes to Deuteronomy, which is understandable since Deuteronomy had existed for hundreds of years by Hosea's time.

Nothing is known about Hosea except that he was the son of Beeri (Hos 1:1), his wife was Gomer (Hos 1:3), and he had at least one child (Hos 1:3) and as many as three children (Hos 1:3-9; this depends on how one interprets Hos 2:4). Hosea evidently lived in Israel, as he called the king of Samaria "our king" (Hos 7:5).

Circumstances

Date: Hosea began prophesying during the prosperous reigns of Jeroboam II in Israel (782-753 BC) and Uzziah in Judah (767-739 BC). His prophecies continued through the reigns of Jotham (739-731 BC), Ahaz (731-715 BC), and Hezekiah (715-686 BC) in Judah, and through the brief reigns of the last six kings of Israel who succeeded Jeroboam II. Therefore, his ministry lasted approximately forty-five years—before, during, and after the captivity of the northern kingdom by Assyria—and overlapped the reigns of eleven kings from the two nations (755-710 BC). He probably compiled this book during the early years of Hezekiah, the last of these eleven kings.

Recipients: The book primarily addresses the northern kingdom of Israel (Hos 4:1), though it contains fifteen references to Judah (Hos 1:1, 7, 11; 4:15; 5:5, 10, 12, 13, 14; 6:4, 11; 8:14; 10:11; 11:12; 12:2), thirteen to Egypt, and eight to Assyria.

Occasion: When Hosea began his ministry, Israel was enjoying a temporary period of prosperity under the rule of Jeroboam II. However, the tide soon turned: In only thirty-two years, seven different kings held the throne. Five of the seven were murdered, and the last one was carried with the nation into exile. Israel's idolatry led to the judgment God had promised.

Characteristics

Some argue that Hosea's marriage to Gomer could not have been literal, only visionary or allegorical, because they feel that God would not ask a prophet to marry someone of disreputable character. However, the account is presented in a straightforward narrative, and God sometimes did ask His prophets to do difficult tasks (e.g., Isa 20:1-4; Ezk 4:1-5:4).

Nevertheless, considering Hosea's book to be a literal historical account does raise some questions.

First, did Gomer become adulterous *before* or *after* her marriage to Hosea? The term "adultery" refers to sexual sin *after* marriage (Hos 2:2, 4; 4:12; 5:4). The emphasis of the book is on Gomer's and Israel's behavior *following* the initiation of their covenants. Therefore, it is best to see her adulterous condition as following, not preceding, her marriage. Thus the Lord's command should be seen as follows: "Go, take to yourself a wife who will prove to be unfaithful…" (Chisholm, *Bible Knowledge Commentary*, 1:1379).

Second, were Gomer's second and third children fathered by Hosea or through one of her adulterous relationships? Hosea is not specifically mentioned in the text regarding Gomer's second two children (Hos 1:6, 9) as he is with the first child (Hos 1:3), leading some to say that he did not father the other two. This is a weak argument based on silence, and in fact, *all three* children are called "children of unfaithfulness" (Hos 1:2). The description of the birth of Leah's children in Genesis 29:32-35, which does not mention Jacob by name, shows that it is not unusual in Scripture to omit the father's name.

Hosea uses the Hebrew word (*hesed*), an equivalent for English phrase "covenantal love," six times (Hos 2:19; 4:1; 6:4, 6; 10:12; 12:6). Although the same word is used by Isaiah eight times and by Jeremiah six times, Hosea uses this term more frequently in his short writing than any other prophet. What does *hesed* really mean? The word is often translated as "loving-kindness," "goodness," or "mercy," and may incorporate acts of devotion, love, kindness, favor, or loyalty.

Nelson Glueck's 1927 study advocated that the term referred not to God's *mercy*, but to His *loyalty* to His covenant obligations made with the nation.

This may seem like a small issue, but it becomes quite important since *hesed* is used in reference to the Ten Commandments (Ex 20:6; Deut 5:10). Are these commandments: (1) *temporary* stipulations stemming from God's *covenant* given only to *Israel,* to whom God remains true and demands loyalty, or (2) are they *eternal* principles of *God's nature* and His creation that compel all men to obedience?

In this study of Hosea, we will follow Glueck's view (#1), which interprets the term as referring to covenant loyalty. A particular example is the Mosaic covenant, which obligates both God and Israel to certain requirements (see Ex 19–20), including Israel's blessings for obedience and curses for disobedience (Deut 28). Therefore, as God continues to show commitment and mercy toward the nation based on the Abrahamic covenant, Israel should respond, demonstrating loyalty toward God by following the Mosaic stipulations. This interpretation best fits the theme of the book, as Gomer's violation of the marriage covenant illustrates Israel's violation of the nation's covenant with God. Also, the covenant name for God, Yahweh, appears 48 times, in contrast to a non-covenantal designation, Elohim, which occurs only 29 times. The terms "loyal love" or "loving loyalty/kindness" will be used when referring to *hesed* in this lesson.

QUESTION 1

The key word for Hosea is _____.

QUESTION 2

Which of the following are correct interpretations of Hosea's situation, as presented in this study? *(Select all that apply.)*

    A. God asked Hosea to marry someone of disreputable character.

    B. The account of Hosea's marriage to Gomer is historical.

    C. Gomer was adulterous before her marriage to Hosea.

    D. Gomer's second and third children were fathered by Hosea.

    E. This situation is unique and may not directly apply to human marriages today.

QUESTION 3

In this study, the Hebrew word *hesed* is believed to refer specifically to God's covenant loyalty, instead of to love in general. *True or False?*

Topic 1 Key Points

- God faithfully accepts His unfaithful people—who show lack of knowledge of God, rejection of loyal love, and faithlessness to His covenant—to motivate them to repentance.

- The account of Hosea's marriage as presented in the book is historical and illustrates God's relationship with Israel and Judah.

- The Hebrew word *hesed,* as used in Hosea and other OT books, refers to the covenant loyalty God shows for His people.

Topic 2: Marriage of Hosea (Hos 1–3)

Although many prophets used object lessons in their prophesying, Hosea's personal tragedies illustrated God's relationship to Israel more than those of any other prophet. Unlike other books in Scripture, the message of Hosea is presented twice: personally, depicted through an adulterous wife and faithful husband (Hos 1–3); and nationally, with an adulterous nation and a faithful God (Hos 4–14).

In this way, Hosea is similar to Ezekiel, who often acted out his messages (e.g., in Ezk 12, where he previewed Israel's experience of going into exile).

Assignment

- Please read Hosea 2:2–3:6 on Judgments and Restoration.
- Please read "Marriage of Hosea."

Marriage of Hosea

Summary Statement for the Book

In order to motivate Israel to repent, God allows Hosea to experience a personal marital tragedy that illustrates God's faithful acceptance of His unfaithful people, who show a lack of knowledge of God, reject His loyal love, and are unfaithful to His covenant.

Hosea's marital tragedy illustrates God's sorrow over Israel's unfaithfulness to the Law to motivate Israel to repent of its sin. Hosea saves his marriage, giving hope to the nation by depicting God's restoration of Israel after captivity (Hos 1–3).

Hosea's prophecy covered a forty-five year period before, during, and after the Assyrian deportation, and demonstrated God's repeated last-effort warnings to His wayward people Israel (Hos 1:1).

Hosea obeyed God's instruction to marry the adulterous Gomer, and she bore three children, who symbolized God's rejection of Israel and compassion on Judah (Hos 1:2-9). She first gave birth to a son named Jezreel, which means "God scatters" (Hos 1:2-5). This predicted and illustrated God's dispersion of the house of Jehu, who had murdered Ahaziah and Ahaziah's relatives (see 2 Kgs 9:27). Next, Gomer bore a daughter named Lo-Ruhamah, which means "not loved," illustrating God's lack of compassion on Israel in comparison to His compassion for Judah (Hos 1:6-7). Gomer's third child, a son, was named Lo-Ammi, which means "not my people," illustrating God's rejection of Israel (Hos 1:8-9).

Despite this discouragement, God promised Israel that He would restore their population, relationship, and land as His beloved people because of His faithfulness to the Abrahamic covenant (Hos 1:10–2:1).

Note: The Church is also called God's people in a quote from Hosea (Rom 9:25-26), yet this does not annul God's promise to the nation of Israel.

In a further example of God's pursuit of His people, Hosea pursued Gomer and redeemed her from prostitution by paying her debts and isolating her from other men (Hos 3:1-3). The way he restored his wife depicted God's future restoration of Israel, after the nation returns to God (Hos 3:4-6).

God had rejected His "wife," Israel, for trusting the Baals, so He withheld the nation's crops to try to motivate the people to come back to Him (Hos 2:2-23). He officially rejected His "wife," Israel, and warned that He would make life difficult because of the nation's idolatry (adultery). But the Lord longed to woo Israel back and promised to restore the covenant relationship (Hos 2:21-23), again because of His commitment to the Abrahamic covenant.

QUESTION 4

Please match the name of the child in Hosea 1:2-9 with its meaning.

Name	Meaning
Jezreel	Not my people
Lo-Ruhamah	God scatters
Lo-Ammi	Not loved

QUESTION 5

The sin Israel was committing that corresponded to adultery was _____.

QUESTION 6

Which of the following steps does Hosea take in Hosea 3 to restore his relationship with Gomer? *(Select all that apply.)*

    A. He isolates her from other men

    B. He moves his family to a Levitical city

    C. He has her take an oath of loyalty

    D. He redeems her by paying her debts

Topic 2 Key Points

- Hosea's children were meaningfully named to illustrate God's changing relationship with Israel before He eventually restoring the nation to Himself.

- Israel's idolatry was her sin that corresponded to adultery.

- Hosea redeemed Gomer, paying her debts and isolated her from other men, to help restore their relationship and illustrate God's eventual restoration of Israel to Himself.

Topic 3: Message of Hosea (Hos 4–14)

Throughout Scripture, God communicates the consistent message that He expects His people to be fruitful. But during Hosea's time, the nation lacked the fruit God desired. He used Hosea to call them to repentance as a first step to that fruitfulness (Hos 14:1-3). In the same way the Jewish leaders were not hearing a new message when John the Baptist demanded:

> Therefore produce fruit that proves your repentance, and don't begin to say to yourselves, 'We have Abraham as our father.' For I tell you that God can raise up children for Abraham from these stones! Even now the ax is laid at the root of the trees, and every tree that does not produce good fruit will be cut down and thrown into the fire" (Lk 3:8-9).

How fruitful are you? Are you in need of repentance before you can bear the fruit God expects?

Assignment

- Please read Hosea 13 on false worship and Hosea 14 on how repentance yields fruitfulness.
- Please read "Message of Hosea."

Message of Hosea

God indicts Israel for its lack of spiritual knowledge, loving loyalty, and faithfulness, but promises fruitfulness if the nation repents, thus encouraging the nation to turn from sin and avoid captivity (Hos 4–14).

Throughout Hosea, in both the example of Hosea's marriage and in God's expression of His disappointment with His chosen people's unfaithfulness, three themes repeat. God condemns His people, explaining how their unfaithfulness to His covenant will lead to their judgment. Then He describes the judgment that will befall them in graphic detail, urging them to repent and avoid it. And then He promises that both Israel and Judah will eventually repent and be restored to Him. We can see that He wanted them to understand why they were being judged, so He cited their grievances in detail.

The Lord was issuing an official lawsuit against His people in both Judah and Israel, whom He was about to judge for breaking the covenantal requirements—knowledge of God (Hos

4:4–6:3), loving loyalty and kindness (Hos 6:4–11:11), and faithfulness (Hos 11:12–13:16; 4:1-3). God had offered them His loving loyalty (*hesed*), but they had replaced it with ritualistic sacrifice, idolatry, and wickedness (Hos 6:4–11:11) as they prostituted themselves to each other and to evilness (Hos 4:4–6:3). Instead of depending on God and His Law and promises, Israel appointed godless kings, created and worshipped false gods, and allied itself with Assyria (Hos 5:13; 8:1-14).

These offenses would result in God's just destruction of Israel. With sadness and anger, God described the dispersion that would come to His people (Hos 8:1–11:11). Israel's alliances with Assyria and Egypt would bring them under foreign oppression (Hos 8:8-10). The people would live in tents once again (Hos 12:7-9), even returning to Egypt as a result of their idolatry (Hos 8:11-14). The land would be barren because of the people's false worship at Baal-peor and Gilgal (Hos 9:7-9), and destruction would come as a result of their faithlessness (Hos 13:1-16). God reminded His people that Israel had historically rejected His prophets, just as they now rejected Hosea (Hos 9:7-9). This explained yet again why the Lord was angry, and justified His chastening (Hos 12:10-14; 9:10-17). He illustrated their idolatry by comparing Israel to a lazy vine that credited idolatry for its prosperity as it became increasingly fruitless (Hos 10:1-10), and also to an ungrateful young cow (Hos 10:11-15).

But God at last drew a comparison that revealed His true heart toward His people: Israel was like a loved son whose father could not reject him despite idolatry and murder (Hos 11:1-11). The warnings of judgment were intended to motivate the people to seek the Lord once again and return to the covenant, just as Jacob had at Bethel (Hos 11:12–13:16). "Turn to Me rather than to idols or alliances!" God pleaded with them (Hos 14:1-3). There was no value in clinging to idols when God alone was the source of prosperity (Hos 14:8). If the wise and righteous who understood the prophecy obeyed the ways of the Lord, and if Israel and Judah turned to Him, He would heal their apostasy and help them bear fruit once again (Hos 14:4-7, 9). Through Hosea's lips, God encouraged both nations to repent, telling them again and again that He was willing to accept them back (Hos 6:1-3).

QUESTION 7

Which of the following were covenantal requirements that Israel was ignoring, which Hosea said would lead to God's judgment on His people? *(Select all that apply.)*

A. Proper sacrifices

B. Spiritual knowledge

C. Loving loyalty and kindness

D. Faithfulness

QUESTION 8

With which of the following countries did Hosea warn Israel **not** to make alliances? *(Select all that apply.)*

A. Assyria

B. Babylon

C. Egypt

D. Philistia

QUESTION 9

Please match the reference with the corresponding call God makes to the wise and righteous in Judah in Hosea 14.

Reference	Call
Hosea 14:1-3	God calls for the nation to repent and turn to Him rather than to idols or alliances.
Hosea 14:4-7	God commands the wise and righteous who understand the prophecy to obey the ways of the Lord.
Hosea 14:8	God promises to heal Israel's apostasy and make the nation fruitful again.
Hosea 14:9	God pleads with Israel to recognize that since He alone provides prosperity, there is no value in clinging to idols.

QUESTION 10

Please open your Life Notebook and explain the connection between Hosea's tragic marriage, God's relationship to wayward Israel, and the Lord's covenant relationship to believers today.

Topic 3 Key Points

- God declared an official lawsuit against Israel, guaranteeing judgment for breaking the covenantal requirements: knowledge of God (Hos 4:4–6:3), loving loyalty and kindness (Hos 6:4–11:11), and faithfulness (Hos 4:1-3; 11:12–13:16).
- God prefers loving loyalty (*hesed*) over sacrifice (Hos 6:4-11).
- God despised Israel's alliances with Assyria and Egypt and consequently would destroy Israel because they should be seeking Him.

Topic 4: Introduction to Micah

Micah's prophecy falls easily into three sections (Mic 1–2; Mic 3–5; Mic 6–7), each beginning with the word "hear." The first section indicts Israel and Judah twice for sins of exploitation and promises judgment in exile, ending with a short section on restoration. The second section

Micah							
Judgment on Israel and Judah for Exploitation							
Israel's Exploitation			Leaders' Exploitation		Wicked Ritualism		
1-2 "Hear…" (1:2)			3-5 "Hear…" (3:1)		6-7 "Hear…" (6:1)		
Punishment & Blessing			Punishment & Blessing		Punishment & Blessing		
Wealth (2:1-12, 8-12)			Wealth (3:1-2, 9-11)		Wealth (6:10-12; 7:1-6)		
Destruction of Samaria & Judah 1:2-16	Judgment for Exploitation 2:1-11	Re-gathering 2:12-13	Judgment for Exploitation 3	Messianic Blessing 4-5	Religious Ritual & Exploitation 6:1-8	Wickedness 6:9-7:6	Confidence 7:7-20
Israel and Judah							
735-710 BC (before, during, and after the Fall of Israel)							

indicts the leaders for the same sins of exploitation but has a much longer hope section. In the third and final section, God twice more indicts His people, but ends with a final hope section to encourage them that, because of His promise in the Abrahamic covenant, He has not abandoned them (Mic 7:7-20). Each of the five indictments from God is answered by Micah, who laments the general lack of godliness in the land (Mic 5:6). But he also prophesies national restoration in order to convince God's people to repent and not give up hope.

Are you in need of encouragement? Living a godly life often seems like a long and treacherous journey. Hope is what keeps us going (Heb 6:18-19). Hope is what keeps us from mourning the Christian dead in the same way unbelievers mourn their dead (1 Thess 4:13). Hope is what Micah continually holds before God's unrepentant people.

- **Key Word:** Exploitation
- **Key Verse:** "He has told you, O man, what is good, and what the Lord really wants from you: He wants you to promote justice, to be faithful, and to live obediently before your God" (Mic 6:8).
- **Summary Statement:** God indicts Israel and Judah for wickedness and exploitation of the poor. While He promises vindication and the blessing of the kingdom in the fulfillment of the Messiah, God declares that He will motivate them to repent through judgment in exile.
- **Application:** Show justice, mercy, and humility rather than getting rich by making others poor.

Assignment

- Please read Micah 1.
- Please read "Introduction to Micah."

Introduction to Micah

Title

The name Micah means "Who is like Yahweh?"

As with nearly all the prophetic writings, the writer is clearly designated in the title: Micah of Moresheth (Mic 1:1; probably Moresheth Gath in Mic 1:14). Some lines of evidence seem to indicate he was a preacher in rural areas about forty kilometers southwest of Jerusalem near the Philistine city of Gath; for example, Micah addresses the crime and corruption in Jerusalem and Samaria as someone who does not live in those areas (Mic 1:1, 5-9; 3:1-4, 12). He painstakingly shows how the coming judgment will affect the towns of his region in southern Judah (Mic 1:10-16). In this respect, Micah contrasts with Isaiah, who felt at home with kings and leaders, but both men held up the covenant with courage and conviction against the flagrant abuses by Israel's people and leaders.

Circumstances

Date: Micah prophesied during the reigns of three kings of Judah (Mic 1:1): Jotham (739-731 BC), Ahaz (735-715 BC), and Hezekiah (715-686 BC). Therefore, his prophecies both preceded and followed the fall of Damascus in 732 BC and the fall of Samaria (which he predicted in Micah 1:6) in 722 BC. Micah's strong denunciations of Judah's sins of exploitation suggest that most of his messages preceded Hezekiah's reforms, but his ministry during Hezekiah's reign nevertheless was significant (see Jer 26:17-18). Idolatry was among the sins he condemned (Mic 1:7; Mic 5:12-14; 6:7, 16).

Recipients: Micah's message was directed toward the capitals of both the northern and southern kingdoms, which are named in the title (Mic 1:1). He spoke of the destruction of Samaria by the Assyrians (Mic 1:6) and of Jerusalem by the Babylonians (Mic 4:10).

Note: The dates for the major events that involve the fall of the Northern Kingdom, and later the Southern Kingdom, are important to remember. The dates for the Northern Kingdom are given in the paragraph above. The ones for the Southern Kingdom are as follows:

- 605 BC: King Nebuchadnezzar of Babylon takes many Jews captive to Babylon, including the prophet Daniel, and defeats Pharaoh Neco at Carchemish.

- 597 BC: The Babylonians capture Jerusalem and replace King Jehoiachin with King Zedekiah.

- 586 BC: The Babylonians destroy Jerusalem and the temple.

- 536 BC: The Jews return to the land, ending their seventy years of captivity.

If you keep these dates in mind while studying through these prophetic books, it will help you to interpret and understand these events.

Characteristics

Micah is the only Old Testament book to specify the exact city in which the Messiah was to be born (Mic 5:2). In proportion to the length of his writing, Micah speaks more of Israel's future, the Messiah, and the kingdom than any other prophet.

Micah predicted the following events:

- The fall of Samaria in 722 BC (Mic 1:6-7)

- The invasion of Judah by Sennacherib (Mic 1:9-16)

- The fall of Jerusalem and destruction of the temple in 586 BC (Mic 3:12; 7:13)

- The exile in Babylon (Mic 4:10)

- The return from captivity, future peace, and supremacy of Israel (Mic 4:1-8, 13; 7:11, 14-17)

- The birthplace of the messianic king—Bethlehem (Mic 5:2)

QUESTION 11

The key word for Micah is _____.

The basic timeline of the period from roughly 750 BC to 550 BC helps in putting events in order and understanding the flow of history.

QUESTION 12

Please match the date with the corresponding event.

Date	Event
732 BC	The Babylonians destroy Jerusalem and the temple.
722 BC	The fall of Damascus to Assyria
605 BC	The end of the Jews' seventy years of captivity
597 BC	The fall of Samaria to Assyria
586 BC	Nebuchadnezzar takes many Jews captive to Babylon and defeats Pharaoh Neco at Carchemish.
536 BC	The Babylonians capture Jerusalem and replace King Jehoiachin with King Zedekiah.

Topic 4 Key Points

- God indicts Israel and Judah for wickedness and warns of judgment in exile to motivate them to repent, but promises kingdom blessing under the Messiah in fulfillment of the Abrahamic covenant.

- Knowing the basic timeline of major events centering on the exiles of Israel and Judah is helpful in interpreting the prophetic books.

Topic 5: Exploitation in Israel (Mic 1–2)

In many ways, the book of Micah is like a miniature Isaiah, as both prophets addressed the same sins of the same people. Compare Micah 1:2 with Isaiah 1:2, and Micah 1:9-16 with Isaiah 10:28-32 (Wilkinson, 264). However, most of Micah's prophecy concerned moral issues rather than eschatology (future things). But Micah, like Isaiah, always had the ultimate restoration under Messiah in view. Isaiah just took more time to write the details of the full gospel, describing both advents of the Messiah (e.g. Isa 61:1-2; see also Lk 4:16-21). Micah focused on the messianic role of restoration and glorification, though he also gave important information about where the Messiah would be born (Mic 5:2).

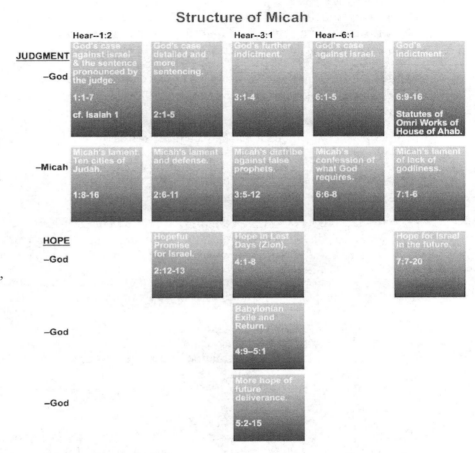

Structure of Micah

Ultimately, the Christian's hope also is for the Messiah's return.

> For the grace of God has appeared, bringing salvation to all people. It trains us to reject godless ways and worldly desires and to live self-controlled, upright, and godly lives in the present age, as we wait for the happy fulfillment of our hope in the glorious appearing of our great God and Savior, Jesus Christ. He gave himself for us to set us free from every kind of lawlessness and to purify for himself a people who are truly his, who are eager to do good. (Tit 2:11-14)

Assignment

- Please read Micah 2.
- Please read "Israel's Exploitation."

Israel's Exploitation

Summary Statement for the Book

God indicts Israel and Judah for wickedness and exploitation of the poor. While He promises vindication and the blessing of the kingdom in the fulfillment of the Messiah, God declares a judgment in exile, in order to motivate them to repent.

God twice indicts Israel for sins of exploitation, to encourage repentance. Micah laments the coming judgment and the discrediting of his ministry by false prophets. However, God promises restoration to instill hope (Mic 1–2).

Micah affirmed God's authority in his prophecy to Judah and Israel during the days preceding and following Israel's fall (Mic 1:1).

- Micah declared his prophecy to be the Word of Yahweh, to affirm to his recipients that God, not man, had spoken these words (Mic 1:1).

- Micah was designated as the country prophet, Micah of Moresheth (Mic 1:1). This emphasizes even more the authority of the Word, because God had chosen one of humble origins as His mouthpiece.

- The prophecy was given in the time of Jotham (739-731), Ahaz (735-715), and Hezekiah (715-686) (Mic 1:1). This places it in the historical context when Israel was at the end of its downward spiral due to neglect of the Law.

- The recipients of the prophecy are designated as Samaria and Jerusalem, the capital cities of the northern and southern kingdoms (Mic 1:1).

God pronounces judgment to motivate the people to repent and avoid future destruction (Mic 1:2-16). He brings a case against both the northern and southern kingdoms and pronounces the judgment of desolation by Assyria on Samaria (Mic 1:2-7). Micah laments, in clever plays on words, the future destruction of nine cities of Judah (Mic 1:8-16); this was fulfilled when the Assyrians destroyed forty-six towns in Judah and the area surrounding Jerusalem (2 Kgs 18–19).

Beginning in Micah 1:10 we see examples of Micah's word play. For each city he mentions, there is a clever twist on the city's name. For example, in Micah 1:10, he names the city of Beth Leaphrah, which means "house of dust" in the original Hebrew; and the prophet is telling them to sit in the dust.

God pronounces a judgment of humiliation on the proud people who exploit others for their own prosperity (Mic 2:1-5). In order to defend his own prophetic ministry, Micah laments the false prophets who exploit people in the name of God for wine and liquor (Mic 2:11).

God predicts Israel's future re-gathering in order to instill hope (Mic 2:12-13).

QUESTION 13

What in Micah's background helped his prophetic word carry more of God's authority?

    A. He was trained in the prophetic schools of the day.

    B. He was designated as the country prophet.

    C. He was a Nazirite from birth.

    D. His had visions of God enthroned in heaven.

QUESTION 14

How does Micah present the destruction of several cities of Judah in Micah 1:8-16?

    A. With clever wordplays involving the cities' names

    B. In an acrostic where each city starts with a consecutive letter of the alphabet

    C. In a predicted direct parallel with how the northern kingdom fell

    D. In a series of visions

Topic 5 Key Points

- God uses the humble country prophet Micah as His mouthpiece, emphasizing the authority of His Word.

- Using clever wordplays, Micah laments the future destruction of nine cities of Judah, which would occur in 701 BC.

Topic 6: Leaders' Exploitation (Mic 3–5)

While Micah preached against the exploitation of Israel and Judah, Assyria committed its own immoral expansion into the west under Tiglath-Pileser (745-727 BC), Shalmaneser V (727-722 BC), Sargon II (722-705 BC), and Sennacherib (705-681 BC). Micah announced that Assyria and Babylon would be God's agents to punish Israel for violating the Mosaic covenant, which had already warned them that spurning His decrees would result in exile (Deut 28:15-68).

The Messiah's deliverance immediately before the kingdom age was so important to the Jews because they faced constant conflict with their neighbors, and domination by Gentile nations was a standing insult! But this condition was clearly predicted in advance as God's discipline for disobeying the covenant (Deut 28:1, 13, 43, 47-68).

Assignment

- Please read Matthew 2:1-18 on the wise men's visit to Jesus.

- Please read Micah 4 and Micah 5 on Messianic blessing.

- Please read "Leaders' Exploitation."

Leaders' Exploitation

God again indicts the prophets and rulers of Israel and Judah for exploitation, but promises that a time of kingdom blessing under the Messiah will come after judgment, in order to comfort the people that God has not abandoned them (Mic 3–5).

God again indicts Israel and Judah for exploiting the poor, and warns that He will not respond when they complain about the judgment (Mic 3:1-4). Micah powerfully declares judgment against the self-serving false prophets and leaders, warning them of the impending destruction (Mic 3:5-12).

Through Micah, God foretells a time of kingdom blessing under the Messiah which will follow the necessary judgment, to encourage the people that He has not abandoned them (Mic 4–5). God predicts Jerusalem's strength, security, and prominence in the world in the coming kingdom (Mic 4:1-8). Micah foretells Israel's exile and subsequent restoration and victory over its enemies that will precede the establishment of the kingdom; this tells the people that God's holiness, shown in judgment, is balanced with His mercy, shown in restoration (Mic 4:9–5:1). Micah describes the messianic ruler who will be born in Bethlehem. Although initially rejected, He will gather the nation and bring in the kingdom by destroying the forces that are destroying Israel (Mic 5:2-15). The Messiah will do the following:

- Reunite and restore the nation (Mic 5:2-3).

- Care for the people and give them security (Mic 5:4).

- Destroy Israel's enemies (Mic 5:5-9).

- Purge Israel of reliance on military power (Mic 5:10-11).

- Destroy false worship within Israel (Mic 5:12-15).

QUESTION 15

According to Micah 5:2, the Messiah would be born in _____.

QUESTION 16

Please match the reference with the corresponding predicted messianic activity.

Reference	Messianic Activity
Micah 5:2-3	He will purge Israel of reliance on military power.
Micah 5:4	He will reunite and restore the nation.
Micah 5:5-9	He will destroy false worship within Israel.
Micah 5:10-11	He will destroy Israel's enemies.
Micah 5:12-15	He will care for the people and give them security.

Topic 6 Key Points

- According to Micah 5:2, the Messiah would be born in Bethlehem.
- Micah predicted the future restoration of the united Jewish nation under the Messiah who would destroy their enemies, purge false worship, and care for the people.

Topic 7: Wicked Ritualism (Mic 6–7)

Jesus addressed the issue of ritualism in His Sermon on the Mount.

> So then, if you bring your gift to the altar and there remember that your brother has something against you, leave your gift there in front of the altar. First go and be reconciled to your brother and then come and present your gift. (Mt 5:23-24)

> When you fast, do not look sullen like the hypocrites, for they make their faces unattractive so that people will see them fasting. I tell you the truth, they have their reward. When you fast, put oil on your head and wash your face, so that it will not be obvious to others when you are fasting, but only to your Father who is in secret. And your Father, who sees in secret, will reward you. (Mt 6:16-18)

God despises ritual for its own sake. Rather, He uses rituals to train us how to express our heart attitude for Him. Without the appropriate heart attitude, the ritual is a despicable, fraudulent expression of hypocrisy. So instead of empty ritual, what does God expect from His people? To make it more personal, what does He expect of you?

Assignment

- Please memorize Micah 6:8, which nicely summarizes what God expects from His people.
- Please read Micah 6–7.
- Please read "Wicked Ritualism."

Wicked Ritualism

God twice more indicts His people's wicked religiosity to convince them to repent, and Micah proclaims the justice of God's judgment balanced with His vindication of His people in fulfillment of the Abrahamic covenant (Mic 6–7).

God again brings His case against His people for their sins in order to show His blamelessness in bringing judgment on them (Mic 6:1-5). Micah responds with the understanding that instead of sacrifices, God prefers justice, mercy and humility. He then proclaims God's displeasure with a people who perform religious rituals while simultaneously exploiting others (Mic 6:6-8).

God gives a final indictment on the people for their wickedness, and warns of destruction as a final attempt to convince Israel to repent (Mic 6:9-16). Micah again laments the lack of godliness in the land, which proves the righteousness of God's actions (Mic 7:1-6).

Micah confidently places his trust in God, who will miraculously shepherd and vindicate His people in accordance with the Abrahamic covenant (Mic 7:7-20). This note closes his prophecy with a sense of expectation, hope, and comfort.

QUESTION 17

Please write Micah 6:8 from memory.

QUESTION 18

Please open your Life Notebook and explain the insights we can gain from Micah's prophecy into God's characteristics of justice, mercy, and humility.

Topic 7 Key Point

- In Micah 6:8 the Lord clearly explains that He wants His people to promote justice, be faithful, and live obediently before Him.

Topic 8: Knowing, Being, Doing

QUESTION 19

Match the theme with the appropriate passage of Hosea.

Outline of Hosea

Instructions

	Hosea 1:1–2:1	Hosea 2:2-23	Hosea 3	Hosea 4:1-3	Hosea 4:4–6:3	Hosea 6:4–11:11	Hosea 11:12–13:16
Gomer Received Back							
Judgments/ Restoration							
Personal Marriage Tragedy							
Spiritual Knowledge							
Faithfulness							
Lawsuit Summary							
Loyal Love							

QUESTION 20

Match the topic with the corresponding chapters of Micah.

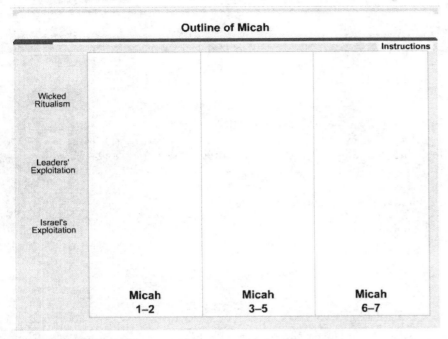

QUESTION 21

Please open your Life Notebook and record anything new you have learned from this lesson, including any applications you should make to your life.

Lesson 3 Self Check

QUESTION 1

The key word for Hosea is _____.

    A. Compassion

    B. Exploitation

    C. Injustice

    D. Loyalty

QUESTION 2

It is most likely that Hosea's wife Gomer was adulterous previous to their marriage. *True or False?*

QUESTION 3

Which child of Hosea was given a name that means "not my people?"

    A. Gomer

    B. Jezreel

    C. Lo-ammi

    D. Lo-ruhamah

QUESTION 4

Which of the following steps does Hosea take in Hosea 3 to restore his relationship with Gomer?

    A. He moves his family to a Levitical city.

    B. He redeems her by paying her debts.

    C. He has her take an oath of loyalty.

    D. He has her lover arrested.

QUESTION 5

Which of the following was NOT a missing covenantal requirement that Hosea says will lead to God's judgment on Israel?

    A. Faithfulness

    B. Loving loyalty and kindness

    C. Proper sacrifices

    D. Spiritual knowledge

QUESTION 6

In what year did Samaria fall to Assyria, sending Israel into exile?

    A. 732 BC

    B. 722 BC

    C. 605 BC

    D. 586 BC

QUESTION 7

Micah's background in the prophetic schools of the day helped his prophetic word carry more of God's authority. *True or False?*

QUESTION 8

Micah presents the destruction of several cities of Judah in Micah 1:8-16 with clever wordplays used with the cities' names. *True or False?*

QUESTION 9

It was Micah who correctly predicted the city of Messiah's birth. *True or False?*

QUESTION 10

Which of the following was NOT mentioned as something God seeks in His people according to the memory verse Micah 6:8?

    A. He wants you to bring proper sacrifice.

    B. He wants you to promote justice.

    C. He wants you to be faithful.

    D. He wants you to live obediently.

Unit 1 Exam: Advanced Studies in the Old Testament, Vol.2

QUESTION 1

Those who claim the name of Christ today and predict things that do not come true can be properly classified as false prophets. *True or False?*

QUESTION 2

Which one of the following is the most distinctive sign of a true prophet?

- A. The character of the prophet is consistent with God's holy nature.
- B. The prophet sees himself as called by a deity to speak with man.
- C. The prophecy is accompanied by signs and wonders.
- D. The prophet gives the message in the name of the Lord (Yahweh).

QUESTION 3

Ethical prophecy refers to future eschatological events. *True or False?*

QUESTION 4

Which of the following is a characteristic of prophecy that can lead to misinterpreting it?

- A. A lack of appreciation for poetry
- B. Religious unfaithfulness on Israel's part
- C. The prophets' depiction of several events now known to be separate as a single event Unprecedented upheaval in the political, military, economic, and social realms

D. QUESTION 5

Generally speaking, all the teachings in the prophets apply to Christians in principle. *True or False?*

QUESTION 6

If you believe the promises to Israel in the Old Testament are now fulfilled by the Church, it is likely you used the normal, grammatical-historical method of interpreting the prophets. *True or False?*

QUESTION 7

What two events of history form the primary focus of the prophets' messages?

- A. The two advents of the Messiah
- B. David's reign and Messiah's reign
- C. The exodus and crossing the Jordan
- D. The two major exiles of Israel and Judah

QUESTION 8

The key word for Obadiah is

- A. Esau
- B. Edom
- C. Arrogance
- D. Hidden

QUESTION 9

Which of the following is the most likely invasion that Obadiah refers to in his prophecy?

A. In 926 BC, Shishak of Egypt plundered both Jerusalem's temple and palace during Rehoboam's reign (1 Kgs 14:25-26).

B. In 848-841 BC, under Jehoram, the Philistines and Arabs looted the palace (2 Chr 21:16-17) and Edom revolted, becoming a bitter enemy (2 Kgs 8:20-22; 2 Chr 21:8-20)

C. In 790 BC, King Jehoash of Israel invaded Judah (2 Kgs 14; 2 Chr 25).

D. In 586 BC, Nebuchadnezzar of Babylon completely destroyed Jerusalem's city and temple (2 Kgs 24–25), which was encouraged by the Edomites (Ps 137:7).

QUESTION 10

The key word for Jonah is _____.

A. Compassion

B. Disobedience

C. Injustice

D. Repentance

QUESTION 11

What is the central point of the literary structure of Jonah 1:4-16?

A. The lot fell on Jonah (Jon 7)

B. "I fear Yahweh the creator" (Jon 1:9-10)

C. The sailors asked Jonah to remedy their plight (Jon 1:11)

D. The sailors cried to Yahweh (Jon 1:14)

QUESTION 12

Since other prophetic books are written as parable, allegory, or fiction, it is reasonable that Jonah could also be interpreted this way. *True or False?*

QUESTION 13

What was the main lesson Jonah was supposed to learn from the plant that shaded him then died?

A. The temporary nature of life

B. That Jonah has no right to be angry

C. That God is concerned about even animals and plants

D. That God should be concerned about wicked people

QUESTION 14

The meaning of Amos' name is especially suited to his prophecy because it means "burden bearer." *True or False?*

QUESTION 15

Which of the following was **not** a self-described occupation of Amos?

    A. Sycamore fig grower

    B. Herdsman

    C. Prophet

    D. Shepherd

QUESTION 16

Which of the following visions was meant to show Israel's moral crookedness?

    A. Locusts

    B. Fire

    C. Plumb line

    D. Ripe fruit

QUESTION 17

Which of the five visions in Amos 7:1–9:7 resulted in God's silence?

    A. Locusts

    B. Fire

    C. Plumb Line

    D. Ripe Fruit

QUESTION 18

The key word for Hosea is _____.

    A. Compassion

    B. Exploitation

    C. Injustice

    D. Loyalty

QUESTION 19

In this unit, the Hebrew word *hesed* is believed to refer to God's covenant loyalty instead of love in general. *True or False?*

QUESTION 20

Which name of Hosea's children means "not loved"?

    A. Gomer

    B. Jezreel

    C. Lo-ammi

    D. Lo-ruhamah

QUESTION 21

The sin Israel was committing that corresponded to adultery was

  A. Blasphemy
  B. Murder
  C. Idolatry
  D. Pride

QUESTION 22

In what year did Samaria fall to Assyria, who carried Israel away into exile?

  A. 722 BC
  B. 605 BC
  C. 586 BC
  D. 536BC

QUESTION 23

What in Micah's background helped his prophetic word carry more of God's authority?

  A. He was a Nazirite from birth.
  B. He had visions of God enthroned in heaven.
  C. He was designated as the country prophet.
  D. He was trained in the prophetic schools of the day.

QUESTION 24

It was Hosea who correctly predicted the city of Messiah's birth. *True or False?*

QUESTION 25

Which of the following was **not** mentioned as something God seeks in His people, according to the memory verse Micah 6:8?

  A. The promotion of justice.
  B. Being faithful
  C. Living obediently
  D. Bringing proper sacrifice

Lesson 3 Answers to Questions

QUESTION 1: Loyal [God faithfully accepts His unfaithful people Israel, who lack knowledge of God, reject His loyal love, and are unfaithful to His covenant.]

QUESTION 2

    A. God asked Hosea to marry someone of disreputable character.

    B. The account of Hosea's marriage to Gomer is historical.

    D. Gomer's second and third children were fathered by Hosea.

    E. This situation is unique and may not directly apply to human marriages today.

[It appears that Gomer became adulterous only after her marriage.]

QUESTION 3: True [In this study, we interpret the term to mean "covenant loyalty." A particular example is the Mosaic covenant, which obligated both God and Israel to certain requirements (see Ex 19–20). This included blessings for Israel's obedience and curses for its disobedience (Deut 28). Therefore, as God continued to show commitment and mercy toward the nation based on the Abrahamic covenant, Israel should respond loyally to God by following the Mosaic stipulations.]

QUESTION 4

Name	Meaning
Jezreel	God scatters
Lo-Ruhamah	Not loved
Lo-Ammi	Not my people

QUESTION 5: Idolatry [God officially rejects His "wife," Israel, for her adulterous idolatry, warning that He will make life difficult so that Israel will realize that returning to Him is best (Hos 2:2-13).]

QUESTION 6

    A. He isolates her from other men

    D. He redeems her by paying her debts

[God uses this to illustrate how He would woo the unfaithful "wife" Israel back to Himself, restoring the Abrahamic covenant relationship (Hos 2:14-23).]

QUESTION 7

    B. Spiritual knowledge

    C. Loving loyalty and kindness

    D. Faithfulness

[God declared an official lawsuit against Israel, guaranteeing judgment for breaking covenantal requirements such as knowledge of God (Hos 4:4–6:3), loving loyalty and kindness (Hos 6:4–11:11), and faithfulness (Hos 11:12–13:16; 4:1-3). God prefers loving loyalty (*hesed*) over sacrifice (Hos 6:4-11).]

QUESTION 8

    A. Assyria

    C. Egypt

[God deplored Israel's external alliances with Egypt and Assyria for trusting them instead of Him (Hos 7:8-16).]

QUESTION 9

Reference	Call
Hosea 14:1-3	God calls for the nation to repent and turn to Him rather than to idols or alliances.
Hosea 14:4-7	God promises to heal Israel's apostasy and make the nation fruitful again.
Hosea 14:8	God pleads with Israel to recognize that since He alone provides prosperity, there is no value in clinging to idols.
Hosea 14:9	God commands the wise and righteous who understand the prophecy to obey the ways of the Lord.

QUESTION 10: *Your answer*

QUESTION 11: Exploitation [God indicts Israel and Judah for wickedness and exploitation of the poor. While He promises vindication and the blessing of the kingdom in the fulfillment of the Messiah, God declares that He will motivate them to repent through judgment in exile.]

QUESTION 12

Date	Event
732 BC	The fall of Damascus to Assyria
722 BC	The fall of Samaria to Assyria
605 BC	Nebuchadnezzar takes many Jews captive to Babylon and defeats Pharaoh Neco at Carchemish.
597 BC	The Babylonians capture Jerusalem and replace King Jehoiachin with King Zedekiah.
586 BC	The Babylonians destroy Jerusalem and the temple.
536 BC	The end of the Jews' seventy years of captivity

QUESTION 13

B. He was designated as the country prophet. [This emphasizes even more the authority of the Word, because God has chosen one of humble origins as His mouthpiece (Mic 1:1).]

QUESTION 14

A. With clever wordplays involving the cities' names [Using clever wordplays, Micah laments the future destruction of several cities of Judah (Mic 1:8-16); this was fulfilled when the Assyrians destroyed forty-six towns in Judah and the area surrounding Jerusalem in 701 BC (2 Kgs 18–19).]

QUESTION 15: Bethlehem [Micah described the messianic ruler who would be born in Bethlehem. Although initially rejected, He would gather the nation and bring in the kingdom by annihilating the forces that were destroying Israel (Mic 5:2-15).]

QUESTION 16

Reference	Messianic Activity
Micah 5:2-3	He will reunite and restore the nation.
Micah 5:4	He will care for the people and give them security.
Micah 5:5-9	He will destroy Israel's enemies.
Micah 5:10-11	He will purge Israel of reliance on military power.
Micah 5:12-15	He will destroy false worship within Israel.

QUESTION 17: *Your answer should be similar to the following:*

He has told you, O man, what is proper, and what the Lord really wants from you: He wants you to promote justice, to be faithful, and to live obediently before your God.

QUESTION 18: *Your answer*

QUESTION 19

Outline of Hosea

						Instructions
Personal Marriage Tragedy	Judgments/ Restoration	Gomer Received Back	Lawsuit Summary	Spiritual Knowledge	Loyal Love	Faithfulness
Hosea 1:1–2:1	Hosea 2:2-23	Hosea 3	Hosea 4:1-3	Hosea 4:4–6:3	Hosea 6:4–11:11	Hosea 11:12–13:16

QUESTION 20

Outline of Micah

		Instructions
Israel's Exploitation	Leaders' Exploitation	Wicked Ritualism
Micah 1–2	Micah 3–5	Micah 6–7

QUESTION 21: *Your answer*

Lesson 3 Self Check Answers

QUESTION 1
   D. Loyalty
QUESTION 2: False
QUESTION 3
   C. Lo-ammi
QUESTION 4
   B. He redeems her by paying her debts.
QUESTION 5
   C. Proper sacrifices
QUESTION 6
   B. 722 BC
QUESTION 7: False
QUESTION 8: True
QUESTION 9: True
QUESTION 10
   A. He wants you to bring proper sacrifice.

Unit 1 Exam Answers

QUESTION 1: True

QUESTION 2
    A. The character of the prophet is consistent with God's holy nature.

QUESTION 3: False

QUESTION 4
    C. The prophets' depiction of several events now known to be separate as a single event
        Unprecedented upheaval in the political, military, economic, and social realms

D. QUESTION 5: True

QUESTION 6: False

QUESTION 7
    D. The two major exiles of Israel and Judah

QUESTION 8
    B. Edom

QUESTION 9
    B. In 848-841 BC, under Jehoram, the Philistines and Arabs looted the palace (2 Chr 21:16-17) and Edom revolted, becoming a bitter enemy (2 Kgs 8:20-22; 2 Chr 21:8-20)

QUESTION 10
    A. Compassion

QUESTION 11
    B. "I fear Yahweh the creator" (Jon 1:9-10)

QUESTION 12: False

QUESTION 13
    D. That God should be concerned about wicked people

QUESTION 14: True

QUESTION 15
    C. Prophet

QUESTION 16
    C. Plumb line

QUESTION 17
    D. Ripe Fruit

QUESTION 18
    D. Loyalty

QUESTION 19: True

QUESTION 20
    D. Lo-ruhamah

QUESTION 21
    C. Idolatry

QUESTION 22
    A. 722 BC

QUESTION 23
    C. He was designated as the country prophet.

QUESTION 24: False

QUESTION 25
    D. Bringing proper sacrifice

Unit 2: Early Prophetic Books

Unit Introduction

This unit covers five prophetic books. Isaiah ministered before, during, and after the fall of Israel to Assyria in 722 BC. The other four—Joel, Zephaniah, Nahum, and Habakkuk—ministered after Israel's fall to Assyria. However, each of these men finished their prophetic ministries before Judah's first deportation to Babylon in 605 BC.

Consequently, each book's message centers around the reason God's people were in danger of destruction and losing their land and temple: their violation of the terms of God's covenant, which in turn led to the curses God had promised (Deut 28:15). The people needed to repent, turning back to the blessings of covenant obedience (Deut 28:1-14).

The fulfillment of God's promises depended on His people's possession of the Promised Land and the temple. Thus, Israel's exile from the land and the destruction of the temple were the ultimate punishment, removing all hope of covenant fulfillment until both land and temple were restored.

Unit Outline

Lesson 4: Isaiah

Lesson 5: Nahum and Habakkuk

Lesson 6: Joel and Zephaniah

Unit Objectives

By the end of this unit you will be able to do the following:

- List the key word for each book in this unit and tell how it relates to the kingdom theme
- Review the historical backgrounds, timelines, and characteristics of the books in this unit
- Discuss how God's program and promises were advanced even through a disobedient people and external opposition
- Discuss the books' purpose: to encourage the Jewish people that God remembers His covenant with them
- Examine how the people's violation of the Palestinian covenant (Deut 28) preceded Israel's exile to Assyria and the warnings of Judah's exile

Lesson 4: Isaiah

Lesson Introduction

As the book of Romans stands at the front of the New Testament epistles and is of prime importance, so the prophecy of Isaiah takes its place at the beginning of the prophetic writings. While to his north the nation of Israel crumbled, this prophet faithfully and eloquently delivered God's message of judgment on Judah as well. Even more significantly, Isaiah promised a full restoration during the Messiah's reign on earth. In this latter sense, Isaiah provides more teaching on the nature of the messianic millennial kingdom than any other book of Scripture.

Isaiah spends a lot of time prophesying about the substitutionary work of the coming Messiah and gives the clearest picture of the gospel of any book in the Old Testament (Isa 52:13–53:12).

Lesson Outline

Topic 1: Introduction to Isaiah

Topic 2: Violations and Deliverance (Isa 1–12)

Topic 3: Judgment on the Nations (Isa 13–23)

Topic 4: Worldwide Judgment and Blessing (Isa 24–35)

Topic 5: Salvation, Sickness, and Sin (Isa 36–39)

Topic 6: Shepherd of Israel (Isa 40–48)

Topic 7: Suffering Servant(Isa 49–59)

Topic 8: Restoration Under Messiah (Isa 60–66)

Topic 9: Knowing, Being, Doing

Lesson Objectives

By the end of this lesson you will be able to do the following:

- Discuss the major objections to the unity of the book of Isaiah
- Discuss how the political situation in Isaiah's day concerning Assyria, Syria, and Israel affected the content of his prophecy
- Discuss the importance of trusting the Lord over any earthly source of strength
- Examine the fulfilled and yet-to-be-fulfilled messianic prophecies in Isaiah
- Discuss how the unique contributions of Isaiah to the future kingdom of the Messiah enable a better interpretation of the New Testament
- Apply Isaiah's prophecies about the future restoration of the earth to help put your priorities in order now

Topic 1: Introduction to Isaiah

The fifty-two-year reign of King Uzziah (Azariah) of Judah ended with his death, likely a few years before Isaiah was called as a prophet (Isa 6:1). During Uzziah's reign, Tiglath-Peleser, king of Assyria, made significant inroads into the west, conquering many lands and taking the Israelites captive (see 2 Kgs 15:29). Jotham, the next king, was a good man, but wicked King Ahaz followed him (2 Kgs 16:1-3). The military threat when Rezin of Damascus and Pekah of Israel rose up against Judah frightened Ahaz into making alliances with the Assyrian king Tiglath-Pileser, which displeased God (Isa 7:1-19).

Isaiah Restoration of The Created Order							
Judgment (and salvation)				Salvation (and judgment)			
Chapters 1-39				Chapters 40-66			
Assyrian invasion				Babylonian captivity			
Prophecy			History	Prophecy			
Mostly condemnation			Interlude	Mostly consolation			
Violations & Deliverance 1-12	Judgment on the Nations 13-23	Worldwide Judgment & Blessing 24-35	Salvation, Sickness, & Sin 36-39	Shepherd of Israel 40-48	Suffering Servant 49-57	God's Initiative 58-59	Restoration under Messiah 60-66
Judah							
739-681 BC (before, during, and after Israel's fall to Assyria in 722 BC)							

Assyria

(from Smith's Bible Dictionary)

Assyria was a great and powerful country lying on the Tigris, (Gen 2:14) the capital of which was Nineveh (Gen 10:11). It derived its name apparently from Asshur, the son of Shem, (Gen 10:22) who in later times was worshipped by the Assyrians as their chief god.

Tiglath-Pileser

(from Easton's Bible Dictionary)

The Assyrian throne-name of Pul (q.v.). He appears in the Assyrian records as gaining, in the fifth year of his reign (about B.C. 741), a victory over Azariah (Uzziah in 2 Chr 26:1), king of Judah, whose achievements are described in 2 Chronicles 26:6-15. He is first mentioned in Scripture, however, as gaining a victory over Pekah, king of Israel, and Rezin of Damascus, who were confederates. He put Rezin to death, and punished Pekah by taking a considerable portion of his kingdom, and carrying off (B.C. 734) a vast number of its inhabitants into captivity (2 Kgs 15:29; 16:5-9; 1 Chr 5:6, 26), the Reubenites, the Gadites, and half the tribe of Manasseh whom he settled in Gozan. In the Assyrian annals it is further related that, before he returned from Syria, he held a court at Damascus, and received submission and tribute from the neighbouring kings, among whom were Pekah of Samaria and "Yahu-khazi [i.e., Ahaz], king of Judah" (comp. 2 Kgs 16:10-16).

- **Key Word:** Restoration
- **Key Verse:** "Look up at the sky! Look at the earth below! For the sky will dissipate like smoke, and the earth will wear out like clothes; its residents will die like gnats. But the deliverance I give is permanent; the vindication I provide will not disappear" (Isa 51:6).
- **Summary Statement:** Isaiah encourages Judah that, while God will judge for breaking His law, He will also restore the original created order of Eden through a godly remnant, a return to the land, and salvation through the Messiah, who will bring universal blessing.

- **Application:** The promise of future restoration of the earth should cause us to get our priorities in order now.

Contrasting Amillennial & Premillennial Views on the Prophets		
	Amillennial	**Premillennial**
Time of the kingdom	Present church age (after Christ's first coming)	Future millennial age (after Christ's second coming)
Interpretative approach	Spiritualizing texts is allowed and even encouraged	Normal, grammatical sense of language is used (figures of speech all have literal referents)
References to Israel	May mean Israel or the church, which is deemed the "new Israel"	Israel always means Israel (the ethnic seed of Abraham)
Location of Christ's reign	Either heaven or the new earth in eternal state (Rev 21:1)	A renewed earth (but no the new earth of Rev 21:1)
Political subjects of Christ's reign	The church in heaven	All people on earth from Jerusalem as the capital of the world (Isa 2:3)
Spiritual life	Some see Jews repentant in mass numbers	Israel & Gentiles repentant and cleansed (Ezek 36)
Topographical changes	No chances in response to prophecy	Mt Olives split (Zech 14:4-5), temple at highest point (Isa 2:2) with river flowing from it (Ezek 47)
Geography	The church spread the gospel throughout the earth	Tribes of Israel allotted new land boundaries (Ezek 47-48)
Physical life	The present age has life-spans generally under 100 years with much death	Most people live past 100 years, babies still born, death only for those in mortal bodies but many live in glorified bodies
Social life	Animals symbolize (or literal) peace between believers and animals today or in the eternal state	Peace between people and animals on renewed earth
Religious life	Amillennial temple and sacrifices viewed as contradicting Hebrews 9	Millennial temple with sacrifices memorial of Christ
Intellectual life	Knowledge of god heightened worldwide as the gospell advances	Worldwide knowledge of God where all people are believers
Emotional life	Christ gives joy to all believers	Jerusalem a city of joy

Assignment

- Please read Isaiah 1.
- Please read "Introduction to Isaiah."

Introduction to Isaiah

Title

The name "Isaiah" means "salvation of Yahweh," a fitting title for the deliverance the book describes.

Authorship

Isaiah, the son of Amoz, authored the book (Isa 1:1). He married a prophetess (Isa 8:3) and had two sons: Shear-Jashub (Isa 7:3) and Maher-Shalal-Hash-Baz (Isa 8:3). Isaiah probably lived in Jerusalem since he had access to the royal court (Isa 7:3; 36:1–38:8; see 2 Kgs 18:3–20:19; 2 Chr 26:22).

Despite reigning tradition, some scholars question whether Isaiah wrote the entire book because of the contrasting emphases of chapters 1–39 and 40–66. They argue that since the perspective of the writing changes, this indicates another author taking over after chapter 39? However, the focus of the writing changes at this point—a shift from the present time to a time to come. This change of emphasis and the events and circumstances of the time of the writing can also explain the differences in language, style, and theology that appear.

Other critics argue that the two messianic personifications that are presented—Messiah as king and Messiah as the suffering servant—are contradictory. However, both personifications appear in each of the two sections, and the concepts are not mutually exclusive.

Furthermore, the New Testament upholds the unity of the book by attributing quotes from both sections to Isaiah. John 12:37-41 quotes Isaiah 6:9-10; 53:1 and Paul in Romans 9:27; 10:16-21 credits Isaiah with quotes from chapters 10, 53, and 65.

Circumstances

Date: Isaiah prophesied both before and after Israel's fall in 722 BC and his lengthy ministry stretched through the reigns of four kings of Judah (Isa 1:1). He began to minister during the rule of King Uzziah (790-739 BC; Isa 6:1), likely a few years before Uzziah's death (2 Chr 26:22). His ministry then spanned the reigns of Jotham (739-731 BC), Ahaz (731-715 BC), and Hezekiah (715-686 BC), since Isaiah wrote Hezekiah's biography (see 2 Chr 32:32). He was still alive at the time of Sennacherib's death in 681 BC (Isa 37:38), which shows that his ministry lasted at least fifty-eight years (739-681 BC).

Recipients: The main hearers of Isaiah's message were Jews in the southern kingdom of Judah who witnessed the destruction of Israel.

Characteristics

Isaiah, probably the best-known prophetic book in the Bible, contains many famous passages (e.g., Isa 1:18; 7:14; 9:6-7; 26:8; 40:3, 31; 53). It is the longest and one of the most influential of the prophetic books, its length granting it placement at the beginning of the prophetic books in the Bible.

Isaiah spoke more than any other prophet of the great kingdom to come at the Messiah's Second Advent (Walvoord 1:1029), describing the nature of this millennial kingdom more thoroughly than even Revelation (Rev 20:1-6).

Isaiah shows *the Bible in miniature*: the first 39 chapters emphasize God's righteousness, holiness, and justice as portrayed in the 39 OT books, and the final 27 chapters (40–66) portray God's glory, compassion, and undeserved favor as seen in the 27 NT books (Wilkinson, 189).

Isaiah is quoted one hundred times in the New Testament, surpassed only by Psalms, which is quoted 119 times.

QUESTION 1

The key word for Isaiah is _____.

QUESTION 2

Please match the critic's objections to the unity of the book of Isaiah with the corresponding explanation.

Objection	Explanation
In general, the events described in Isaiah 1–39 involve the nation of Assyria, but in Isaiah 40–66 the events involve the nation of Babylon	The shift is one of perspective, from the present to a future time.
The language, style, and theology of the two sections differ radically.	Focus, time of writing, and circumstances normally affect an author's style, viewpoints, and method of presenting facts.
Messiah is primarily portrayed as king in 1–39, but as the suffering servant in 40–66.	These two concepts are not contradictory, and both are present in each section.
Israel's return under Cyrus is predicted 150 years in advance, and Cyrus is named.	This objection assumes the impossibility of predicting the future. Nothing is impossible with God, who knows the future.

QUESTION 3

At least two books in the New Testament uphold the unity of Isaiah by quoting from both sections and attributing both to Isaiah. *True or False?*

QUESTION 4

Only Isaiah gives the length of the reign of Messiah in Israel's future great kingdom. *True or False?*

Topic 1 Key Points

- The key word for Isaiah is "restoration," as God will restore the created order through a godly remnant, a return to the Promised Land, and salvation through Messiah, who will bring universal blessing.
- Objections to Isaiah's unity can be explained by shifts in perspective from present to future, changes in emphasis and current circumstances, the two Advents of Messiah, and God's knowledge of the future.
- The New Testament books of John and Romans uphold the unity of Isaiah by quoting from both sections and attributing both to Isaiah.
- Isaiah describes the *nature* of the millennial kingdom the most thoroughly of any book in the Bible.

Topic 2: Violations and Deliverance (Isa 1–12)

The book of Isaiah divides neatly into two major sections. Isaiah 1–39 concerns the judgment that Israel and the surrounding nations faced, and Isaiah 40–66 comforts God's people with the salvation and restoration He promises. The first section probably was written before Judah's Assyrian exile, and the second section after the fall of Samaria. Since Judah looked to its neighboring nations for security, both sections encourage a return to God in repentance—especially since He will restore all creation to a glorious kingdom under Messiah.

Assignment

- Please read Isaiah 6–7.
- Please read "Violations and Deliverance."

Violations and Deliverance

Summary Statement for the Book

Isaiah encourages Judah that, while God will judge for breaking His law, He will also restore the original created order of Eden through a godly remnant, a return to the land, and salvation through the Messiah, who will bring universal blessing.

The heading of the book identifies the author, date, and nature of the prophecies that dealt with Judah's present condition and its future as a nation. Isaiah's name, which means "Yahweh is salvation," summarizes the message of the book; and his message spanned at least fifty-eight years through the reigns of four kings of Judah (Isa 1:1).

Judah had broken God's covenant by forming ungodly alliances, so God's judgment of the nation through exile was justified (Isa 1–6). But despite the impending judgment on Israel and Judah, God promised to preserve a godly remnant and provide blessing in the distant future through the Messiah.

Isaiah joined the other prophets in indicting Judah for breaching the covenant and substituting ritual for repentance. The people should be motivated to repent rather than be judged for rebellion (Isa 1:2-31).

Isaiah contrasted the future restored nation to the present sinful nation, demonstrating the value of the people's repentance (Isa 2–4). Isaiah affirmed that Judah would be restored to the land in the future kingdom, encouraging the people to turn from their sin now (Isa 2:1-5). Then he warned of the impending day of the Lord, which would come in the form of a Babylonian invasion. This would occur because of the pride and rebellion of Judah, and Isaiah exhorted the people to repent *now* on both personal and national levels (Isa 2:6–4:1). Holy survivors of Judah would be fruitful as a holy nation under the rule of Messiah, "the Branch of the Lord" (Isa 4:2-6).

But for now, they were not fruitful. Isaiah's song of the vineyard is a parable form of the case against Judah. It highlights its worthless deeds in response to God's goodness (Isa 5:1-7) and promised woes and judgment in captivity (Isa 5:8-30). God was clearly justified in allowing the nation to suffer the consequences of its sin.

God commissioned Isaiah to his prophetic ministry. His rebellious people had hardened their hearts, and His judgment was forthcoming—but a holy remnant would remain (Isa 6).

God encourages the people, promising to deliver Judah in both the immediate and distant futures. Even though He will judge them, He will bless them as promised, through Messiah's reign (Isa 7–12).

Through the births of two sons, Isaiah's own son Maher-Shalal-Hash-Baz as well as the still-distant Messiah, Isaiah prophesied God's present and future deliverance of Judah (Isa

7:1–9:7). Isaiah's son was given the name "Maher-Shalal-Hash-Baz" (meaning "one who hurries to the spoils") as a sign to Ahaz of God's timely deliverance of Judah from Israel and Damascus (Isa 7). Isaiah also prophesied the distant birth of the Messiah, who will reign in righteousness (Isa 9:1-7), a promise of Judah's deliverance from sin through God's own presence.

God's first deliverance of Judah would come with the fall of the nation He had used to mete out His justice: Assyria (Isa 10:5-34). And yet again, the far-off promise of God's ultimate deliverance by the coming of Messiah showed how He remained faithful to His righteous remnant, which would result in praise for Him (Isa 11–12).

QUESTION 5

What parable or picture does God use to illustrate Judah's worthless deeds?

   A. An olive tree

   B. A fig tree

   C. A vineyard

   D. An abandoned field

QUESTION 6

Please explain the significance, in both the near and distant future, of the name and birth of Isaiah's son Maher-Shalal-Hash-Baz.

Topic 2 Key Points

   • In a parable, God indicts Judah for its worthless deeds by depicting it as a vineyard, imagery Jesus also used in the New Testament (see Mk 12:1-12).

   • The prediction of the birth of Isaiah's son was a sign to Ahaz of God's timely deliverance of Judah, and also of the future birth of a Messiah who would deliver Judah from sin through God's own presence (Isa 7).

Topic 3: Judgment on the Nations (Isa 13–23)

During the reign of Ahaz, the northern kingdom fell to the Assyrians (722 BC) and Jerusalem was besieged by Israel and Syria (2 Kgs 16:5, 6; 2 Chr 28:5-15). Under Hezekiah, the final king during Isaiah's ministry, Judah saw some positive reforms (2 Chr 29:1–31:21). However, Isaiah ministered in a turbulent time in Judah's history. His message was that Judah should trust in God rather than in Assyria—whose intentions were to defeat Israel and Syria—or Egypt, or any of the other nations in the twelve-nation anti-Assyrian coalition (Isa 13–23). After all, only God could ultimately protect the nation, and He alone had promised the glorious kingdom that Judah was seeking.

Assignment

   • Please read "Judgment on the Nations."

Judgment on the Nations

God pronounces judgment on the twelve-nation anti-Assyrian coalition in order to show Ahaz the futility of making alliances rather than trusting Him for protection from Assyria, the nation that would become God's agent of judgment (Isa 13–23).

God pronounced judgment on:

- Babylon, to show Judah the futility of trusting in it for protection (Isa 13:1–14:27). Babylon is judged for its pride, which is also characteristic of Satan at his fall (Isa 13:1–14:23).

- Assyria, to show Judah that He will punish even the instrument of His discipline (Isa 14:24-27).

- Philistia, for rejoicing in the destruction of Israel, in order to show Judah that God protects His people (Isa 14:28-32).

- Moab (Isa 15–16), Damascus, Israel (Isa 17), Ethiopia (Isa 18), Egypt (Isa 19–20), Edom (Isa 21:11-12), Arabia (Isa 21:13-17), and Tyre (Isa 23), to show Judah the futility of trusting in them for protection.

- The uprising against Babylon by invaders from the desert near the Persian Gulf in 722 BC, to show Judah the futility of relying on this revolt (Isa 21:1-10).

- Jerusalem, to show Judah the futility of trusting in its own defenses (Isa 22).

QUESTION 7

Please match the reference with the corresponding nation or city on which God pronounced judgment.

Reference	Nation or City
Isaiah 13:1–14:27	Babylon
Isaiah 14:28-32	Philistia
Isaiah 15–16	Ethiopia
Isaiah 17	Egypt
Isaiah 18	Damascus and Israel
Isaiah 19–20	Moab

QUESTION 8

Please match the reference with the corresponding nation or city on which God pronounced judgment.

Reference	Nation or City
Isaiah 21:1–10	Edom
Isaiah 21:11-12	Jerusalem
Isaiah 21:13-17	Arabia
Isaiah 22	Tyre
Isaiah 23	The desert near the Persian Gulf

QUESTION 9

In Isaiah's time, the nation was tempted to trust in foreign alliances instead of in God's promises for their deliverance. Please open your Life Notebook and describe what temptation in your life you think corresponds to Israel placing their trust in foreign alliances.

Topic 3 Key Points

- God pronounces judgment on each nation in the anti-Assyrian coalition to show Ahaz the futility of making alliances rather than trusting Him for protection against Assyria.

- Assyria, God's agent of judgment will also be judged, so Judah should trust in God.

Topic 4: Worldwide Judgment and Blessing (Isa 24–35)

It is sometimes hard to imagine God's miraculous deliverance of His people from Egypt, drying up the sea before them. He provided supernatural deliverance through Joshua and the various judges. Then He made Israel the dominant nation of the known world during the reigns of David and Solomon. Yet, instead of trusting in God to deliver them, Israel and Judah trusted in alliances with their neighboring nations to keep them safe.

How often do we do the same today?

Assignment

- Please read Isaiah 27.
- Please read "Worldwide Judgment and Blessing."
-

Worldwide Judgment and Blessing

God declares a period of global tribulation to refine the nation, followed by a great restoration of the people and world order in the kingdom, to encourage Judah that He has not forgotten His covenant (Isa 24–27).

God's judgments on individual nations (Isa 13–23) will culminate in judgment on the entire world during the tribulation (Isa 24).

Isaiah sang a song of praise for God's protection, prophesying both the Wedding Banquet of the Lamb for resurrected saints and the defeat of all of Israel's enemies (Isa 25; see Rev 19). The redeemed, Isaiah predicted, will praise God in song for His protection in their time of judgment (Isa 26). God declared that His people will be forgiven and restored in the kingdom age after the world and the nation have been refined, to encourage Judah that He had not forgotten His covenant (Isa 24, 27).

God pronounces six woes on Israel, Judah, and Assyria, to affirm that deliverance from Assyria will come from Him rather than from Egypt, and to establish His Messianic King on the throne (Isa 28–33).

1. The first woe is on the drunkards of Israel and scoffers of Jerusalem, for not trusting in Him (Isa 28). They would be replaced with a restored Israel and Judah.

2. The second woe is on Jerusalem for practicing only external religion without changed hearts (Isa 29:1-14). This attitude would result in a successful siege of the city.

3. The third woe addressed the kings of Judah who sought security in foreign alliances rather than in the Lord (Isa 29:15-24). This states that the kings would be replaced by people in awe of God's holy name.

4. The fourth woe is directed to Judah for the stubbornness it displayed when it made alliances with Egypt rather than trusting in God (Isa 30). This woe included Egypt, which would also be destroyed.

5. The fifth woe is on the women of Judah for seeking security in Egypt (Isa 31–32). God promises that the messianic king will bring in an age of true security and blessing, to motivate Judah to recognize that their luxurious lifestyle was short-lived.

6. For the last woe, God comes against Assyria, the destroyer, for afflicting Judah (Isa 33). God assured that His judgment on Assyria would make Jerusalem a place of justice and righteousness.

God promises His vengeance on all nations for mistreating Israel, which will precede Israel's blessing and restoration to the land (Isa 34–35).

God affirmed that His vengeance would fall on all nations who mistreated Israel (Isa 34). Following the judgment of the nations, Israel would be restored to the land in renewed belief and would enjoy kingdom blessings (Isa 35).

QUESTION 10

While defeat is predicted for all of Israel's enemies, what is promised to resurrected saints in Isaiah 25?

- A. Eternal life
- B. The wedding banquet of the Lamb
- C. Shining like the stars forever
- D. A crown of gold

QUESTION 11

From Isaiah 28–33, please match the people who did not trust God, and therefore received God's pronouncement of "Woe!" with their corresponding consequence or disproval.

Those Who Doubted	*Consequence or Disproval*
The drunkards of Israel and scoffers of Jerusalem (Isa 28)	Egypt also will be destroyed
Jerusalem, for practicing only external religion without changed hearts (Isa 29:1-14)	A devastating and successful siege of the city
Kings of Judah who sought security in foreign alliances (Isa 29:15-24)	The messianic king will bring in an age of true security and blessing
Judah, for the stubbornness it displayed by making alliances with Egypt (Isa 30)	Judgment on Assyria that would make Jerusalem a place of justice and blessing
The falsely secure women of Judah with luxurious lifestyles (Isa 31–32)	People who are in awe of God's holy name
Assyria, the destroyer, for afflicting Judah (Isa 33)	A restored Israel and Judah

Topic 4 Key Points

- Isaiah 25 predicts defeat for all of Israel's enemies, but the wedding banquet of the Lamb is promised for resurrected saints.

- God pronounced six woes on Israel, Judah, and Assyria to show that deliverance from Assyria is through Him. He would establish His messianic king on the throne.

Topic 5: Salvation, Sickness, and Sin (Isaiah 36-39)

In these chapters, Isaiah illustrates the dilemma Israel and Judah had entered by trusting in foreign alliances instead of the Lord. Who was the strongest? Who had been their helper in the past? Who had promised help for the future?

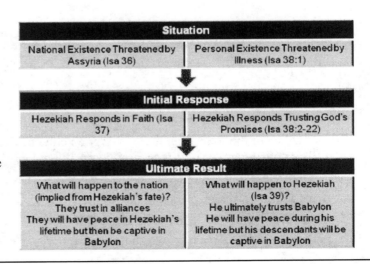

Situation	
National Existence Threatened by Assyria (Isa 36)	Personal Existence Threatened by Illness (Isa 38:1)

Initial Response	
Hezekiah Responds in Faith (Isa 37)	Hezekiah Responds Trusting God's Promises (Isa 38:2-22)

Ultimate Result	
What will happen to the nation (implied from Hezekiah's fate)? They trust in alliances They will have peace in Hezekiah's lifetime but then be captive in Babylon	What will happen to Hezekiah (Isa 39)? He ultimately trusts Babylon He will have peace during his lifetime but his descendants will be captive in Babylon

In Isaiah 36, the nation faced a seemingly hopeless situation. Better-supplied and greater in number, the mighty Assyrian army sat outside Israel's gates with Judah at its mercy (Isa 36–37). Would Judah trust in the Lord and His promises? In a parallel situation, Hezekiah faced death from an illness (Isa 38). After receiving word from the prophet that the illness was terminal, would he trust in the Lord and His promises (Isa 39)? Isaiah used Hezekiah's life to illustrate the nation's predicament, its options, and its ultimate fate.

Assignment

- Please read Isaiah 36 and Isaiah 37.
- Please read "Salvation, Sickness, and Sin."

Salvation, Sickness, and Sin

A historical interlude in this prophetic book records how Judah escapes Assyria due to God's sovereignty over the nations, but predicts its exile in Babylon for trusting alliances more than God (Isa 36–39).

King Hezekiah and his nation were saved from the immediate threat of Sennacherib of Assyria, demonstrating God's sovereignty over the gods of the surrounding nations (Isa 36-37). Sennacherib's chief advisor ridiculed the Lord before the Hebrews and threatened to conquer Jerusalem if the people did not surrender (Isa 36). Hezekiah responded in faith, bringing the matter before God, who responded by killing 185,000 Assyrian soldiers as well as the Rabshakeh himself, thus demonstrating God's sovereignty over the gods of the surrounding nations and Assyria (Isa 37).

Isaiah later warned Hezekiah that he would die, and soon. But Hezekiah responded in faith to God, and the Lord saved him miraculously from sickness, granting him fifteen additional years of life and proving God's sovereignty even over death and the movements of the sun (Isa 38). However, Hezekiah's foolish reliance on Babylonian messengers who came to the kingdom, rather than on God, would result in the nation being taken into Babylonian exile. This narrative provides a bridge to chapters 40–66, which primarily concern Babylon (Isa 39).

QUESTION 12

In Isaiah 36, in whom did the Assyrian chief advisor suggest that Hezekiah was trusting? *(Select all that apply.)*

A. Babylon

B. Egypt

C. Philistia

D. The Lord

QUESTION 13

In Isaiah 36, which of the following did the Assyrian chief advisor suggest were reasons that the Lord would NOT be able to deliver Jerusalem? *(Select all that apply.)*

A. Because Hezekiah removed the high places where the Jews had worshiped the Lord

B. Because the Lord himself sent the Assyrians

C. Because the Assyrians had defeated the gods of all the lands they had conquered

D. Because the Assyrians had broken through Jerusalem's walls

Topic 5 Key Points

- The Assyrian chief advisor suggested Hezekiah must be trusting vainly either in Egypt or in the Lord.

- The Assyrian chief advisor suggested Hezekiah could not trust in the Lord because he had removed His high places; the Lord himself had sent the Assyrians; and the Assyrians had defeated the gods of all the lands (so of course they would defeat the Lord also).

Topic 6: Shepherd of Israel (Isa 40–48)

Recurring Strands in Isaiah 40–48

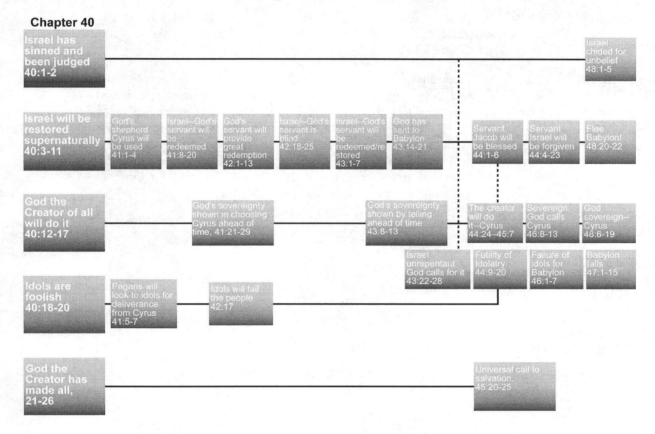

Israel's covenant with God promised blessings for obedience, and consequences for disobedience (Deut 30:3). But even before the southern kingdom was exiled, God was working on their deliverance (Isa 40:1-12). He is the one with true military power, not the temporal nations (Isa 40:10). He, not the nations, is the shepherd of His people: "Like a shepherd he tends his flock; he gathers up the lambs with his arm; he carries them close to his heart; he leads the ewes along" (Isa 40:11). He would accomplish this through His Servant (Isa 42:1-7).

Assignment

- Please read Isaiah 40–41.
- Please read "Shepherd of Israel."

Shepherd of Israel

In order to comfort His people with His shepherd's heart and His sovereign knowledge of the future, God promises to punish Babylon and restore Judah to the land through Cyrus of Persia (Isa 40–48).

Despite the ominous foretelling of Judah's exile, God's majesty and His gentle shepherding of Judah comforted His people, who would have suffered enough for their sin by the exile's end in 539 BC (Isa 40). He promised to demonstrate to the nations His sovereignty over His servant Judah by appointing Cyrus (Isa 41:25), who would allow the people to return to their land after a period of captivity. Isaiah predicted this more than 150 years before it happened! God was indeed adequate to redeem Judah from the Babylonians (Isa 41).

In order to comfort His people, God contrasts His Servant the Messiah with His servant Israel. (*Note:* "Servant" refers both to Israel [Isa 41:8; 42:19; 43:10; 44:1-2, 21; 45:4; 48:20] and to the Messiah [Isa 42:1; 49:3, 5-7; 50:10; 52:13; 53:11].)

Though the people had been judged, God offered them comfort through the prophecy of His messianic servant, who would defeat Israel's enemies and rule the world (Isa 42). In order to further comfort His people so that they could trust Him, God promised to restore the unworthy nation to the land (Isa 43:1–44:5). This provided sovereign comfort for His people as they saw the futility of trusting idols, the divine appointment of Cyrus, and the promised restoration to their land (Isa 44:6–45:25). The empire of Babylon and its idols would be destroyed because God was sovereign over them (Isa 46–47), and the Lord would deliver the people from Babylon's grasp, returning them to their land to signify His commitment to the covenant (Isa 48).

QUESTION 14

The Persian whom God predicted would come to redeem Judah from the Babylonians was named _____.

QUESTION 15

Both Israel and the Messiah are named as God's servants in Isaiah 40–48. *True or False?*

Topic 6 Key Points

- God appointed Cyrus the Persian to redeem Israel from the Babylonians; Isaiah prophesied this over 150 years before it happened.
- Both Israel and the Messiah are named as God's servants in Isaiah 40–48.

Topic 7: Suffering Servant (Isaiah 49–59)

When Philip met the Ethiopian eunuch on the road to Gaza, he was reading these verses in Isaiah:

> He was treated harshly and afflicted, but he did not even open his mouth.

Like a sheep led to the slaughtering block, like an ewe silent before her shearers, he did not even open his mouth. He was led away after an unjust trial. But who even cared? Indeed, he was cut off from the land of the living; because of the rebellion of his own people he was wounded. (Isa 53:7-8).

The eunuch wondered who these words referred to, saying, "'Please tell me, who is the prophet saying this about — himself or someone else?' So Philip started speaking, and beginning with this scripture proclaimed the good news about Jesus to him" (Acts 8:34-35). This passage, in chapters 52 and 53 of Isaiah, contains the clearest look into the passion of Christ—the gospel—of any book in the Old Testament.

Diagram of Isaiah 40–46

Comfort	Deliverance	Encouragement for Jews	for Gentiles	Cleansing from Sin	Condition of Glory
40–45	46–48	49–52	53 54–57	58–59	60–66

Deliverance from Babylon   Deliverance from Sin   Deliverance in the Millennium

Assignment

- Please read Isaiah 52:13–53:12.
- Please memorize Isaiah 52:7.
- Please read "Suffering Servant."
-

Suffering Servant

God promises that His Suffering Servant will both restore the nation and bring blessing to the Gentiles through His vicarious death; this promise encourages His righteous remnant to trust Him now (Isa 49—57).

God promised that the rejected Messiah, or Suffering Servant, would save the Gentiles and restore Israel to its land, showing that He had not forsaken Israel (Isa 49–50). He exhorted the righteous remnant to trust Him since they would be exalted (Isa 51:1–52:12). In a preview of the New Testament gospel, God also promised that the Suffering Servant would bring salvation through His vicarious death, but afterward would be exalted (Isa 52:13–53:12). God continued His promises by saying that the Servant's salvation would extend to both Israel and the Gentiles, as evidence of His loving loyalty (Isa 54:1–56:8). Israel would prosper again, re-gathering as a nation, becoming numerous, and ruling over the world (Isa 54). Then God blessed the Gentiles as well with the promise of salvation, showing just how far His loving loyalty extends (Isa 55:1–56:8). God then condemned the vile leaders of Israel to teach them that blessings in the kingdom come only to the contrite in heart (Isa 56:9–57:21).

God indicted the nation for making a false declaration of godliness in response to the threat of exile, urging the people to be characterized by true worship (Isa 58). God also revealed the nation's sinful practices that caused His judgment, reminding them that salvation and restoration would result from God's initiative rather than the nation's goodness (Isa 59).

QUESTION 16

Please write Isaiah 52:7 from memory.

QUESTION 17

If someone came to you and said they'd be open to Christianity if you could show them the gospel from the Old Testament, which passage would be best to use?

A. Isaiah 51:1–52:12

B. Isaiah 52:13–53:12

C. Isaiah 54

D. Isaiah 55:1–56:8

E. Isaiah 56:9–57:12

Topic 7 Key Points

- God's message of salvation brings delight to the enlightened hearer.
- Isaiah 52:13–53:12 prophesies the New Testament gospel message of Jesus' vicarious death and resurrection for our sin (see also Acts 8:26-40).

Topic 8: Restoration Under Messiah (Isaiah 60–66)

Up to this point in Isaiah, God has taught Israel that it needs to trust Him. He has shown them that neither alliances with foreign nations, nor any other god or idol can deliver them or bring security. Instead, Israel must trust in Him. Only He can fulfill the promises He made to them.

When they do trust Him and call to Him for deliverance, the wonderful promises of a glorious future can come true (Lk 13:35). But, as is clear from the final words of the prophecy, they will not come true for everyone (Isa 66:22-24).

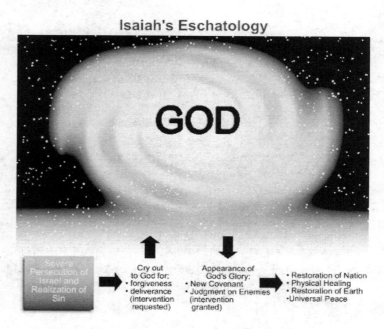

Isaiah's Eschatology

Assignment

- Please read "Restoration Under Messiah."

Restoration Under Messiah

In order to comfort His people that He will fulfill the Abrahamic covenant, God promises Israel a glorious future restoration under Messiah's rule of prosperity and peace (Isa 60–66).

God promised Israel a glorious future of prosperity and peace in the kingdom (Isa 60). He also promised that the Servant would prepare the way in Jerusalem for the Father to usher in this eternal lifestyle (Isa 61:1–63:6). The people of Israel responded by praying to be forgiven for their past rebellion so they could be restored through God's grace, and God declared His reasons for judging them, still offering restoration (Isa 63:7–64:12; 65).

God promised restoration to Israel's land and descendants forever, fulfilling His promises in the Abrahamic covenant (Isa 66). However, the unfaithful and hypocrites were warned that they would justly suffer throughout eternity,

Differences between the Millennium and Heaven		
	Millennium	**Heaven**
Duration	1000 years (Rev 20:1-6)	Eternal (Rev 22:5)
Death	Possible	Impossible
Longevity of life	"Never again will there be an infant who lives a few days. He who dies at a hundred will be thought a mere youth" (Isa 65:20)	No aging (implied in Rev 21:4)
Sin nature	Active (Rev 20:7-9)	Abolished (Rev 21:27)
Inhabitants	Initially Christians, but later includes unbelievers—no living with angels? (Mt 25:34; Rev 20:7-9)	Saints and angels alone (Rev 21:27)
Bodies	Mortal and immortal living together (Isa 65:20; 1 Cor 15:42-44)	Only immortal--glorified (1 Cor 15:42-44)
Satan	Bound, but then released after 1000 years (Rev 20:3, 7)	In lake of burning sulfur, never to be released again (Rev 20:10)
Political & religious center	Jerusalem (Isa 2:2-3; Mic 4:1-2, 7)	New Jerusalem (Rev 21)
Place	Earth (Rev 5:10)	New heavens and new earth (Rev 21:1)
Key passages	Psalm 72; Isaiah 2, 11, 65-66; Revelation 20:1-6	Revelation 21-22

QUESTION 18

God answers the prayer of Israel's remnant for forgiveness from past rebellion and for future restoration with _____ and restoration (Isa 63:7–64:12).

QUESTION 19

Which of the following are present in Isaiah 66? *(Select all that apply.)*

    A. Peace proceeding from God's temple

    B. Judgment on the unclean

    C. Sabbath worship

    D. Evangelism to distant lands

    E. Everyone in eternal peace

QUESTION 20

Isaiah teaches about the future restoration of the earth, first in the millennium, then on into eternity. Please open your Life Notebook and record your thoughts on how this relates to getting your priorities in order now.

Topic 8 Key Points

- The judgments of the tribulation lead to Israel's forgiveness at Christ's Second Advent, which in turn precedes its restoration in the millennial kingdom.

- The rebellious will suffer eternal punishment, and true worship will be reestablished that will extend into eternity.

Topic 9: Knowing, Being, Doing

QUESTION 21

Outline of Isaiah

	Isaiah 1–12	Isaiah 13–35	Isaiah 36–39	Isaiah 40–48	Isaiah 49–57	Isaiah 60–66
Salvation, Sickness & Sin						
Suffering Servant						
Violations & Deliverance						
Worldwide Judgment & Blessing						
Restoration under Messiah						
Shepherd of Israel						

QUESTION 22

Please open your Life Notebook and record anything new you have learned from this lesson, including any applications you should make to your life.

Lesson 4 Self Check

QUESTION 1

The key word for Isaiah is _____.

QUESTION 2

Which of the following is true for Isaiah 40–66?

    A. Assyria is the foreign power in the background.

    B. Messiah is the Suffering Servant.

    C. The time frame is mainly in the present.

    D. A Davidic king is on the throne of Judah

QUESTION 3

Isaiah describes the nature of the millennial kingdom more thoroughly than any other Bible book. *True or False?*

QUESTION 4

In a parable in Isaiah 5:1-7, God indicts Judah for the nation's worthless deeds by picturing it as what?

    A. A fig tree

    B. A vineyard

    C. An olive tree

    D. An abandoned field

QUESTION 5

In Isaiah 13–23, how did God show Ahaz the futility of trusting in foreign alliances?

    A. God appeared to him in a dream.

    B. God gave Isaiah a vision of the siege of Jerusalem.

    C. God gave the sign of Maher-Shalal-Hash-Baz.

    D. God pronounces judgment on several neighboring countries.

QUESTION 6

While defeat is predicted for all of Israel's enemies, what is promised to resurrected saints in Isaiah 25?

    A. A name written in gold

    B. Reigning in the kingdom

    C. The wedding banquet of the Lamb

    D. Shining like the stars forever

QUESTION 7

In Isaiah 36, the Assyrian chief advisor suggested that Hezekiah could not trust in the Lord because he had removed the high places where the Jews had worshipped the Lord. *True or False?*

QUESTION 8

In Isaiah 41:25, the name of the Persian whom God foretold would come to redeem Judah from the Babylonians is _____.

QUESTION 9

If someone came to you and said they'd be open to Christianity if you could show them the gospel from the Old Testament, which passage would be best to use?

    A. Isaiah 52:13-53:12

    B. Isaiah 54

    C. Isaiah 55:1-56:8

    D. Isaiah 56:9-57:12

QUESTION 10

The last verse in Isaiah ends with a beautiful picture of an eternity with all people at peace and in fellowship with God. *True or False?*

Lesson 4 Answers to Questions

QUESTION 1: Restoration [God will restore the original created order of Eden through a godly remnant, a return to the land, and salvation through Messiah, who will bring universal blessing.]

QUESTION 2

Objection	Explanation
In general, the events described in Isaiah 1–39 involve the nation of Assyria, but in Isaiah 40–66 the events involve the nation of Babylon	The shift is one of perspective, from the present to a future time.
The language, style, and theology of the two sections differ radically.	Focus, time of writing, and circumstances normally affect an author's style, viewpoints, and method of presenting facts.
Messiah is primarily portrayed as king in 1–39, but as the suffering servant in 40–66.	These two concepts are not contradictory, and both are present in each section.
Israel's return under Cyrus is predicted 150 years in advance, and Cyrus is named.	This objection assumes the impossibility of predicting the future. Nothing is impossible with God, who knows the future.

QUESTION 3: True [John 12:37-41 quotes Isaiah 6:9-10 and 53:1; and Paul quotes Isaiah in Romans 9:27 and 10:16-21 with quotes from Isaiah 10, 53, and 65.]

QUESTION 4: False [Only the book of Revelation gives the length of this kingdom— one thousand years (Rev 20:1-6). However, Isaiah describes the nature of this millennial kingdom the most thoroughly of any book in the Bible.]

QUESTION 5

C. A vineyard [Isaiah's song of the vineyard uses parable form to indict Judah for its worthless deeds in response to God's goodness (Isa 5:1-7). Isaiah's image of Judah (Israel) as a vineyard is continued in the New Testament (see Mk 12:1-12).]

QUESTION 6: *Your answer should be similar to the following:*

In the near future, this was a sign to Ahaz of God's speedy deliverance of Judah from Israel and Damascus. It also prophesied the birth, in the distant future, of the Messiah who would deliver Judah from sin through God's own presence (Isa 7).

QUESTION 7

Reference	Nation or City
Isaiah 13:1–14:27	Babylon
Isaiah 14:28-32	Philistia
Isaiah 15–16	Moab
Isaiah 17	Damascus and Israel
Isaiah 18	Ethiopia
Isaiah 19–20	Egypt

QUESTION 8

Reference	Nation or City
Isaiah 21:1-10	The desert near the Persian Gulf
Isaiah 21:11-12	Edom
Isaiah 21:13-17	Arabia
Isaiah 22	Jerusalem
Isaiah 23	Tyre

QUESTION 9: *Your answer*

QUESTION 10

    B. The wedding banquet of the Lamb [Isaiah sings a song of praise for God's protection and prophesies both the wedding banquet of the Lamb for resurrected saints, and the defeat of all of Israel's enemies (Isa 25; see Rev 19).]

QUESTION 11

Those Who Doubted	Consequence or Disproval
The drunkards of Israel and scoffers of Jerusalem (Isa 28)	A restored Israel and Judah
Jerusalem, for practicing only external religion without changed hearts (Isa 29:1-14)	A devastating and successful siege of the city
Kings of Judah who sought security in foreign alliances (Isa 29:15-24)	People who are in awe of God's holy name
Judah, for the stubbornness it displayed by making alliances with Egypt (Isa 30)	Egypt also will be destroyed
The falsely secure women of Judah with luxurious lifestyles (Isa 31–32)	The messianic king will bring in an age of true security and blessing
Assyria, the destroyer, for afflicting Judah (Isa 33)	Judgment on Assyria that would make Jerusalem a place of justice and blessing

QUESTION 12

    B. Egypt

    D. The Lord

[He said, "Look, you must be trusting in Egypt, that splintered reed staff" and "Perhaps you will tell me, 'We are trusting in the Lord our God'" (Isa 36:6, 7).]

QUESTION 13

    A. Because Hezekiah removed the high places where the Jews had worshipped the Lord

    B. Because the Lord himself sent the Assyrians

    C. Because the Assyrians had defeated the gods of all the lands they had conquered

QUESTION 14: Cyrus [God's sovereignty over His servant Israel is demonstrated to the nations "in court" by His appointment of Cyrus, who will allow the people to return to their land after a period of captivity (Isa 41:25).]

QUESTION 15: True [God's Servant, the Messiah, is contrasted with His servant, Israel, to comfort His people. Though they have been judged, they should be comforted by the prophecy of His messianic servant, who would defeat Israel's enemies and rule the world (Isa 42).]

QUESTION 16: *Your answer should be similar to the following:*

"How delightful it is to see coming over the mountains the feet of a messenger who announces peace, a messenger who brings good news, who announces deliverance, who says to Zion, 'Your God reigns!'"

QUESTION 17

    B. Isaiah 52:13–53:12 [In this passage God promises that the rejected Messiah, or Suffering Servant, will bring salvation through His vicarious death, but afterwards will be exalted, so that Israel might take comfort in His ultimate sacrifice for its sin (Isa 52:13–53:12; see also Acts 8:26-40).]

QUESTION 18: Judgment [Israel will experience judgment, the tribulation, forgiveness, and Christ's Second Advent before its restoration and the establishment of the millennial kingdom (Isa 66:6-8; Zech 12:1-10).]

QUESTION 19

    B. Judgment on the unclean

    C. Sabbath worship

    D. Evangelism to distant lands

[In this chapter, judgment comes from God's temple on the unclean, the idolaters, and those who rebelled. The rebellious suffer eternal punishment. But true worship will be reestablished for all eternity.]

QUESTION 20: *Your answer*

QUESTION 21

Outline of Isaiah

					Instructions
Violations & Deliverance	Worldwide Judgment & Blessing	Salvation, Sickness & Sin	Shepherd of Israel	Suffering Servant	Restoration under Messiah
Isaiah 1–12	Isaiah 13–35	Isaiah 36–39	Isaiah 40–48	Isaiah 49–57	Isaiah 60–66

QUESTION 22: *Your answer*

Lesson 4 Self Check Answers

QUESTION 1: Restoration

QUESTION 2
    B. Messiah is the Suffering Servant.

QUESTION 3: True

QUESTION 4
    B. A vineyard

QUESTION 5
    D. God pronounces judgment on several neighboring countries.

QUESTION 6
    C. The wedding banquet of the Lamb

QUESTION 7: True

QUESTION 8: Cyrus

QUESTION 9
    A. Isaiah 52:13–53:12

QUESTION 10: False

Lesson 5: Nahum and Habakkuk

Lesson Introduction

Just as Isaiah had predicted, God used the mighty nation of Assyria to judge Israel's sin. But God's instruments of judgment are not above judgment themselves. Nahum's short prophecy explicitly details how Babylon will conquer Assyria. Likewise, the book of Habakkuk shows how Babylon itself will undergo God's discipline after completing its divine task of judging Judah's sin. These books together remind God's people to place their trust in His divine timing and plan to bring in His kingdom. They also address common questions people have today:

- Why does evil go unpunished?
- Why is justice so slow?
- Why not do evil in order to get ahead?
- Why not sin so that grace may abound (Rom 6:1)?
- Why trust God under the current circumstances?

Lesson Outline

Topic 1: Introduction to Nahum

Topic 2: Destruction Decreed (Nah 1)

Topic 3: Destruction Described (Nah 2)

Topic 4: Destruction Deserved (Nah 3)

Topic 5: Introduction to Habakkuk

Topic 6: Habakkuk's Perplexity (Hab 1–2)

Topic 7: Habakkuk's Praise (Hab 3)

Topic 8: Knowing, Being, Doing

Lesson Objectives

By the end of this lesson you will be able to do the following:

- Discuss the timelines and historical backgrounds for the books and the authors of Nahum and Habakkuk
- Explain God's purpose and plan for Judah, Assyria, and Babylon
- Discuss why God's people are punished by evildoers and why they should observe the destruction of evil
- Look at God's plan and why God's people should trust Him despite current circumstances
- Evaluate how God's people are encouraged by God's majesty

Topic 1: Introduction to Nahum

The city of Nineveh, the capital of the Assyrian Empire, had repented under the brief preaching of Jonah more than one hundred years earlier (about 760 BC; see Jon 3). However, the revival was short lived, and the city returned to its evil practices. In 722 BC, during the reign of one of Assyria's greatest kings, Sargon II, Assyria destroyed Israel's capital, Samaria, located forty-eight kilometers north of Jerusalem. In 701 BC, Assyria invaded Judah under the leadership of Sennacherib, Sargon II's son, though King Hezekiah was delivered from his hand (see Isa 36–37). By the time of Nahum five decades later, God felt it was time to announce to His people the doom of this evil empire.

Nahum — Nineveh's Destruction								
Certain			Detailed			Justified		
Chapter 1			Chapter 2			Chapter 3		
Destruction Decreed			Destruction Described			Destruction Deserved		
Verdict of Vengeance			Vision of Vengeance			Vindication of Vengeance		
What God will do			How God will do it			Why God will do it		
God's Anger			God's Actions			God's Accusation		
God's Predictions for Judah			God's Power for Judah			God's Justice for Judah		
Title 1:1	God's Attributes 1:2-8	Plotting Against God 1:9-11	Destruction is Judah's Deliverance 1:12-15	Battling vs Judah's Splendor 2:1-2	Destruction & Despoiling 2:3-13	Judgment for Cruelty 3:1-7	Drunk when Destroyed 3:8-11	Burned with Fire 3:12-19
In Judah Against Assyria's Capital, Nineveh								
c. 660 BC								

- **Key Word:** Nineveh

- **Key Verse:** "The Lord is slow to anger but great in power; the Lord will certainly not allow the wicked to go unpunished" (Nah 1:3).

- **Summary Statement:** Nahum prophesies certain destruction for Nineveh for its scheming against God and cruelty to man, comforting Judah that God will powerfully protect it in accordance with His justice.

- **Application:** Have you ever thought God was less powerful because He did not answer your prayer immediately?

Assignment

- Please read "Introduction to Nahum."

Introduction to Nahum

Title

Nahum means "comfort"—an appropriate name for the prophet who comforted Judah by decreeing the fall of the Assyrians who had severely persecuted Israel.

Authorship

Nahum is mentioned only in this book of prophecy. He resided in the town of Elkosh (Nah 1:1), but its location is unknown. The most likely options for its location are Capernaum, which means "city of Nahum," or an unnamed city about thirty-six kilometers southwest of Jerusalem, as Nahum had a keen interest in the triumph of the southern kingdom of Judah (Nah 1:12, 2:1-2).

Circumstances

Date: This short book mentions the fall of Thebes in Egypt (Nah 3:8-10), which occurred in 664 BC, yet Nineveh's fall (612 BC) had not yet occurred at the time of Nahum's writing. Therefore, the date of composition probably falls between 663 and 654 BC. This time period falls during the reign of Manasseh (686-642 BC). Since Manasseh was Judah's most wicked king, it is understandable that Nahum made no mention of him in the superscription.

Recipients: Although the message concerned Nineveh (Nah 1:1), the capital of Assyria, no record exists of it having reached this empire. The recipients were likely the people of Judah, who needed to know that God would judge the nation that persecuted them.

This book was written after Samaria fell to the Assyrians (722 BC) but before the fall of Nineveh itself (612 BC), during which time Judah greatly feared that Samaria's fate also awaited the southern nation. God used this prophecy against Assyria to encourage His people in Judah that they would not fall to Assyria as well. Apparently, only Judah received this word about Nineveh's fate (Nah 1:15).

Characteristics

Nahum is the only prophetic book in the Bible that is entirely concerned with Assyria. While Jonah also wrote about this nation, his was a narrative account rather than a prophetic pronouncement. The only other prophets who preached against non-Israelite nations were Habakkuk (against Babylon) and Obadiah (against Edom). These three empires—Assyria, Babylon, and Edom—were the ones that afflicted the Jewish people most during the ninth to sixth centuries BC.

Unlike most prophets, Nahum did not preach a call to repentance, but rather an announcement of irreversible judgment. By Nahum's time, Assyria had already filled her quota of sins, similar to Judah by the time of Jeremiah.

Nineveh's destruction is one of the most clearly documented prophetic fulfillments in archaeology today. See the chart titled "Fulfillments of Nahum's Prophecies" in the lesson.

QUESTION 1

The key word for Nahum is _____.

QUESTION 2

Please match the following events with the dates they occurred.

Date	Event
722 BC	Fall of Israel
664 BC	Fall of Thebes
612 BC	Fall of Nineveh
586 BC	Fall of Jerusalem

QUESTION 3

The preaching of Nahum can be characterized as a call to repentance. *True or False?*

Topic 1 Key Points

- The key word for Nahum is "Nineveh," for the people in that city faced certain destruction for their scheming against God and cruelty to man.

- Nahum prophesied between the fall of Thebes in 664 BC and the fall of Nineveh in 612 BC.

Topic 2: Destruction Decreed (Nah 1)

Nahum's prophecy, though directed toward the powerful and cruel Assyrian capital city of Nineveh, was given for the benefit of Judah. He prophesied certain destruction on Nineveh for its scheming against God (Nah 1–2). The city would also be punished for its cruelty against man (Nah 3). Judah could find comfort in the fact that God would powerfully protect His people by destroying Nineveh in accordance with His justice. The prophecy decreed irreversible destruction and described it in detail because such judgment was deserved by the formerly repentant but now backslidden nation.

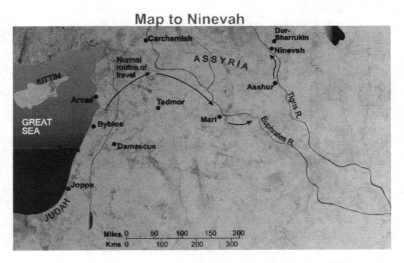

Map to Ninevah

Assignment

- Please read Nahum 1.
- Please read "Destruction Decreed."

Destruction Decreed

Summary Statement for the Book

Nahum prophesies certain destruction for Nineveh for its scheming against God and cruelty to man, comforting Judah that God will powerfully protect it in accordance with His justice.

Nahum declares the certainty of God's judgment on Nineveh for scheming against the powerful and just God in order to comfort Judah that God will protect it by destroying Nineveh (Nah 1).

Nahum declared divine authority for his message, stating that his prophecy was a vision from God regarding Nineveh's impending doom (Nah 1:1). He described the justice and power of God that would lead to the overthrow of Nineveh (Nah 1:2-6). Nahum described the goodness of God to justify His vengeance on Nineveh and to demonstrate His covenant loyalty towards Judah (Nah 1:2-8). No one can withstand the Lord's wrath (Nah 1:4-8).

Nineveh's plotting against the Lord would result in its own destruction, which would deliver Judah; a fact that should comfort Judah with the assurance of God's protection (Nah 1:9-15).

QUESTION 4

In Nahum 1:9-11, what is Assyria accused of?

    A. Killing widows and orphans

    B. Plotting against the Lord

    C. Stealing from the poor

    D. Unusual cruelty against mankind

QUESTION 5

God gave this promise of Assyria's destruction so that His people could find

    A. A reason to boast

    B. Strength for battle

    C. Vengeance

    D. Comfort and safety

Topic 2 Key Points

- In Nahum 1:9-11, God accuses Assyria of plotting, (Nah 1:11), against the Lord.

- God promises Assyria's destruction so that His people may find comfort and safety.

Topic 3: Destruction Described (Nah 2)

Often, when judgment comes from God in response to great evil, God allows His people to view the destruction.

> The LORD rained down sulfur and fire on Sodom and Gomorrah. …Abraham got up early in the morning and went to the place where he had stood before the LORD. He looked out toward Sodom and Gomorrah and all the land of that region. As he did so, he saw the smoke rising up from the land like smoke from a furnace (Gen 19:24, 27-28).

In Jeremiah 4:22-26, Jeremiah prophetically previewed the destruction soon coming on Judah from the Babylonians:

> The Lord answered, "This will happen because my people are foolish. They do not know me. They are like children who have no sense. They have no understanding. They are skilled at doing evil. They do not know how to do good." I looked at the land and saw that it was an empty wasteland. I looked up at the sky, and its light had vanished. I looked at the mountains and saw that they were shaking. All the hills were swaying back and forth! I looked and saw that there were no more people, and that all the birds in the sky had flown away. I looked and saw that the fruitful land had become a desert and that all of the cities had been laid in ruins. The Lord had brought this all about because of his blazing anger.

Contrasts Between Jonah and Nahum

JONAH	NAHUM
First Book (4 chapters)	Sequel (3 chapters)
c. 760 BC	c. 660 BC
Repentance from Sin	Return to Sin
Nineveh Delivered	Nineveh Destroyed
Israel Responsible for Salvation	Israel Protected by Destruction
Opportunity to Repent	No Opportunity to Repent
Narrative	Declarative
Focus on the Messenger	Focus on the Message
Prophet Disobeys	Prophet Obeys
Nineveh Obeys	Nineveh Disobeys
Deliverance from Water	Destruction by Water
Repented then Relented	No Repenting, No Relenting
Jonah's Wrath Refused	Jonah's Wrath Revisited
God's Compassion	God's Judgment

Just as the destruction of evil seen by Jeremiah would encourage God's people to continue doing good, the destruction described in Nahum 2 is an example of this principle.

Assignment

- Please read Nahum 2.
- Please read "Destruction Described."

Destruction Described

Nahum prophesies the future destruction of Nineveh in detail in order to enable Judah to see that God is more powerful than Assyria and more than adequate for protection (Nah 2).

Nahum warned Nineveh to prepare for battle because God considered the restoration of Judah's splendor an accomplished fact (Nah 2:1-2). Judah could visualize God's power over the Assyrians (Nah 2:3-8), and they could see how the proud city would be reduced to ruins (Nah 2:9-10). Nineveh, Nahum said, was like a lion's den filled with torn flesh. God had ultimate power over the powerful Assyrians (Nah 2:11-13).

QUESTION 6

Which of the following is more true of the book of Nahum than of the book of Jonah?

A. Israel is held responsible for Nineveh's fate.

B. The focus is on the messenger more than the message.

C. There is no opportunity for Nineveh to repent.

D. The prophecy happens about 760 BC.

QUESTION 7

What illustration does God use to show His power over the Assyrians in Nahum 2:11-13?

A. A lion's den filled with torn flesh

B. Bees swarming around an attacker

C. A field destroyed by locusts

D. Trees torn out by the roots

Topic 3 Key Points

- Unlike Jonah's prophecy to Nineveh, Nahum's prophecy does not hold Israel responsible for Nineveh's fate. The focus is on the message, and there is no opportunity to repent.
- God compares the results of His judgment of the Assyrians with a lion's den filled with torn flesh.

Topic 4: Destruction Deserved (Nah 3)

Fulfillments of Nahum's Prophecies

	Nahum's Prophecies	Historical Fulfillments
1	The Assyrian fortresses surrounding the city would be easily captured (3:12).	According to Babylonian Chronicle the fortified towns in Nineveh's environs began to fall in 614 B.C. including Tabris, present-day Sharif-Khan, a few miles northwest of Nineveh.
2	The besieged Ninevites would prepare bricks and mortar for emergency defense walls (3:14).	A.T. Olmstead reported: "To the south of the gate, the moat is still filled with fragments of stone and of mud bricks from the walls, heaped up when they were breached" (*History of Assyria*. Chicago: University of Chicago Press, 1951, p. 637).
3	The city gates would be destroyed (3:13).	Olmstead noted: "The main attack was directed from the northwest and the brunt fell upon the Hatamti gate at this corner...Within the gate are traces of the counterwall raised by the inhabitants in their last extremity" (*History of Assyria*, p. 637).
4	In the final hours of the attack the Ninevites would be drunk (1:10; 3:11).	Diodorus Siculus (ca. 20 B.C.) wrote, "The Assyrian king...distributed to his soldiers meats and liberal supplies of wine and provisions...While the whole army was thus carousing, the friends of Arbakes learned from some deserters of the slackness and drunkenness which prevailed in the enemy's camp and made an unexpected attack by night" (*Bibliotheca Historica* 2. 26. 4).
5	Nineveh would be destroyed by a flood (1:8; 2:6; 8).	Diodorus wrote that in the third year of the siege heavy rains caused a nearby river to flood part of the city and break part of the walls (*Bibliotheca Historica* 2. 26. 9; 2. 27. 13). Xenophon referred to terrifying thunder (presumably with a storm) associated with the city's capture (*Anabasis*, 3. 4. 12). Also the Khosr River, entering the city from the northwest at the Ninlil Gate and running through the city in a southwesterly direction, may have flooded because of heavy rains, or the enemy may have destroyed its sluice gate.
6	Nineveh would be destroyed by fire (1:10; 2:13; 3:15).	Archeological excavations at Nineveh have revealed charred wood, charcoal, and ashes. "There was no question about the clear traces of the burning of the temple (as also in the palace of Sennacherib), for a layer of ash about two inches thick lay clearly defined in places on the southeast side about the level of the Sargon pavement" (R. Campbell Thompson and R.W. Hutchinson, *A Century of Exploration at Nineveh*. London: Luzac, 1929, pp. 45,77).

Fulfillments of Nahum's Prophecies (cont'd)

	Nahum's Prophecies	Historical Fulfillments
7	The city's capture would be attended by a great massacre of people (3:3).	"In two battles fought on the plain before the city, the rebels defeated the Assyrians...So great was the multitude of the slain that the flowing stream, mingled with their blood, changed its color for a considerable distance" (Diodorus, *Bibliotheca Historica* 2. 26. 6-7).
8	Plundering and pillaging would accompany the overthrow of the city (2:9-10)	According to the Babylonian Chronicle, "Great quantities of spoil from the city, beyond counting, they carried off. The city [they turned] into a mound and ruin heap" (Luckenbill, *Ancient Records of Assyria and Babylonia*, 2:420).
9	When Nineveh would be captured its people would try to escape (2:8).	"Sardanapalus [another name for King Sin-shar-ishkun] sent away his three sons and two daughters with much treasure into Paphlagonia, to the governor of Kattos, the most loyal of his subjects" (Diodorus, *Bibliotheca Historica*, 2. 26. 8).
10	The Ninevite officers would weaken and flee (3:17).	The Babylonian Chronicle states that "[The army] of Assyria deserted [lit., ran away before] the king" (Luckenbill, *Ancient Records of Assyria and Babylonia*, 2:420).
11	Nineveh's images and idols would be destroyed (1:14).	R. Campbell Thompson and R.W. Hutchinson reported that the statue of the goddess Ishtar lay headless in the debris of Nineveh's ruins ("The British Museum Excavations on the Temple of Ishtar at Nineveh, 1930-1," *Annals of Archaeology and Anthropology*. 19, pp. 55-6).
12	Nineveh's destruction would be final (1:9, 14).	Many cities of the ancient Near East were rebuilt after being destroyed (e.g., Samaria, Jerusalem, Babylon) but not Nineveh.

The description of the destruction of "Babylon," whether literal or figurative, in Revelation 18 continues this theme—reviewing victories over evil—through the end of the Bible (Rev 18:1-3, 17-20). An angel proclaims fallen Babylon as a place for every evil and unclean thing. People mourn Babylon's death and destruction, but heaven rejoices in God's judgment against her.

Just as in Nahum 3, the destruction of "Babylon" as described in Revelation encourages God's faithful people that God will not let evil go unpunished.

Assignment

- Please read Nahum 3.
- Please read "Destruction Deserved."

Destruction Deserved

In order to help Judah realize that God's justice will not let the city go unpunished,

Nahum claims that Nineveh will be destroyed because of its cruelty (Nah 3).

God vowed that Nineveh would be made a spectacle before other nations because of its treatment of others (Nah 3:1-7). Its bloodshed, lying, and insatiable lust for plunder had caused great violence and cruelty (Nah 3:1-4). Therefore, God's justice would not let the city go unpunished.

Nineveh would be drunk when it was destroyed, and it would go into hiding after treating Thebes cruelly in Egypt in 663 BC (Nah 3:8-11). Nineveh would be burned with fire because its defensive efforts could not stand up against God's vengeance (Nah 3:12-19).

QUESTION 8

Nineveh would be drunk when destroyed and go into hiding for its cruel treatment of which city (Nah 3:8-11)?

    A. Damascus

    B. Jerusalem

    C. Samaria

    D. Thebes

QUESTION 9

In Nahum, God promises to avenge Judah's national enemies, and Judah sees that God's justice will not let Nineveh's evil deeds go unpunished. This should also motivate us to live a godly life. Please open your Life Notebook and explain how this knowledge motivates you.

Topic 4 Key Points

- When God punished Assyria, Judah realized that God's justice will not let evil go unpunished.

- Understanding God's justice should motivate us to live a godly life.

Topic 5: Introduction to Habakkuk

The rise of Babylon over Assyria provoked terror among the people of Judah as the Babylonians swept westward toward them (Hab 1:6). But God was more concerned about the *internal* affairs of His people. King Josiah's reforms were short-lived and incomplete, and his son Jehoahaz was deposed by Egypt after only three months. Jehoahaz's brother and successor, Jehoiakim, was evil and rebellious (2 Kgs 23:36–24:7; 2 Chron

Habakkuk Faith in Babylon's Destruction						
Judah						
c. 607-605 BC						
Punishment of Babylon				Praise Song		
1-2				3		
Habakkuk's Perplexity				Habakkuk's Praise		
God's Actions Challenged and Examined				God's Actions Commended and Extolled		
Faith Troubled				Faith Triumphant		
Problem				Resolution		
Habakkuk	God	Habakkuk	God	Habakkuk		
Why aren't you judging Judah's sin, God? 1:1-4	I will. I'll judge Judah with the Babylonians! 1:5-11	But can you use a nation *more* wicked than Judah? 1:12-2:1	Sure, but I'll judge them too. 2:2-20	In wrath remember mercy 3:1-2	Our God is an awesome God! 3:3-15	I'll wait patiently for Babylon's judgment and rejoice in God. 3:16-19

36:5-8). Habakkuk therefore saw Judah's internal problems: violence (Hab 1:2), injustice (Hab 1:3, 4), strife and conflict (Hab 1:3), disobedience to the law (Hab 1:4), and the oppression of the righteous by the wicked (Hab 1:4). With both internal and external problems, Habakkuk cried out to God, "Lord, why don't you do something?" The prophecy records God's response.

- **Key Word:** Faith

- **Key Verse:** (God regarding Babylon) "Look, the one whose desires are not upright will faint from exhaustion, but the person of integrity will live because of his faithfulness" (Hab 2:4).

- **Summary Statement:** Habakkuk questions God's use of Babylon to discipline Judah. God promises to punish Babylon, and Habakkuk responds by praising the sovereign and faithful work He has done in the past. This encourages Judah to trust Him in the future, despite the circumstances.

- **Applications**: Do you trust in God despite the perplexities of your life?

Assignment

- Please read "Introduction to Habakkuk."

Introduction to Habakkuk

Title

The name Habakkuk comes from a verb which means "to clasp or to embrace." However, we can only guess whether the name intends the one who embraces or the one who receives the embrace. Confusing matters even more is the related Assyrian word *hambakuku*, which is the name of a plant. In light of the argument of the book, which traces how Judah is to be disciplined by God through Babylon, who then will also be disciplined, it seems that the passive sense of Judah being "embraced by God" may make the best sense. However, until further evidence is presented, the meaning of the name must remain a mystery.

Authorship

Like many of the minor prophets, Habakkuk is mentioned only in his prophecy. Discussion abounds about his identity, but nothing conclusive is known.

Habakkuk is called a prophet (Hab 1:1; 3:1). He also notes at the end of the book, "For the director of music. On my stringed instruments" (Hab 3:19), which may suggest that he was a musician of the Levitical office as well (Walvoord 1:1506). This evidence suggests that he may have been a priest connected with the temple worship in Jerusalem, and perhaps also a poet, as evidenced by his educated, sensitive, and articulate poetic style.

Circumstances

Date: The author gives no references to a king in the superscription, but dates ranging from 700 to 300 BC have been speculated (LaSor, 449). However, the reference to the attacking Babylonians (Hab 1:6) places the time of the prophecy between 625 BC, when Nabopolassar seized the throne and gave birth to the Neo-Babylonian kingdom, and 605 BC, during Nebuchadnezzar's first attack on Jerusalem, when the prophet Daniel was taken captive. The imminence of the Babylonian invasion (Hab 2:1; 3:16) argues for a date just before or during 605 BC. In May or June of that year, Babylon routed Egypt in the battle of Carchemish before attacking Jerusalem in September (Walvoord, 1:1326). A date between these months for Habakkuk's prophecy therefore would make good sense, but 607-605 is nearly certain. This places it after the fall of Nineveh in 612 BC and before the first deportation of the Jews in 605 BC.

Recipients: Even though the prophecy concerned Babylon, it was directed toward the people of Judah. Since the northern kingdom had fallen more than one hundred years earlier, only Judah could have received it.

Characteristics

Habakkuk is the only pre-exilic prophet who is specifically designated as a prophet by profession in the title of his book (Hab 1:1). He is also unique among the prophets in that most prophets declared God's message *to people*, but Habakkuk dialogued with God *about people*. Also, normally the prophetic process was initiated by God—but Habakkuk initiated the dialogue, taking up two thirds of the book (Wilkinson, 275). Whereas most Old Testament prophets *proclaimed* God's judgment, Habakkuk *pleaded for* God's judgment.

QUESTION 10

The key word for Habakkuk is _____.

QUESTION 11

Which of the following are considered likely to be true about Habakkuk? *(Select all that apply.)*

    A. He was the Shunammite woman's son whom Elijah restored to life.

    B. He was a priest connected with the temple worship.

    C. He was an aide to the prophet Daniel.

    D. He was an excellent poet.

QUESTION 12

Please select the most likely time of writing for Habakkuk.

    A. Between 722 BC and 664 BC

    B. Between 664 BC and 612 BC

    C. Between 612 BC and 586 BC

    D. After 586 BC

Topic 5 Key Points

- Habakkuk's key word is "faith," and the prophecy encourages Judah to trust God based on His past faithfulness, despite current circumstances.

- Besides being a prophet, Habakkuk was probably also a priest connected with the temple worship and an excellent poet.

- Habakkuk likely prophesied about 607 BC, when the Babylonians had become the major world power and were a threat to Jerusalem.

Topic 6: Habakkuk's Perplexity (Hab 1–2)

Habakkuk's prophecy actually is in the form of a dialogue as much as a prophetic pronouncement. In the first two chapters, Habakkuk questions God about why Judah's sin has gone unpunished. God answers that Babylon will be His means of judgment, but that this nation will also be punished as a demonstration of His sovereignty over the nations. In recognition of God's sovereign and just ways, the prophet concludes by writing a praise song. The song acknowledges His faithful workings in the past in order to encourage Judah to trust Him in the future, despite the circumstances (Hab 3). The prophet's purpose is to express that God has everything under control and knows what He is doing.

Assignment

- Please read Habakkuk 1–2.
- Please read "Habakkuk's Perplexity."

Man and God Contrasted in Habakkuk

MAN	GOD
Accuses God of injustice (1:2-4)	Justly uses whoever He wants (1:12)
Asks "Why?" (1:3)	Answers "Who?" (2:20)
Tolerates sin (1:3-4)	Cannot tolerate wrong (1:13)
Feels things are out of control (1:14-17)	Has all things in control (1:5)
Says God can't use the wicked (1:13)	Uses even the wicked in His plan (1:6)
Impatient with God's judging sin (1:2)	Patient in judgment of sin (2:3; cf. 2 Pet. 3:9)
Wants God to show him by sight (2:1)	Wants men to trust Him by faith (2:4)

Habakkuk's Perplexity

Summary Statement for the Book

Habakkuk questions God's use of Babylon to discipline Judah. God promises to punish Babylon, and Habakkuk responds by praising the sovereign, faithful work He has done in the past. This encourages Judah to trust Him in the future, despite the circumstances.

Habakkuk questions God why Judah's sin has gone unpunished, and God answers that Babylon will be His means of judgment, but that this nation will also be punished; this encourages Judah to trust His sovereignty (Hab 1–2).

Habakkuk affirmed the divine authority of his message by identifying himself as God's prophet who had a message from God to give the people (Hab 1:1).

Habakkuk complained that he doubted God's justice because it seemed God had allowed the injustices in Judah to go unpunished for so long (Hab 1:2-4). Habakkuk asked how long he must point out the violence in the land to the deaf ears of God (Hab 1:2). He asked why he must see continued injustice, destruction, violence, strife, and conflict while it seemed to him that God stood by without punishing the evildoers (Hab 1:3). Habakkuk noted that the result of this evil is spurned law, injustice, and the oppression of the righteous by the wicked (Hab 1:4).

God responded to Habakkuk's questions by declaring that He was about to do something amazing and unbelievable (Hab 1:5). He explained that He would raise up the fierce and arrogant Babylonians as His instrument of judgment on Judah (Hab 1:6–11). This would be evidence of His sovereignty over the nations.

Habakkuk doubted God's justice, complaining that the Lord could not punish Judah with a nation as evil as Babylon (Hab 1:12–2:1). Habakkuk questioned why God would employ a nation with even more iniquity, injustice, and idolatry than Judah (Hab 1:12-17). Habakkuk compared his anticipation of God's reply to a sentinel anxiously watching for the approaching enemy on the watchtower (Hab 2:1).

God responded to Habakkuk's doubts by commanding him to record woes against Babylon for its injustices (Hab 2:2-20). He told Habakkuk to record His revelation regarding the demise of Babylon so that everyone would know of His just dealings with the wicked nation (Hab 2:2-3). He then contrasted the demise of the proud, debauched, greedy, and bloodthirsty Babylonians with the preservation of the righteous remnant of Judah (Hab 2:4-5). Lastly, God prophesied that the nations conquered by Babylon would sing a taunting song of woe against the arrogant, unjust nation after its fall (Hab 2:6-20).

Woe was pronounced on Babylon for its:

- Greed, therefore, it would also be plundered (Hab 2:6-8)

- Material gain by exploitation, which would return on its own head (Hab 2:9-11)

- Violence, in contrast to God filling the earth with His glory (Hab 2:12-14)

- Immorality, which was forced on others (Hab 2:15-17)

- Powerless idols, in contrast to the sovereign majesty of God, which the whole world would recognize when the nation fell (Hab 2:18-20)

QUESTION 13

Habakkuk's first question to God was why Babylon's evil hadn't been punished (Hab 1:2-4). *True or False?*

QUESTION 14

Please match the reference with the corresponding reason Habakkuk thought Babylon was a bad choice to discipline Judah.

Reference	Reason
Habakkuk 1:12-13	They practiced even more *idolatry* than Judah
Habakkuk 1:14-15	They practiced even more *iniquity* than Judah
Habakkuk 1:16-17	They practiced even more *injustice* than Judah

But God would also punish the punisher for its sins.

QUESTION 15

Based on Habakkuk 2:2-20, which of the following are reasons woe is pronounced on Babylon? *(Select all that apply.)*

   A. Its greed

   B. Its powerless idols

   C. Its immorality forced on others

   D. Its material gain by exploitation

   E. Its excessive violence

God pronounces these judgments on Babylon so that a righteous remnant of Judah will trust Him (Hab 2:2-20).

Topic 6 Key Points

- Habakkuk first questioned God about why the evil in Judah had gone unpunished.

- Habakkuk next asked how God could use Babylon to punish Judah when it practiced more iniquity, injustice, and idolatry than Judah did (Hab 1:12-17).

- God's answered Habakkuk by pronouncing woe on Babylon, which would eventually also be punished for its sins.

Topic 7: Habakkuk's Praise (Hab 3)

Habakkuk has several of the same emphases as Revelation. Revelation portrays God's people going through extremely tough circumstances. Chapters 6–19 give a prophetic vision of God's people going through the tribulation, the seventieth week of Daniel (Dan 9:24-27), which Jeremiah called the time of Jacob's trouble (Jer 30:7). Habakkuk predicts tough times for God's people at the hand of evil Babylon and so does Revelation (Hab 1:1-11; Rev 18:20). But God eventually will judge the wicked nations (Hab 2; Rev 18).

One of the main points both books teach is that God's faithful people should trust His plan. Despite appearances, God is in control, and He ultimately wins (Rev 19–22).

Assignment

- Please read Habakkuk 3.

- Please read "Habakkuk's Praise."

Habakkuk's Praise

Habakkuk responds to God's promise of Babylon's demise by praising His sovereign, faithful works of the past. Those works are the basis for confident rejoicing that He can be trusted in the future, despite the circumstances (Hab 3).

Habakkuk prayed for the mercy God demonstrated in the past, showing his acceptance of God's method of judgment using the Babylonians (Hab 3:1-2). Then he pondered God's majesty as demonstrated in His past works on the nation's behalf, to encourage Judah to trust Him for the future as well.

God's splendor and majesty at Mount Sinai showed His sovereign control (Hab 3:3-4). His power over nature was demonstrated in the plagues of Egypt (Hab 3:5). Then, God's eternality was demonstrated when He destroyed age-old mountains by earthquake (Hab 3:6). His workings on behalf of Israel distressed nations on both sides of the Red Sea (Hab 3:7). God had sovereign control of rivers (Hab 3:8-10). His power was also seen when He caused the sun and moon to stand still in order to defeat Joshua's enemies (Hab 3:11). God's faithfulness to the Davidic covenant was shown in His delivering Israel from destruction by the nations, to preserve the Davidic line for the Messiah (Hab 3:12-13). God's protection of Israel was shown when He caused the Midianites to destroy themselves under Gideon (Hab 3:14) and when He destroyed Pharaoh and his men in the Red Sea as if with "God's horses" (Hab 3:15).

Habakkuk confessed his fear of the Babylonians, but he continued to wait patiently for God's Word to come true regarding Babylon's fall (Hab 3:16). In a song, Habakkuk committed himself to have confidence and rejoice in the Lord despite the worst of circumstances (Hab 3:17-18). His final words were a note to the music director, indicating that this song was to be accompanied by stringed instruments (Hab 3:19).

QUESTION 16

Please match the reference with the corresponding teaching about the mercy God has shown in the past.

Reference	God's Mercy
Habakkuk 3:3-4	God's power was shown in His sovereign control of rivers.
Habakkuk 3:5	God's splendor and majesty at Mount Sinai showed His sovereign control.
Habakkuk 3:6	God demonstrated His eternal nature when He destroyed age-old mountains by earthquake.
Habakkuk 3:7	God demonstrated His power over nature in the plagues of Egypt.
Habakkuk 3:8-10	God's workings on behalf of Israel distressed nations on both sides of the Red Sea.

QUESTION 17

Please match the reference with the corresponding teaching about God's mercy shown in the past.

Reference	God's Mercy
Habakkuk 3:11	God's protection of Israel was shown when He destroyed Pharaoh and his men in the Red Sea as if with "God's horses."
Habakkuk 3:12-13	God's power was shown when He caused the sun and moon to stand still in order to defeat Joshua's enemies.
Habakkuk 3:14	God's protection of Israel was shown when He caused the Midianites to destroy themselves under Gideon.
Habakkuk 3:15	God's faithfulness to the Davidic covenant was shown in His delivering Israel from destruction by the nations to preserve the line for the Messiah.

QUESTION 18

When Habakkuk wanted to encourage Judah to trust God with the future, he listed events that showed God's majesty in His past workings. If someone came to you for counsel who had just lost their job and needed to trust the Lord for the future, what Bible story would you recommend they read and why? Record your answer in your Life Notebook.

Topic 7 Key Points

- Habakkuk recalled several memorable historic events that showed God's mercy on Israel's behalf, in order to encourage Israel to trust God for the future, despite the current circumstances.

- One way to counsel a discouraged person is to use an appropriate Bible passage that shows God's historic mighty and majestic work on His people's behalf.

Topic 8: Knowing, Being, Doing

QUESTION 19

Match the events in Nahum with the corresponding passage from the book.

Events in Nahum

		Instructions
Nineveh's Cruelty against Man		
Nineveh's Scheming against God		
Certain Destruction upon Nineveh		
Nahum 1	**Nahum 2**	**Nahum 3**

QUESTION 20

Match the events in Habakkuk with the corresponding passage from the book.

Themes in Habakkuk

	Habakkuk 1:1-4	Habakkuk 1:5–2:1	Habakkuk 2:2-20	Habakkuk 3
				Instructions
God pronounces woes against Babylon				
Habakkuk praises God's past works				
How can God use an evil nation to punish Judah?				
Why does evil in Judah go unpunished?				

QUESTION 21

Please open your Life Notebook and record anything new you have learned from this lesson, including any applications you should make to your life.

Lesson 5 Self Check

QUESTION 1

The keyword for Nahum is _____.

    A. Babylon

    B. Faith

    C. Nineveh

    D. Plan

QUESTION 2

What is the correct date for the fall of Thebes?

    A. 722 BC

    B. 664 BC

    C. 612 BC

    D. 586 BC

QUESTION 3

In Nahum 1, besides crimes against mankind, Assyria is accused of plotting against God. *True or False?*

QUESTION 4

Which of the following is true in the book of Jonah more than the book of Nahum?

    A. Israel is held responsible for Nineveh's fate.

    B. The focus is on the message more than the messenger.

    C. The prophecy happens about 660 BC.

    D. There is opportunity to repent.

QUESTION 5

Nineveh will be drunk when it is destroyed and will go into hiding for its cruel treatment of which city (Nah 3:8-11)?

    A. Damascus

    B. Jerusalem

    C. Samaria

    D. Thebes

QUESTION 6

Which of the following is likely true about Habakkuk?

    A. He was a musician of the Levitical office.

    B. He was the Shunammite woman's son, whom Elijah restored to life.

    C. He was an aide to the prophet Daniel in Babylon.

    D. His letter was written primarily as a message to Babylon.

QUESTION 7

The book of Habakkuk was most likely written just before the fall of Assyria. *True or False?*

QUESTION 8

In the book's first chapter, Habakkuk asks God why the evil in Judah has gone unpunished. *True or False?*

QUESTION 9

One purpose for God's pronouncement of woes on Babylon in Habakkuk 2 was to prove His anger against it. *True or False?*

QUESTION 10

Which of the following was connected with five of the nine events mentioned in Habakkuk 3 to remind the people of God's majestic acts?

    A. The account of creation

    B. The conquest of Canaan

    C. The exodus from Egypt

    D. The period of the judges

Lesson 5 Answers to Questions

QUESTION 1: Nineveh [Nahum prophesies certain destruction on Nineveh for its scheming against God and cruelty to man, in order to comfort Judah that God will powerfully protect it in accordance with His justice.]

QUESTION 2

Date	Event
722 BC	Fall of Israel
664 BC	Fall of Thebes
612 BC	Fall of Nineveh
586 BC	Fall of Jerusalem

QUESTION 3: False [Unlike most of the prophets, Nahum's preaching was not a call to repentance, but rather an announcement of irreversible judgment.]

QUESTION 4

    B. Plotting against the Lord [Assyria was promised destruction no matter what they plotted against the Lord (Nah 1:9).]

QUESTION 5

    D. Comfort and safety

QUESTION 6

    C. There is no opportunity for Nineveh to repent.

QUESTION 7

    A. A lion's den filled with torn flesh

QUESTION 8

    D. Thebes [Therefore Judah would realize that God's justice would not let Nineveh go unpunished.]

QUESTION 9: *Your answer*

QUESTION 10: Faith [Habakkuk responded to God's discipline of Judah by praising the sovereign, faithful work He has done in the past. This encouraged Judah to trust Him in the future, despite the circumstances.]

QUESTION 11

    B. He was a priest connected with the temple worship.

    D. He was an excellent poet.

QUESTION 12

    C. Between 612 BC and 586 BC [The book was written after the fall of Nineveh (612 BC) and before the first deportation of Jews to Babylon in 605 BC. Nineveh's fall allowed Babylon to become the next world power; they were the foreign power referred to in Habakkuk's prophecy.]

QUESTION 13: False [His first question actually was, "Why has evil in Judah gone unpunished?"]

QUESTION 14

Reference	Reason
Habakkuk 1:12-13	They practiced even more *iniquity* than Judah
Habakkuk 1:14-15	They practiced even more *injustice* than Judah
Habakkuk 1:16-17	They practiced even more *idolatry* than Judah

QUESTION 15

    A. Its greed

    B. Its powerless idols

    C. Its immorality forced on others

    D. Its material gain by exploitation

QUESTION 16

Reference	God's Mercy
Habakkuk 3:3-4	God's splendor and majesty at Mount Sinai showed His sovereign control.

Habakkuk 3:5	God demonstrated His power over nature in the plagues of Egypt.
Habakkuk 3:6	God demonstrated His eternal nature when He destroyed age-old mountains by earthquake.
Habakkuk 3:7	God's workings on behalf of Israel distressed nations on both sides of the Red Sea.
Habakkuk 3:8-10	God's power was shown in His sovereign control of rivers.

QUESTION 17

Reference	*God's Mercy*
Habakkuk 3:11	God's power was shown when He caused the sun and moon to stand still in order to defeat Joshua's enemies.
Habakkuk 3:12-13	God's faithfulness to the Davidic covenant was shown in His delivering Israel from destruction by the nations to preserve the line for the Messiah.
Habakkuk 3:14	God's protection of Israel was shown when He caused the Midianites to destroy themselves under Gideon.
Habakkuk 3:15	God's protection of Israel was shown when He destroyed Pharaoh and his men in the Red Sea as if with "God's horses."

QUESTION 18: *Your answer*

QUESTION 19

Events in Nahum

Instructions

Nineveh's Scheming against God	Certain Destruction upon Nineveh	Nineveh's Cruelty against Man
Nahum 1	**Nahum 2**	**Nahum 3**

QUESTION 20

Themes in Habakkuk

Instructions

Why does evil in Judah go unpunished?	How can God use an evil nation to punish Judah?	God pronounces woes against Babylon	Habakkuk praises God's past works
Habakkuk 1:1-4	**Habakkuk 1:5–2:1**	**Habakkuk 2:2-20**	**Habakkuk 3**

QUESTION 21: *Your answer*

Lesson 5 Self Check Answers

QUESTION 1
   C. Nineveh

QUESTION 2
   B. 664 BC

QUESTION 3: True

QUESTION 4
   D. There is opportunity to repent.

QUESTION 5
   D. Thebes

QUESTION 6
   A. He was a musician of the Levitical office.

QUESTION 7: False

QUESTION 8: True

QUESTION 9: False

QUESTION 10
   C. The exodus from Egypt

Lesson 6: Joel and Zephaniah

Lesson Introduction

One of the most common concepts found in the prophetic writings is the day of the Lord. Although we have not used this term until this point in our study, every prophet notes this time of judgment, which is followed by blessing. However, Joel and Zephaniah have the highest percentage of their material devoted to this day.

The day of the Lord refers in general to any visitation of special judgment or blessing by God on humanity. But the fulfillment of the day of the Lord refers specifically to the seventieth week of Daniel, also known as the tribulation, or the time of Jacob's trouble. This includes Jesus' Second Advent at the end of the tribulation and the millennium. The prophets predict that this time will be accompanied by many signs and judgments.

Lesson Outline

Topic 1: Introduction to Joel

Topic 2: Zion's Discipline (Joel 1:1–2:17)

Topic 3: Zion's Deliverance (Joel 2:18–3:21)

Topic 4: Introduction to Zephaniah

Topic 5: Day of Punishment (Zeph 1:1-3:8)

Topic 6: Day of Praise (Zeph 3:9-20)

Topic 7: Knowing, Being, Doing

Lesson Objectives

By the end of this lesson you will be able to do the following:

- Understand the backgrounds of the Joel and Zephaniah
- Discuss the near and far judgments and blessings called the day of the Lord
- Examine the call to repentance in hopes of avoiding these judgments because of God's compassion
- Discuss the sins that lead to the promised judgments of the day of the Lord
- Discuss the blessings promised to Israel and to the Gentiles during the day of the Lord

Topic 1: Introduction to Joel

The prophet Joel masterfully illustrates both the judgment and grace of God, using the devastation from a recent locust plague in the land of Judah. In the first of two major movements in the book (Joel 1:1–2:17), Joel declares that the judgment of locusts should cause the people to repent, as a more dreadful day of the Lord is coming on the land through the invasion of the Babylonian army. This is followed by Joel proclaiming God's forgiveness and future deliverance of His people through the judgment of the nations and the restoration of Judah (Joel 2:18–3:21).

Joel Day of the Lord				
Judah				
c. 607-605 BC				
Past			Future	
"Locust" Plagues 1:1-2:17			Blessing 2:18-3:21	
Zion's Discipline			Zion's Deliverance	
The Lord fights *against* His people			The Lord fights *for* His people	
Introduction 1:1-3	Repent from literal locusts 1:4-20	Repent after Babylonian/ Armageddon "locusts" 2:1-17	Forgiveness after repentance 2:18-2:27	Spiritual awakening 2:28-3:21

Therefore, the book follows the common pattern—judgment followed by blessing—that many of the prophetic writings use. It is written to encourage repentance based on God's mercy.

- **Key Word:** Locusts

- **Key Verse:** "…Yes, the day of the Lord is awesome and very terrifying—who can survive it? 'Yet even now,' the Lord says, 'return to me with all your heart—with fasting, weeping, and mourning'" (Joel 2:11-12).

- **Summary Statement:** A recent judgment of locusts should cause the people of Judah to repent, as a more dreadful day of the Lord will come in a Babylonian invasion and eventually at Armageddon. Yet God promises forgiveness, deliverance, and restoration by judging the nations.

- **Application:** Do you need God to strip you of everything before you repent?

Assignment

- Please read "Introduction to Joel."

Introduction to Joel

Title

The name Joel is usually interpreted to mean "Yahweh is God," but other possible meanings may be "strong-willed" and "take refuge."

Authorship

External Evidence: The Joel of this prophecy is mentioned nowhere else in the Old Testament.

Internal Evidence: The title declares the author to be Joel, the son of Pethuel (Joel 1:1). Although several men named Joel are mentioned in Scripture, nothing is known of the author of this prophecy except what may be determined from the book. Because of the several references to Zion and the Temple (Joel 1:9, 13-14; 2:15-17, 23, 32; 3:1, 5-6, 16-17, 20-21), he probably lived close to Jerusalem. The references to religious activities and priestly ceremonies (Joel 1:13-14; 2:17) may suggest that Joel was a temple prophet (LaSor, 438).

Circumstances

Date: The time of Joel's writing remains a problem, as the book makes no explicit references to time in the superscription. Until recently, most dating estimates fell into two general periods (1 and 2 below).

1. The first date proposed is *early pre-exilic*, usually during the time of Joash (835 BC). Support for this date is found in: (a) the reference to Israel's early enemies, Tyre, Sidon, Philistia, Egypt and Edom (Joel 3:4, 19); (b) the government of elders (Joel 1:2; 2:16) and priests (Joel 1:9, 13; 2:17); these were in power while Joash was a boy, as he was crowned at age seven (see 2 Chr 24:1); (c) the position of Joel between Hosea and Amos in the Hebrew canon; and (d) Amos' dependence on Joel (Amos 1:2 on Joel 3:16; Amos 9:13 and Joel 3:18).

Response: Old Testament prophets in even the much-later Babylonian era preached against the nations mentioned above (see Jer 46–47; 49:7-22; Ezek. 27–30; Zeph 2:4-7). The government of elders and priests was in power again at a later, post-exilic date, which makes this argument inconclusive. The Septuagint (Greek) order is different from the Hebrew, thus making the order in the canon insignificant concerning date. One cannot tell whether Amos quotes Joel or vice versa. Further, the Greek slave trade (mentioned in Joel 3:6) was not characteristic of this early time period.

2. Others suggest a *post-exilic* date near the end of the exile in 540 BC or even as late as 350 BC. Four arguments rally to defend this position: (a) the Babylonian destruction of Jerusalem and Judah's exile in 586 BC are mentioned (Joel 3:1-2, 17), and other temple references (Joel 1:9, 13; Joel 2:17) could apply to the post-exilic temple of 516 BC; (b) the government of elders was in power after the last king of Judah was carried into exile; (c) Joel quotes the exilic prophet Ezekiel (Joel 2:3 with Ezk 36:35; Joel 2:10 with Ezk 32:7; Joel 2:27-28 with Ezk 39:28-29), and (d) the mention of the Greek slave trade (Joel 3:6) could refer to the post-exilic time, when the Greek empire had its greatest control of Palestine.

Response: (a) Joel 3 could record a future restoration which will follow captivity; it does not require captivity to have already occurred; (b) the absence of a monarchy in the book does not disprove its existence at the time of writing, especially since elders were also prominent *before* the exile (2 Kgs 23:1; Jer 26:17; Lam 5:12, 14); (c) dependency on parallel quotations is speculative, as it is difficult to know who quoted whom; and (d) the slave trade between the Phoenicians and Greeks flourished as early as the seventh and early sixth centuries (Ezk 27:13). Also, Greek control of Palestine (331-143 BC) was even later than the post-exilic date proposed above.

3. A *late pre-exilic* time period between the two periods proposed above (597-586 BC) is supported by affinities between Joel, Zephaniah, and Jeremiah, especially since Zephaniah refers to the day of the Lord as a time of darkness. Further, this perspective is consistent with the fact that the Greek slave trade existed in the seventh-sixth centuries BC. Finally, a date between 597 and 586 BC seems best because the invasion described in Joel 3:2 could refer to the Babylonian invasion, which deported 10,000 men in 597 BC (see 2 Kgs 24:10-16). This occurred before the final exile and destruction of the temple in 586 BC, thus explaining why the temple is still prominent in the book.

Recipients: The total lack of reference to Israel indicates that Joel had in mind those living in Judah when he penned the prophecy. This is also supported by the many references to Zion and the temple (Joel 1:9, 13-14; 2:15-17, 23, 32; 3:1, 5-6, 16-17, 20-21). The prophecy's focus on Judah may also provide additional evidence that it was written just before Judah's fall in 586 BC rather than more than two centuries earlier in 835 BC.

Characteristics

The locust plague in Joel's prophecy was not merely a natural disaster. It was a supernatural disaster, for Moses had predicted that when locusts invaded the land, the people should see it as divine judgment on their sin (Deut 28:38, 42; see Lev 26:20).

Although calls to repentance are made in the book (Joel 2:12, 15-17), the sins of the nation are never specifically spelled out. The coming day of the Lord, a time of awesome judgment on people who have rebelled against God, is the preeminent theme of the prophecy (Joel 1:15; 2:1, 11, 31; 3:14, 18). The day of the Lord theme pervades this prophecy perhaps more than any other with the possible exception of Zephaniah (e.g., Zeph 1:14-18; 2; 3), though it is mentioned throughout the Bible (see Amos 1:3–2:3; Zech 12–14; Isa 13:6, 9; 14:28-32; 17:1; 20:1-6; Isa 31:1-5; Jer 46:10; Ezk 30:3; 1 Thess 5:2, 4; 2 Thess 2:2; 2 Pet 3:10). Joel mentions this "day" several times (Joel 1:15; 2:1-2, 11, 31; 3:14, 18), indicating that it actually refers to a time period of judgment for the unrighteous.

When is this day? The mention of apocalyptic phenomena—wonders in the heavens like the sun being turned to darkness and the moon to blood (Joel 2:30-31)—indicates that *near* judgment will strike Judah for disobedience, but the *ultimate* judgment will befall the nation at Christ's Second Advent (see Mt 24:29-30). However, this day will not just be a day of wrath on the unbelieving; it will also be a day of blessing as well for the righteous (Joel 2:32; Zech 14; Zeph 3:8-20; Isa. 2; 11; 65–66; Amos 9:11-15; Ezk 20:33-44, etc.).

The difficult relationship between the literal locusts in chapter 1 and the "locusts" in 2:1-11 has produced at least 15 different views. Who are these "locusts" in Joel 2:1-11? The following views are adapted from a chart by John Martin, "Views on the Locust Plague in Joel 2":

Views on the Locust Plague in Joel 2
Supernatural Creatures
1. Distant Future (scorpions/supernatual insects; see Rev 9:3-10)
Armies (Allegorical View)
2. Near Future (Assyria, Babylon, Greece, Rome)
Armies (Literal/Apocalyptic Views)
3. Near Future (Assyria)
4. Near Future (Egypt) referring to Pharaoh Shishak (1 Kings 14:25; 1 Chron 12:2-9)
5. Near Future (Egypt) referring to Pharaoh Neco (2 Chron 35:20-36:4)
6. Distant Future (Armageddon)
7. Distant Future (Gog and Magog)
8. Distant Future (Army of God leader Brother Amos)
9. Near Future (Assyria) and Distant Future (Armageddon)
10. Near Future (identity unknown) and Distant Future (Armageddon)
11. Near Future (Babylon) and Distant Future (Armageddon)
Locusts (Literal Views)
12. Pas (same locust invasion as in chapter 1)
13. Near Future (in Joel's Day)
14. Distant Future (in the Tribulation)
Locusts and Army (Combination View)
15. Near Future (literal locusts) and Distant Future (figurative army at Armageddon)

This course holds to the apocalyptic view, which sees both a near army, Babylon, and a far army, at Armageddon. This finds support in several lines of evidence, four of which are listed here:

1. The imagery of chapter 2 can't simply describe a locust plague, since it includes an earthquake, signs in the skies, and ominous events (Joel 2:10, 30-31; see Mt 24:29).

2. The invaders of chapter 2 are called "people" (Joel 2:2), an "army" (Joel 2:11), and "the northern army" (Joel 2:20).

3. Literal locusts never invade Palestine from the north as does this "army" (Joel 2:20).

4. The term "northern one" (Joel 2:20) would be an unsuitable designation for locusts since it is an adjective ("northern") with a prefixed article, thus meaning "the northerner," or "the northern one." In contrast, Israel's eschatological enemies are often said to be ones who will invade from the north (see Zech 6:8; Jer 1:14-15; 6:1, 22; Ezk 38:6, 15; 39:2; Isa 14:31; Zeph 2:13).

QUESTION 1

The key word for the book of Joel is _____.

QUESTION 2

Joel's prophecy follows the pattern of judgment followed by blessing, as seen in many of the prophetic writings. *True or False?*

QUESTION 3

To which of the following views of the locust plague in Joel 2 does this course hold?

    A. Past—it was the same locust invasion as in chapter 1

    B. Near Future—Babylon and Distant Future—Armageddon

    C. Near Future—Assyria and Distant Future—Armageddon

    D. Near Future—Egypt, referring to Pharaoh Neco

Topic 1 Key Points

- Joel teaches that a recent judgment of locusts should cause the people of Judah to repent, as a more dreadful day of the Lord will come in a Babylonian invasion and at Armageddon.

- Joel proclaims God's promise of forgiveness and future deliverance of His people through the judgment of the nations and the restoration of Judah (Joel 2:18–3:21)

- Joel prophesies a near judgment on Judah, prefiguring the distant judgment on Israel at Christ's Second Advent, which will also bring blessing for the righteous.

Topic 2: Zion's Discipline (Joel 1:1–2:17)

Due to uncertainty about the correct date of the book, it is equally speculative to posit an exact occasion for the prophecy. However, it is evident that the people of Judah were recovering from a severe and recent devastation from locusts, as Joel graphically described (Joel 1–2). The catastrophe thoroughly plagued the land for at least two years (Joel 1:4; 2:25). Joel used this calamity to illustrate an even more serious future devastation of the land by the Babylonian army (Joel 2:1-11; 3:2). The people needed to see that the ultimate devastation was not the loss of their crops, but the loss of their existence as a nation. Joel prophesied the latter loss unless the people repented of their sins.

Assignment

- Please read Joel 1 and Joel 2:1-17.
- Please read "Zion's Discipline."

Zion's Discipline

Summary Statement for the Book

A recent judgment of locusts should cause the people of Judah to repent, as a more dreadful day of the Lord will come in the Babylonian invasion and eventually at Armageddon. Yet God promises forgiveness, deliverance, and restoration by judging the nations.

The recent judgment of locusts should cause the people of Judah to repent, as a more dreadful day of the Lord is coming on the land in the Babylonian army invasion (Joel 1:1–2:17).

In his introduction (Joel 1:1-3), Joel notes that the following prophecy came to him from God Himself, affirming the authority of the prophecy (Joel 1:1). He notes that nothing like what he is about to tell them had ever happened before, so the people should pass this word on to the succeeding generations (Joel 1:2-3).

Joel called the people to seek God's deliverance from the terrible locust invasion (Joel 1:4-20). He called the drunkards, land, farmers, and priests to mourn because the invasion had eaten everything in its path in Judah (Joel 1:4-13). The locust plague and accompanying drought should cause man and animal alike to seek God's face for deliverance (Joel 1:14-20).

Repentance was vital, however, because an even more dreadful judgment was coming on the land— through the Babylonian army in the near future and at Armageddon in the distant future (Joel 2:1-17). Joel reiterated that the locust plague prefigured a future day of the Lord, a judgment even worse than the Egyptian plagues (Joel 2:1-2; see Ex 10:14). The havoc created by the invasion of these figurative "locusts" will leave the land totally devastated (Joel 2:3-5). The people will respond to the "locusts" in terror as the army advances quickly and thoroughly (Joel 2:6-9), accompanied by cosmic disorder (Joel 2:10-11).

God Himself called Judah to sincere repentance that was demonstrated outwardly by fasting, weeping, and mourning (Joel 2:12). Sincere repentance could change God's mind about sending calamity because of His grace, compassion, patience, and love (Joel 2:13-14). Joel pled with the nation to show repentance by gathering together for fasting and prayer (Joel 2:15-17).

QUESTION 4

Please match the reference with the corresponding teaching that Joel gives on the day of the Lord.

Reference	Teaching
Joel 1:14	The locusts are compared to a fire which destroys everything in its path
Joel 1:15	The religious leaders should call the people to repentance, fasting, and prayer
Joel 1:16-18	The locust invasion indicates that an even greater day of the Lord is imminent
Joel 1:19-20	The locust plague is accompanied by a severe drought

QUESTION 5

Joel warns that the destruction prefigured by the locust plague is like none the world has ever seen. *True or False?*

QUESTION 6

Joel makes it clear that even repentance will not change God's mind about sending the calamity. *True or False?*

Topic 2 Key Points

- Joel 1:14 called Judah to repentance, fasting and prayer in hopes that God's grace, compassion, patience and love would cause Him to relent from the coming catastrophe (Joel 2:13-14).

- The locust plague prefigures a judgment like none the world has ever known, even worse than the Egyptian plagues (Joel 2:2; see Ex 10:14).

Topic 3: Zion's Deliverance (Joel 2:18–3:21)

Another difficult issue in Joel's book is how Joel 2:28-32 relates to the day of Pentecost:

Joel 2: Joel's prophecy details the coming of a "day of the LORD," which follows a recent locust invasion in Judah. The prophet's point is that while the people are concerned about the existence of their *crops* due to the locusts, even more serious "locusts" (eschatological armies) are coming that threaten the existence of their *nation*.

Then Joel declares that in the last days, the Lord will pour out His Spirit on all flesh (all of Judah) so that young men will dream dreams and old men will see visions (Joel 2:28-32). This is a clear prophecy of the Holy Spirit's coming and His future role. In other words, deliverance in Joel's time foreshadows deliverance in the end times.

Acts 2: When Peter and the apostles experienced the coming of the Holy Spirit on the day of Pentecost, several unusual things occurred. Each of the apostles praised God in new languages that could be understood by pilgrims visiting Jerusalem. Further, tongues of fire appeared on their heads. With these new languages and strange fiery phenomena, the apostles were accused of being drunk with wine. Peter refuted this claim by quoting Joel 2:28. He declared that what they were witnessing was actually a fulfillment of Joel's prophecy of the giving of the Holy Spirit. This is clear in his designation, "This is *that* which was spoken…" (Acts 2:16), which leaves no question that the reception of the Spirit was what Joel had in mind.

However, Joel's prophecy also mentioned strange events in the sky as well—the sun darkening and the moon turning blood red. Acts 2 records no such phenomena, suggesting that the prophecy was left incomplete due to Israel's unbelief. These elements are reserved for a future time, just prior to the return of Christ, when the nation will believe.

Assignment
- Please read Joel 2:18-32 and Joel 3.
- Please read "Zion's Deliverance."

Zion's Deliverance

Joel notes God's forgiveness and promises that He will eventually deliver His people by judging the nations and restoring Judah during the tribulation period as a motivation for the nation to repent (Joel 2:18–3:21).

God promised that if Judah did repent, He would forgive and *physically* bless His covenant people (Joel 2:18-20). He would give them fertility of crops, reputation above reproach, and He would remove the Babylonian army (Joel 2:18-20). He also promised to make up for the years of food lost because of the locusts (Joel 2:21-27). Then the people would know that He is the only God and never be ashamed again.

As further motivation toward repentance, God promised a great time of *spiritual* awakening (Joel 2:28-3:21). In this future day of the Lord—when the Jewish nation repents at the return of Christ—God will marvelously intervene on His people's behalf, delivering them by judging the nations (Joel 2:28-32). Through the outpouring of the Spirit, prophecies, dreams, and visions will characterize people of every class (Joel 2:28-29).

Through celestial signs and an offer of salvation, some of His people will be delivered (Joel 2:30-32).

God promised that when Israel is restored as a nation, He will judge the neighboring nations for their harsh treatment of Judah (Joel 3:1-17). He promised a restoration to the land (Joel 3:1). He also promised a judgment for the nations, to comfort Judah with His loyal love and justice (Joel 3:2-8). Joel even described the warfare between God and the nations, so the people would know that God's judgment will be complete (Joel 3:9-17).

God would be faithful to His covenant people. Joel described the fruitfulness of Judah, in contrast to the desolation of Edom and Egypt, to show that Judah will be inhabited forever (Joel 3:18-21).

QUESTION 8

In Acts 2, Peter makes it clear that the prophecy of Joel 2:28-32 was completely fulfilled on the day of Pentecost. *True or False?*

Contrasts between Joel 1 and 2:21-27	
IN JOEL'S DAY	IN THE DAY OF THE LORD
Land mourned (1:10)	Land will rejoice and be glad (2:21)
Animals groan, wander, and hunger (1:18)	Animals will not be afraid (2:22a)
Fields and orchards were barren and nonproductive (1:7, 10-12)	Fields and orchards will grow and be fruitful and productive (2:22)
Drought--with dryness causing fire (1:20)	Rain will pour down in abundance (2:23)
Grain, wine, and oil are ruined and dried (1:10)	Grain, wine, and oil will be plentiful (2:24)
Crops damaged by locusts (1:4)	Crop damage will be replaced with productivity (2:25-26)

Note: From Dallas Theological Seminary

QUESTION 8

Which of the following does God promise to *physically* bless His people with, if Judah repents (Joel 2:18-20)? *(Select all that apply.)*

    A. Fertility of crops

    B. Increased population

    C. Reputation above reproach

    D. Incineration of the attacking army

QUESTION 9

Which of the following does God promise to *spiritually* bless His people with, if Judah repents (Joel 2:18-3:21)? *(Select all that apply.)*

    A. The outpouring of the Spirit

    B. Common Jews will see visions

    C. The return of a Davidic King

    D. Signs in the sky

QUESTION 10

First, read Joel 2:28-32 and then read Mark 15:21-41 on Christ's crucifixion and death. If we consider the time of Christ's crucifixion as one of the possible prophetic fulfillments of this passage, can you draw any conclusions about the darkness that came over the land when Jesus was crucified? How should the Jews of Jesus' time have responded to this phenomenon? Please open your Life Notebook and record your thoughts.

Topic 3 Key Points

- Certain elements of Joel's prophecy in Joel 2:28-32 were fulfilled, but the signs in the sky have still not appeared because of Israel's unbelief.

- To motivate the people of Judah to repent, God promises that after they repent, He will forgive and *physically* bless His covenant people (Joel 2:18-20).

- God also promises to *spiritually* bless His repentant people with the outpouring of the Spirit, with visions, signs in the sky, and an offer of salvation.

Topic 4: Introduction to Zephaniah

Zephaniah follows the prophets' common theme of judgment followed by blessing, but emphasizes the former. The bulk of his prophecy conveys judgment on Judah for its sin. This is followed by the hope of ultimate deliverance (Zeph 3:9-20). His aim is to encourage Judah that while God will judge, He will still restore a remnant, in faithfulness to His covenants.

Zephaniah Day of the Lord							
Judgment						Salvation	
1:1-3:8						3:9-20	
Day of Punishment						Day of Praise	
D-Day						V-Day	
Destruction						Deliverance	
Ruin						Restoration	
God's Righteousness						God's Faithfulness	
Warning						Encouragement	
Title 1:1	Earth 1 2-3	Judah 1 4-2:3	Nations 2 4-15	Jerusalem 3 1-7	Earth 3:8	Remnant Regathered 3 9-10	Redeemed & Restored 3 11-20
Judah, Nations, and Whole Earth							
c. 630 BC							

- **Key Word:** Day
- **Key Verse:** "Bunch yourselves together...before the day of the Lord's angry judgment overtakes you! Seek the Lord's favor, all you humble people of the land who have obeyed his commands! Strive to do what is right! Strive to be humble! Maybe you will be protected on the day of the Lord's angry judgment" (Zeph 2:1-3).

- **Summary Statement:** To exhort Judah to repent because of God's righteous character and His promise to restore a remnant, Zephaniah prophesies the day of the Lord's judgment on Judah, the surrounding nations, and the entire earth.

- **Application:** If you insist on living like a pagan, then you will die like a pagan. How can you live according to the Lord's commands and not like a pagan?

Assignment

- Please read "Introduction to Zephaniah."

Introduction to Zephaniah

Title

The name Zephaniah literally means "Yahweh hides" or "Yahweh treasures up." Zephaniah's name may recall the suppression of prophetic activity under the wicked King Manasseh, as prophets may very well have had to go into hiding in order to survive the purges of the evil king.

Authorship

External Evidence: Nothing is known about Zephaniah outside of his prophecy.

Internal Evidence: That Zephaniah is the author is indisputable (Zeph 1:1), but his residence in Jerusalem can only be inferred from his use of the phrase "this place" (Zeph 1:4) and the familiarity he had with the city (Zeph 1:9-10). As the great-great-grandson of King Hezekiah (Zeph 1:1), Zephaniah is the only prophet who is of royal descent, and also the only prophet related to the king under whose reign he prophesied (Josiah). Perhaps the author states his extensive four-generation genealogy to substantiate his intimate knowledge of the sins of Jerusalem's leaders (Zeph 1:11-13; 3:3-5).

Circumstances

Date: Zephaniah ministered during the reign of Josiah from 640-609 BC (Zeph 1:1). Since Nineveh had not yet fallen (Zeph 2:13-15), his prophecy must pre-date the fall of the great city, which occurred in 612 BC. Also, his preaching about the idolatrous practices in Judah and Jerusalem make it likely that his prophecy preceded the reforms Josiah put in place after discovering the book of the Law in 622 BC. Therefore, the likely date of composition is 640-622 BC. This means that Jeremiah, who was called in 627 BC, and Zephaniah could have been contemporaries.

Recipients: The northern kingdom had fallen to the Assyrians approximately one hundred years earlier (722 BC). Zephaniah's preaching was directed toward the southern kingdom of Judah, about forty years before Judah fell to Babylon.

As noted above, Zephaniah is unique in that it is the only prophecy by a man of royal blood, who prophesied to his relative the king.

Judgment and Blessing in the Prophets

	JUDGMENT (J)	BLESSING (B)
Explanation	Retribution for Sin	Restoration from Sin
Recipients	Nations and Israel	Nations through Israel
Covenant	Mosiac	Abrahamic
Nature of the Covenant	Conditional	Unconditional
God's Attribute	Justice	Faithfulness
Key Covenant Texts	Ex 19–20; Deut 28	Gen 12:1-3; 15:17-21; 17:8
Isaiah	1–39	40–66
Jeremiah (J-B-J pattern)	1–29, 34–52	30–33
Lamentations	1:1–5:18	5:19-22
Ezekiel	1–32	33–48
Daniel	1–7	8–12
Hosea (J-B-J pattern 2x)	1:1–2:13; 4–13	2:14–3:5; 14
Joel	1:1–2:17	2:18–3:21
Amos	1:1–9:7	9:8-15
Obadiah	1-14	15-21
Jonah	1:1–39	3:10–4:10
Micah (J-B-J pattern 2x)	1:1–2:11; 3:1-12; 6:1–7:6	2:12-13; 4:1–5:15; 7:7-20
Nahum (J-B-J pattern)	1:1-11; 2–3	1:12-15
Habakkuk	1–2	3
Zephaniah	1:1–3:8	3:9-20
Haggai (J-B-J pattern 2x)	1:1-15; 2:10-19	2:1-9; 2:20-23
Zechariah	1:1-6	1:7–14:21
Malachi	1–3	4

QUESTION 11

The key word for the book of Zephaniah is _____.

QUESTION 12

Which of the following are most likely true about Zephaniah? *(Select all that apply.)*

    A. He was related to the king he ministered to.

    B. He was a musician in the temple.

    C. He wrote after Josiah's reforms.

    D. He wrote between 640 and 622 BC.

QUESTION 13

Zephaniah follows the prophets' common theme of judgment followed by blessing, but emphasizes the judgment. *True or False?*

Topic 4 Key Points

- The key word for Zephaniah is day (of the Lord). God promises judgments on that day, but if Judah and the nations repent, He will fulfill His promise to restore a remnant.

- Zephaniah was related to the king he ministered to and most likely wrote between 640 and 622 BC.

- Zephaniah's prophecy conveys judgment on Judah for its sin (Zeph 1:1–3:8), followed by the hope of ultimate deliverance (Zeph 3:9-20), to encourage Judah to covenant faithfulness.

Topic 5: Day of Punishment (Zeph 1:1–3:8)

Zephaniah ministered at the close of one of the darkest periods of Judah's history, after the evil Manasseh occupied the throne—an infamous fifty-five-year reign from which the nation never recovered. Manasseh made altars to several foreign deities: Ashtoreth of the Canaanites, Chemosh of the Moabites, Milcom of the Ammonites, and Baal of the Canaanites. He reestablished child sacrifice (2 Kgs 21) and even sacrificed two of his own sons in the Valley of Hinnom, near the walls of Jerusalem. Astrology, occultism, witchcraft, spiritism, and divination were common (2 Chr 33:5-6). Manasseh even placed a carved idol in the temple (2 Chr 33:7). His son Amon was named after an Egyptian god.

Although later, under the influence of some unnamed prophets of God (2 Chr 33:12-19), Manasseh made some token efforts at reforming Yahweh worship, the people had gone too far into idolatry (2 Chr 33:17). After his son, Amon, assumed the throne briefly in 642-640 BC, Josiah became king. The false worship still continued in the early part of Josiah's reign during the ministry of Zephaniah (Zeph 1:4-5, 8, 9, 12). Zephaniah was God's spokesman to turn a people of false worship back to the true God.

Assignment

- Please read Zephaniah 1 and Zephaniah 2.
- Please read "Day of Punishment."

Day of Punishment

Summary Statement for the Book

To exhort Judah to repent because of God's righteous character and His promise to restore a remnant, Zephaniah prophesies the day of the Lord's judgment on Judah, the surrounding nations, and the entire earth.

Judgment in the day of the Lord will come on Judah, the surrounding nations, and the entire earth, so Judah should repent because of God's righteous character (Zeph 1:1–3:8).

Zephaniah noted that the prophecy came to him during Josiah's reign, 640-609 BC (Zeph 1:1). He also noted it came from God Himself.

Judgment will come on the *whole earth* for its wickedness, so Judah should realize that it is not alone (Zeph 1:2-3).

Judgment would come on *Judah* for its idolatry and social injustice, so the nation should repent to avoid the terrible calamity (Zeph 1:4–2:3):

- Judgment would come on the pagan priests who had led the people into all forms of idolatrous and false worship (Zeph 1:4-6).

    1. Some people had been led into Baal worship (Zeph 1:4).

    2. Some people had become involved in astrology (Zeph 1:5).

    3. Some people had a religious syncretism which mixed worship of Yahweh with that of the Ammonite god Milcom (Zeph 1:5).

    4. All the people had simply rejected Yahweh, having turned their backs on Him (Zeph 1:6).

- Judgment would come on the princes and aristocracy, who evidenced their disobedience by adopting foreign dress and practices (Zeph 1:7-8).

- Judgment would come on those who oppressed fellow citizens by robbing them to offer up objects for pagan worship (Zeph 1:9).

- Judgment would come on the people throughout the city and the merchants in the business district who had grown rich by taking advantage of others (Zeph 1:10-11).

- Judgment would come on the indifferent who felt that God would keep neither His promises nor His threats (Zeph 1:12-13).

Earth-ravaging bloodshed and celestial signs will characterize the day of the Lord (Zeph 1:14-18). Consequently, Judah was urged to gather together in humble and righteous repentance to try to avert the judgments of that day (Zeph 2:1-3).

Judgment would come on *the nations* all around Judah for their arrogance and mistreatment of Judah, who would inhabit some of their territory (Zeph 2:4-15).

- Judgment would come on *Philistia in the west* so that the devastated land would be inhabited by a remnant of Judah (Zeph 2:4-7).

- Judgment would come on *Moab and Ammon in the east* for their arrogance against Judah, who would also inhabit that land (Zeph 2:8-11).

- Judgment would come on *Ethiopia in the south*, who would die from an invading army (Zeph 2:12).

- Judgment through the Babylonians would come on *Assyria in the north* for its arrogance, leaving Nineveh inhabited only by wild beasts (Zeph 2:13-15).

- Judgment would come justly on *Jerusalem* for arrogantly spurning God's righteous and just warnings against its depraved spiritual condition (Zeph 3:1-7).

God had given Jerusalem chances to repent, but the city still spurned His warnings (Zeph 3:7). Judah should wait on the Lord, because judgment was coming to the whole earth (Zeph 3:8).

QUESTION 14

Please match the reference with the corresponding description of the judgment that will come.

Reference	Judgment
Zephaniah 1:4-6	Judgment will come on the pagan priests who have led in idolatry.
Zephaniah 1:7-8	Judgment will come on the princes and aristocracy who have adopted foreign practices.
Zephaniah 1:9	Judgment will come on the indifferent who feel that God can keep neither His promises nor His threats.
Zephaniah 1:10-11	Judgment will come on the people who have grown rich by taking advantage of others.
Zephaniah 1:12-13	Judgment will come on those who oppress fellow citizens by robbing them to offer up objects for pagan worship.

QUESTION 15

Please match the reference with the corresponding description of the judgment that will come on the specified area.

Reference	Judgment
Zephaniah 2:4-7	On *Moab and Ammon in the east* for their arrogance against Judah, who will also inhabit their land.
Zephaniah 2:8-11	On *Jerusalem* for arrogantly spurning God's righteous and just warnings against its depraved spiritual condition.
Zephaniah 2:12	On *Ethiopia in the south* who will die from an invading army.
Zephaniah 2:13-15	On *Assyria in the north* for its arrogance, leaving Nineveh inhabited only by wild beasts.
Zephaniah 3:1-7	On *Philistia in the west* so that the devastated land will be inhabited by a remnant of Judah.

QUESTION 16

Which of the following characterized the reign of Manasseh? *(Select all that apply.)*

A. The abomination of desolation

B. Child sacrifice

C. Token efforts at reform late in his reign

D. Witchcraft

Topic 5 Key Points

- God's judgment will come on various groups in Judah, each for their own particular sins.

- God's judgment will come on Jerusalem for its spiritual depravity, and on several neighbor nations for arrogance against Judah and other sins.

- The reign of Manasseh, Judah's previous king, was characterized by sin, including child sacrifice; he made token efforts at reform late in his reign.

Topic 6: Day of Praise (Zeph 3:9-20)

Zephaniah's predominant theme is the same as that of Joel—the day of the Lord. This term refers to a time in the future when Israel will be disciplined; this will be followed by blessings in the kingdom era.

Zephaniah is a short prophecy, yet it uses the phrase "day of the LORD" more than any other prophetic book. Variations of the term occur twenty-three times in only three chapters:

Zephaniah "Day of the Lord" Use			
Term	Chapter 1	Chapter 2	Chapter 3
"day of the LORD"	v. 7, 8, 14b		
"great day of the LORD"	v. 14a		
"that day"	v. 9, 10, 15	v. 2a	v. 11, 16
"at that time"	v. 12		v. 19, 20
"a day"	v. 15 (5 times), 16		
"day of the LORD's wrath"	v. 18	v. 2b	
"day of the LORD's anger"		v. 3	
"the day"			v. 8

Assignment

- Please read Zephaniah 3.
- Please read "Day of Praise."

> # Day of Praise
>
> **The day of the Lord also includes the salvation of a remnant from the nations and the restoration of Judah, which is declared in order to encourage the nation (Zeph 3:9-20).**
>
> The day of the Lord will include worship by a remnant from the nations beyond Egypt (Zeph 3:9), as well as the redemption and restoration of Judah under the protection of the Lord Himself (Zeph 3:10-20).
>
> The remnant of the nation will be redeemed in humility (Zeph 3:10-13). Judah should rejoice since the Lord will protect it from enemies forever (Zeph 3:14-17). Judah will be gathered again and restored to the land, as preparation for entrance into the Millennial Kingdom (Zeph 3:18-20).

QUESTION 17

Zephaniah's predominant theme is the same as that of Joel. *True or False?*

QUESTION 18

The day of the Lord includes worship of God by a remnant from the nations beyond Egypt. *True or False?*

QUESTION 19

Many Christians feel that studying prophecy is a waste of time or at least impractical. But obviously neither Joel nor Zephaniah felt that way. Please open your Life Notebook and explain how the prophetic message of these two books helped steer the righteous remnant toward living a godly life. Also explain how this can be applied in your own life.

Topic 6 Key Points

- The predominant theme of both Zephaniah and Joel is the day of the Lord, a day in the future when Israel will be disciplined, which will be followed by blessings in the kingdom era.

- The day of the Lord includes worship by a remnant from the nations beyond Egypt.

Topic 7: Knowing, Being, Doing

QUESTION 20

Match the event in Joel with the corresponding passage.

Outline of Joel

	Instructions		
Spiritual Awakening			
Forgiveness after Repentance			
Repent from Babylonian/ Armageddon "Locusts"			
Repent from Literal Locusts			
Joel 1:4-20	Joel 2:1-17	Joel 2:18-27	Joel 2:28-3:21

QUESTION 21

Match the event in Zephaniah with the corresponding passage.

Events in Zephaniah

Instructions

Warning to the Earth			
Remnant Restored			
Warning to Judah and Jerusalem			
Warning to the Nations			
Zephaniah 1:2-3; 3:8	**Zephaniah 1:4–2:3; 3:1-7**	**Zephaniah 2:4-15**	**Zephaniah 3:9-20**

QUESTION 22

Please open your Life Notebook and record anything new you have learned from this lesson, including any applications you want to make to your life.

Lesson 6 Self Check

QUESTION 1

What is the key word for Joel?

- A. Day
- B. Locusts
- C. Repent
- D. Spirit

QUESTION 2

This course takes the view that the locust plague in Joel 2 refers to both the near future—Babylon—and distant future—Armageddon. *True or False?*

QUESTION 3

Joel warns that the destruction prefigured by the locust plague will be a judgment no worse than any other. *True or False?*

QUESTION 4

Joel makes it clear that _____ may possibly change God's mind about sending the predicted judgment.

- A. Repentance
- B. Sacrifice
- C. Nothing
- D. Worship

QUESTION 5

Which of the following does God promise to *physically* bless His people with if Judah repents (Joel 2:18-20)?

- A. The early and latter rains
- B. Increased population
- C. Reputation above reproach
- D. Fullness of health

QUESTION 6

Which of the following is most likely true of Zephaniah?

- A. He is mentioned in several other Bible books.
- B. He was related to the king he ministered to.
- C. He wrote after Josiah's reforms.
- D. He was a musician in the temple.

QUESTION 7

In Zephaniah 1, when God pronounced judgment on various sinners in Judah, He included judgment on the indifferent. *True or False?*

QUESTION 8

In Zephaniah 2, when God pronounced judgment on various nations, which nation did He predict would have their land devastated and inhabited by a remnant of Judah?

 A. Philistia

 B. Syria

 C. Ethiopia

 D. Assyria

QUESTION 9

Wicked King Manasseh never attempted any reforms during his reign. *True or False?*

QUESTION 10

Zephaniah and Joel had different 'predominant themes. *True or False?*

Unit 2 Exam: Advanced Studies in the Old Testament, Vol.2

QUESTION 1

The key word for Isaiah is _____.

- A. Day
- B. Faith
- C. Nineveh
- D. Restoration

QUESTION 2

Which of the following is true for Isaiah 1–39?

- A. Babylon is the foreign power in the background.
- B. Messiah is the Suffering Servant.
- C. The time frame is mainly in the present.
- D. Israel is in captivity.

QUESTION 3

In a parable, how does God picture Judah's worthless deeds when He indicts the nation?

- A. An abandoned field
- B. An olive tree
- C. A fig tree
- D. A vineyard

QUESTION 4

Which of the following Bible books is the only one that gives the length in years of Christ's reign in the millennium?

- A. Psalms
- B. Isaiah
- C. Matthew
- D. Revelation

QUESTION 5

In Isaiah 13–23, how does God show Ahaz the futility of trusting in foreign alliances?

- A. God appears to him in a dream.
- B. He gives the sign of Maher-Shalal-Hash-Baz.
- C. He pronounces judgment on several neighboring countries.
- D. Isaiah visualizes the siege of Jerusalem.

QUESTION 6

The Assyrian chief advisor suggested to Hezekiah that the Lord would **not** be able to deliver Jerusalem because they had already broken through Jerusalem's walls (Isa 36–37). *True or False?*

QUESTION 7

The Persian whom God predicted would come to redeem Judah from the Babylonians was named
_____.

    A. Cyrus

    B. Nebuchadnezzar

    C. Darius

    D. Tiglath-Pileser

QUESTION 8

Both Israel and the Messiah are named as God's servant in which prophecy?

    A. Joel

    B. Isaiah

    C. Nahum

    D. Habakkuk

‘

QUESTION 9

The last passage in Isaiah shows a scene in eternity with everyone in eternal peace. *True or False?*

QUESTION 10

What is the correct date for the fall of Nineveh?

    A. 722 BC

    B. 664 BC

    C. 612 BC

    D. 586 BC

QUESTION 11

Basically, the preaching of Nahum can be characterized as a call to repentance. *True or False?*

QUESTION 12

Which of the following is more true of the book of Nahum than of the book of Jonah?

    A. There is no opportunity for Nineveh to repent.

    B. The prophecy is written about 760 BC.

    C. Israel is held responsible for Nineveh's fate.

    D. The focus is on the messenger more than the message.

QUESTION 13

What illustration does God use to show His power over the Assyrians in Nahum 2:11-13?

    A. Trees torn out by the roots

    B. A field destroyed by locusts

    C. A lion's den filled with torn flesh

    D. Bees swarming around an attacker

QUESTION 14

Which of the following is considered likely to be true about Habakkuk?

- A. He was the son of the Shunammite woman, whom Elijah restored to life.
- B. He was a priest connected with the temple worship.
- C. He was an aide to the prophet Daniel.
- D. He was related to the reigning king

QUESTION 15

The book of Habakkuk was most likely written just after the fall of Judah to Babylon. *True or False?*

QUESTION 16

In Habakkuk's first chapter, he asks God why the evil in Judah has gone unpunished. *True or False?*

QUESTION 17

Which of the following events was connected with five of the nine events in mentioned in Habakkuk 3 to recall God's majestic acts?

- A. The account of creation
- B. The exodus from Egypt
- C. The conquest of Canaan
- D. The period of the judges

QUESTION 18

This course takes the view that the locust plague in Joel 2 refers to only to the near future. *True or False?*

QUESTION 19

Joel warns that the destruction prefigured by the locust plague will be a judgment worse than anything including the plagues of Egypt. *True or False?*

QUESTION 20

Joel makes it clear that _____ may possibly change God's mind about sending the predicted judgment.

- A. Sacrifice
- B. Nothing
- C. Repentance
- D. Worship

'

QUESTION 21

In Acts 2, Peter makes it clear that the prophecy of Joel 2:28-32 was fully fulfilled on the day of Pentecost. *True or False?*

QUESTION 22

The key word for the book of Zephaniah is _____.

    A. Day

    B. Faith

    C. Nineveh

    D. Restoration

QUESTION 23

Which of the following is most likely true about Zephaniah?

    A. He wrote between 605 and 587 BC.

    B. He was a musician in the temple.

    C. He wrote after Josiah's reforms.

    D. He was related to the king he ministered to.

QUESTION 24

Zephaniah rejects the prophets' common theme of judgment followed by blessing and emphasizes the blessings. *True or False?*

QUESTION 25

Zephaniah's predominant theme is the same as that of Joel. *True or False?*

Lesson 6 Answers to Questions

QUESTION 1: *Your answer should be one of the following:*
    Locusts, Locust [A recent judgment of locusts should cause the people of Judah to repent, as a more dreadful day of the Lord will come in a Babylonian invasion and at Armageddon.]

QUESTION 2: True [After declaring that the recent judgment of locusts should cause the people of Judah to repent (Joel 1:1–2:17), Joel proclaims God's promise of forgiveness and future deliverance of His people through the judgment of the nations and the restoration of Judah (Joel 2:18–3:21).]

QUESTION 3
    B. Near Future—Babylon and Distant Future—Armageddon [The mention of apocalyptic phenomena—wonders in the heavens like the sun being turned to darkness and the moon to blood (Joel 2:30-31)—indicates that near judgment will strike Judah for disobedience, but the ultimate judgment will befall the nation at Christ's Second Advent (see Mt 24:29-30). However, this day will not just be a day of wrath on the unbelieving; it will also be a day of blessing for the righteous (Joel 2:32; Zech 14; Zeph 3:8-20; Isa 2, 11; 65–66; Amos 9:11-15; Ezk 20:33-44).]

QUESTION 4

Reference	Teaching
Joel 1:14	The religious leaders should call the people to repentance, fasting, and prayer
Joel 1:15	The locust invasion indicates that an even greater day of the Lord is imminent
Joel 1:16-18	The locust plague is accompanied by a severe drought
Joel 1:19-20	The locusts are compared to a fire which destroys everything in its path

QUESTION 5: True [The locust plague of God's judgment and destruction prefigures a judgment like none the world has ever known, even worse than the Egyptian plagues (Joel 2:2; see Ex 10:14).]

QUESTION 6: False [Joel adds that sincere repentance may change God's mind about sending calamity because of His grace, compassion, patience, and love (Joel 2:13-14). Joel calls Judah to show national repentance by gathering the nation together for fasting and prayer (Joel 2:15-17).]

QUESTION 7: False [Joel's prophecy also mentioned strange events in the sky as well—the sun darkening and the moon turning blood red. These elements are reserved for a future time, just prior to the return of Christ, when the Jewish nation will believe.]

QUESTION 8
    A. Fertility of crops
    C. Reputation above reproach
    [In order to motivate Judah to repent, God promises that if they do, He will forgive and physically bless His covenant people (Joel 2:18-20). Then the people will know that He is the only God, and therefore will never be ashamed again.]

QUESTION 9
    A. The outpouring of the Spirit
    B. Common Jews will see visions
    D. Signs in the sky
    [There is no mention by Joel of a Davidic King. God promised to bless His repentant people with the outpouring of the Spirit, with visions, signs in the sky, and an offer of salvation (Joel 2:30-32).]

QUESTION 10: *Your answer*

QUESTION 11: Day [Zephaniah prophesies the day of the Lord's judgment on Judah, the surrounding nations, and the entire earth, to exhort Judah to repent because of God's righteous character and His promise to restore a remnant.]

QUESTION 12

   A. He was related to the king he ministered to.

   D. He wrote between 640 and 622 BC.

[We do not know if he was a musician. He most likely wrote before Josiah's reforms.]

QUESTION 13: True [The bulk of his prophecy conveys judgment on Judah for its sin. This is followed by the hope of ultimate deliverance (Zeph 3:9-20). His aim is to encourage Judah that while God will judge, He will still restore a remnant, in faithfulness to His covenants.]

QUESTION 14

Reference	Judgment
Zephaniah 1:4-6	Judgment will come on the pagan priests who have led in idolatry.
Zephaniah 1:7-8	Judgment will come on the princes and aristocracy who have adopted foreign practices.
Zephaniah 1:9	Judgment will come on those who oppress fellow citizens by robbing them to offer up objects for pagan worship.
Zephaniah 1:10-11	Judgment will come on the people who have grown rich by taking advantage of others.
Zephaniah 1:12-13	Judgment will come on the indifferent who feel that God can keep neither His promises nor His threats.

QUESTION 15

Reference	Judgment
Zephaniah 2:4-7	On *Philistia in the west* so that the devastated land will be inhabited by a remnant of Judah.
Zephaniah 2:8-11	On *Moab and Ammon in the east* for their arrogance against Judah, who will also inhabit their land.
Zephaniah 2:12	On *Ethiopia in the south* who will die from an invading army.
Zephaniah 2:13-15	On *Assyria in the north* for its arrogance, leaving Nineveh inhabited only by wild beasts.
Zephaniah 3:1-7	On *Jerusalem* for arrogantly spurning God's righteous and just warnings against its depraved spiritual condition.

QUESTION 16

   B. Child sacrifice

   C. Token efforts at reform late in his reign

   D. Witchcraft

[Although Manasseh, under the influence of some unnamed prophets of God, later made some token efforts at reforming Yahweh worship, the people had gone too far into idolatry (see 2 Chr 33:12-19).]

QUESTION 17: True [His theme also is the day of the Lord. This term refers to a time in the future when Israel will be disciplined; this will be followed by blessings in the kingdom era.]

QUESTION 18: True [After the judgments of the tribulation, there will be worship of God by a remnant of Gentile nations.]

QUESTION 19: *Your answer*

QUESTION 20

Outline of Joel

			Instructions
Repent from Literal Locusts	Repent from Babylonian/ Armageddon "Locusts"	Forgiveness after Repentance	Spiritual Awakening
Joel 1:4-20	Joel 2:1-17	Joel 2:18-27	Joel 2:28-3:21

QUESTION 21

Events in Zephaniah

			Instructions
Warning to the Earth	Warning to Judah and Jerusalem	Warning to the Nations	Remnant Restored
Zephaniah 1:2-3; 3:8	Zephaniah 1:4–2:3; 3:1-7	Zephaniah 2:4-15	Zephaniah 3:9-20

QUESTION 22: *Your answer*

Lesson 6 Self Check Answers

QUESTION 1
   B.   Locusts
QUESTION 2: True
QUESTION 3: False
QUESTION 4
   A.   Repentance
QUESTION 5
   C.   Reputation above reproach
QUESTION 6
   B.   He was related to the king he ministered to.
QUESTION 7: True
QUESTION 8
   A.   Philistia
QUESTION 9: False
QUESTION 10: False

Unit 2 Exam Answers

QUESTION 1
   D. Restoration

QUESTION 2
   C. The time frame is mainly in the present.

QUESTION 3
   D. A vineyard

QUESTION 4
   D. Revelation

QUESTION 5
   C. He pronounces judgment on several neighboring countries.

QUESTION 6: False

QUESTION 7
   A. Cyrus

QUESTION 8
   B. Isaiah

QUESTION 9: False

QUESTION 10
   C. 612 BC

QUESTION 11: False

QUESTION 12
   A. There is no opportunity for Nineveh to repent.

QUESTION 13
   C. A lion's den filled with torn flesh

QUESTION 14
   B. He was a priest connected with the temple worship.

QUESTION 15: False

QUESTION 16: True

QUESTION 17
   B. The exodus from Egypt

QUESTION 18: False

QUESTION 19: True

QUESTION 20
   C. Repentance

QUESTION 21: False

QUESTION 22
   A. Day

QUESTION 23
   D. He was related to the king he ministered to.

QUESTION 24: False

QUESTION 25: True

Unit 3: Exilic Prophets

Unit Introduction

All three of the prophets in this unit—Jeremiah, Daniel and Ezekiel—ministered both before and after the fall of Jerusalem in 586 BC. Only Jeremiah ministered in Jerusalem, experiencing the terrible reality of a siege. Daniel was taken to Babylon as a youth in the first deportation in 605 BC, where he shared the fate of God's people. Ezekiel also ministered to the exiles in Babylon, first warning them that Jerusalem would fall and later giving them hope—first of national restoration (Ezk 37) and then spiritual restoration, including a new temple (Ezk 40–48).

Of these prophets, only Daniel lived until the end of the captivity. He prayed for the restoration of the exiles to the land, trusting in Jeremiah's promises of an end to captivity after seventy years (Dan 9).

Unit Outline

Lesson 7: Jeremiah and Lamentations

Lesson 8: Daniel

Lesson 9: Ezekiel

Unit Objectives

By the end of this unit you will be able to do the following:

- Discuss the key word for each book in this unit and how it relates to the kingdom theme
- Review the historical background, timeline, and characteristics of the books
- Explore how God's program and promises are advanced, despite disobedient people and external opposition
- Discuss the books' purpose: to encourage the Jewish people that God remembers His covenant with them
- Understand how the fall of Jerusalem and the destruction of the temple by Babylon occurred because of covenant disobedience

Lesson 7: Jeremiah and Lamentations

Lesson Introduction

Jeremiah has been called "the weeping prophet" for good reason. While many men predicted Jerusalem's destruction, Jeremiah was the only prophet to experience it firsthand. His extensive prophecy in the book of Jeremiah anticipates this catastrophe as inevitable, while his book of Lamentations looks back on the ruined temple and models confession for the nation. Yet, amidst this ruin, God promised renewal in a new covenant for His people.

Lesson Outline

Topic 1: Introduction to Jeremiah and Call

Topic 2: Pre-Captivity

Topic 3: Captivity

Topic 4: Introduction to Lamentations

Topic 5: Lamentations

Topic 6: Knowing, Being, and Doing

Lesson Objectives

By the end of this lesson you will be able to do the following:

- Understand the backgrounds and characteristics of Jeremiah and Lamentations
- Discuss Jeremiah's use of symbolism to communicate his basic message
- Examine how God's promise of judgment came to those disobedient to His Word and warnings
- Discuss how the warnings against covenant disobedience in Deuteronomy 28 were literally fulfilled in Lamentations
- Evaluate Jeremiah's example of prayerful confession, repentance, obedience, and hope as an example for God's people in exile

Topic 1: Introduction to Jeremiah and Call (Jer 1)

Jeremiah's prophecies follow a thematic, not a chronological, arrangement. This explains why the fall of Jerusalem appears twice in his book (Jer 39; 52). Following the introductory chapter, which reveals Jeremiah's mission to proclaim God's judgment on the nation (Jer 1), the material is arranged to demonstrate the deserved judgment of Judah (Jer 2–45) and the nations (Jer 46–51). The

Jeremiah										
Deserved Captivity & Undeserved Restoration										
c. 627-580 BC										
Jeremiah's Call	Judgment Judah Deserved				Judgment Nations Deserved				Jerusalem's Fall	
1	2-45				46-51				52	
Commission	Condemnation & Comfort				Condemnation				Captivity	
Judgment Message but God's Presence	Pre-Fall 2-38	Fall 39	Post-Fall 40-44	Baruch 45	South-west 46-47	East 48:1-49:22	North 49:23-33	North-east 49:34-51:64	Fall 52:1-30	Rise 52:31-34
Prologue	Ministry								Epilogue	
	Judah				The Nations				Babylon	

final chapter (Jer 52) describes how God fulfilled His promise of judgment in the fall of Jerusalem but would soon return the people to their land. Throughout the prophecy, Jeremiah lists the moral and spiritual causes for God's judgment and balances them with His gracious promise of hope through restoration to the land under a new covenant.

- **Key Word:** Inevitable
- **Key Verse:** "…The Lord our God has condemned us to die. He has condemned us to drink the poison waters of judgment because we have sinned against him" (Jer 8:14).
- **Summary Statement:** Jeremiah prophesies, at great personal cost, the deserved fall of Jerusalem, the seventy-year captivity, the judgment of Gentiles, and restoration under a new covenant, to give hope and to exhort Judah to accept God's inevitable discipline by yielding to Babylon.
- **Application:** If we choose to continue in sin, we will eventually come to the point where God's discipline is inevitable (i.e., resisting repentance requires breaking before remaking). Have you ever come to a point where God's discipline was inevitable? What are some ways that you could avoid this discipline in the future?

Assignment

- Please read Jeremiah 1, which contains the call of Jeremiah.
- Please read "Introduction to Jeremiah."

Introduction to Jeremiah

Title

The meaning of the name Jeremiah is difficult to determine. It could come from one of two roots, meaning "cast, shoot" or possibly "loosen." Some say it has the connotation "Yahweh throws," perhaps in the sense of laying a foundation, or even "Yahweh establishes, appoints or sends" (Wilkinson, 198), but no one really knows.

Authorship

External Evidence: Daniel 9:2 calls Jeremiah 25:11-14 and Jeremiah 29:10 prophetic writing from Jeremiah's hand, as does the New Testament explicitly in Matthew 2:17-18 (Jer 31:15) and implicitly in Matthew 21:13; Mark 11:17; Luke 19:46 (Jer 7:11); Romans 11:27 (Jer 31:33); and Hebrews 8:8-13 (Jer 31:31-34). Other historical writings, such as the Talmud, Josephus, and Ecclesiasticus, also affirm Jeremiah as author (Wilkinson, 198).

Internal Evidence: Despite the above external support, critical scholars continue to doubt Jeremiah's authorship on several internal grounds, arguing that the poetic styles of Lamentations and Jeremiah are different and that the books do not share the same viewpoint. However, the author is clearly designated as Jeremiah (Jer 1:1, 11) who was appointed a prophet by God before his birth (Jer 1:5) and officially called to the prophetic office as a youth (Jer 1:6). So it seems clear that Jeremiah was the author of the majority of the book. However, Jeremiah 52 is nearly identical to 2 Kings 24:18–25:30, and the postscript (Jer 52:31-34) says Jehoiachin was released thirty-seven years into his exile (ca. 560 BC) and lived at the king's table until his death. It is likely that chapter 52 was recorded, under the direction of the Holy Spirit, by the same author as the 2 Kings postscript, especially since "the words of Jeremiah end here" (Jer 51:64, NIV. [Note: Verses 58-64 are omitted in the NET Bible.]).

Circumstances

Date: Jeremiah prophesied in the darkest days of Judah's history, starting in the thirteenth year of Josiah (627 BC; see 1:2) and extending past the fall of Judah (586 BC) to about 580 BC. Thus, his ministry spanned over four decades during the reigns of Josiah and his four successors, the last kings of Judah (Jehoahaz, Jehoiakim, Jehoiachin, and Zedekiah). Most of his material, however, concerns events after Josiah's tragic death in 609 BC (LaSor, 404).

Recipients: The majority of the prophecy addresses Judah before the fall of Jerusalem, but some directs itself to the exiles following the fall (Jer 38–44, 52). One chapter (Jer 29) was sent to the exiles in Babylon *before* the fall of Jerusalem.

Characteristics

Jeremiah communicated his messages through many symbols and symbolic acts, including a rotten waistband (Jer 13), remaining unmarried (Jer 16), a potter's clay (Jer 18), a broken jar (Jer 19), wearing a yoke (Jer 27), purchasing a field (Jer 32), hiding stones in the palace of Egypt (Jer 43), and throwing scrolls into a river (Jer 51).

- Several types of literary materials compose the prophecy: poetic discourse (e.g., Jer 30–31), prose discourse (e.g., Jer 32; 33), and prose narrative (e.g., Jer 46–51).

- Jeremiah edited his own material, arranging it thematically rather than chronologically (as Ezekiel also did). Therefore, the dates of his prophecies move from the reigns of earlier kings to later ones and back several times. This has been charted by Charles H. Dyer (Walvoord, 1:1126):

- Jeremiah was the only prophet to specify the length of the exile as seventy years (Jer 25:11-12; Jer 29:10).

- Jeremiah was the only prophet to chronicle the fall of Jerusalem twice in the same book (Jer 39, Jer 52). He also wrote a poetic description on the same theme in Lamentations.

- Jeremiah was the only prophet whose ministry in Judah stretched through the fall of the southern kingdom. Thus he alone provides personal perspectives before, during, and after Jerusalem's downfall.

- Jeremiah is the longest book in the Bible in terms of the number of words.

- Jeremiah 31:31-34 is the longest OT quote found in the NT (Heb 8:8-13).

- Only Jeremiah recorded that judgment for Judah was inevitable. In other words, the nation had gone so far in its sin that even if it repented, the judgment would still come. This is seen in the book in several ways:

  1. The people were encouraged to repent only up until chapter 19 (e.g., Jer 15:19; 17:24; 18:8; see Jer 5:3; 8:6). After this point, no exhortations to repent were forthcoming.

  2. Jeremiah was instructed by God not even to pray for the people of Judah (Jer 11:14; 14:11).

  3. Jeremiah told the people that each could individually have life instead of death if that person would surrender to the Babylonians, but destruction still would come on the nation as a whole (Jer 21:8-9; 24:1-10; 27:5-12, 16-17; 32:5; 38:17-23; 42:9-22; 52:24-27).

  4. God's decided length of the captivity (seventy years) indicates that judgment was unavoidable (Jer 25:11-12; 29:10).

5. Jeremiah smashed a pot to illustrate that God's decision to destroy the city was not retractable (Jer 19:1-2, 10-11).

6. Jeremiah instructed those already in exile to settle down (Jer 29:4-14), in contrast to the false prophet, Hananiah, who said the exile would last only two years (Jer 28:1-3, 10-12). This indicates that the "die was already cast" and even repentance of the people could not forestall the judging hand of God.

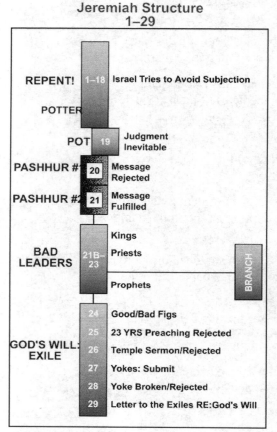

QUESTION 1

The key word for Jeremiah is _____.

QUESTION 2

Please match the reference with the corresponding symbolic act Jeremiah used to communicate his message.

Reference	Symbolic Act
Jeremiah 13	Rotten waistband
Jeremiah 16	Remaining single
Jeremiah 18	Wearing a yoke
Jeremiah 19	A potter's clay
Jeremiah 27	Purchasing a field
Jeremiah 32	Hiding stones in the palace of Egypt
Jeremiah 43	A broken jar

Another symbolic act used by Jeremiah (but not listed above) is throwing scrolls into a river (Jer 51).

QUESTION 3

Which of the following are likely true of either the book or the person Jeremiah? *(Select all that apply.)*

A. He wrote every chapter of Jeremiah.

B. He chronicled the fall of Jerusalem twice.

C. Most of the book was written about events before Josiah's death.

D. He alone of the prophets ministered in Jerusalem before and after its fall.

E. It is one of the longest books in the Bible.

QUESTION 4

After Jeremiah 19, the people were no longer asked to repent, because after that time even the repentance of the people would not have forestalled the judgment of God. *True or False?*

Topic 1 Key Points

- The key word for Jeremiah is "inevitable," and it shows that if we continue in sin, God's judgment is inevitable.

- Jeremiah used several symbolic acts to help communicate his message.

- Most of Jeremiah's message came after Josiah's death in 609 BC. He chronicled the fall of Jerusalem twice and ministered in Jerusalem before and after its fall to Babylon.

- After Jeremiah 19, the people were no longer asked to repent. After that time, even the repentance of the people would not have forestalled the judgment of God.

Topic 2: Pre-Captivity (Jer 1–38)

Rule over Judah during Jeremiah's time shifted between several powers:

Assyria: Since before 722 BC—nearly one hundred years before Jeremiah's birth—Assyria had been the foreign power dominating Jerusalem.

Babylon: In 612 BC, Assyria's capital, Nineveh, fell to Babylon, the rising power to its south. This meant Judah would be subject to Babylon.

Egypt: But conflicts between Assyria and Babylon in the east gave Egypt control of Israel in the west. Pharaoh Neco killed Josiah, king of Judah, in 609 BC, then Josiah's son Jehoahaz ruled for three months before Neco deposed him and replaced him with Jehoahaz's brother, Jehoiakim.

Babylon: When Egypt was defeated by Nebuchadnezzar of Babylon at the Battle of Carchemish (605 BC), Jehoiakim switched his allegiance from Egypt to Babylon.

Egypt: Then, only four years later (601 BC), Nebuchadnezzar was defeated by Egypt and Jehoiakim switched his allegiance back to Egypt.

Babylon: Jehoiakim's trusting again in Egypt as the main power force was a fatal mistake. Within three years, Nebuchadnezzar regrouped, successfully attacked Jerusalem, and killed Jehoiakim. Nebuchadnezzar put Jehoiakim's son, Jehoiachin, on the throne, but three months later deported him to Babylon with ten thousand others and replaced him with his uncle, Zedekiah, as Judah's vassal king. Zedekiah's control was unstable and defiant toward Babylon, which soon besieged Jerusalem, leading to the city's final fall in 586 BC.

Assignment

- Please read Jeremiah 7:1–8:3, part of Jeremiah's temple address that explains that judgment will come on Judah.
- Please read Jeremiah 35 on the Rechabites.
- Please read "Pre-Captivity."

Pre-Captivity

Summary Statement for the Book

Jeremiah prophesied, at great personal cost, the deserved fall of Jerusalem, the seventy-year captivity, the judgment of Gentiles, and restoration under a new covenant, to give hope and to exhort Judah to accept God's inevitable discipline by yielding to Babylon.

Jeremiah records his prophetic call in order to express the divine approval of his prophecy (Jer 1).

Jeremiah claimed authorship of the book and gave the span of his ministry, which lasted over four decades, from Josiah's thirteenth year in 627 BC to the exile in 586 BC (Jer 1:1-3). He was called by God as a prophet to proclaim judgment and restoration to the nation (Jer 1:4-10).This was confirmed through the signs of the blossoming almond branch and the boiling pot (Jer 1:11-16). Jeremiah was assured of God's presence, which encouraged him to speak God's entire message without fear (Jer 1:17-19).

Jeremiah prophesies to Judah of its deserved captivity—before, during, and after Jerusalem's fall—to encourage the people to submit to a seventy-year Babylonian exile before being restored under a new covenant (Jer 2–45).

Before the fall of Jerusalem, Jeremiah prophesied messages that revealed God's justified reasons for judging the nation (Jer 2–38). God indicted the people for their sinful *treatment of God*, as seen in its ingratitude, idolatry, immorality, and irrationality (Jer 2:10-11).Thus, the people should submit to seventy years of captivity in Babylon, until they would be restored under a new covenant. Unfortunately, Jeremiah's message to submit to captivity was violently opposed.

God called the nation to repent from spiritual adultery and warned them of the impending destruction by Babylon to motivate the people to escape the impending judgment by the Babylonians (Jer 3–6).

Jeremiah's temple address aimed to convince the people to turn from false dependence on the temple and idolatry, in order to avoid the impending judgment (Jer 7–10). Jeremiah preached that God's judgment would still fall on their false worship, even with the temple in their midst (Jer 7:1–8:3). God described the coming judgment (Jer 8:4–9:26). Imminent and terrible, this coming judgment would give the people a glimpse of God's perspective (Jer 8:4-17; 9:3-26).Jeremiah's lament modeled the kind of repentant response God desired of the entire nation (Jer 8:18–9:2).

God proclaimed that the judgment would come on the nation for its idolatry, and Jeremiah requested judgment on the other nations also (Jer 10).

Jeremiah delivered his covenant sermon, detailing how Judah had violated God's statutes and the consequences of its idolatry (Jer 11–12). Subsequently, the men of Anathoth, Jeremiah's own home town, plotted against his life because they did not want to listen to his prophecy (Jer 11:18-23). Jeremiah complained to God about the prosperity of the wicked, and God says that worse events were coming, but that destruction would bring Judah to repentance (Jer 12).

God illustrated Judah's judgment and captivity several ways, graphically portraying the severity of Judah's sin and His response (Jer 13–20).

- A *rotten waistband* and a proverb about drunkenness depict how useless the nation had become to God (Jer 13).

- Jeremiah identified with Judah during God's judgment of *drought* (Jer 14–15).

- God *restricted* Jeremiah from marrying or attending funerals or parties, to illustrate the seriousness of His judgment coming on the land (Jer 16:1-9).

In Jeremiah 16:10—17:18, God promised restoration after Judah experienced the consequences of its sin, and Jeremiah expressed his trust in Yahweh.

- Jeremiah rebuked the people for *disobeying the Sabbath* by carrying loads on this day, which was set aside for God as a sign of the Mosaic covenant (Jer 17:19-27).

- God's sovereign decision to destroy Judah was announced by Jeremiah through the *imagery of pots,* and Jeremiah was persecuted by Pashhur as a result (Jer 18–20).

    1. God is sovereign, like a potter with clay (Jer 18).

2. God would destroy Judah like a broken pot (Jer 19).

3. The priest, Pashhur, persecuted Jeremiah because he compared the judgment of Judah to the broken pot. Jeremiah lamented to God (Jer 20).

Jeremiah prophesied to Judah's leaders, through another man named Pashhur and the priest Zephaniah, of unavoidable seventy-year captivity. He encouraged the people to submit to Babylon but received stiff opposition to his message (Jer 21:1–22:9). He prophesied that Judah's godless leaders would be replaced with ones who genuinely cared for the people; the Messiah (Righteous Branch) will be the preeminent leader, who would lead the nation justly (Jer 21:1–23:8).

- Shallum (Jehoahaz) would be judged through his death in exile (Jer 22:10-12).

- Jehoiakim would be judged through a terrible death without burial (Jer 22:13-23).

- Jeconiah (Jehoiachin) would be judged by not having any of his immediate descendants sit on the throne (Jer 22:24-30).

Jeremiah prophesied destruction on Judah's false prophets, who claimed that God sent them to prophesy safety for the unrepentant land (Jer 23:9-40).

God used baskets of good and bad figs to represent Jews who went into exile and those who stayed in Judah, respectively. This was to encourage the nation to submit to God's chastisement through Babylon even though Jeconiah (Jehoiachin) had been deported (597 BC) (Jer 24). Jeremiah predicted seventy years of captivity (605-536 BC), putting an endpoint on Judah's punishment—their exile would not be permanent (Jer 25). But Jeremiah and his message received stiff opposition from the leaders of Jerusalem, and their unbelief made capitivity unavoidable (Jer 26–29).

Priests and false prophets opposed Jeremiah's second temple sermon, but the common people and Ahikam son of Shaphan saved him. In contrast, the prophet Uriah also prophesied for God, but died trying to save his own life (Jer 26).

Note the following genealogy of Shaphan (26:24), which depicts how his sons righteously stood for the truth in various ways (with the exception of the youngest, who rebelled against his father's values)

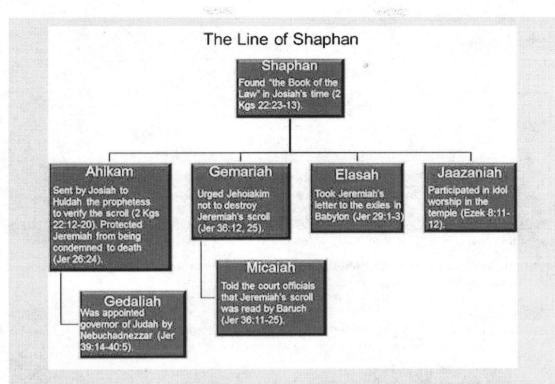

The Line of Shaphan

Shaphan
Found "the Book of the Law" in Josiah's time (2 Kgs 22:23-13).

Ahikam
Sent by Josiah to Huldah the prophetess to verify the scroll (2 Kgs 22:12-20). Protected Jeremiah from being condemned to death (Jer 26:24).

Gemariah
Urged Jehoiakim not to destroy Jeremiah's scroll (Jer 36:12, 25).

Elasah
Took Jeremiah's letter to the exiles in Babylon (Jer 29:1-3).

Jaazaniah
Participated in idol worship in the temple (Ezek 8:11-12).

Micaiah
Told the court officials that Jeremiah's scroll was read by Baruch (Jer 36:11-25).

Gedaliah
Was appointed governor of Judah by Nebuchadnezzar (Jer 39:14-40:5).

Jeremiah used a yoke to convince the people of Judah as well as the neighboring nations to submit to Babylon (Jer 27). But he still met opposition. The false prophet Hananiah opposed Jeremiah by claiming that the captivity would last only two years (Jer 28), and another false prophet, Shemaiah, opposed Jeremiah's open letter to the exiles, which told them to unpack their bags for a long stay (Jer 29).

Messages of hope for Israel, of a future restoration to the land under Messiah and a new covenant, encouraged the remnant that God had not forgotten His promises to Abraham (the Book of Comfort, Jer 30–33). Israel and Judah will be reunited in the land, the Lord said, with a new heart under a new covenant, after Messiah's second coming (Jer 30–31). Jeremiah exemplified this by purchasing and redeeming a field, which demonstrated Israel's future restoration to the land, and comforted the people that they would return (Jer 32). Not only would the people be restored, but so would the land and the Davidic line, under the Messiah (Jer 33).

Jeremiah gave final warnings against disobedience as Jerusalem was besieged (Jer 34–38). Zedekiah freed Jewish slaves in supposed repentance, but then he took them back (Jer 34). Jehoiakim burned Jeremiah's scroll in disdain for God's Word and refused to submit to Babylon, but Jeremiah rewrote an expanded prophecy (Jer 36). His messages contrasted the disobedience of Zedekiah and Jehoiakim with the obedience of the Rechabites, who abstained from wine as an example of obedience that resulted in blessing (Jer 35) For his efforts, Jeremiah was imprisoned in both a dungeon and a cistern (Jer 37-38).

Four Covenants

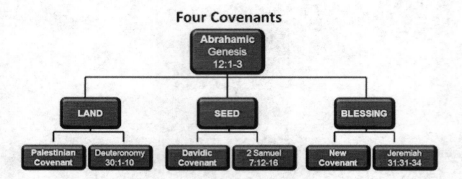

Jeremiah contains the key passage in the entire Bible on the new covenant (Jer 31:31-34). The significance of this covenant can be seen in the following:

1. **Definition**: God's unconditional amplification of the *blessing* promise in the Abrahamic covenant, in which Israel and Judah will experience national and spiritual redemption.

2. **Provisions**

    a. Indwelling of the Holy Spirit (Jer 31:33; Ezk 36:27). Fulfilled for the church in Acts 2; will be fulfilled for Israel at Christ's second advent (Acts 2:14-21).

    b. New nature, heart, and mind (Jer 31:33; Isa 59:21). Fulfilled for the church now; will be fulfilled for Israel at Christ's second advent. (1 Cor 2:16; 2 Cor 5:17; Tit 3:5)

    c. Forgiveness of sins (Jer 31:34). Fulfilled for the church; will be fulfilled for Israel at Christ's second advent (Col 2:14).

    d. Everyone will know the Lord (Jer 31:34). Not yet fulfilled, though the church is commanded to proclaim His name everywhere (Mat 28:18).

    e. Israel and Judah will be reunited (Jer 31:31). This was fulfilled when Israel became a unified nation once again in 1948.

3. **Unconditional Nature**

    a. Eternal (Jer 31:36, 40; 32:40; 50:5; Isa 61:2, 8-9; 24:5; Ezek 37:26)

    b. Amplification of the Abrahamic covenant, which is unconditional

    c. Unqualified "I will" statements of God (Jer 31:31-34; Ezek 16:60-62)

4. **Time of Fulfillment**

    a. *Partial* fulfillment in the *present* church age: Three pre-millennial views have been given on how to correlate Jeremiah 31:31 with various NT passages (Lk 22:20; 1 Cor 11:25; 2 Cor 3:6; Heb 8:8; 9:15)

        1. Only one new covenant for Israel

        2. Two new covenants: one for Israel and one for the church

        3. One new covenant with a two-fold application: to the church now and to Israel in the future

    b. *Complete* fulfillment in the *future* after the return of Christ

QUESTION 5

According to Jeremiah 7, even if the people do evil deeds, as long as the temple stands, it sanctifies them. *True or False?*

QUESTION 6

Please match the symbolic act Jeremiah used to communicate his message with its meaning.

Symbolic Act	Meaning
Rotten waistband	How useless the nation has become to God
Restrictions on marrying or partying	Illustrates the nation's future restoration to the land
A potter's clay	The sovereignty of God
A broken jar	The seriousness of the coming judgment
Wearing a yoke	Represents how Judah will be destroyed
Purchasing a field	Represents Jeremiah's advice to submit to Babylon

QUESTION 7

Please briefly explain what God used the baskets of good and bad figs to represent (Jer 24).

Figs: Jeremiah 24

QUESTION 8

Please match the reference with the corresponding teaching about the new covenant.

Reference	New Covenant Teaching
Jeremiah 30–31	Jeremiah redeems a field by purchasing it; this illustrates Israel's future restoration to the land, to comfort the people that they will return.
Jeremiah 32	Israel and Judah will be reunited in the land with a new heart under a new covenant, after the Messiah's second coming.
Jeremiah 33	Jeremiah prophesies restoration of the people, land, and the Davidic line under the Messiah, who will sit on the throne.

QUESTION 9

God used the Rechabites as an example because they had exactly followed His commands throughout their generations. *True or False?*

Topic 2 Key Points

- The temple was not a sanctuary from God's just judgment if His people continued in evil deeds.

- Jeremiah used symbolism to communicate God's certain, severe judgment on His now-useless people, who should submit to Babylonian chastisement and repent in hopes of future restoration.

- God used baskets of good and bad figs to represent the obedient people of Judah who would go to Babylon and the disobedient who would stay in Judah.

- God used the Rechabites as an example of obedience even though they were faithful merely to their ancestor's commands.

Topic 3: Captivity (Jer 39–52)

Although Jeremiah preached for more than forty years, most of his prophecy (all except Jer 1–6; 11–12; 52) was delivered in a twenty-two-year period before Jerusalem's fall (around 607-586 BC). At times he encouraged the people of Judah to repent, but after chapter 19 he indicated to Judah that God's warnings against the nation's sin would soon stop since the captivity was inevitable. Many of his sermons noted the people's sins, which demonstrated that God was just in punishing the nation.

Assignment

- Please read Jeremiah 39 on the fall of Jerusalem.

- Please read "Captivity."

Nebuchadnezzar's Six Deportations to Babylon

SEQUENCE & SIZE	DATE	KING OF JUDAH	NUMBER TAKEN	KEY CAPTIVES	RESULTS/ COMMENTS
1 Minor	605 BC	Jehoiakim	Few (Dan. 1:3)	Daniel, his 3 friends, & other nobility & royalty	Tribute imposed. Egypt powerful.
2 Moderate	598 BC	Jehoiakim	3,023 (Jer. 52:28)	—	Before the deportation fo 597 BC.
3 Major	597 BC	Jehoiachin	10,000 (2 Kings 24:14)	Jehoiachin (2 Kings 24:12b), Ezekiel (Ezek. 1:2), Mordecai (Esther 2:6)	Large deportation. Jehoiachin replaced by his uncle Zedekiah.
4 Minor	587 BC	Zedekiah	832 (Jer. 52:29)	—	Before the destruction of 586 BC.
5 Major	586 BC	Zedekiah	ca 10,400* (2 Kings 25:11)	Zedekiah	Jerusalem & temple destroyed after 30 month siege.
6 Minor	582 BC	—	745 (Jer. 52:30)	—	Four years after Jerusalem's destruction.

Captivity

Jerusalem fell, fulfilling God's promise of destruction on the disobedient Israelites, but Ebed-Melech, God's foreign servant, was spared for protecting Jeremiah's life (see Jer 38:7-13); this shows the benefits of obedience (Jer 39). Meanwhile at Riblah, the King of Babylon had Zedekiah's sons and all the nobles of Judah put to death while Zedekiah looked on showing God's discipline for disobedience (Jer 39:6).

Jeremiah was not required to go to Babylon, so he ministered to the remnants in Judah and Egypt as an evidence of God's blessing for his faithfulness (Jer 40–44). After the slaughter of Gedaliah by Ishmael, he exhorted the remnant in Judah to remain in the land under Babylon's rule rather than going to Egypt (Jer 40–42). Then he rebuked the remnant in Egypt who disobeyed God's command by fleeing Israel, warning against claiming to want God's will when one's mind is already made up (Jer 43–44).

Twenty years earlier, Jeremiah had encouraged a man named Baruch, who was depressed over Jehoiakim's burning of the scroll. The account of that event was placed here to show how God's promise to save Baruch's life was fulfilled (Jer 45).

God's judgment against the nations that persecuted Judah encourages Judah that God will also judge others who defy Him (Jer 46–51).

The title introduces chapters 46–51 as oracles against nations that persecuted Judah (Jer 46:1).

- God prophesied judgment against Egypt at Carchemish and within its own borders, as a testimony to Judah that God would re-gather it from exile (Jer 46:2-28). Judgment was also proclaimed against Philistia (Jer 47), Moab (Jer 48), Ammon (Jer 49:1-6), Edom (Jer 49:7-22), Damascus (Jer 49:23-27), Kedar and Hazor (Jer 49:28-33), Elam (Jer 49:34-39), and Babylon (Jer 50–51; key verse is 51:49) to encourage Judah that its enemies would be punished.

An epilogue describes how God fulfilled His promise of judgment in the fall of Jerusalem, but would soon return the people to their land. This teaches Judah that His justice is balanced with mercy and faithfulness (Jer 52).

Jeremiah detailed the fall of Jerusalem, declaring God's faithfulness to fulfill His promise of judgment on His unrepentant people (Jer 52:1-30). Evil-Merodach's elevation of Jehoiachin (a Davidic King) encourages the exiles that they too will soon be elevated (returned to the land) as evidence of God's mercy and faithfulness to His land promise (Jer 52:31-34).

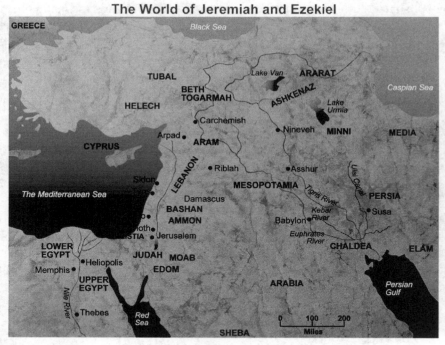

The World of Jeremiah and Ezekiel

QUESTION 10

Which of the following did not survive the siege of Jerusalem by the Babylonians in Jeremiah 39:6? *(Select all that apply.)*

    A. King Zedekiah

    B. King Zedekiah's sons

    C. The nobles of Judah

    D. Jeremiah

    E. Ebed-Melech the Ethiopian

QUESTION 11

The book of Jeremiah ends with the encouraging note that the Davidic king in captivity in Babylon is treated well (Jer 52: 31-34). *True or False?*

QUESTION 12

What do we learn from Jeremiah about God's wrath? Can we reach a point where He is no longer open to our repentance? What does that mean for you, if you're aware of sin in your life and allow it to continue? Please open your Life Notebook and record your answer.

Topic 3 Key Points

- When the Babylonians breached Jerusalem's walls, the disobedient Jewish nobles and heirs to the throne tried to flee and were put to death at Riblah.

- Jeremiah ends on the encouraging note that the Davidic king in captivity in Babylon was being treated well, hinting at future restoration as promised.

Topic 4: Introduction to Lamentations

Lamentations				
Emotions of and Reasons for the Fall				
Jerusalem				
586 BC				
Fall Described	Judgment Acknowledged	Jeremiah's Feelings	Trusting Leaders	Prayer
1	2	3	4	5
The Suffering	The cause	The Hope	The Reason	The Lament
People	God	Prophet	God	People
Third Person Singular (she) 1:1-11 / First Person Singular (I) 1:12-22	Third Person Singular (he) 2:1-10	First Person Singular (I) 2:11-4:22		First Person Plural (us/our) 5:1-22

Jeremiah's book of Lamentations consists of five poems that express in deeply emotional terms the siege conditions and the reasons God caused the fall of Jerusalem. The purpose of documenting such an unpleasant situation is to serve as a model of national confession, so that the remnant will repent and trust God for His merciful restoration. Jeremiah begins with two acrostic poems of equal length which describe the siege (Lam 1) resulting from God's withdrawal of His hand (Lam 2). Then he expresses, in an extended poem, his own feelings of affliction, hope, and repentant confidence in God, as a model for the suffering people to follow (Lam 3). The fourth acrostic poem indicates that the city fell because it trusted in its leaders rather than in God (Lam 4). The final, non-acrostic poem laments, acknowledges national sin, and requests restoration (Lam 5). The structure of the book makes chapter 3 the focal point, in which Jeremiah models the repentant attitude needed in Judah.

- **Key Word:** Confession

- **Key Verse:** "The Lord's loyal kindness never ceases; his compassions never end. They are fresh every morning; your faithfulness is abundant" (Lam 3:22-23).

- **Summary Statement:** Jeremiah expresses in deeply emotional terms the siege conditions and the reasons God caused the fall of Jerusalem, modeling national confession so that the remnant will repent and trust God for His merciful restoration.

- **Application:** When God punishes us, our only hope lies in turning to Him instead of running from Him.

Assignment

- Please read Lamentations 1–2.
- Please memorize Lamentations 3:22-23.
- Please read "Introduction to Lamentations."

Introduction to Lamentations

Title

The Hebrew title for the book is the exclamation "How!" or "Oh!", and it is taken from the first word of chapters 1, 2, and 4 (Lam 1:1; 2:1; 4:1, 2; see Isa 1:21; Jer 48:17). Lamentations is the only prophetic book not named after its author. Rather, the title conveys the deep personal and national loss that the author felt after the fall of Jerusalem.

Authorship

External Evidence: The Masoretic (Hebrew) text does not claim a particular author, but Jewish tradition attributes the authorship to Jeremiah (LaSor, 617). The Septuagint introduction reads: "And it came to pass after Israel was taken captive and Jerusalem laid waste that Jeremiah sat weeping and raised this lament over Jerusalem…"

Internal Evidence: The book is anonymous, yet its contents reveal an author who was an eyewitness, a profound theologian, a skillful poet, and a true patriot (LaSor, 618). The similarities between the books of Jeremiah and Lamentations are striking: Lamentations 1:2 (Jer 30:14); Lamentations 1:15 (Jer 8:21); Lamentations 1:16; 2:11 (Jer 9:1, 18); Lamentations 2:20; 4:10 (Jer 19:9); Lamentations 2:22 (Jer 6:25); Lamentations 4:21 (Jer 49:12). Both books express the same compassion, sympathy, and grief over Judah's downfall (Wilkinson, 207). It is no wonder that Jeremiah has been called "the weeping prophet."

Circumstances

Date: Nearly all scholars agree that the book was composed in conjunction with the fall of Jerusalem to Nebuchadnezzar of Babylon in 586 BC. Nothing indicates that it was written during the exile. The vividness and deep emotions in the account indicate that an eyewitness composed it shortly after the events took place.

Recipients: Jeremiah was never exiled to Babylon (see Jer 40–44), so Lamentations shows to the remnant left in the land the devastating effects of God's judgment on His people.

Characteristics

- This is the saddest of all books in Scripture. In 2 Kings 25 and Jeremiah 52 one can find the *facts* of the destruction of Jerusalem and the temple, but only Lamentations captures the *emotions* (LaSor, 617).

- The book has a chiastic structure. In other words, certain elements reappear in a deliberate order later in the book. Chapters 1 and 5 both depict Jerusalem's destruction from the viewpoint of the inhabitants; chapters 2 and 4 both describe God's view; and the center of the book (Lam 3) shows Jeremiah's response. These connections can be seen in the graphic below:

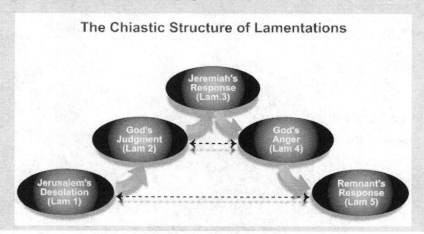

Nearly eight hundred years before Lamentations was written, Deuteronomy 28 prophesied the terrible judgments that would result from sin. The parallels between these writings are striking:

Parallels Between Lamentations and Deuteronomy

LAMENTATIONS		DEUTERONOMY	
1:3	She dwells among the nations; she finds no resting place.	28:65	Among those nations you will find no repose, no resting place for the sole of your foot.
1:5	Her foes have become her master.	28:44	He will be the head, but you will be the tail.
1:5	Her children have gone into exile, captive before the foe.	28:32	Your sons and daughters will be given to another nation.
1:6	In weakness they have fled before the pursuer.	28:25	The Lord will cause you to be defeated before your enemies. You will come at them from one direction but flee from them in seven.
1:18	My young men and maidens have gone into exile.	28:41	You will have sons and daughters but you will not keep them, because they will go into captivity.
2:15	All who pass your way clap their hands at you; they scoff and shake their heads at the Daughter of Jerusalem.	28:37	You will become a thing of horror and an object of scorn and ridicule to all the nations where the Lord will drive you.
2:20	Should women eat their offspring, the children they have cared for?	28:53	Because of the suffering that your enemy will inflict on you during the siege, you will eat the fruit of the womb, the flesh of the sons and daughters the Lord your God has given you.
2:21	Young and old lie together in the dust of the streets.	28:50	...a fierce-looking nation without respect for the old or pity for the young.
4:10	With their own hands compassionate women have cooked their own children.	28:56-57	The most gentle and sensitive woman among you...will begrudge the husband she loves and her own son or daughter the afterbirth from her womb and the children she bears. For she intends to eat them secretly during the siege.
5:2	Our inheritance has been turned over to aliens, our homes to foreigners.	28:30	You will build a house, but you will not live in it.
5:5	We are weary and find no rest.	28:65	Among those nations you will find no repose.
5:10	Our skin is hot as an oven, feverish from hunger.	28:48	In hunger and thirst...you will serve the enemies the Lord sends against you.
5:11	Women have been ravished in Zion, and virgins in the towns of Judah.	28:30	You will be pledged to be married to a woman, but another will take her and ravish her.
5:12	Elders are shown no respect (4:16).	28:50	...a fierce-looking nation without respect for the old...
5:18	Mount Zion...lies desolate, with jackals prowling over it.	28:26	Your carcasses will be food for all the birds of the air and the beasts of the earth, and there will no one to frighten them away.

QUESTION 13

The key word for Lamentations is _____.

QUESTION 14

Please write Lamentations 3:22-23 from memory.

QUESTION 15

Which chapter is the focal point of Lamentations, based on its chiastic structure?

- A. Chapter 5
- B. Chapter 3
- C. Chapter 1
- D. Chapter 4

QUESTION 16

Please match the chapters with the corresponding main point they teach.

Chapters	Main Point
Lamentations 1 and Lamentations 5	Jerusalem's destruction from the viewpoint of the inhabitants
Lamentations 2 and Lamentations 4	Jeremiah's view of the destruction of Jerusalem
Lamentations 3	God's view of the destruction of Jerusalem

QUESTION 17

Please match the reference from Lamentations with the corresponding prediction from Deuteronomy.

Lamentations Reference	Deuteronomy Reference
Lamentations 1:3	Deuteronomy 28:25
Lamentations 1:5	Deuteronomy 28:37
Lamentations 1:6	Deuteronomy 28:65
Lamentations 2:15	Deuteronomy 28:53
Lamentations 2:20	Deuteronomy 28:26
Lamentations 5:18	Deuteronomy 28:32

QUESTION 18

As you saw in the previous question, there is a striking parallel between the warnings in Deuteronomy 28 and their fulfillments in Lamentations. Since this connection was true in the Old Testament, how should we then understand the warnings in the New Testament for disobedience? Please open your Life Notebook and record your thoughts.

Topic 4 Key Points

- The key word for Lamentations is "confession," and Jeremiah expresses a model of national confession so that the remnant will repent and trust God for His merciful restoration.

- Lamentations 3:23 tells us "The Lord's loyal kindness never ceases; his compassions never end. They are fresh every morning; your faithfulness is abundant."

- The chiastic structure of Lamentations makes chapter 3, in which Jeremiah models the repentant attitude needed in Judah, the focal point.

- Chapters 1 and 5 depict Jerusalem's destruction from the viewpoint of the inhabitants; chapters 2 and 4 describe God's view of the destruction of Jerusalem; and chapter 3 describes Jeremiah's view of the destruction of Jerusalem.

- The warnings against covenant disobedience that appeared in Deuteronomy 28 were literally fulfilled in Lamentations, and we can apply the same principle to new covenant warnings.

Topic 5: Lamentations (Lam 1–5)

In 586 BC, Nebuchadnezzar destroyed Jerusalem and its temple, and the nation of Judah went into exile. This followed years of prophetic warnings by Jeremiah, Zephaniah, Habakkuk, and others—warnings that stretched back even as far as the giving of the Law (see Deut 28:41, 49-57, 64). On the heels of such a catastrophic defeat, Jeremiah mourned the loss in the five poems that comprise Lamentations. These poems express the anguish of the remnant and the reasons for God's judgment, to motivate the nation to repent.

The worst disaster ever to befall the Jewish nation was certainly this destruction of Jerusalem and its temple, which included the departure of the Spirit of God from the Holy of Holies. The two scriptural books written by Jeremiah focus on this tragic event:

Jeremiah's Two Glimpses of Jerusalem's Fall

Book of Jeremiah — Looking Ahead (Warning)

Book of Lamentations — Looking Back (Mourning)

Assignment
- Please read Lamentations 3–5.
- Please read "Lamentations."

Lamentations

Summary Statement for the Book

Jeremiah emotionally describes the siege conditions and the reasons God caused the fall of Jerusalem, then his personal confession provided a model for the remnant who needed to repent and trust God for His merciful restoration.

Jeremiah provides a vivid, dramatic description of Jerusalem's fall, to remind Judah of the awful effects of rebellion against God and to stimulate the nation to repentance and future obedience (Lam 1).

Jeremiah recorded Jerusalem's fall from the height of its prominence to a new, lowly position (Lam 1:1-11). This was meant as a reminder of the extent of the blessing the city had enjoyed by grace before God's judgment. Next, Jeremiah switched from third person to first person, confessing Jerusalem's deserved desolation because of her sin (Lam 1:12-22). Thus he conveyed the agony the people felt, to remind them of the awful effects of rebelling against God and to stimulate them to repent and obey in the future

Jeremiah acknowledges that God caused the destruction of the city, and exhorts all involved to acknowledge the city's fall as His judgment so that He will act mercifully (Lam 2).

Jeremiah acknowledged that God caused the destruction of the city and its covenantal institutions, trying to help his readers associate their sin with God's judgment (Lam 2:1-10). Jeremiah lamented the suffering that had come because the people listened to false prophets, so their enemies controlled them as God foretold (Lam 2:11-17; see Deut 28). He implored the people to cry out to God in prayer to save them from death by starvation (Lam 2:18-19), and called to God, pleading with Him to observe the cannibalism, murders, and terrors on every side and to give them relief (Lam 2:20-22).

Jeremiah voices his own feelings of affliction, hope, and repentant confidence in God, as a model for the suffering people to follow (Lam 3).

Jeremiah's afflictions were described in general, poetic terms to show how he identified with the suffering people (Lam 3:1-18). His hope was in God (Lam 3:19-39). Jeremiah's prayer of repentance and acknowledgment of God's deliverance was a model of the needed national repentance and confident faith in God (see Daniel's prayer seventy years later, Dan 9:1-19; Lam 3:40-66). He encouraged the suffering to penitent prayer, so that those still living after the holocaust would repent (Lam 3:40-42). Then he lamented the sad state of the people to remind them of the awful consequences of disobedience (Lam 3:43-54). Finally, he expressed confidence that God would uphold the case of the repentant Israelites and pay back the Babylonians, to encourage the nation toward repentance and confident faith in God's justice (Lam 3:55-66).

Jeremiah asserts that the siege conditions came as a judgment for trusting in Jerusalem's leaders rather than God, and notes that Edom also will be punished, as an encouragement to rely on God (Lam 4).

Jeremiah contrasted the glory of pre-siege Jerusalem with the contemptible conditions of the siege to recall God's wrath for breaking the covenant (Lam 4:1-11).

Parallelism in Lamentations 4:1-11			
4:1-2	The value of the sons of Zion is despised.	4:7-8	The value of the princes is despised.
4:3-5	The little children and adults suffer.	4:9-10	The little children and adults suffer.
4:6	Conclusion: This is God's punishment.	4:11	Conclusion: This is God's punishment.

Jeremiah noted that the city fell because the people trusted their prophets, priests, elders, alliances, and king rather than God, as a stimulus to rely on God even now (Lam 4:12-20). Jeremiah sarcastically called to Edom to rejoice over Jerusalem's doom but warned that Edom's judgment was coming; this encouraged Judah that God would punish its enemies for their sin also (Lam 4:21-22).

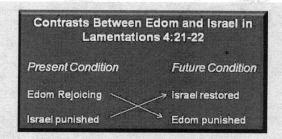

Jeremiah prays a lament, acknowledges sin, and requests restoration, to motivate the remnant to repentance and hope for renewal (Lam 5).

Jeremiah lamented to God on behalf of the remnant, identifying with their suffering (Lam 5:1-15). He acknowledged the nation's sin on behalf of the remnant to exhort the people to repentance (Lam 5:16-18). Then he prayed for restoration, encouraging the remnant to not relinquish hope of renewal (Lam 5:19-22).

QUESTION 19

Please briefly explain what the parallelism in Lamentations 4:1-11 teaches.

QUESTION 20

The last four verses of Lamentations end on a note of hope for restoration. *True or False?*

Topic 5 Key Points

- The parallelism in Lamentations 4:1-11 teaches that Judah's princes are despised and the children and elders suffer because the calamity is God's punishment.

- Lamentations ends with Jeremiah's prayer for restoration, encouraging the remnant to not relinquish hope of renewal (Lam 5:19-22).

Topic 6: Knowing, Being, and Doing

QUESTION 21

Match the event with the corresponding passage of Jeremiah.

Events in Jeremiah

	Jeremiah 1	Jeremiah 2–45	Jeremiah 46–51	Jeremiah 52	Instructions
Jeremiah's Call					
Jerusalem's Fall					
Judah's Judgment Deserved					
Nations' Judgment Deserved					

QUESTION 22

Match the topic with the corresponding passage of Lamentations.

Events in Lamentations

	Lamentations 1	Lamentations 2	Lamentations 3	Lamentations 4	Lamentations 5	Instructions
Trusting Leaders						
Judgment Acknowledged						
Fall Described						
Prayer						
Jeremiah's Feelings						

QUESTION 23

Please open your Life Notebook and record anything new you have learned from this lesson, including any applications you should make to your life.

Lesson 7 Self Check

QUESTION 1

The key word for Jeremiah is.

    A. Lament

    B. Repentance

    C. Judgment

    D. Inevitable

QUESTION 2

Which of the following is true of either the book or the prophet Jeremiah?

    A. He wrote every chapter of Jeremiah.

    B. He chronicled the fall of Jerusalem twice.

    C. Most of the book was written about events before Josiah's death.

    D. Jeremiah is the longest book in the Bible in number of chapters.

QUESTION 3

After Jeremiah 19, the people were no longer asked to repent, because even their repentance would not have forestalled the judgment of God. *True or False?*

QUESTION 4

Which of the following did the symbol of the rotten waistband represent?

    A. How useless the nation had become to God

    B. The seriousness of the coming judgment

    C. Jeremiah's advice to submit to Babylon

    D. How Judah would be destroyed

QUESTION 5

God used the Rechabites as an example even though their obedience was merely to their ancestor's commands, not necessarily God's. *True or False?*

QUESTION 6

Which of the following did not survive the siege of Jerusalem by the Babylonians in Jeremiah 39?

    A. King Zedekiah

    B. The nobles of Judah

    C. Jeremiah

    D. Ebed-Melech the Ethiopian

QUESTION 7

What literary feature identifies the chapter that is the focal point of Lamentations?

    A. The acrostic structure

    B. The allegory in the focal chapter

    C. The chiastic structure

    D. The parallelism in its poetry

QUESTION 8

Lamentations is the saddest book in Scripture, and Lamentations 3:23 probably the saddest verse in the book. *True or False?*

QUESTION 9

Many of the consequences for covenant disobedience that are fulfilled in Lamentations were warned about in Deuteronomy 28. *True or False?*

QUESTION 10

Lamentations is one of the few biblical books that end on a negative note. *True or False?*

Lesson 7 Answers to Questions

QUESTION 1: Inevitable [If we choose to continue in sin, we will eventually come to the point where God's discipline is inevitable (i.e., resisting repentance requires breaking before remaking).]

QUESTION 2

Reference	Symbolic Act
Jeremiah 13	Rotten waistband
Jeremiah 16	Remaining single
Jeremiah 18	A potter's clay
Jeremiah 19	A broken jar
Jeremiah 27	Wearing a yoke
Jeremiah 32	Purchasing a field
Jeremiah 43	Hiding stones in the palace of Egypt

QUESTION 3

B. He chronicled the fall of Jerusalem twice.
D. He alone of the prophets ministered in Jerusalem before and after its fall.
E. It is one of the longest books in the Bible.
[Chapter 52 was probably written as a postscript by an unknown author after Jeremiah's death. Most of the book was written after Josiah's death in 609 BC.]

QUESTION 4: True [Only Jeremiah recorded that judgment for Judah was inevitable. In other words, the nation had gone so far in its sin that even if it repented, God would still bring judgment.]

QUESTION 5: False [In Jeremiah 7:11, God lists the peoples' sins, then asks if they think they are safe because of the temple. He tells them to look at how He destroyed the former worship center at Shiloh when the people did wicked things (Jer 7:12).]

QUESTION 6

Symbolic Act	Meaning
Rotten waistband	How useless the nation has become to God
Restrictions on marrying or partying	The seriousness of the coming judgment
A potter's clay	The sovereignty of God
A broken jar	Represents how Judah will be destroyed
Wearing a yoke	Represents Jeremiah's advice to submit to Babylon
Purchasing a field	Illustrates the nation's future restoration to the land

QUESTION 7: *Your answer should be similar to the following:*
God used baskets of good and bad figs to represent the people who would go into exile and those who would stay in Judah, respectively. This encouraged the nation to submit to God's chastisement through Babylon even though Jeconiah (Jehoiachin) had been deported in 597 BC (Jer 24).

QUESTION 8

Reference	New Covenant Teaching
Jeremiah 30–31	Israel and Judah will be reunited in the land with a new heart under a new covenant, after the Messiah's second coming.
Jeremiah 32	Jeremiah redeems a field by purchasing it; this illustrates Israel's future restoration to the land, to comfort the people that they will return.
Jeremiah 33	Jeremiah prophesies restoration of the people, land, and the Davidic line under the Messiah, who will sit on the throne.

QUESTION 9: False [God used them as an example because they were obedient to their ancestor's commands, even though those commands were not the Lord's. The main point was that they were faithful, and that was the lesson God wanted Judah to learn (Jer 35:12-19).]

QUESTION 10

B. King Zedekiah's sons
C. The nobles of Judah

[There at Riblah the king of Babylon had Zedekiah's sons put to death while Zedekiah was looking on. The king of Babylon also had all the nobles of Judah put to death (Jer 39:6).]

QUESTION 11: True [This shows God's continued blessing on His people and hints at the fulfillment of His promises of restoration under a Davidic King in the future.]

QUESTION 12: *Your answer*

QUESTION 13: Confession [Jeremiah expresses in deeply emotional terms the siege conditions and the reasons God caused the fall of Jerusalem, modeling national confession so that the remnant will repent and trust God for His merciful restoration.]

QUESTION 14: *Your answer should be similar to the following:*
"The Lord's loyal kindness never ceases; his compassions never end. They are fresh every morning; your faithfulness is abundant."

QUESTION 15

    B. Chapter 3

QUESTION 16

Chapters	Main Point
Lamentations 1 and Lamentations 5	Jerusalem's destruction from the viewpoint of the inhabitants
Lamentations 2 and Lamentations 4	God's view of the destruction of Jerusalem
Lamentations 3	Jeremiah's view of the destruction of Jerusalem

QUESTION 17

Lamentations Reference	Deuteronomy Reference
Lamentations 1:3	Deuteronomy 28:65
Lamentations 1:5	Deuteronomy 28:32
Lamentations 1:6	Deuteronomy 28:25
Lamentations 2:15	Deuteronomy 28:37
Lamentations 2:20	Deuteronomy 28:53
Lamentations 5:18	Deuteronomy 28:26

QUESTION 18: *Your answer*

QUESTION 19: *Your answer should be similar to the following:*
It teaches that the value of the sons of Zion has become despised. Consequently, the little children and elders suffer. Conclusion: The calamity is God's punishment.

QUESTION 20: True [Jeremiah prays for restoration, encouraging the remnant to not relinquish hope of renewal (Lam 5:19-22).]

QUESTION 21

Events in Jeremiah

Instructions

Jeremiah's Call	Judah's Judgment Deserved	Nations' Judgment Deserved	Jerusalem's Fall
Jeremiah 1	**Jeremiah 2–45**	**Jeremiah 46–51**	**Jeremiah 52**

QUESTION 22

Events in Lamentations

Instructions

Fall Described	Judgment Acknowledged	Jeremiah's Feelings	Trusting Leaders	Prayer
Lamentations 1	**Lamentations 2**	**Lamentations 3**	**Lamentations 4**	**Lamentations 5**

QUESTION 23: *Your answer*

Lesson 7 Self Check Answers

QUESTION 1
 D. Inevitable
QUESTION 2
 B. He chronicled the fall of Jerusalem twice.
QUESTION 3: True
QUESTION 4
 A. How useless the nation had become to God
QUESTION 5: True
QUESTION 6
 B. The nobles of Judah
QUESTION 7
 C. The chiastic structure
QUESTION 8: False
QUESTION 9: True
QUESTION 10: False

Lesson 8: Daniel

Lesson Introduction

Kings rise and fall, but God's rule over the nations remains constant. The book of Daniel illustrates this great truth, both in Daniel's prophecies and in his seventy-year ministry, which spanned the reigns of several kings. His message of the restoration of the nation provided hope for an exiled Judah serving Babylon. It also instructed the people how to remain pure amidst many temptations to defile themselves.

Lesson Outline

Topic 1: Introduction to Daniel

Topic 2: Sovereignty Over Daniel (Daniel 1)

Topic 3: Sovereignty Over Gentiles

Dream Image (Dan 2)

Golden Image (Dan 3)

King Nebuchadnezzar (Dan 4)

King Belshazzar (Dan 5)

King Darius (Dan 6)

Kings of the Future (Dan 7)

Topic 4: Sovereignty Over Jews (Dan 8–12)

Medo-Persia to Greece (Dan 8)

Return to Seventy "Sevens" (Dan 9)

Intertestamental Period to Tribulation (Dan 10–12)

Topic 5: Knowing, Being, Doing

Lesson Objectives

By the end of this lesson you will be able to do the following:

- Discuss Daniel's purpose: encouraging the Judean exiles and future believers
- Discuss Daniel's distinctions and the timelines of his life and visions
- Explore the meanings of the symbols and visions in Daniel
- Discuss Daniel's seventy weeks and its timeline
- Examine Daniel's outstanding character

Topic 1: Introduction to Daniel

Daniel										
Universal Sovereignty in Times of the Gentiles										
Sovereignty over Daniel			Sovereignty over Gentiles						Sovereignty over Jews	
1			2-7						8-12	
Narrative			Visions in Narrative						Visions	
Hebrew			Aramaic						Hebrew	
Gentile names for God			Gentile names for God						Jewish names for God	
Third Person ("Daniel")			Third Person ("Daniel")						First Person ("I")	
Daniel's Example			Daniel Interprets King's Dreams						Angel Interprets Daniel's Dreams	
Exile 1:1-7	Food 1:8-16	Exaltation 1:17-21	Images			Kings			Return to Seventy "7s" 9	Intertestamental Period to Tribulation 10-12
			Varied 2 Promoted	Gold 3 Furnace	Neb 4 Exile	Bel 5 Party	Dar 6 Lions	All 7 Beasts	Medo-Persia to Greece 8	
Babylon										
605-536 BC										

The book of Daniel aims to encourage the exiles in Babylon that God is sovereign over any and all nations, including Babylon. Daniel records this in two ways: through his personal history, which tells of God's sovereign work in his own life as an exemplary exile (Dan 1); and more importantly, by revealing God's sovereign timetable in the prophetic history of the Gentiles (Dan 2–7) and of His own covenant people (Dan 8–12). Since God is sovereign, a practical application of this truth is that His people should keep themselves pure from the godless (e.g., polytheistic) influences of the Gentile world.

- **Key Word:** Sovereignty

- **Key Verse:** (Daniel to God) "Let the name of God be praised forever and ever, for wisdom and power belong to him. He changes times and seasons, deposing some kings and establishing others" (Dan 2:20-21).

- **Summary Statement:** Daniel writes to affirm for the Judean exiles God's sovereign control over all nations. God will preserve Israel between Nebuchadnezzar's invasion of Jerusalem (605 BC) and the establishment of the kingdom blessings under the Messiah.

- **Application:** Believers need not fear political and personal trouble since God rules all nations. How can you trust God to rule in your nation?

Assignment

- Please read "Introduction to Daniel."

Introduction to Daniel

Title

Daniel (*dani'el*, Ezek. 14:14, 20; 28:3; *daniye'l*, Dan 1:3, etc.) means literally "God is my judge." This meaning is fitting because the main focus of Daniel's writing declares God's sovereign right to judge. Although liberals have said that the difference in spelling above indicates two separate persons, Ezekiel, one of Daniel's contemporaries, was about fifty miles away. He may never have seen how Daniel spelled his name, but only heard it spoken.

Authorship

External Evidence: Ezekiel listed Daniel along with Noah and Job as a model of righteousness and wisdom (Ezk 14:14, 20; 28:3). This shows that his reputation as a man of character spread quickly. Christ acknowledged Daniel 9:27 as *spoken* by "Daniel the prophet" (Mt 24:15), although He did not say that it was *written* by Daniel. But evidence from the Jewish Talmud attributes the work to Daniel (Wilkinson, 221). The fact that Jews accepted the work into the canon of Scripture bears witness that Daniel indeed was the author.

Internal Evidence: While many have sought to discredit Daniel's authorship, the internal factors support it. Daniel is expressly referred to as author (Dan 7:2; 8:1; 9:2; 12:4), and he uses the autobiographical first person throughout the prophetic section (Dan 7:2–12:13). Since the first section has historical—not prophetic—material written in the third person, some have inferred a multiplicity of authors, especially since the book uses two different languages. However, the fact that the content is different, dealing with God's sovereignty over the nations in chapters 2–7, and with prophecy concerning Israel in chapters 8–12, can explain the change in languages, and this practice was not unusual. Also, ancient literature often used different literary forms (e.g., historical and prophetic) to heighten contrast, as is the case in the book of Job, which consists mainly of poetry with the exception of the prologue (Job 1; 2) and epilogue (Job 42:7-17).

Circumstances

Date: The biographical data indicates that Daniel recorded his prophecy from 605 (Dan 1:1) to sometime after 536 BC (Dan 10:1). Nevertheless, the date of Daniel's writing has been debated more than that of any other biblical book (LaSor, 665). A large number of liberal scholars date the work at about 164 BC, and others place it in the fourth or fifth century BC (e.g., LaSor, 666). The late–date view is held generally for three reasons (Wilkinson, 222):

1. *The prophetic argument* holds that Daniel could not have accurately made as many predictions as were fulfilled between the exile and the Maccabean era (ca. 164 BC). Chapter 8 very specifically foretells the rise of the Persian and Greek empires, and chapter 11 details more than one hundred specific prophecies, including those about Alexander the Great and the four generals who succeeded him (Dan 11:3-4); the Ptolemies and Seleucids (Dan 11:5); and particularly the desolation of the temple by Antiochus IV Epiphanes in 168 BC (Dan 11:31). Late-date advocates believe that such specificity could only be known after the fact and therefore consider Daniel's account recounted history rather than predictive prophecy. They claim that the kingdoms mentioned in chapters 2 and 7 were accurately recorded as history ending at 168 BC. Then Daniel's prophecy would have been written within the next four years (168-164) since there is no historical evidence that 11:40-45 can be applied to Antiochus (he died in 164 BC). Since Daniel 11:40-45 was not historically fulfilled, the prophecies in these verses must be inaccurate.

2. *The linguistic argument* claims that the book uses a late Aramaic dialect in chapters 2–7, as well as Persian and Greek words that could not have been known in Babylon before the second century BC. A median date of the fourth or fifth century has also been advocated based upon linguistic evidence (e.g., by LaSor, 666).

3. *The historical argument* asserts that Daniel inaccurately recorded the reigns of some kings in the book. Especially attacked is the lack of external evidence that Nebuchadnezzar was insane for seven years (as Daniel claimed in Dan 4:25, 32).

What can be said in response to these claims? Their support for the late-date theory is flawed on several fronts:

1. *The prophetic argument* assumes that true prophecy is impossible, an idea contrary to the entire tenor of Scripture. Daniel repeatedly stated that his prophecies came from God, not man (Dan 2:27-28; 4:9), and God certainly knows the future. Also, it is impossible that Daniel's prophecy could have been written after 168 BC. It would need time to be copied and circulated quickly enough to gain acceptance within four years, before the "never-fulfilled" prophecies of 11:40-45 could be exposed as unfulfilled through Antiochus.

2. *The linguistic argument* is also invalid, as the language of Daniel is earlier than the second century BC (LaSor, 666). The Hebrew resembles the language used in the Chronicles, and the Aramaic (2:4–7:28) is closer to that of Ezra and the fifth-century papyri than to that of Qumran (second century). Similarly, one should not be surprised to find Persian words since Daniel lived in the Persian period under Cyrus! Finally, the only Greek words used refer to musical instruments, which could be expected since Greek mercenaries served in the Assyrian and Babylonian armies. More Greek words would be expected if the book had been composed in the second-century Greek period.

3. *The historical argument* also has recently been proven wrong, as recent inscriptions found at Haran show Belshazzar reigning in Babylon while his father Nabonidus was fighting the Persians. Further, while liberals once thought Darius the Mede (Dan 5:31; 6:1) to be fictitious, archaeological finds have now identified him as Gubaru, a governor appointed by Cyrus (Wilkinson 222). Finally, there exists no attested activity by Nebuchadnezzar from 581-573 BC except the ongoing, drawn-out siege of Tyre (Hill and Walton, 350), so his seven years of insanity could have occurred during this period.

4. The late-date view denies Daniel's authorship of the book (see Internal Evidence above). Daniel lived before (Dan 1:1-6), throughout (Dan 1–9), and after (Dan 10:1) the seventy-year captivity (605-536 BC). This means that the writing must have occurred during this time.

5. The Dead Sea Scrolls discovered in the Qumran Community in 1947 included a Daniel scroll dated around 100 BC–AD 68. This find makes the late date of 164 BC impossible, as it requires as a period of less than six decades between the date of composition in Babylon and the appearance of the final, copied form in this small community in Palestine!

6. Daniel is found even earlier, as it appeared in the Septuagint (Greek translation of the OT) in 250 BC. How, then could it have been written around 164 BC?

Recipients: Daniel wrote primarily to the Jews in captivity in Babylon.

Characteristics

Daniel is the most symbolic of the Old Testament books. Since nine of its twelve chapters include unusual symbolic depictions of trees, animals, beasts, and statues, Daniel has sometimes been referred to as the "Apocalypse of the Old Testament."

The man Daniel was unique among the prophets in regard to his profession. While God called some prophets to leave their "secular" vocations (for instance, Amos), Daniel remained a politician throughout his ministry. Additionally, he is not called a prophet in the book itself, as he did not deliver a message *publicly* to the nation of Israel (Walvoord, 1:1323).

Daniel and Ezra are the only biblical works that were penned in two languages: Hebrew (Dan 1:1–2:4; 8:1–12:13) and Aramaic (Dan 2:4–7:28).

Daniel is one of two OT prophetic books that were recorded outside of Israel. The other is Ezekiel.

While both Job and Daniel teach on God's sovereignty, Job emphasizes God's sovereignty over individuals, whereas Daniel focuses on God's rule over the nations.

Daniel records more about the "times of the Gentiles" than any other book in Scripture. Jesus also referred to the "times of the Gentiles" in His Olivet Discourse (Luke 21:24).

1. *Beginning*: The "times of the Gentiles" refers to the period in Israel's history in which the nation was ruled and disciplined by Gentile powers rather than exercising its own self-rule. The beginning date for this situation was 605 BC, when Nebuchadnezzar invaded Judah the first of six times, deported some of its citizens (including Daniel), and brought the nation under his control through puppet kings. Daniel acknowledges twice that Nebuchadnezzar began this era: in chapter 2, through the image of a statue made of many materials, and in chapter 4, in the vision of Nebuchadnezzar as a large tree cut down.

2. *Continuation*: Chapters 2 and 7 indicate the broad scope of this time period in a prophetic history of four nations: Babylon, Medo-Persia, Greece, and Rome. While each of these nations defeated the one before it in the succession of intertestamental kingdoms, none of them will be defeated in an ultimate sense until the Kingdom of Messiah is established. This finds support in the fact that the various layers of material in the statue (Dan 2) lay one upon another without replacing the former, and the entire image will be destroyed simultaneously by the "Rock" (Christ; Dan 2:44). Similarly, the beasts of chapter 7 are not specifically declared defeated until they all die at once (Dan 7:17-18, 27). History bears this out, in that each of these kingdoms is still operative in some sense: Babylon (mystical religions), Medo-Persia (systems of government), Greece (art, literature, sciences), and Rome (also art, literature, etc.). Daniel contains more information about the Hellenistic (Greek) era than any other biblical book. Chapter 11 includes over one hundred pointed predictions that were fulfilled during Alexander the Great's conquest and the subsequent Seleucid and Ptolemaic attempts to control Palestine. The final acts of the times of the Gentiles recorded by Daniel relate to the Antichrist (Dan 11:36-45). After an initial time of peace in his covenant with Israel (Dan 9:27), he will seek worship for himself and cause the slaughter of many in a battle of rage.

3. *Culmination*: The end of the times of the Gentiles can arrive only when Israel as a nation chooses to accept its Messiah at the second coming of Christ. This will not occur until the end of the great rribulation, which Daniel specifies as three and a half years in length (the latter half of the tribulation noted in Dan 9:24-27; see also Dan 12). At Israel's acceptance of Christ, the times of the Gentiles will come to a close because Jesus Himself will rule the nation.

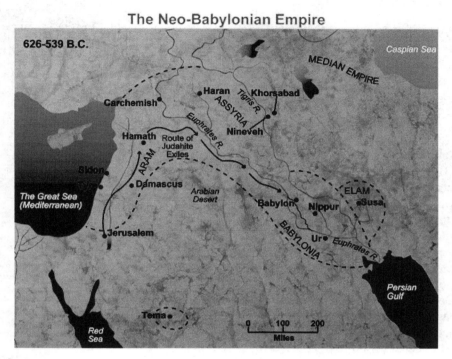

The Neo-Babylonian Empire

QUESTION 1

The key word for Daniel is _____.

QUESTION 2

The prophetic argument that supports a late date for the writing of Daniel assumes that prophecy cannot happen. *True or False?*

QUESTION 3

Which of the following are characteristic of the book or person of Daniel? *(Select all that apply.)*

A. It was originally written in two languages

B. Though Daniel was called to ministry he remained in his secular profession

C. Daniel is the most symbolic of the Old Testament books

D. It was the only Old Testament book written outside of Israel

Topic 1 Key Points

- Daniel writes to affirm for the Judean exiles God's sovereign control over all nations. God will preserve Israel between Nebuchadnezzar's invasion of Jerusalem (605 BC) and the establishment of the kingdom blessings under the Messiah.

- The prophetic argument that supports a late date for the writing of Daniel assumes that prophecy cannot happen, which is foreign to the entire pattern of Scripture.

- Daniel was originally written in two languages and is the most symbolic of all the Old Testament books.

- The author fulfilled his call to ministry, yet remained in his secular profession.

Topic 2: Sovereignty Over Daniel (Dan 1)

Who was Daniel? The book refers to him as a youth in 605 BC, taken captive by Nebuchadnezzar because he was of nobility or from the royal family (Dan 1:3). Daniel was trained in the Babylonian court because of his health, good looks, intelligence, and ability to learn quickly (Dan 1:4). He possessed an unusual commitment to the Lord and held to his standards without compromise (Dan 1:5, 8-20), could understand dreams (Dan 2:27), and possessed great administrative skill. As a result, he served under several administrations during the entire seventy-year exile that ended in the third year of Cyrus (536 BC; Dan 10:1). If he was 16 when captured, then he would have been 85

Names of Daniel and His Friends

HEBREW NAMES	BABYLONIAN NAMES
Daniel "God is judge"	Belteshazzar "Bel [master god],protect his life!"
Hananiah "The Lord is gracious"	Shadrach "Command of Aku [moon god]"
Mishael "Who is what God is?"	Meshach "Who is what Aku is?"
Azariah "The Lord helps" (or "Whom the Lord helps")	Abednego "Servant of Nego" (or Nebo, i.e., the god Nabu)

in Cyrus' third year, after which he retired. This chronology places his birth year at about 621 BC, nearly the same as Ezekiel, who was born about 622 BC—although he was taken to Babylon eight years after Daniel, in 597 BC.

Cyrus

(Smith's Bible Dictionary)

(The sun), the founder of the Persian empire—see (2 Chr 36:22, 23; Dan 6:28; 10:1, 13)—was, according to the common legend, the son of Cambyses, a Persian of the royal family of the Achaemenidae. When he grew up to manhood his courage and genius placed him at the head of the Persians. His conquests were numerous and brilliant. He defeated and captured the Median king B.C. 559. In B.C. 546 (?) he defeated Croesus, and the kingdom of Lydia was the prize of his success. Babylon fell before his army, and the ancient dominions of Assyria were added to his empire B.C. 538. The prophet Daniel's home for a time was at his court. (Dan 6:28) The edict of Cyrus for the rebuilding of the temple, (2 Chron 36:22,23; Ezra 1:1-4; 3:7; 4:3; 5:13,17; 6:3) was in fact the beginning of Judaism;

and the great changes by which the nation was transformed into a church are clearly marked. His tomb is still shown at Pasargadae, the scene of his first decisive victory.

Assignment

- Please read Daniel 1.
- Please read "Sovereignty Over Daniel."

Sovereignty Over Daniel

Summary Statement for the Book

Daniel writes to affirm for the Judean exiles God's sovereign control over all nations. God will preserve Israel between Nebuchadnezzar's invasion of Jerusalem (605 BC) and the establishment of the kingdom blessings under the Messiah-ruler.

Daniel explains God's sovereign workings in his own personal history of deportation, faithfulness to the Law, and reward for his obedience. He uses himself as an example of devotion to God for Judeans living in a pagan land and culture (Daniel 1).

In the first deportation of Jews to Babylon (605 BC), Daniel and his friends were taken hostage (Dan 1:1-7). During Babylon's conquest of Judah, the young men were prepared educationally and administratively for ministry in Babylon's court. Daniel and his friends demonstrated their faithfulness to the Law of God, even while in captivity, which encouraged other exiles to remain true to God (Dan 1:8-16). They also impressed the king with their wisdom and understanding and entered his service as a reward from God for their commitment to obey the Law (Dan 1:17-21).

QUESTION 4

In what year was Daniel taken to Babylon?

- A. 609 BC
- B. 605 BC
- C. 597 BC
- D. 586 BC

QUESTION 5

Daniel and his friends were prepared educationally and administratively for ministry in Babylon's court. *True or False?*

Topic 2 Key Points

- Daniel was taken to Babylon in the first deportation in 605 BC.
- Daniel and his friends were prepared educationally and administratively for ministry in Babylon's court.

Topic 3: Sovereignty Over Gentiles (Dan 2–7)

Identification of the Four Kingdoms

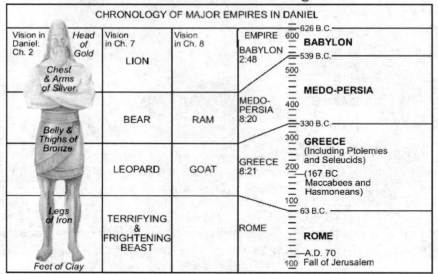

During the dark days of captivity, the Jews certainly wondered whether they would ever return to their homeland and regain independence. In all probability, those who did believe expected the Kingdom of God to be established upon their return from exile. Daniel answered by proclaiming that they would indeed return, but the Gentile domination which began with the captivity would last many years. It will be followed by the Messianic kingdom, which will last forever. Therefore, Daniel's message is one of hope for the captives: God is sovereign over all nations. It also includes elements that encourage continued purity before God while awaiting restoration to the land of Israel.

Dream Image (Dan 2)

Kings of the Neo-Babylonian Empire

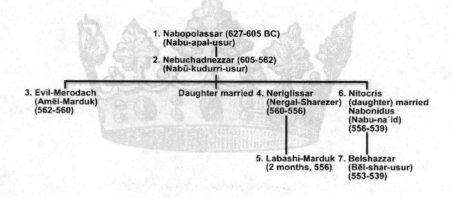

Assignment

- Please read Daniel 2.
- Please read "Sovereignty Over Images."

Sovereignty Over Images

Through Daniel's interpretation of dreams and the devotion of Daniel and his friends, God reveals the prophetic history of "the times of the Gentiles," showing His sovereignty over the nations (Dan 2–7).

In 604 BC, Nebuchadnezzar had a dream that he concealed from his wise men. But they failed to discern the dream or interpret its message from God (Dan 2:1-13). Daniel was able both to reveal and to interpret the king's undisclosed dream (Dan 2:14-45), offering Nebuchadnezzar a solution to his puzzle.

Nebuchadnezzar's dream was of a multi-material image, or statue, that was destroyed, depicting God's power over him and all kingdoms of the world. Usually, the representations are considered to be gold (Babylon), silver (Medes), bronze (Persia), iron (Greece), iron/clay (Maccabean), and rock (God's kingdom). The usual view of critical scholars on this section is lion (Babylon), bear (Medes), leopard (Persia), horrible beast (Greece), and ten horns/little horn (Maccabean). However, in the author's opinion, the critical scholars' conclusion is invalid because their conclusions are based on the assumption that detailed predictive prophecy is not possible.

The angel Gabriel interpreted the beasts as the kingdoms of Babylon, Medo-Persia, Greece, and Rome, which will be followed by the Millennial Kingdom under the rule of Christ. This demonstrates God's sovereignty over all worldly kingdoms (Dan 7:15-28).

But note also that the kingdoms here follow one another in dominion, but are simultaneous in influence (Dan 2:44), as *all of the "kings" [plural] are destroyed at once, not just the last one*.

After seeing Daniel do what no man could do, Nebuchadnezzar acknowledged God's sovereignty and promoted Daniel to a high position in the kingdom (Dan 2:46-49). This is typical of a witness of God during any age: God's prophet does something no human can do, and then the person witnessed to responds subconsciously—with amazement!—to that supernatural act (e.g., Mk 1:23-28).

QUESTION 6

Please match the symbolism of Nebuchadnezzar's statue with the kingdom it represents according to the author's preferred interpretation.

Symbol	*Kingdom*
Gold	Rome
Silver	Babylon
Bronze	Medo-Persia
Iron/Clay	Greece
Rock	Messiah

QUESTION 7

In Daniel 2, Daniel not only interpreted the king's dream but also told the king what he had dreamed. *True or False?*

Golden Image (Dan 3)

Assignment

- Please read Daniel 3.
- Please read "Golden Image."

Golden Image

Nebuchadnezzar erected a golden image, 27.4 meters tall and 2.7 meters wide (60 cubits by 6 cubits), and ordered everyone to worship it. Everyone in Babylon bowed before it (Dan 3:1-7). However, Daniel's friends, Shadrach, Meshach, and Abednego, refused to worship the image (Dan 3:8-23). Theirs was an example to Israel and Babylon of loyalty to the true God. However, Nebuchadnezzar was angered, and ordered them to be thrown into a hot, hot furnace. But even when faced with death, Daniel's friends did not back down. They were careful not to presume that God would physically rescue them, though they affirmed that He was able to save them, admitting they didn't know if He would choose to do so. But God delivered these three faithful young men from the flames, showing His ability to protect those who fear Him (Dan 3:24-27). After witnessing this display of the Lord's power, Nebuchadnezzar confessed God as the true God (Dan 3:28-30).

QUESTION 8

In Daniel 3, Daniel's friends could face the prospect of the fiery furnace without fear because they knew in advance that God was going to save them. *True or False?*

QUESTION 9

Like Daniel's friends in Daniel 3:17-18, we normally don't know in advance if God will deliver us from difficult situations. Our delivery doesn't depend on how much faith we have that He will deliver us. Please open your Life Notebook and describe how this should affect how you pray in a similar situation.

King Nebuchadnezzar (Dan 4)

Assignment

- Please read Daniel 4.
- Please read "King Nebuchadnezzar."

King Nebuchadnezzar

Nebuchadnezzar made an official proclamation: Through his own experience, he now knew that God's kingdom was supreme and eternal (Dan 3:31). He then related the events of his humiliation by God that led him to his conclusion (Dan 4:1-34).

Nebuchadnezzar expressed confidence that though his wise men *could not* interpret his vision of the destruction of a large tree, Daniel, through his God, *could* (Dan 4:21-24). Daniel interpreted the dream for Nebuchadnezzar, saying that the king himself was the great tree, and needed to repent and acknowledge God's sovereignty to avoid God's judgment (Dan 4:24). But instead of repenting, Nebuchadnezzar exalted himself. True to

His Word, God brought judgment, causing the king to live like a wild animal for seven years (Dan 4:28-30). But as a result of the judgment, Nebuchadnezzar acknowledged God's sovereignty over him and all nations (Dan 4:31-34).

QUESTION 10

Briefly summarize the dream that led King Nebuchadnezzar to acknowledge God's sovereignty in Daniel 4.

King Belshazzar (Dan 5)

Assignment

- Please read Daniel 5.
- Please read "King Belshazzar."

King Belshazzar

In 539 BC, Belshazzar denied God's sovereignty at a huge party by irreverently drinking from the temple goblets and praising the gods of gold, silver, bronze, iron, and stone—the same materials that represented the future kingdoms in Daniel 2 (Dan 5:1-4).

God concealed his message of judgment on the prideful Belshazzar in an unreadable inscription on the wall. The wise men could not decipher it, despite Belshazzar's offer of third rank in the kingdom for the one who read it correctly (Dan 5:5-9). But Daniel, in the power of God, interpreted the inscription as God's judgment on Belshazzar, demonstrating that God's wisdom was given to those who acknowledge His sovereignty (Dan 5:10-28). Thus, Daniel was promoted to the third position in the kingdom as Belshazzar had promised (Dan 5:29). True to Daniel's prediction, Belshazzar died that very night, and his kingdom was given to Darius the Mede—Daniel 6:28—to demonstrate the cost of denying God's sovereignty (Dan 5:30).

QUESTION 11

From Daniel 5, please match the word written on the wall with the corresponding meaning of that word.

Word	Meaning
MENE	"Your kingdom is divided and given over to the Medes and Persians."
TEQEL	"You are weighed on the balances and found to be lacking."
PHARSIN	"God has numbered your kingdom's days and brought it to an end."

King Darius (Dan 6)

Assignment

- Please read Daniel 6.
- Please read "King Darius."

King Darius

In 539 BC, under the new rule of Darius the Mede, Daniel distinguished himself by his extraordinary spirit and was promoted to administer one third of the empire. This showed the exiles that a pure lifestyle is possible even among pagans (Dan 6:1-3). Jealous of Daniel's anticipated further promotion, and unable to show negligence on his part, Daniel's fellow officers tricked Darius into publishing a decree stating that anyone who petitioned any god or man except Darius should be killed by lions (Dan 6:4-9).

But faithful Daniel continued to openly worship God, despite the death penalty for disobeying the decree (Dan 6:10-15). He consequently served as a model of faithfulness to God for the exiled captives who were tempted daily to worship Babylonian gods. Distressed at being tricked, Darius was still forced to follow through with his edict, and reluctantly threw Daniel to the lions. But God delivered His faithful servant, demonstrating His sovereignty and power (Dan 6:16-24). Even Darius had to admit that God was the true God after he saw the man who should have been dead alive and well (Dan 6:25-27).

Daniel continued his work with integrity and was rewarded during the reigns of Darius the Mede, 539-525 BC, and Cyrus, 550-530 BC (Dan 6:28).

QUESTION 12

Which of the following are repeated at least three times in Daniel 6? *(Select all that apply.)*

- A. Daniel kneeling and offering prayers
- B. Den of lions
- C. It cannot be altered
- D. Rescue
- E. Spirit
- F. Supervisors and satraps

Kings of the Future (Dan 7)

Comparison of Daniel 2, 7, 8, 9, 11, and Revelation 13

CHAPTER 2	CHAPTER 7	CHAPTER 8	CHAPTER 9	CHAPTER 11	REVELATION 13
Head of Gold (Babylon)	Lion				Leopard
Breast of Silver (Medo-Persia)	Bear	Ram (Two Horns)	Decree to Build the City	11:2	Bear
Belly & Thighs of Bronze (Greece)	Leopard	Goat (1 Horn) (4 Horns) (Little Horn)		11:3-35	Lion
Legs of Iron (Rome)	Awful Beast		Messiah the Prince		Beast
Feet/Toes of Clay/Iron (Last Days Kingdom)	Ten Horns Little Horn		Seventieth Seven	11:36	Ten Horns Seven Heads
			Covenant Broken		
Stone from Mountain (God's Kingdom)	Thrones Set (God's Judgment)				
	Son of Man				
Kingdoms Destroyed	Beasts Killed				
Kingdom Established	Kingdom Established				

Assignment

- Please read Daniel 7.
- Please read "Kings of the Future."

Kings of the Future

In 553 BC, during the reign of Belshazzar, Daniel saw a vision of four beasts succeeded by "one like a son of man." These will rule before the coming of the "Ancient of Days," whose Kingdom lasts forever with sovereign power over all peoples (Dan 7:1-14). The interpretation of critical scholars on this section is generally lion (Babylon), bear (Medes), leopard (Persia), horrible beast (Greece), and ten horns/little horn (Maccabean). However, the author believes this viewpoint to be invalid because the scholars base their conclusions on the assumption that detailed predictive prophecy is impossible.

The angel Gabriel interpreted the beasts as the kingdoms of Babylon, Medo-Persia, Greece, and Rome, which will be followed by the Millennial Kingdom under the rule of Christ. This demonstrates God's sovereignty over all worldly kingdoms (Dan 7:15-28).

QUESTION 13

Please match the symbol from Daniel's vision with the corresponding kingdom.

Symbol	Kingdom
Lion	Rome
Bear	Medo-Persia
Leopard	Babylon
Beast	Greece

Topic 3 Key Points

- In the symbolism of Nebuchadnezzar's dream image, gold represents Babylon; silver, Medo-Persia; bronze, Greece; iron/clay, Rome; and the rock, the Messiah's kingdom.

- In contrast to the wise men, Daniel was able to reveal and interpret the king's undisclosed dream, proving that the true God had revealed it to him (Dan 2:14-45).

- In Daniel 3, Daniel's friends faced the prospect of the fiery furnace. They were certain that God could save them, and even though they did not know He would, they were determined to remain faithful.

- In Daniel 4, Nebuchadnezzar was humbled by being assigned a place with the wild animals for seven years until he acknowledged God's sovereignty.

- In Daniel 5, King Belshazzar received a handwritten message from God saying he had been judged and found wanting, so his kingdom was being given to the Medes and Persians.

- The repetition in Daniel 6 shows that Daniel's continued devotion to God in the face of the king's edicts, along with his rescue from impossible circumstances, testified to God's sovereign work in Daniel's life during the exile.

- In the symbolism of Daniel's dream in Daniel 7, the lion represents Babylon; the bear, Medo-Persia; the leopard, Greece; and the beast, Rome.

Topic 4: Sovereignty Over Jews (Dan 8–12)

Daniel reveals more about the tribulation period, Daniel's Seventieth Week, than any other Old Testament book. Events and rulers in Israel's near future would prefigure events in the more distant future time of tribulation. Events are detailed, even down to the day. Why is this so important in Daniel? As mentioned before, he and the rest of faithful Israel probably expected the immediate fulfillment of God's Kingdom promises when they returned to the land. So when it was revealed that the nation was in for more times of wars, Daniel mourned for three weeks (Dan 10:1-3). Daniel and all believers need to know Israel's future because our understanding of the fulfillment of God's promises depends on it (Dan 10:1-19).

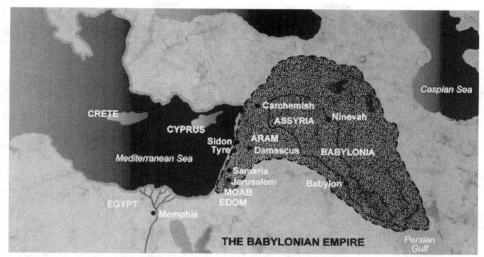

THE BABYLONIAN EMPIRE

THE MEDO-PERSIAN EMPIRE

THE GREEK EMPIRE

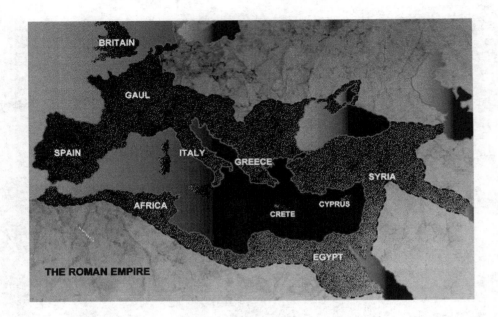

Medo-Persia to Greece (Dan 8)

Assignment

- Please read Daniel 8.
- Please read "Medo-Persia to Greece."

> # Medo-Persia to Greece
>
> **Daniel records visions of Israel's future during "the times of the Gentiles" to encourage Israel that God's sovereignty over the nations includes faithfulness to His covenant with Israel (Dan 8–12).**
>
> In 551 BC, during the reign of Belshazzar, Daniel saw a vision of a double-horned ram (Dan 8:1-14). This ram was destroyed by a large horned goat, whose horn then broke off and was replaced by four smaller horns, one of which gained prominence and desecrated the temple. The angel Gabriel interpreted the ram as Medo-Persia and the goat as Alexander the Great (Dan 8:15-26). From Alexander's four generals would come four kingdoms, the most powerful of which was the Seleucid dynasty under Antiochus IV Epiphanes. Antiochus would desecrate the temple, foreshadowing the desecration by the Antichrist that will occur near the middle of the tribulation (see Dan 9:27). As a result of the vision, Daniel got sick, and even after recovering, he did not understand the significance of the vision (Dan 8:27).

QUESTION 14

Please match the symbol with the nation, group or person it represents in Daniel 8.

Symbol	Represents
Double-horned ram	Alexander the Great
A large horned goat (horn broken off)	The Seleucid dynasty under Antiochus IV
The large horned goat with four new horns	Medo-Persia
The most prominent horn on the goat	The kingdoms of Alexander's four generals

QUESTION 15

In Daniel 8, Antiochus IV foreshadowed the desecration of the temple that will occur during the middle of the tribulation at the hand of the future _____.

Return to Seventy Sevens (Dan 9)

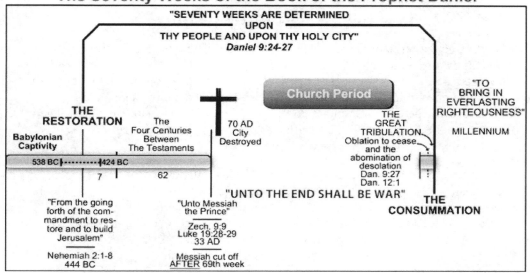

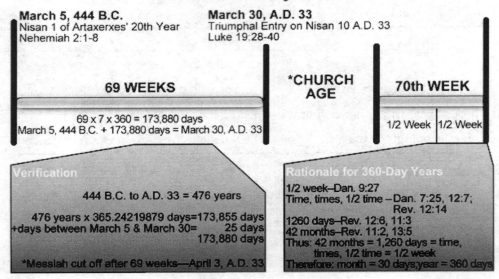

Daniel's Seventy Weeks

March 5, 444 B.C.
Nisan 1 of Artaxerxes' 20th Year
Nehemiah 2:1-8

March 30, A.D. 33
Triumphal Entry on Nisan 10 A.D. 33
Luke 19:28-40

69 WEEKS

*CHURCH AGE

70th WEEK

69 x 7 x 360 = 173,880 days
March 5, 444 B.C. + 173,880 days = March 30, A.D. 33

1/2 Week | 1/2 Week

Verification

444 B.C. to A.D. 33 = 476 years

476 years x 365.24219879 days=173,855 days
+days between March 5 & March 30=   25 days
                                                        173,880 days

*Messiah cut off after 69 weeks—April 3, A.D. 33

Rationale for 360-Day Years

1/2 week–Dan. 9:27
Time, times, 1/2 time –Dan. 7:25, 12:7;
                                        Rev. 12:14
1260 days–Rev. 12:6, 11:3
42 months–Rev. 11:2, 13:5
Thus: 42 months = 1,260 days = time,
        times, 1/2 time = 1/2 week
Therefore: month = 30 days;year = 360 days

Assignment

- Please read Daniel 9.
- Please read "Return to Seventy Sevens."

Return to Seventy Sevens

In 539 BC, during the reign of Darius, Daniel discovered from Jeremiah's prophecy (Jer 25:11-12) that the exile was to last seventy years (605-536 BC), which meant the end was only three years away (Dan 9:1-2). He responded with confession of the sin of Israel through disobedience to the Law of Moses (Dan 9:3-11). He acknowledged that God had faithfully judged His people by subjugating them to Gentiles as He said He would (Dan 9:12-15; see Deut 28:48-57, 64-68). So Daniel asked God to mercifully restore the Jerusalem temple for His own name's sake (Dan 9:16-19).

The angel Gabriel appeared while Daniel was confessing and petitioning God for restoration (Dan 9:20-23). Then he introduced God's message of seventy sevens, which concerned the completion of the captivity, the coming of the Messiah, and events preceding the second coming of Christ (Dan 9:24-27). Seventy sevens were decreed yet to be completed after the completion of the captivity before Israel will embrace Christ's atonement and experience kingdom blessings at His second coming (Dan 9:24). These 490 years are not continuous, since the church age occurs between the sixty-ninth and seventieth sevens.

In Daniel 9:24, we see that at the end of these 490 years, Israel's disobedience, which previously went unpunished, will come to an end and be removed at Christ's second coming, when it embraces Him as Messiah and Savior based on His atoning death on the cross. Then they will experience the blessings of the Millennial Kingdom in an age of righteousness when the 490 years (and the church age) have passed after the completion of the captivity. The kingdom of Israel will be inaugurated when Christ is enthroned as the Holy Ruler (or at the dedication of the holy Millennial temple described in Ezekiel 40–46). Israel will completely fulfill all that God spoke through visions and prophecies concerning His covenant with them.

The seventy sevens are divided into seven sevens (49 years), sixty-two sevens (434 years) and one seven (seven years). They cover the period from Artaxerxes' decree to rebuild Jerusalem (444 BC) to the end of the tribulation (Dan 9:25-27). The church age, a period of undisclosed length, occurs between the sixty-ninth and seventieth sevens.

- Events during the sixty-nine "sevens" (483 years) (Dan 9:25)

    1. Seven sevens (49 years) after Artaxerxes' decree to completely rebuild Jerusalem (March 5, 444 BC), the city will be fully rebuilt (395 BC). Jerusalem will surely be rebuilt with streets and trenches, but only amid much opposition (i.e., during Nehemiah's time) (Dan 9:25).

    2. Sixty-two sevens (434 years) later, Jesus Christ will be officially presented to Israel as the Messiah at the Triumphal Entry (March 30, AD 33) (Dan 9:25). (Note: this period [395 BC to AD 33] appears to us as only 427 years because of differences in the Jewish and Gregorian calendars. See the table in the main text for further explanation.)

- Events after first sixty-nine sevens (Dan 9:26)

    1. After the sixty-two sevens (following the Triumphal Entry on March 30, AD 33), Christ the Messiah will die and will have no Messianic Kingdom over Israel due to the nation's rejection; this inaugurates the church age (Dan 9:26).

    2. During this intervening period between the sixty-ninth and seventieth weeks (between AD 33 and Christ's second coming), the Romans general Titus will destroy Jerusalem and the temple; this occurred in AD 70 (Dan 9:26).

    3. Israel's suffering will stretch throughout the church age, as the nation is set aside from AD 70 until it is freed from Gentile bondage at Christ's second coming (Dan 9:26).

- Events at the middle of the last seven (Dan 9:27)

    1. At the midpoint of the final seven (the seven-year tribulation), the Antichrist, who is an antitype of Titus (see 9:26), will break his seven-year covenant by ending the revived Levitical sacrifices and offerings (Dan 9:27).

    2. The False Prophet will set up an image of the Antichrist in the temple and force people to worship it until the end of the tribulation, when both will be cast into the Lake of Fire (see Rev 13:14; 20:10) (Dan 9:27).

The 483 Years in the Jewish and Gregorian Calendars

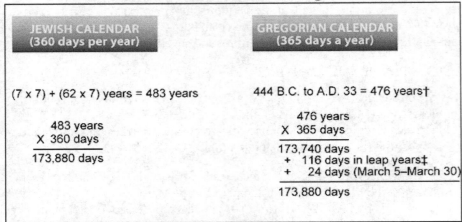

JEWISH CALENDAR (360 days per year)

(7 x 7) + (62 x 7) years = 483 years

```
    483 years
X   360 days
  173,880 days
```

GREGORIAN CALENDAR (365 days a year)

444 B.C. to A.D. 33 = 476 years†

```
      476 years
X     365 days
  173,740 days
  +   116 days in leap years‡
  +    24 days (March 5–March 30)
  173,880 days
```

†Since only one year expired between 1 B.C. and A.D. 1, the total is 476, not 477.
‡A total of 476 years divided by four (a leap year every four years) gives 119 additonal days. But three days must be subtracted from 119 because centennial years are not leap years, though every 400th year is a leap year.

QUESTION 16

Please give the three main elements of Daniel's prayer for Israel's restoration to the Promised Land (Dan 9:1-19).

Daniel's 70 Weeks (Dan 9:24-27)

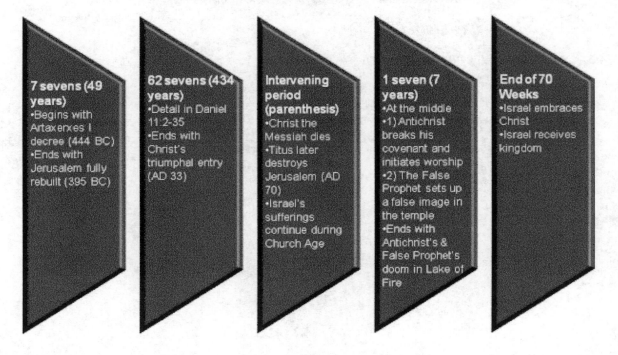

7 sevens (49 years)
•Begins with Artaxerxes I decree (444 BC)
•Ends with Jerusalem fully rebuilt (395 BC)

62 sevens (434 years)
•Detail in Daniel 11:2-35
•Ends with Christ's triumphal entry (AD 33)

Intervening period (parenthesis)
•Christ the Messiah dies
•Titus later destroys Jerusalem (AD 70)
•Israel's sufferings continue during Church Age

1 seven (7 years)
•At the middle
•1) Antichrist breaks his covenant and initiates worship
•2) The False Prophet sets up a false image in the temple
•Ends with Antichrist's & False Prophet's doom in Lake of Fire

End of 70 Weeks
•Israel embraces Christ
•Israel receives kingdom

QUESTION 17

Please match the reference with the corresponding teaching about Daniel's "seventy weeks."

Reference	Teaching
Daniel 9:24	At the midpoint of the last "seven" (the seven-year tribulation), Antichrist will break his covenant and will replace temple sacrifices with worship of himself until his doom.
Daniel 9:25	Sixty-nine "sevens" (483 years by the Jewish calendar) will transpire between Artaxerxes' decree to rebuild Jerusalem (444 BC) and Jesus Christ's presentation to Israel as Messiah at the Triumphal Entry (AD 33).
Daniel 9:26	Israel will embrace Christ's atonement on the cross at Christ's second coming and experience the blessings of the Millennial Kingdom after 490 years, or seventy "sevens."
Daniel 9:27	After the sixty-two "sevens" (following March 30, AD 33) Christ the Messiah would die, Titus would destroy Jerusalem, and Israel's suffering will continue throughout the church age until Christ's second coming.

Intertestamental Period to Tribulation (Dan 10-12)

Assignment

- Please read Daniel 10-12.
- Please read "Intertestamental Period to Tribulation."

Intertestamental Period to Tribulation

In 536 BC, during the rebuilding of the temple under Cyrus, Daniel received a message indicating that Israel would be in a great war with its neighbors rather than enjoying immediate peace in the land, so he mourned for three weeks (Dan 10:1-3).

Gabriel appeared in great splendor at the Tigris River. The men with Daniel ran away in fear without even seeing Gabriel, leaving Daniel alone in a deep sleep (Dan 10:4-9). So when Daniel awoke, Gabriel explained that he had appeared to Daniel because Daniel was highly esteemed (Dan 10:10-11). He had tried to come to Daniel at the beginning of Daniel's mourning, but had been delayed by the demon assigned to Persia (Dan 10:12-13). Daniel needed to know Israel's future, so Gabriel promised him strength to understand the message he was about to receive

(Dan 10:14-11:1).

Gabriel explained what would happen to Israel during the intertestamental era, prophesying events that would demonstrate God's sovereignty over the nations (Dan 11:2-35).

- Israel would be ruled by Persia during the reigns of four more Persian kings, the fourth being the wealthy Xerxes, who would fight against Greece (Dan 11:2).

- Israel's tumultuous history under Hellenistic (Greek) rulers would culminate in the desecration of the temple by Antiochus IV; these events were prophesied beforehand to demonstrate God's sovereignty (Dan 11:3-35).

Alexander the Great would rule with great power, but then his kingdom would be divided into four empires (Dan 11:3-4). Then, various rulers of the Ptolemies and the Seleucids would battle against one another over the land of Israel (Dan 11:5-20). Finally, Antiochus IV Epiphanes of the Seleucids would defeat the Ptolemies at first, but later he would be defeated (Dan 11:21-35). Once victorious, he would desecrate the temple in Jerusalem by offering a pig on the altar on his way back home.

The Antichrist, who is the antitype of Antiochus, will set himself up as a god to rule by military strength (Dan 11:36-39). Soldiers from the east and Arab nations from the north, as well as Egypt and its allies from the south, will attack. In a rage of retaliation, the Antichrist will defeat them all and conquer many other countries (Dan 11:40-43). Then, posing as Christ, the Antichrist will rule from Jerusalem over a one-world government and religion. But when Christ returns at the glorious second coming, the Antichrist and his dominion will be destroyed (Dan 11:45; see also Rev 19:19-20).

Just prior to the ushering in of the Millennial kingdom, the archangel Michael will protect the nation of Israel during the final difficult times (Dan 12:1). And when the Millennium finally arrives, the righteous will be resurrected to eternal life, and the wicked to eternal punishment, though the resurrection of the wicked will not occur until after the Millennial Kingdom (Dan 12:2-3; Rev 20:6, 11-15).

Gabriel told Daniel to write and protect these prophecies so that Israel would be able to understand them in the tribulation. God's sovereignty over the nations includes faithfulness to His covenant promises (Dan 12:4).

Daniel observed two angels standing on opposite sides of the Tigris River (Dan 12:5; see also Dan 10:4), and two questions arose. In response to the first question, which came from an angel, Gabriel said that the great tribulation (the second half of the seven-year tribulation) will last three and one half years—1260 days (Dan 12:6-7). In response to the second question, which came from Daniel, Gabriel said that the end of the great tribulation will bring judgment for ignorant unbelievers who worship the Antichrist, but blessing for wise Israel, who will enter the kingdom (Dan 12:8-13).

Gabriel told Daniel not to inquire too deeply about the period after the great tribulation, since those persecuted during that period will understand while others remain ignorant (Dan 12:9-10). The restored daily Levitical sacrifices will be replaced by Antichrist worship beginning thirty days before the midpoint of the seven-year tribulation (1290 days before the end of the 1260-day great tribulation) (Dan 12:11). Judgment will remove the unbelieving at the end of the 1290 days, but believing Israel (with some Gentiles) will last forty-five more days, for a total of 1335 days, and will then receive kingdom blessings (Dan 12:12).

Gabriel assured Daniel that, although he would die, he would receive his inheritance after the great tribulation to enjoy during the kingdom (Dan 12:13).

QUESTION 18

Which of the following explanations does Gabriel give Daniel when he appears to him in Daniel 10? *(Select all that apply.)*

    A. "I came in response to your prayers, but I was delayed by a demon."

    B. "You are greatly esteemed."

    C. "You need to know Israel's future."

    D. "Jeremiah's predicted seventy-year captivity will be extended."

QUESTION 19

Please match the reference with the corresponding teaching about the future, beginning with the seventieth week and ending with the Millennial reign of Christ.

Reference	Teaching
Daniel 11:36-39	Gabriel says the great tribulation will last three and one half years—1260 days.
Daniel 11:40-45	Gabriel says the end of the great tribulation will bring judgment for ignorant unbelievers who worship the Antichrist but blessing for wise Israel, who will enter the kingdom.
Daniel 12:1-3	The Antichrist will set himself up as a god to rule by military might.
Daniel 12:4	Israel will be protected by Michael prior to the ushering in of the Millennial kingdom, and resurrections will precede, providing two options for the resurrected: either entrance into the Millennium or punishment at God's hand.
Daniel 12:6-7	The Antichrist will be attacked repeatedly and will die at the second coming of Christ.
Daniel 12:8-13	Gabriel tells Daniel to write and protect these prophecies so that Israel can understand them in the tribulation.

Timeline of Daniel 12:11-12

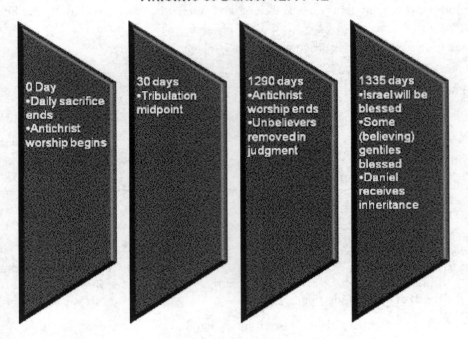

0 Day
•Daily sacrifice ends
•Antichrist worship begins

30 days
•Tribulation midpoint

1290 days
•Antichrist worship ends
•Unbelievers removed in judgment

1335 days
•Israel will be blessed
•Some (believing) gentiles blessed
•Daniel receives inheritance

QUESTION 20

Read Daniel 10:1-3. Why do you think Daniel was in such great mourning? Recall, if you can, the last time you felt that way. What was Daniel's response, and what was God's solution for His servant? Please open your Life Notebook and record your thoughts, along with how you can respond next time you feel this way.

Topic 4 Key Points

- In the symbolism for Daniel's dream image in Daniel 8, the double horned ram represents Medo-Persia; the large-horned goat whose horn is broken off represents Alexander the Great; the four new horns represent the kingdoms of Alexander's four generals; and the most prominent of the four horns represents the Seleucid dynasty under Antiochus IV.

- Antiochus IV foreshadowed the desecration of the temple, which will be repeated at the middle of the tribulation by the future Antichrist.

- Israel will embrace Christ's atonement on the cross and experience the blessings of the Millennial Kingdom after seventy "sevens", which will be at Christ's second coming

- Sixty-nine of the "sevens" (483 years by the Jewish calendar) would transpire between Artaxerxes' decree to rebuild Jerusalem (444 BC) and Jesus Christ's presentation to Israel as Messiah at the Triumphal Entry (AD 33).

- The church age occurs as a parenthesis between the sixty-ninth and seventieth weeks of Daniel. It began on the day of Pentecost (Acts 2), fifty days after Jesus' resurrection. Daniel had predicted that at the end of sixty-nine weeks, the Messiah would be "cut off and have nothing" (Dan 9:26).

Topic 5: Knowing, Being, Doing

QUESTION 21

Daniel--Sovereignty over Gentiles

	Daniel 2	Daniel 3	Daniel 4	Daniel 5	Daniel 6	Daniel 7 Instructions
Handwriting on the Wall						
Nebuchadnezzar's Pride						
Image of Beasts						
Golden Image						
Daniel Promoted						
Lion's Den						

QUESTION 22

Match the event with the corresponding chapter of Daniel.

Event	Chapter
The ram, goat and little horn	Daniel 9
Daniel's seventy weeks	Daniel 12
Daniel's prayer and explanation	Daniel 11
Daniel's prophecies about the Gentile nations	Daniel 8
Daniel's prophecies about Israel	Daniel 10

QUESTION 23

Please open your Life Notebook and record anything new you have learned from this lesson, including any applications you should make to your life.

Lesson 8 Self Check

QUESTION 1

What is the key word for Daniel?

    A. Sovereignty

    B. Babylon

    C. Prophecy

    D. Millennium

QUESTION 2

In what year was Daniel taken to Babylon?

    A. 612 BC

    B. 609 BC

    C. 605 BC

    D. 597 BC

QUESTION 3

In the vision of the statue in Daniel 2, what nation is represented by bronze?

    A. Babylon

    B. Rome

    C. Medo-Persia

    D. Greece

QUESTION 4

In Daniel 3, when Daniel's friends were thrown into the furnace, they showed great faith by telling the king they were sure that God would deliver them. *True or False?*

QUESTION 5

What happened to Nebuchadnezzar that humbled his pride in Daniel 4?

    A. He lost his kingdom to the Medo-Persians

    B. He became like an animal for seven years

    C. He was captured by a rival

    D. He became like a tree

QUESTION 6

When King Belshazzar received the handwritten message on the wall in Daniel 5, saying, "MENE, MENE, TEQEL and PHARSIN," what did the word PHARSIN mean?

    A. "God has numbered your kingdom's days and brought it to an end."

    B. "You are weighed on the balances and found to be lacking."

    C. "Your kingdom is divided and given over to the Medes and Persians."

    D. "Tonight you will lose your kingdom."

QUESTION 7

In the story of Daniel in the lion's den in Daniel 6, the statement "it cannot be altered" is repeated at least three times. *True or False?*

QUESTION 8

In Daniel 7's vision of the four beasts, which nation was represented by the bear?

A. Babylon

B. Rome

C. Medo-Persia

D. Greece

QUESTION 9

Which of the following events ends the sixty-ninth week of Daniel?

A. Jesus enters Jerusalem a week before His resurrection

B. Antichrist places an idol in the Jewish Temple

C. Titus destroys the temple in 70 AD

D. Jerusalem is completely rebuilt

QUESTION 10

The archangel Gabriel is specially appointed to defend Israel during the great tribulation. *True or False?*

Lesson 8 Answers to Questions

QUESTION 1: Sovereignty [Daniel writes to affirm for the Judean exiles God's sovereign control over all nations. God will preserve Israel between Nebuchadnezzar's invasion of Jerusalem (605 BC) and the establishment of the kingdom blessings under the Messiah.]

QUESTION 2: True [This is foreign to the entire tenor of Scripture. Daniel repeatedly states that his prophecies come from God, not man (Dan 2:27-28; 4:9), and God certainly knows the future.]

QUESTION 3

    A. It was originally written in two languages

    B. Though Daniel was called to ministry he remained in his secular profession

    C. Daniel is the most symbolic of the Old Testament books

    [Ezekiel is the other prophetic Old Testament book recorded outside of Israel]

QUESTION 4

    B. 605 BC [Daniel was taken to Babylon in the first deportation to Babylon in 605 BC. Ezekiel was taken eight years later, in 597 BC.]

QUESTION 5: True [They also impressed the king with their wisdom and understanding and entered his service as a reward by God for their commitment to obey the Law (Dan 1:17-21).]

QUESTION 6

Symbol	Kingdom
Gold	Babylon
Silver	Medo-Persia
Bronze	Greece
Iron/Clay	Rome
Rock	Messiah

QUESTION 7: True [In contrast to the wise men, Daniel was able to reveal and interpret the king's undisclosed dream, proving that the true God had revealed it to him (Dan 2:14-45).]

QUESTION 8: False [In Daniel 3:17-18, they affirmed to the king that God was able to save them, but even if He didn't choose to, they still would not worship the golden statue. They had determined to do what was right, whether or not they would be delivered.]

QUESTION 9: *Your answer*

QUESTION 10: *Your answer should be similar to the following:*

Nebuchadnezzar dreamed of a tall tree that reached to the heavens. It had enough provisions to shelter many wild animals and birds. But a holy sentinel chopped it down, leaving only its taproot; this represented Nebuchadnezzar being assigned a place with the wild animals for seven years until he acknowledged God's sovereignty.

QUESTION 11

Word	Meaning

MENE	"God has numbered your kingdom's days and brought it to an end."
TEQEL	"You are weighed on the balances and found to be lacking."
PHARSIN	"Your kingdom is divided and given over to the Medes and Persians."

QUESTION 12

    A. Daniel kneeling and offering prayers

    B. Den of lions

    C. It cannot be altered

    D. Rescue

    F. Supervisors and satraps

[Repetition is often used to emphasize elements in a story. In this case, Daniel's continued devotion to God in the face of the king's edicts—which by law "cannot be altered"—along with his rescue from impossible circumstances show God's sovereign work in Daniel's life among the exiles.]

QUESTION 13

Symbol	Kingdom
Lion	Babylon
Bear	Medo-Persia
Leopard	Greece
Beast	Rome

QUESTION 14

Symbol	Represents
Double-horned ram	Medo-Persia
A large horned goat (horn broken off)	Alexander the Great
The large horned goat with four new horns	The kingdoms of Alexander's four generals
The most prominent horn on the goat	The Seleucid dynasty under Antiochus IV

QUESTION 15: Antichrist [See more teaching on the Antichrist in Daniel 9:27.]

QUESTION 16: *Your answer should be similar to the following:*

Daniel based his prayer on God's promise that the captivity would last only seventy years (Jer 25:11-12). (1) He confessed that Israel has sinned (Dan 9:3-11); (2) he acknowledged that God faithfully judged His people as He said He would (Deut 28:48-57, 64-68); (3) he asked God to mercifully restore the Jerusalem temple for His name's sake.

QUESTION 17

Reference	Teaching
Daniel 9:24	Israel will embrace Christ's atonement on the cross at Christ's second coming and experience the blessings of the Millennial Kingdom after 490 years, or seventy "sevens."
Daniel 9:25	Sixty-nine "sevens" (483 years by the Jewish calendar) will transpire between Artaxerxes' decree to rebuild Jerusalem (444 BC) and Jesus Christ's presentation to Israel as Messiah at the Triumphal Entry (AD 33).
Daniel 9:26	After the sixty-two "sevens" (following March 30, AD 33) Christ the Messiah would die, Titus would destroy Jerusalem, and Israel's suffering will continue throughout the church age until Christ's second coming.
Daniel 9:27	At the midpoint of the last "seven" (the seven-year tribulation), Antichrist will break his covenant and will replace temple sacrifices with worship of himself until his doom.

QUESTION 18

A. "I came in response to your prayers, but I was delayed by a demon."

B. "You are greatly esteemed."

C. "You need to know Israel's future."

[In 536 BC, Gabriel appeared to Daniel in great splendor and explained that, though delayed by a demon, he had come to strengthen Daniel and to help him understand Israel's future (Dan 10:1—11:1).]

QUESTION 19

Reference	Teaching
Daniel 11:36-39	The Antichrist will set himself up as a god to rule by military might.
Daniel 11:40-45	The Antichrist will be attacked repeatedly and will die at the second coming of Christ.
Daniel 12:1-3	Israel will be protected by Michael prior to the ushering in of the Millennial kingdom, and resurrections will precede, providing two options for the resurrected: either entrance into the Millennium or punishment at God's hand.
Daniel 12:4	Gabriel tells Daniel to write and protect these prophecies so that Israel can understand them in the tribulation.
Daniel 12:6-7	Gabriel says the great tribulation will last three and one half years—1260 days.

Daniel 12:8-13	Gabriel says the end of the great tribulation will bring judgment for ignorant unbelievers who worship the Antichrist but blessing for wise Israel, who will enter the kingdom.

QUESTION 20: *Your answer*

QUESTION 21

Daniel--Sovereignty over Gentiles					
					Instructions
Daniel Promoted	Golden Image	Nebuchadnezzar's Pride	Handwriting on the Wall	Lion's Den	Image of Beasts
Daniel 2	**Daniel 3**	**Daniel 4**	**Daniel 5**	**Daniel 6**	**Daniel 7**

QUESTION 22

Event	Chapter
The ram, goat and little horn	Daniel 8
Daniel's seventy weeks	Daniel 9
Daniel's prayer and explanation	Daniel 10
Daniel's prophecies about the Gentile nations	Daniel 11
Daniel's prophecies about Israel	Daniel 12

QUESTION 23: *Your answer*

Lesson 8 Self Check Answers

QUESTION 1

    A. Sovereignty

QUESTION 2

    C. 605 BC

QUESTION 3

    D. Greece

QUESTION 4: False

QUESTION 5

    B. He became like an animal for seven years

QUESTION 6

    C. "Your kingdom is divided and given over to the Medes and Persians."

QUESTION 7: True

QUESTION 8

    C. Medo-Persia

QUESTION 9

    A. Jesus enters Jerusalem a week before His resurrection

QUESTION 10: False

Lesson 9: Ezekiel

Lesson Introduction

While Daniel's prophecy provides extensive political predictions, the prophecy of his fellow exilic prophet, Ezekiel, provides a religious perspective. Ezekiel depicts the departure and subsequent return of the glory of God from the temple, to instruct Judah that God disciplines us for our sin but restores us by His grace. The natural response of His people is to be holy as He is holy. "For without (holiness), no one will see the Lord" (Heb 12:14).

Significantly, the glory of the Lord would depart from the temple, Jerusalem, and Israel following the same path that Jesus Christ would follow after his Triumphal Entry and cleansing of the temple (Mk 11:11, 15-19). In Ezekiel 10:3-5, Ezekiel saw the glory of the Lord "(arise) from the cherub and (move) to the threshold of the temple." It soon moved to the entrance of the *east* gate of the temple (Ezk 10:19). After seeing more evil in Jerusalem, the glory departed the city "to *the mountain east of it (Olivet)*" (Ezk 11:23).

Many years later, Jesus, the true "glory of the Lord," would track the same path, first touring the evil practices in the temple and sharing in God's fury with those practices (Ezk 8). He first visited the temple, cleansed it, and then went out into Jerusalem (Mk 11:11, 15-19, 27-33; Mk 12). He departed through the temple courts to the *east*, and then sat for a while on *the Mount of Olives* "opposite the temple" (Mk 13: 1-3). Within forty years of both Ezekiel's and Jesus' times, the temple would be destroyed and left desolate (Ezk 24; Mk 13).

But that wasn't the end of the story. Ezekiel 33–48 details the final restoration of Israel and God's glory to the future millennial temple.

Lesson Outline

Topic 1: Introduction to Ezekiel

Topic 2: Glory Departs

> Judgment Necessary

> Optimism Futile

> Judgment Deserved

Topic 3: Nations Judged—No Glory

Topic 4: Glory Returns

> New Life

> New Order

Topic 5: Knowing, Being, Doing

Lesson Objectives

By the end of this lesson you will be able to do the following:

- Examine Ezekiel's purpose to encourage the Judean exiles and future believers
- Evaluate Ezekiel's distinctions and the timelines of his life and visions
- Discuss the meanings of the symbols and visions in Ezekiel
- Discuss Ezekiel's emphasis on the glory of the Lord
- Look at Israel's new life and temple services after the return of Christ

Topic 1: Introduction to Ezekiel

God's promise to bless the world through Abraham will see fulfillment in the millennial reign of Christ. But the book of Ezekiel records one of the darkest times in Jerusalem's history, as Judah, Jerusalem and the temple faced destruction because of the nation's disobedience—though this also was a fulfillment of God's promise of discipline for sin (Deut 28). Ezekiel shows Israel first under discipline (Ezk 1–24), but eventually restored to their land and blessed under Christ's reign in His kingdom (Ezk 33–48).

Ezekiel Sovereign Departure and Return of the Glory						
Glory Departs		Nations Judged (no glory)			Glory Returns	
1-24		25-32			33-48	
Exile		Sovereignty Vindicated			Restoration	
Judgment of Judah		Judgment of Nations			Blessing of Israel	
Judah's Fall		Judah's Foes			Judah's Future	
Before the Siege (592-588 BC)		Through the Siege (587-586 BC)			After the Siege (586-573 BC)	
Call in Glory 1-3	Pre-Exile Hopelessness 4-24	Ammon, Moab, Edom, Philistia 25	Tyre and Sidon 26-28	Egypt 29-32	New Life 33-39	New Order 40-48
Babylon (592-570 BC)						

Millennial

Most evangelical Christians believe that the kingdom of God will have universal sway over the earth, and that righteousness and peace and the knowledge of the Lord will prevail everywhere. This happy time is commonly called the millennium, or the thousand-years' reign.

- **Key Word:** Glory
- **Key Verse:** "I will take you from the nations and gather you from all the countries; then I will bring you to your land. I will sprinkle you with pure water and you will be clean from all your impurities. I will purify you from all your idols. I will give you a new heart, and I will put a new spirit within you. I will remove the heart of stone from your body and give you a heart of flesh. I will put my Spirit within you; I will take the initiative and you will obey my statutes and carefully observe my regulations" (Ezk 36:24-27).
- **Summary Statement:** Ezekiel prophesies two messages, one of judgment and one of blessing. He encourages the exiles that, although God will sovereignly judge His people, He will also

destroy their adversaries and restore the glory of the Lord, which departed before the destruction of the temple.

- **Application:** God disciplines us for our sin, but restores us by His grace. In what ways can you see God's grace at work in your life?

Assignment

- Please read "Introduction to Ezekiel."

Introduction to Ezekiel

Title

The name Ezekiel (*yehezke'l*) means literally "God strengthens." Ezekiel was indeed strengthened by the God who called him to a hard-hearted people (Ezk 3:8-9).

Authorship

External Evidence: The unity, authorship, and exilic date for Ezekiel were never challenged until long after the book had been written. The first to question the authorship was Spinoza (1632-1677), whose work was later taken up by Oeder and published in 1771. This work claimed that the prophecy concluded with chapter 39, and that chapters 40–48 were a "spurious addition to the genuine work." Tradition preserved in rabbinic circles said that the men of the Great Synagogue wrote Ezekiel, as well as the twelve minor prophets, but this probably means that they copied or edited the books.

Internal Evidence: Two verses in the book itself mention Ezekiel as author, but he appears nowhere else in the Old Testament. The text clearly indicates that Ezekiel, a priest and the son of Buzi (Ezk 1:3), penned the work (Ezk 24:24). He grew up in Palestine, probably in Jerusalem, but lived in Babylon "among the exiles" in a transplanted Jewish colony most of his life (Ezk 1:1). His wife died as a sign to Judah of the mourning that was to come when Nebuchadnezzar began his final siege on Jerusalem (Ezk 24:16-24). Some scholars have questioned the book's unity, but the text (1) identifies the author as Ezekiel, (2) maintains a consistent style, language, and theme throughout, and (3) repeats key phrases throughout, such as "they shall know that I am the LORD," "Son of man," "the word of the LORD came to me," and the "glory of the LORD" (Wilkinson, 213).

Circumstances

Date: Ezekiel's Babylonian exile began in 597 BC (Ezk 33:21), when he was twenty-five. We know this because five years after he and Jehoiachin had been exiled to Babylon (Ezk 1:2-3), he began his prophetic office at thirty years old (Ezk 1:1). This makes his birth year 622 BC. Therefore, he ministered from 593-592 to at least 573 BC, which is the last recorded date in the prophecy.

Recipients: Ezekiel directed his message towards the captives in Babylon (Ezk 1:1) who had been there from five to twelve years when he began prophesying. Some, like Daniel, were taken captive in 605 BC and had been there twelve years. Others, taken into exile with Ezekiel himself, had waited in Babylon for five years to see what would happen to Judah.

Characteristics

Ezekiel has one of the key texts on the New Covenant (Ezk 36:24-28), perhaps second in importance only to Jeremiah 31:31-34.

Ezekiel uses prophecies, signs, symbols, drama, and parables to express God's Word in creative and interesting ways. Because of this "strange behavior" he has been called ecstatic, visionary, neurotic, psychotic, and schizophrenic (see LaSor, 462).

Ezekiel and Daniel are the only prophets of God whose entire prophetic ministry was outside the borders of Palestine. Ezekiel writes only in the first person (except Ezk 1:3).

God's glory first hovered over the waters of creation (Gen 1:2), then descended on Mount Sinai (Ex 19:16-17), and later filled the tabernacle (Ex 40:34-35). Since Solomon's time (ca. 959 BC) the *shekinah* glory had been above the ark in the Holy of Holies in the Jerusalem temple (1 Kgs 8:10-11). After Ezekiel sees God's glory in Babylon (Ezk 1:28; 3:23), he sadly reports God's glory departing from the temple in stages, though he said that it would eventually return.

Scripture	Stage of Departure
Ezekiel 8:4	North gate of inner court (assuming "there" means *outside* the sanctuary)
Ezekiel 9:3	Ark to temple threshold
Ezekiel 10:4	Ark to Temple court
Ezekiel 10:18-19	Threshold to east gate of the temple court
Ezekiel 11:23	City to east mountain (Mount of Olives)
Ezekiel 43:1-5	Glory returns to Millennial temple (in the future)

Ezekiel also provides one of the two most important passages in all of Scripture (see Isa 14:12-15) on the sin and fall of Satan from heaven, giving it a double meaning, since it refers to the King of Tyre as well as to the devil (Ezk 28:11-19). There are several views of this passage:

1. A **literal ruler** alone is in view (not Satan in any sense).

- A literal ruler based upon a *myth* is depicted.

- An *exaggerated*, satirical, hyperbolic view of a literal ruler is portrayed.

- The literal ruler is the *king of Tyre* alone.

2. **Satan** is in view.

- The "literal ruler" is *Satan*, who is *behind the human ruler*.

- *Only Satan* is in view (no literal king).

- Both *Satan and the literal king of Tyre* are in view (double reference—the view this course holds).

3. **Man** is in view (Zuck, 384).

Contrasting the Exilic Prophets		
	Daniel	Ezekiel
Date	605-536	597-570
Beginning of Ministry	First invasion of Nebuchadnezzar	Second invasion of Nebuchadnezzar
End of ministry	After the exile	In the exile
Length of ministry	Longer (70 years)	Shorter (27 years)
Restoration	Political	Religious
God's	Sovereignty	Glory/Holiness
Occupation	Administrator/prophet	Prophet
Style	Abstract	Concrete
Length	12 chapters	48 chapters
Subjects	Nations & Israel	Israel & Nations
Proclamations	Private	Public

QUESTION 1

The key word for Ezekiel is _____.

QUESTION 2

In what year was Ezekiel taken to Babylon?

- A. 609 BC
- B. 605 BC
- C. 597 BC
- D. 586 BC

QUESTION 3

Which of the following are true of Ezekiel? *(Select all that apply.)*

- A. He provided one of the most important passages on the fall of Satan.
- B. He and his family were protected from the dangers of God's judgment.
- C. He ministered both before and after the fall of Jerusalem.
- D. He prophesied using many parables and symbols

QUESTION 4

Why did God choose not to separate His holy prophet from the judgmental effects of the exile experience? What were the advantages of allowing him to personally experience those effects, and what does that mean for you in your ministry? Please open your Life Notebook and record your thoughts.

Topic 1 Key Points

- Ezekiel encourages the exiles that, although God will sovereignly judge His people, He will also destroy their adversaries and restore the *glory* of the Lord, which had departed before the destruction of the temple.

- Ezekiel was taken to Babylon in the second major deportation in 597 BC. Daniel had been taken in 605 BC, and Jerusalem would fall when the nation was taken in 586 BC.

- Ezekiel was not isolated from the trials of his people during this time, but was deeply and personally affected by the conditions of the exile. His wife died as a sign of the mourning that was to come.

Topic 2: Glory Departs (Ezk 1–24)

Dates in Ezekiel

REFERENCE	YEAR	MONTH	DAY	MODERN RECKONING	EVENT
1. 1:1 1:2 3:16	30 5 "At the end of seven days"	4 — 	5 5 	July 31, 593 B.C.	Inaugural vision
2. 8:1	6	6	5	Sept. 17, 592	Transport to Jerusalem
3. 20:1-2	7	5	10	Aug. 14, 591	Negative view of Israel's history
4. 24:1	9	10	10	Jan. 15, 588	Beginning of siege (see also 2 Kings 25:1)
5. 26:1	11	—	1	Apr. 23, 587 to Apr. 13, 586	Oracle against Tyre
6. 29:1	10	10	12	Jan. 7, 587	Oracle against Egypt
7. 29:17	27	1	1	Apr. 26, 571	Egypt in exchange for Tyre
8. 30:20	11	1	7	Apr. 29, 587	Oracle against Pharoah
9. 31:1	11	3	1	June 21, 587	Oracle against Pharoah
10. 32:1	12	12	1	Mar. 3, 585	Lament over Pharoah
11. 32:17	12	—	15	Apr. 13, 586 to Apr. 1, 585	Egypt dead
12. 33:21	12	10	5	Jan. 8, 585	Arrival of first fugitive
13. 40:1 40:1	25 "14th year after the fall of the city"	1 	10 	Apr. 28, 573	Vision of the future

The predominant theme of Ezekiel's writing is the sovereignty and glory of God, as shown in the repeated phrases "they shall know that I am the LORD" and "the glory of the LORD." God's sovereignty and glory is demonstrated in the threefold outline of the book: (1) His calling of Ezekiel and impending judgment upon the nation (Ezk 1–24); (2) His judgment of nations which oppressed Judah (Ezk 25–32); and (3) His unconditional restoration of the nation, which would mark the return of the glory of the Lord (Ezk 33–48). Within these sections, three visions of this glory appear that demonstrate His holiness (Ezk 1:1–3:27; 8:1–11:25; 40–48). The book first traces the glory of God that resides with the people (Ezk 1:28; 3:23) before the fall of Jerusalem but departs at the destruction of the temple (Ezk 10:4, 18). This "glory of the LORD" is not present in chapters 12–32, which deal with the surrounding nations rather than with Judah, although God does declare that even in their judgments, His glory would be displayed (Ezk 25:9; 28:22; 30:13; 39:21). However, His glory will return fully when the millennial temple is constructed (Ezk 43:1-5).

Despite exile and the departure of God's glory, Ezekiel comforts the people with the message that that glory will dwell with them again. Therefore, these revelations of God's holiness and sovereignty are given to encourage the exiles in Babylon that, although God will judge them by removing His glory from the temple, He will also restore His glory to the temple according to His sovereign purpose.

Judgment Necessary (Ezk 1–11)

Assignment

- Please read "Judgment Necessary."

Judgment Necessary

Summary Statement for the Book

Ezekiel prophesies two messages, one of judgment and one of blessing. He encourages the exiles that, although God will sovereignly judge His people, He will also destroy their adversaries and restore the glory of the Lord, which departed before the destruction of the temple.

God commissions Ezekiel, who prophesies that His glory will leave the nation at Jerusalem's fall. This proves His sovereignty by warning of His necessary, irrevocable, and justified judgment (Ezk 1–24).

God commissioned Ezekiel to deliver His messages of judgment and blessings for Judah while His glory still resided with the people (Ezk 1–3). Before the fall of Jerusalem, Ezekiel saw a vision of God in His glory (Ezk 1). This shows that God's sovereignty and holiness were the foundation for the message of the book. God called Ezekiel to be Israel's watchman and empowered him to prophesy despite opposition and physical restraints (Ezk 2–3):

Ezekiel was told to deliver God's message to Israel fearlessly, despite the nation's rebellion, so that the people would know that a prophet was among them (Ezk 2:1-7). Obediently, he ate a scroll to receive God's word of judgment upon the nation (Ezk 2:8–3:3), and God sent him to the house of Israel to deliver the message of judgment written on the scroll, even though he was warned that the nation will not listen (Ezk 3:4-11). Ezekiel was empowered by the Spirit to perform his ministry, despite physical restraints (Ezk 3:12-27).

Ezekiel prophesied a pre-exilic message of judgment: God's glory would leave the nation because of its disobedience, Jerusalem's fate was sealed; optimism was futile; and God's righteousness in judgment was justified due to Judah's corrupt history (Ezk 4–24).

- Ezekiel revealed Judah's disobedience through four prophesied signs (Ezk 4–5).

    1. He symbolized Jerusalem under attack by using a clay tablet (Ezk 4:1-3).

    2. He symbolized Israel's 390 years of sin and Judah's forty years of sin by lying on his sides for more than fourteen months (Ezk 4:4-8).

    3. He symbolized the scarcity of clean food and water during Jerusalem's siege by eating food cooked over cow dung (Ezk 4:9-17).

    4. He symbolized the division and destruction of Jerusalem, the city's punishment for its disobedience despite God's revelations, by using the illustration of hair divided and burned (Ezk 5).

- Two sermons showed that judgment upon the nation was necessary (Ezk 6–7).

    1. Prophecies against the mountains of Israel depicted judgment upon the nation for its idolatry on the high places (Ezk 6).

    2. Prophecies against the people of the land showed that judgment was certain, soon, complete, and continuous (Ezk 7).

- Four visions showed that God was justified in judging the nation for its disobedience, and they culminated in the actual departure of God's glory (Ezk 8–11).

    1. A vision of idolatry in the doomed temple itself showed the evil that was practiced on the temple grounds: worship of the jealousy idol, paintings, Tammuz (a Babylonian god), and the sun (Ezk 8).

    2. A vision of the execution of the godless people of Jerusalem, leaving a righteous remnant, showed that God would not allow open rebellion to continue (Ezk 9).

    3. A vision of God's glory departing from the temple in the form of wheels and cherubim showed that God could not dwell among a wicked, idolatrous people (Ezk 10).

    4. A vision showed those remaining in Jerusalem being judged for their wicked rulers, the people in captivity being restored, and God's glory departing from the city (Ezk 11).

Signs in Ezekiel

SIGN	TEACHING	PASSAGE
1. Sign of the Brick	Jerusalem's siege and fall	4:1-3
2. Sign of the Prophet's Posture	Discomforts of captivity	4:4-8
3. Sign of Famine	Deprivations of captivity	4:9-17
4. Sign of the Knife and Razor	Utter destruction of the city	5:1-17
5. Sign of House Moving	Removal to another land	12:1-7,17-20
6. Sign of the Sharpened Sword	Judgment imminent	21:1-17
7. Sign of Nebuchadnezzar's Sword	Babylon the captor	21:18-23
8. Sign of the Smelting Furnace	Judgment and purging	22:17-31
9. Sign of Ezekiel's Wife's Death	Blessings forfeited	24:15-27
10. Sign of the Two Sticks	Reunion of Israel and Judah	37:15-17

QUESTION 5

At the time Ezekiel started prophesying, Judah could have still avoided judgment by repenting. *True or False?*

QUESTION 6

Please match the reference with the corresponding symbolic prophecy.

Reference	Symbolic Prophecy
Ezekiel 4:1-3	By using a clay tablet, Ezekiel depicts Jerusalem under attack.
Ezekiel 4:4-8	By lying on his sides for more than fourteen months, Ezekiel illustrates Israel's 390 years of sin and Judah's forty years of sin.
Ezekiel 4:9-17	By eating food cooked over cow dung, Ezekiel demonstrates the future need to eat unclean food, illustrating that food and water will be scarce during Jerusalem's siege.
Ezekiel 5	By using the illustration of hair divided and burned, Ezekiel symbolizes the division and destruction of Jerusalem because it has disobeyed despite God's revelations.

QUESTION 7

Please match the reference with the corresponding vision.

Reference	Vision
Ezekiel 8	Those remaining in Jerusalem are judged for their wicked rulers, the the people in captivity are restored, and God's glory departs from the city.
Ezekiel 9	God's glory departing from the temple in the form of wheels and cherubim shows that God cannot dwell among a wicked, idolatrous people.
Ezekiel 10	The idolatry in the doomed temple itself shows the evil practiced on the temple grounds: worship of the jealousy idol, paintings, Tammuz, and the sun.
Ezekiel 11	The execution of the godless people of Jerusalem, leaving a righteous remnant, shows that God will not allow open rebellion to continue.

Optimism Futile (Ezk 12–19)

Restoration of Edenic Ideals

The ideal characteristics of life in Eden were forfeited because of sin. The OT prophets developed the theme of restoration of these ideals and the hope of a coming ideal community. Ezekiel developed every aspect of this restoration hope of a new Eden (Ezek. 36:35).		
Life Genesis 2:7-9	Death Genesis 3:19; 4:8	NEW LIFE (everlasting) Ezekiel 36:25-27; 37:1-14; 47:1-2, 5-10; Revelation 22:1-2, 14
Work Genesis 2:15	Toil, Labor Genesis 3:17-19	WORK (rewards for labor) Jeremiah 31:15-17; Ezekiel 36:8-11, 33-36; 1 Corinthians 3:11-15; 15:58
Rest Genesis 2:3	No Rest Genesis 3:19a	REST (cessation of human efforts) Jeremiah 6:16; Ezekiel 34:27-28; Matthew 11:28; Hebrews 4:8-11; Revelation 14:13
Peace (harmony) Genesis 2:8-20	Enmity Genesis 3:15; 4:8	PEACE (new harmony) Isaiah 9:6; 11:6-8; Ezekiel 34:25; 37:26; Jeremiah 31:31-34; Micah 4:1-3; Ephesians 2:14; Revelation 22–23
Companionship Genesis 2:18, 21-25	Discord Genesis 3:12, 16 (polygamy 4:19)	COMPANIONSHIP Isaiah 11:11-12; Ezekiel 34:13, 16, 23-24, 30; 36:28; 37:15-28; Revelation 22:3
Knowledge Genesis 2:9, 17 (by revelation and discernment)	Knowledge Genesis 3:7 (by experience) Amos 8:11-12; Hosea 4:6	KNOWLEDGE (by revelation and experience) Jeremiah 31:31-34; Ezekiel 34:30; 36:26-27; Colossians 1:9; 1 Timothy 2:3-4; 2 Timothy 3:16-17
Dominion (stewardship) Genesis 1:26-28; 2:19-20	Domination Genesis 3:6; 4:17; 6:5	DOMINION (stewardship renewal) Ezekiel 34:39; 36:28-38; Zechariah 9:10; Revelation 22:3-5
Productivity	Unproductivity Genesis 3:17-18	PRODUCTIVITY Joel 2:23-34; Ezekiel 29:21; 34:26-31; 36:8-12, 30-32, 37-38; 47:12; Amos 9:11-15; Revelation 22:2-3
Security (garden = sheltered, protected area) Genesis 2:8	Fear	SECURITY (eternal) Ezekiel 34:28; 37:27-28; Micah 4:4; 1 John 4:18; Revelation 7:14-17; 21:3, 8; 22:3-4

Assignment

- Please read "Optimism Futile."

Optimism Futile

Two signs, six messages, and five parables pronounced judgment so the people could see that Jerusalem's fate had been sealed and that optimism was utterly futile (Ezk 12–19).

- Two signs demonstrated the inescapable judgment (Ezk 12:1-20).

  1. Ezekiel packed and carried his baggage with him so the people would know that Yahweh is the Lord and that exile is unavoidable (Ezk 12:1-16).

  2. Ezekiel trembled while he ate to show the nearness of the judgment (Ezk 12:17-28).

- Five messages on the certainty of God's judgment removed any doubt about whether Ezekiel's preaching was of divine origin (Ezk 12:21–14:23).

1. His message of doom would surely come true despite the people's skepticism (Ezk 12:21-25).

2. The predicted judgment would be soon, not far off as the people had supposed (Ezk 12:26-28).

3. The false peace proclaimed by the false prophets and prophetesses was exposed in order to keep the people from having a false sense of security (Ezk 13).

4. Ezekiel preached against the elders engaged in idolatry, warning them to repent or suffer judgment (Ezk 14:1-11).

5. Judgment was inescapable for those who had sinned, but a righteous remnant would be spared. This message comforted the people with the knowledge that even though judgment would come, the righteous may escape (Ezk 14:12-23).

- Three parables stress the impossibility of deliverance for Israel (Ezk 15–17).

   1. The parable of a fruitless vine depicts the certainty of God's judgment upon Jerusalem for its lack of spiritual fruit (Ezk 15).

   2. The parable of the adulterous wife shows that God has cared for Jerusalem from birth but she has betrayed Him by worshipping other gods (Ezk 16). This will result in judgment but will be followed by restoration.

   3. The parable of the eagles and vine depicts God's judgment upon Jerusalem and King Zedekiah for turning to Egypt to escape from Nebuchadnezzar instead of to Him (Ezk 17). This will result in more judgment followed by restoration.

- Ezekiel stated that God holds each person individually responsible for his sin, encouraging each individual to repent in order to escape judgment (Ezk 18).

- Two more parables lamented the false optimism of kings in Jerusalem, which led to their captivity (Ezk 19).

   1. The parable of two lions laments the reckless reigns of Jehoahaz and Jehoiakim, who ended up in exile in Egypt and Babylon, respectively (Ezk 19:1-9).

   2. The parable of the withered vine lamented Zedekiah's rule, which will culminate in the nation (vine) in exile in Babylon (Ezk 19:10-14).

QUESTION 8

Which of the following best explains why Ezekiel trembled when he ate in Ezekiel 12:17-20?

    A. A sign of the sureness of the exile

    B. A sign of the nearness of the exile

    C. A sign of the severity of the exile

    D. A sign of the scarce provisions after the exile

QUESTION 9

Please match the reference with the corresponding message.

Reference	Message
Ezekiel 12:21-25	Judgment is inescapable for those who have sinned, but a righteous remnant will be spared.
Ezekiel 12:26-28	His prediction of doom will surely come true despite the people's skepticism.
Ezekiel 13	The predicted judgment will be soon, not far off as the people had supposed.
Ezekiel 14:1-11	The false peace proclaimed by the false prophets and prophetesses is exposed.
Ezekiel 14:12-23	Ezekiel preaches against the elders engaged in idolatry, warning them to repent or suffer judgment.

QUESTION 10

Please match the reference with the corresponding parable.

Reference	Parable
Ezekiel 15	The parable of two lions laments the reckless reigns of Jehoahaz and Jehoiakim, who ended up in exile in Egypt and Babylon, respectively.
Ezekiel 16	The parable of the eagles and vine depicts God's judgment upon Jerusalem and King Zedekiah for turning to Egypt to escape from Nebuchadnezzar instead of to Him.
Ezekiel 17	The parable of the withered vine laments Zedekiah's rule, which will culminate in the nation (vine) in exile in Babylon.
Ezekiel 18	The parable of the adulterous wife shows that God has cared for Jerusalem from birth, but she has betrayed Him by worshipping other gods.
Ezekiel 19:1-9	Ezekiel states that God holds each person individually responsible for his sin, encouraging each individual to repent in order to escape judgment.
Ezekiel 19:10-14	The parable of a fruitless vine depicts the certainty of God's judgment upon Jerusalem for its lack of spiritual fruit.

Judgment Deserved (Ezk 20–24)

Chiastic Structure of Ezekiel

A. Chapter 1-11 Glory departs from Jerusalem
  B. Chapter 12 Exile prophesied. Rebellious house.
    C. Chapter 13-15 Defiled land-Dead
      D. Chapter 16 Harlot/Unclean
        E. Chapter 17 Proud rulers. Rebellious kings.
          F. Chapter 18 Man accountable for own sin
            G Chapter 19 Lamentation (for Israel)
              H. Chapter 20 Speak to Elders [idolatry and disobedience]
                I. Chapter 21 Prophecy against Israel and the Nations
                  J. Chapter 22-23 Judge Jerusalem
                    K. Chapter 24 The seige of Jerusalem
                  J. Chapter 25-29 Judge Nations
                I. Chapter 30 Prophecy against Nations
              H. Chapter 31 Speak to the King of Egypt [pride]
            G. Chapter 32 Lamentation (for Egypt)
          F. Chapter 33 Man accountable for own sin
        E. Chapter 34 Shepherds out. God, the king, in.
      D. Chapter 35-36 Israel rebuilt/made clean
    C. Chapter 37 Israel restored-revived
  B. Chapter 38-39 Brought back from exile. Rebellion punished
A. Chapter 40-48 Glory of God dwells in the New Jerusalem

Assignment

- Please read "Judgment Deserved."

Judgment Deserved

A recap of Israel's unfaithfulness in Egypt, the wilderness, and the Promised Land reminded the nation that God's righteous judgment was justified (Ezk 20:1-31). Although the nation wanted to imitate its idolatrous neighbors, God would restore Israel to Himself in the future (Ezk 20:32-44, see also 1 Sam 8:5).

The "fire" in Judah was God's judgment, and all would see it as God's doing (Ezk 20:45-49). God would use Nebuchadnezzar as His sword against the nations of both Israel and Ammon (Ezk 21).

Three messages revealed Jerusalem's sins, the resultant punishment under Nebuchadnezzar, and the various recipients of judgment (Ezk 22).

1. The parable of two harlot sisters depicted how God's righteousness in judgment was justified because of the sins of Samaria and Jerusalem (Ezk 23).

2. The parable of the cooking pot foretold that Nebuchadnezzar would begin his siege of Jerusalem on that very day (Ezk 24:1-14).

3. The death of Ezekiel's wife was a sign to all that everyone will lose relatives dear to them in the siege of Jerusalem (Ezk 24:15-27).

QUESTION 11

In Ezekiel 20:1-31, when God wanted to show that His judgment of Judah was justified, on which events did He focus?

QUESTION 12

The fire Ezekiel talked about in Ezekiel 20:45-49 refers to God's judgment. *True or False?*

QUESTION 13

Which parable was a sign that Nebuchadnezzar would begin his siege of Jerusalem on that very day?

    A. The harlot sister Samaria

    B. The harlot sister Jerusalem

    C. The cooking pot

    D. The death of Ezekiel's wife

Topic 2 Key Points

- At the time Ezekiel starts prophesying, Judah could not avoid judgment by repenting.
- God's glory departing from the temple in the form of wheels and cherubim showed that God cannot dwell among a wicked, idolatrous people.
- In Ezekiel 4–5, Ezekiel illustrated Judah's sin, the consequent judgment of it, and its resulting uncleanliness, which led to God's glory departing.
- In Ezekiel 8–11, four visions show the open rebellion of Jerusalem, God's refusal to let it continue, and the consequent departure of His glory.
- Ezekiel trembled when he ate in Ezekiel 12:21-28 as a sign of the nearness of the exile.
- In Ezekiel 12–14, Ezekiel said in several messages that near judgment was inescapable for those who had sinned, but a righteous remnant would be spared.
- In five parables in Ezekiel 15–19 God judged the people of Judah for their individual sins, their unrighteous leaders, their trust in other gods and nations, and their lack of spiritual fruit.
- When God wanted to show that his judgment of Judah was justified, He recapped Israel's history of unfaithfulness in Egypt, in the wilderness, and in the Promised Land (Ezk 20:1-31).
- The "fire" in Judah was God's judgment, and all would see it as God's doing (Ezk 20:45-49).
- The parable of the cooking pot signified that Nebuchadnezzar would begin his siege of Jerusalem on that very day (Ezk 24:1-14).

Topic 3: Nations Judged—No Glory (Ezk 25–32)

Nebuchadnezzar destroyed Jerusalem in three stages: 605 BC (Daniel and friends taken), 597 BC (Ezekiel, Jehoiachin, and ten thousand hostages taken), and 586 BC (the final stage which leveled Jerusalem and destroyed the temple). Between this second and third siege, the captives in Babylon waited with anticipation as they watched Judah. Ezekiel proclaimed that the exiles waited with a false hope, as God had decreed that the entire nation must pay for its sins through exile. However, he also prophesied a future restoration of the nation. The people needed to know the truth about their punishment, but also the reality that they would be restored once again.

Assignment

- Please read "Nations Judged."

Nations Judged

A message of destruction upon Gentile nations that have oppressed Judah shows that God's sovereignty would be vindicated and His glory demonstrated (Ezk 25–32).

- Ammon would be judged for rejoicing when the sanctuary was destroyed (Ezk 25:1-7).

- Moab would be judged for thinking that Israel was like all of the other nations (Ezk 25:8-11).

- Edom would be judged for taking vengeance on Judah (Ezk 25:12-14).

- Philistia would be judged for taking vengeance on Judah; this judgment vindicates God's sovereignty (Ezk 25:15-17).

- Tyre would be destroyed by Nebuchadnezzar and others so thoroughly that it would not be found or rebuilt; this prophecy was fulfilled in 573-72 after a thirteen-year siege (585-573/72 BC) (Ezk 26). Its beauty, might and trade would be lamented after its fall (Ezk 27). The prince of Tyre would be overthrown for his claim to deity (Ezk 28:1-10), and just as Satan was cast to the earth at his fall, so the king of Tyre would be overthrown (Ezk 28:11-19).

- Sidon would be judged for its maliciousness against Judah (Ezk 28:20-26). God would gain glory in the judgment and His sovereign judgment would be vindicated.

A series of oracles, each beginning with "The word of the LORD came to me," predicted that Egypt would be judged by Nebuchadnezzar and taken to Babylon; these were fulfilled in 571 BC (Ezk 29–32).

Egypt would be exiled for forty years because of its violence and arrogance. It would then be restored, but never to its former power over other nations—prophesied January 5, 587 (Ezk 29:1-16). Egypt would be plundered by Nebuchadnezzar (unlike Tyre, which gave him no reward), but both Egypt and Israel would be restored—prophesied April 26, 571 (Ezk 29:17-21). The destruction of Egypt is foretold in a lament, to show, in poetic form, God's sovereign workings (undated, Ezk 30:1-19).

God would use Babylon as His instrument to break Pharaoh—prophesied April 29, 587 BC (Ezk 30:20-26). As Assyria was like a large and important tree cut down by Babylon (612-605 BC), so Pharaoh would be cut down by Nebuchadnezzar so that his pride might be humiliated—prophesied June 21, 587 (Ezk 31).

The downfall of Pharaoh by Babylon was foretold in a lament, to show, in poetic form, God's sovereign workings—prophesied March 3, 585 BC (Ezk 32:1-16).

Babylon would destroy Egypt just as it had Assyria, Persia (Elam), Meshech, Tubal, Edom, and Sidon; this shows God's sovereignty—prophesied March 17, 585 BC (Ezk 32:17-21).

QUESTION 14

Please match the reference with the corresponding country God will judge.

Reference	Parable
Ezekiel 25:1-7	Moab will be judged for thinking that Israel was like all of the other nations.
Ezekiel 25:8-11	Sidon will be judged for its maliciousness against Judah.
Ezekiel 25:12-14	Edom will be judged for taking vengeance on Judah.
Ezekiel 25:15-17	Philistia will be judged for taking vengeance on Judah; this judgment vindicates God's sovereignty.
Ezekiel 26:1–28:19	Ammon will be judged for rejoicing when the sanctuary was destroyed.
Ezekiel 28:20-26	Tyre will be destroyed and never rebuilt because of its arrogance in its beauty, might, and trade.
Ezekiel 29-32	Egypt will be judged by Nebuchadnezzar and taken to Babylon (fulfilled in 571 BC).

QUESTION 15

In Ezekiel 25–32, the fall of Satan is compared to the fall of which earthly king?

A. Edom

B. Egypt

C. Philistia

D. Tyre

Topic 3 Key Points

- Judgment would also come on the surrounding nations to show Israel the mistake of trusting them; this would vindicate God's sovereignty and demonstrate His glory.

- As Satan was cast to the earth at his fall, so the king of Tyre would be overthrown for his claim to deity (Ezk 26–28).

Topic 4: Glory Returns (Ezk 33–48)

Ezekiel 40–48 refers to a rebuilt temple and sacrificial system. This is one of the most difficult OT texts, as the temple dimensions and modified sacrificial system find no parallel in Scripture or in history. The views abound—some saying that it refers to an "ideal" temple, Solomon's temple, Zerubbabel's temple, Herod's temple, or even the church—but this study takes the perspective that it refers to a literal, Millennial temple.

The Millennial Temple Proper

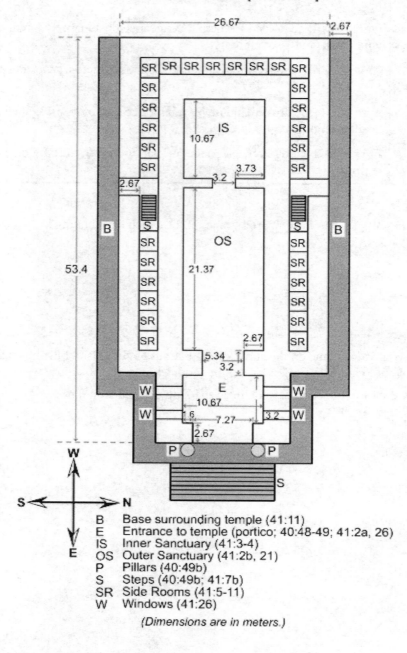

B   Base surrounding temple (41:11)
E   Entrance to temple (portico; 40:48-49; 41:2a, 26)
IS   Inner Sanctuary (41:3-4)
OS   Outer Sanctuary (41:2b, 21)
P   Pillars (40:49b)
S   Steps (40:49b; 41:7b)
SR   Side Rooms (41:5-11)
W   Windows (41:26)

(Dimensions are in meters.)

New Life (Ezk 33–39)

When Will the Invasion of Gog Occur (Ezekiel 38–39)?

TIME PERIOD VIEWS	DESCRIPTION
1. This passage is entirely symbolic. It does not refer to any literal army.	But would a symbolic battle be described in such detail? How are the various details accounted for in the symbolic view?
2. It will occur before the tribulation, either just prior to or at the time of the Church's rapture.	Since the tribulation has not yet begun, this may explain the security and peace faced by Israel. But this does not accord with the scheme of end-time events, which requires a period of preparation after which Israel will enjoy a time of peace (Dan. 9:27; cf. Eze 38:8b, 11, 14). Furthermore it could hardly be the period where the Lord's name would not be profaned (Eze. 39:7, 22) with the Tribulation still ahead.
3. It will occur in the middle of the tribulation.	This battle is associated with Revelation 14:14-20 and Daniel 11:40-41. It also happens at the time when the Antichrist will break his covenant with Israel. It will happen at a time when Israel is already in the land enjoying a period of false security through her treaty with the Antichrist. But, Cooper indicates that there is no battle mentioned at mid-Tribulation. The peace and security in Ezekiel does not seem to be false. Judgment is at its height during the Tribulation not peace.
4. It will occur at the end of the tribulation.	There is an allusion to the great feast of Ezekiel 39:17-20 in Revelation 19:17-21. Israel is restored to her land after the battle of Armageddon (Rev 16:12-16). However, this view has the same problems as the previous one.
5. It will occur in the transitional period between the end of the tribulation and the Millennium.	This can explain the fact that Israel is restored to her land after the Tribulation and enjoying a true sense of peace and security, while awaiting the arrival of the Millennium. But, is there scriptural support for such a transitional period? Some sees the extra 45 days in Daniel 12:12 as postulating this period. However, there is no biblical evidence that a battle will occur during this period. Then, there is hardly time to include the burning of weapons and the burial of bodies.
6. It will occur at the end of the Millennium.	This battle is associated with Revelation 20:7-10. The support that it draws upon is the explicit mention of Gog and Magog in Revelation 20:8. The Millennium would certainly explain Israel's time of peace and security. It also provides the time for the burning of weapons and the burial of bodies. But, as mentioned above, it is the debatable whether Gog and Magog in Revelation is the same as the one in Ezekiel.
7. A combination of the fourth and sixth views.	That is, Ezekiel 38-39 is a description of the battles in Revelation 19:17-21 and 20:7-10. It has the advantages of both of these views.

Assignment

- Please read "New Life."

New Life

A message of blessing, which will come through restoration to a new life in the land and a new order in the Millennial Kingdom, provides encouragement for the people that God's glory will return to them once again (Ezk 33–48).

Prophecies of blessings for Judah in a new life—through Ezekiel's reappointment, the replacement of false shepherds, judgment on Israel's enemies, and a restoration to the land—helped prepare Judah for the return of God's glory (Ezk 33–39).

Ezekiel was reappointed as a watchman, and he announced the recent fall of Jerusalem and explained the reasons for God's judgment (Ezk 33). National restoration was emphasized to prepare for the return of the glory of God.

At the time of the Millennial kingdom new life will be given to Judah. The false, self-serving shepherds will be replaced by the Lord, the true, selfless Shepherd (Ezk 34). This true Shepherd will guide the nation after the glory has returned.

Israel's enemies, represented by Edom, which opposed Israel with arrogance against God, will be judged and no longer oppose the people (Ezk 35). Judah will be restored by national blessing, cleansing, and restoration to the land under the New Covenant (see Jer 31:31-34), in order that God's holy character might be shown (Ezk 36).

Judah, a "dead nation," will be restored to life once again in the land, in fulfillment of the Palestinian Covenant (see Deut 30:1-10). Fulfillment began in AD 1948 with the reestablishment of the State of Israel (Ezk 37:1-14).

Judah and Israel will no longer be two nations, but will be united as one under the Messiah's rule in fulfillment of the Davidic Covenant (see 2 Sam 7:13-14); this is a witness to other nations of God's holiness (Ezk 37:15-28).

An attack against Israel by the area of Gog and its allies (an alliance of northern Arab armies) will be turned back by God during the tribulation period (Ezk 38–39). This will ensure Israel's safety and demonstrate God's sovereignty.

An alliance of northern Arab armies (Gog and her allies), will unite to attack Israel with strength so great they will look unconquerable (Ezk 38:1-16).

> Note: Many dispensationalists [who interpret the Bible with a literal hermeneutic, believing that the church and Israel are separate entities] argue that Magog is Russia, but arguing against this are Bible atlases which equate this area with modern-day Turkey. J. Paul Tanner, in "Daniel's 'King of the North': Do We Owe Russia an Apology?" [*Journal of the Evangelical Theological Society* 35 (September 1992): 315-28] believes a confederation of northern Arab nations is in view.

These enemies of Israel will be turned back by God through setbacks in nature, destruction, and fire during the tribulation period (Ezk 38:17–39:29). This will ensure Israel's safety and demonstrate God's sovereignty.

End Time Battles: Armageddon; Gog and Magog

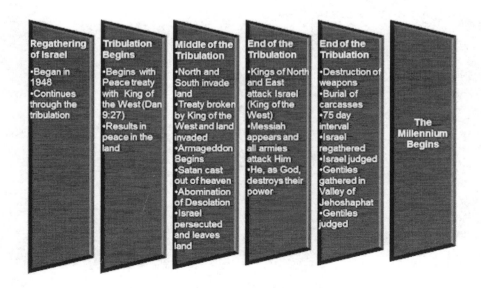

QUESTION 16

Which of the following are predicted to restore new life to the future united Israel and Judah in Ezekiel 33–37? *(Select all that apply.)*

A. The sprinkling of the nation with cleansing water

B. The replacement of the false shepherds with the true, selfless Shepherd

C. Judgment on Israel's enemies

D. Fulfillment of the Abrahamic, Palestinian, Davidic, and new covenants

QUESTION 17

According to this study, during what time period will the battle of Gog and Magog take place?

    A. Before the tribulation period

    B. In the first half of the tribulation period

    C. At the beginning of the second half of the tribulation period

    D. At the end of the millennium

New Order (Ezk 40–48)

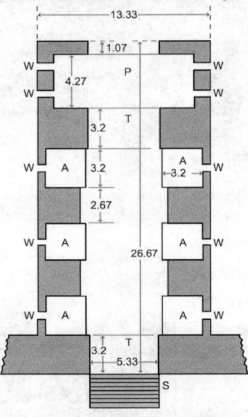

Gate to the Millennial Temple

A Alcoves for the guards (40:7a, 10, 12)
P Portico (40:8-9)
S Steps (40:6a)
T Thresholds (40:6b, 7b)
W Windows (41:16)

(Dimensions are in meters.)

The Millennial Altar

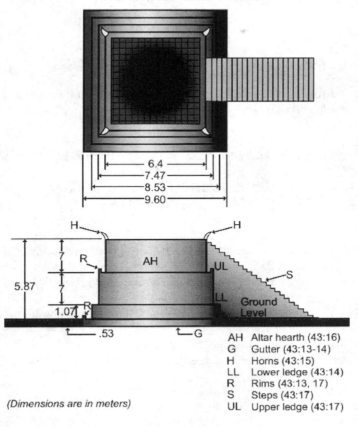

AH	Altar hearth (43:16)
G	Gutter (43:13-14)
H	Horns (43:15)
LL	Lower ledge (43:14)
R	Rims (43:13, 17)
S	Steps (43:17)
UL	Upper ledge (43:17)

(Dimensions are in meters)

Assignment

- Please read "New Order."

New Order

At the new temple, established in the millennium and filled with God's glory, commemorative sacrifices will be offered (Ezk 40–43). These will visibly show Israel's new relationship with God under the New Covenant. This temple will also testify of God's presence with Israel.

Ezekiel saw the magnificent temple buildings from a distance (Ezk 40:1-4). This would have been a tremendous encouragement to Israel, both during the time that their temple was destroyed and during the time of the inferior postexilic temple (vision in 573 BC).

The inner and outer courts are described in detail as perfect squares (Ezk 40:5-47).

- The outer court, with its gates and chambers, forms a square (Ezk 40:5-27).

- The inner court, with its gates, slaughtering tables, and priests' chambers, also forms a perfect square (Ezk 40:28-47).

The temple building itself contains a rectangular nave, the most holy place, a square separate building and an interior filled with galleries of carvings (Ezk 40:48–41:26).

Two sets of chambers are there for the priests' use when they dined or changed their clothes (Ezk 42:1-14).

The walls surrounding the entire complex form another perfect square, which separates the holy from the profane (Ezk 42:15-20).

The glory of the Lord fills the temple, proving that the temple is God's earthly dwelling place among His people and that God will fulfill His promise to once again dwell with His people (Ezk 43:1-12).

The altar of burnt offering is measured and consecrated so that sin offerings which commemorate the sacrificial death of Christ may begin; this shows the complete restoration of God's fellowship with Israel (Ezk 43:1-12). A new service of worship, which will include priests, Levites and Jewish ceremonies, will be established in the millennium (Ezk 44–46).

The duties and land of the temple priests and Levites are given to establish standards for temple ministers (Ezk 44:1–45:8). The temple priests will exercise oversight of the temple, and the sons of Zadok will offer sacrifices and teach the people (Ezk 44). The land of the temple priests and Levites comprises two separate rectangles, with the temple in the midst of the priests (Ezk 45:1-8).

Honesty among the princes is commanded. Offerings, feasts, Sabbath worship and the Year of Jubilee will be reinstituted and serve as memorials to the death of Christ during the millennium (Ezk 45:9–46:24).

The land will be newly divided, and the city will be renamed as testimony to the returned glory of God (Ezk 47–48). A river will flow from the temple eastward in ever-increasing depth. The salty Dead Sea will become fresh water teeming with fish, which symbolizes the cleansing power of the temple (Ezk 47:1-12). New, equal boundaries (from the southern boundary of the Wadi of Egypt to Lebo Hamath in the north) will be given to each tribe, and a land inheritance is also given to the aliens; this indicates that the Abrahamic Covenant is finally fulfilled (Ezk 47:13-23; see also Gen 15:18).

Inheritances for each tribe include seven areas for the northern tribes; a center portion for priests, Levites, the city, and David the prince; and five areas for the southern tribes, with the maidservants' sons on the extreme north and south (Ezk 48:1-29; Gen 35:23-26).

Twelve gates (one per tribe) will surround the city for access from any side (Ezk 48:30-34). The circumference of the city will be 18,000 cubits—about nine and a half kilometers (Ezk 48:35). The name of the city will be "the LORD is there," thus emphasizing the return of God in His glory to dwell with His people during the millennium (Ezk 48:36).

QUESTION 18

What types of sacrifices are offered in the new millennial temple?

    A. Commemorative

    B. Propitiatory

    C. Atoning

    D. None

QUESTION 19

The land boundaries for the tribes will be returned to the original boundaries that were given before Israel crossed into the Promised Land in the book of Joshua. *True or False?*

QUESTION 20

If Old Testament believers needed to be holy to enjoy God's blessing, what does that mean for you personally, if you want to enjoy God's blessing? Please open your Life Notebook and record your thoughts.

Topic 4 Key Points

- New life will be restored to Israel as described in Ezekiel 33–37, when false shepherds are replaced with the true selfless Shepherd, judgment comes upon Israel's enemies, and the Abrahamic, Palestinian, Davidic and New Covenants are fulfilled.

- The Battle of Gog and Magog will take place during the second half of the tribulation period after the King of the West breaks the covenant.

- The sacrifices offered in the Millennial temple will commemorate the propitiatory sacrifice of Christ on the cross.

- New, equal boundaries will be given to each tribe, and a land inheritance given to the aliens, indicating that the Abrahamic Covenant is finally fulfilled.

Topic 5: Knowing, Being, Doing

QUESTION 21

Match the title with the appropriate section of Ezekiel.

Outline of Ezekiel

				Instructions
Call in Glory				
Nations Judged				
New Life				
New Order				
Pre-Exile Hopelessness				
Ezekiel 1–3	Ezekiel 4–24	Ezekiel 25–32	Ezekiel 33–39	Ezekiel 40–48

QUESTION 22

Please open your Life Notebook and record anything new you have learned from this lesson, including any applications you should make to your life.

Lesson 9 Self Check

QUESTION 1

The key word for Ezekiel is

    A. Temple

    B. Judgment

    C. Glory

    D. Restoration

QUESTION 2

As God's prophet, Ezekiel and his family were protected from the dangers of the exile. *True or False?*

QUESTION 3

At the time Ezekiel started prophesying, Judah could still avoid judgment by repenting. *True or False?*

QUESTION 4

What were the Jews worshipping at the time Ezekiel toured the temple?

    A. God

    B. The sun

    C. A golden image

    D. A beast

QUESTION 5

Which of the following best explains why Ezekiel trembled when he ate in Ezekiel 12:17-20?

    A. A sign of the nearness of the exile

    B. A sign of the severity of the exile

    C. A sign of the scarce provisions after the exile

    D. A sign of the sureness of the exile

QUESTION 6

The parable of the cooking pot denotes that Nebuchadnezzar would begin his siege of Jerusalem

    A. The next day

    B. The following year

    C. That very day

    D. Never

QUESTION 7

The fall of Satan is compared to the fall of which city/nation in Ezekiel 25–32?

    A. Tyre

    B. Philistia

    C. Egypt

    D. Edom

QUESTION 8

According to this study, the battle of Gog and Magog will take place during the first half of the tribulation period. *True or False?*

QUESTION 9

According to Ezekiel 40–48, what type of sacrifices will be offered in the new Millennial temple?

   A. Commemorative

   B. Atoning

   C. Guilt

   D. Fellowship

QUESTION 10

New, equal boundaries will be given to each tribe in the Millennial Kingdom. *True or False?*

Unit 3 Exam: Advanced Studies in the Old Testament, Vol.2

QUESTION 1

What is the key word for Jeremiah?

- A. Confession
- B. Glory
- C. Inevitable
- D. Sovereignty

QUESTION 2

Which of the following is likely true of the book or the person Jeremiah?

- A. He wrote every chapter of Jeremiah.
- B. He chronicled the fall of Jerusalem twice.
- C. Most of the book was written about events before King Josiah's death.
- D. Jeremiah is the longest book in the Bible in number of chapters.

QUESTION 3

According to Jeremiah 7, having the Lord's temple in their land sanctified the people of Judah from their evil deeds. *True or False?*

QUESTION 4

In Jeremiah 24, the bad figs represented the people in Jerusalem who would be exiled to Babylon. *True or False?*

QUESTION 5

God used the Rechabites as an example of obedience, even though the commands they followed were merely their ancestor's, not God's. *True or False?*

QUESTION 6

Which of these men did NOT survive the siege of Jerusalem by the Babylonians in Jeremiah 39?

- A. King Zedekiah
- B. The nobles of Judah
- C. Jeremiah
- D. Ebed-Melech the Ethiopian

QUESTION 7

What literary feature tells us which chapter is the focal point of Lamentations?

- A. The acrostic structure
- B. The allegory in the focal chapter
- C. The chiastic structure
- D. The parallelism in its poetry

QUESTION 8

Many of the warnings for covenant disobedience that are fulfilled in Lamentations were predicted in Deuteronomy 28. *True or False?*

QUESTION 9

In what year was Jeremiah taken to Babylon?

A. 605 BC

B. 597 BC

C. 586 BC

D. Never

QUESTION 10

The prophetic argument that supports a late date for the writing of Daniel assumes that prophecy cannot happen. *True or False?*

QUESTION 11

In the vision of the statue in Daniel 2, what nation is represented by iron?

A. Babylon

B. Rome

C. Medo-Persia

D. Greece

QUESTION 12

In Daniel 3, when Daniel's friends were thrown into the furnace, they showed great faith by telling the king they were sure God that would deliver them. *True or False?*

QUESTION 13

In Daniel 5, when King Belshazzar received the handwritten message on the wall saying, "MENE, MENE, TEQEL, PHARSIN," what did the word TEQEL mean?

A. "God has numbered your kingdom's days and brought it to an end."

B. "You are weighed on the balances and found to be lacking."

C. "Your kingdom is divided and given over to the Medes and Persians."

D. "Tonight you will lose your kingdom."

QUESTION 14

In Daniel 8, who foreshadowed the desecration of the temple, which will be repeated at the middle of the tribulation by the future Antichrist?

A. Antiochus IV

B. The Seleucids

C. Alexander the Great

D. Cyrus

QUESTION 15

Which of the following events ends the sixty-ninth week of Daniel?

A. Antichrist places an idol in the Jewish temple

B. Titus destroys the temple in AD 70

C. Jesus enters Jerusalem a week before His resurrection

D. Jerusalem is completely rebuilt

QUESTION 16

Part of Daniel's prophecy was that Tyre would be destroyed so thoroughly that it would not be found or rebuilt. *True or False?*

QUESTION 17

The archangel Michael is specially appointed to defend Israel during what time period?

    A. The exile

    B. The great tribulation

    C. The church age

    D. The Old Testament period

QUESTION 18

As God's prophet, Ezekiel and his family were protected from the dangers of the exile. *True or False?*

QUESTION 19

At the time Ezekiel started prophesying, Judah could still avoid judgment by repenting. *True or False?*

QUESTION 20

What does the fire Ezekiel mentions in Ezekiel 20:45-49 refer to?

    A. God's judgment

    B. The altar in the temple

    C. The Babylonian army

    D. The restoration of the temple

QUESTION 21

The parable of the cooking pot was a sign that Nebuchadnezzar would begin his siege of Jerusalem that very day (Ezk 24:1-14) *True or False?*

.

QUESTION 22

The fall of Satan is compared to the fall of which city/nation in Ezekiel 25–32?

    A. Edom

    B. Egypt

    C. Philistia

    D. Tyre

QUESTION 23

According to this study, the battle of Gog and Magog will take place during the first half of the tribulation period. *True or False?*

QUESTION 24

According to Ezekiel 40–48, which type of sacrifice will be offered in the new Millennial temple?

    A. Propitiatory

    B. None

    C. Commemorative

    D. Fellowship

QUESTION 25

New, equal boundaries will be given to each tribe in the Millennial Kingdom. *True or False?*

Lesson 9 Answers to Questions

QUESTION 1: Glory [Ezekiel encourages the exiles that God would sovereignly judge His people, destroy their adversaries, and restore the glory of the Lord, which had departed before the destruction of the temple.]

QUESTION 2

C. 597 BC [Ezekiel was taken to Babylon during the second major deportation to Babylon, in 597 BC. Daniel had been taken in 605 BC, and Jerusalem would fall when the nation was taken in 586 BC. Ezekiel's ministry actually began in 593 BC.]

QUESTION 3

A. He provided one of the most important passages on the fall of Satan.
C. He ministered both before and after the fall of Jerusalem.
D. He prophesied using many parables and symbols

[Ezekiel's wife died as a sign to Judah of the mourning that was to come when Nebuchadnezzar began his final siege on Jerusalem (Ezk 24:16-24).]

QUESTION 4: *Your answer*

QUESTION 5: False [Ezekiel prophesied a pre-exilic message of judgment: God's glory would leave the nation because of its disobedience, Jerusalem's fate is sealed (which shows the futility of optimism), and God's righteousness in judgment was justified due to Judah's corrupt history (Ezk 4–24).]

QUESTION 6

Reference	Symbolic Prophecy
Ezekiel 4:1-3	By using a clay tablet, Ezekiel depicts Jerusalem under attack.
Ezekiel 4:4-8	By lying on his sides for more than fourteen months, Ezekiel illustrates Israel's 390 years of sin and Judah's forty years of sin.
Ezekiel 4:9-17	By eating food cooked over cow dung, Ezekiel demonstrates the future need to eat unclean food, illustrating that food and water will be scarce during Jerusalem's siege.
Ezekiel 5	By using the illustration of hair divided and burned, Ezekiel symbolizes the division and destruction of Jerusalem because it has disobeyed despite God's revelations.

QUESTION 7

Reference	Vision
Ezekiel 8	The idolatry in the doomed temple itself shows the evil practiced on the temple grounds: worship of the jealousy idol, paintings, Tammuz, and the sun.
Ezekiel 9	The execution of the godless people of Jerusalem, leaving a righteous remnant, shows that God will not allow open rebellion to continue.
Ezekiel 10	God's glory departing from the temple in the form of wheels and cherubim shows that God cannot dwell among a wicked, idolatrous people.
Ezekiel 11	Those remaining in Jerusalem are judged for their wicked rulers, the the people in captivity are restored, and God's glory departs from the city.

QUESTION 8

B. A sign of the nearness of the exile [Ezekiel trembled while he ate to show the nearness of the judgment (Ezk 12:21-28). He also packed and carried his baggage so that the people would know that Yahweh was the Lord and that their exile was unavoidable (Ezk 12:1-16).]

QUESTION 9

Reference	Message
Ezekiel 12:21-25	His prediction of doom will surely come true despite the people's skepticism.

Ezekiel 12:26-28	The predicted judgment will be soon, not far off as the people had supposed.
Ezekiel 13	The false peace proclaimed by the false prophets and prophetesses is exposed.
Ezekiel 14:1-11	Ezekiel preaches against the elders engaged in idolatry, warning them to repent or suffer judgment.
Ezekiel 14:12-23	Judgment is inescapable for those who have sinned, but a righteous remnant will be spared.

QUESTION 10

Reference	Parable
Ezekiel 15	The parable of a fruitless vine depicts the certainty of God's judgment upon Jerusalem for its lack of spiritual fruit.
Ezekiel 16	The parable of the adulterous wife shows that God has cared for Jerusalem from birth, but she has betrayed Him by worshipping other gods.
Ezekiel 17	The parable of the eagles and vine depicts God's judgment upon Jerusalem and King Zedekiah for turning to Egypt to escape from Nebuchadnezzar instead of to Him.
Ezekiel 18	Ezekiel states that God holds each person individually responsible for his sin, encouraging each individual to repent in order to escape judgment.
Ezekiel 19:1-9	The parable of two lions laments the reckless reigns of Jehoahaz and Jehoiakim, who ended up in exile in Egypt and Babylon, respectively.
Ezekiel 19:10-14	The parable of the withered vine laments Zedekiah's rule, which will culminate in the nation (vine) in exile in Babylon.

QUESTION 11: *Your answer should be similar to the following:*
A recap of Israel's history of unfaithfulness in Egypt, in the wilderness, and in the Promised Land reminded the nation that God's righteous judgment was justified (Ezk 20:1-31).

QUESTION 12: True [The "fire" in Judah is God's judgment, and all would see it as God's doing (Ezk 20:45-49).]

QUESTION 13

C. The cooking pot [The parable of the cooking pot signified that Nebuchadnezzar would begin his siege of Jerusalem on that very day (Ezk 24:1-14).]

QUESTION 14

Reference	Parable
Ezekiel 25:1-7	Ammon will be judged for rejoicing when the sanctuary was destroyed.
Ezekiel 25:8-11	Moab will be judged for thinking that Israel was like all of the other nations.
Ezekiel 25:12-14	Edom will be judged for taking vengeance on Judah.
Ezekiel 25:15-17	Philistia will be judged for taking vengeance on Judah; this judgment vindicates God's sovereignty.
Ezekiel 26:1–28:19	Tyre will be destroyed and never rebuilt because of its arrogance in its beauty, might, and trade.
Ezekiel 28:20-26	Sidon will be judged for its maliciousness against Judah.
Ezekiel 29–32	Egypt will be judged by Nebuchadnezzar and taken to Babylon (fulfilled in 571 BC).

QUESTION 15

D. Tyre [Tyre would be destroyed by Nebuchadnezzar and others so thoroughly that it would not be found or rebuilt; this prophecy was fulfilled in 573-72 after a thirteen-year siege (Ezk 26–28). As Satan was cast to the earth at his fall, so the king of Tyre would be overthrown for his claim to deity.]

QUESTION 16

B. The replacement of the false shepherds with the true, selfless Shepherd

C. Judgment on Israel's enemies

D. Fulfillment of the Abrahamic, Palestinian, Davidic, and new covenants

[What a blessing and encouragement that in our age, the predicted physical restoration of Israel to its land has already occurred (AD 1948).]

QUESTION 17

C. At the beginning of the second half of the tribulation period [At the mid-point of the tribulation, the King of the West breaks the covenant, which brings the King of the North into the battle.]

QUESTION 18

A. Commemorative [It can seem somewhat surprising that any sacrifices are offered, because Christ's sacrifice eliminated the need for any atoning or propitiating sacrifices (Heb 10:8-10). However, the idea seems to be that commemorative sacrifices will remind those future Jewish believers of the connection between the Old Testament sacrifices and Jesus' sacrificial work (Ezk 45:13-17). So they are a memorial, similar to the memorial the Lord's Supper is for Christians today.]

QUESTION 19: False [New, equal boundaries (from the southern boundary of the Wadi of Egypt to Lebo Hamath in the north) will be given to each tribe, and a land inheritance will be given to the aliens; this indicates that the Abrahamic Covenant is finally fulfilled (Ezk 47:13-23; see also Gen 15:18).]

QUESTION 20: *Your answer*

QUESTION 21

Outline of Ezekiel

				Instructions
Call in Glory	Pre-Exile Hopelessness	Nations Judged	New Life	New Order
Ezekiel 1–3	Ezekiel 4–24	Ezekiel 25–32	Ezekiel 33–39	Ezekiel 40–48

QUESTION 22: *Your answer*

Lesson 9 Self Check Answers

QUESTION 1
    C. Glory

QUESTION 2: False

QUESTION 3: False

QUESTION 4
    B. The sun

QUESTION 5
    A. A sign of the nearness of the exile

QUESTION 6
    C. That very day

QUESTION 7
    A. Tyre

QUESTION 8: False

QUESTION 9
    A. Commemorative

QUESTION 10: True

Unit 3 Exam Answers

QUESTION 1
   C. Inevitable

QUESTION 2
   B. He chronicled the fall of Jerusalem twice.

QUESTION 3: False

QUESTION 4: False

QUESTION 5: True

QUESTION 6
   B. The nobles of Judah

QUESTION 7
   C. The chiastic structure

QUESTION 8: True

QUESTION 9
   D. Never

QUESTION 10: True

QUESTION 11
   B. Rome

QUESTION 12: False

QUESTION 13
   B. "You are weighed on the balances and found to be lacking."

QUESTION 14
   A. Antiochus IV

QUESTION 15
   C. Jesus enters Jerusalem a week before His resurrection

QUESTION 16: True

QUESTION 17
   B. The great tribulation

QUESTION 18: False

QUESTION 19: False

QUESTION 20
   A. God's judgment

QUESTION 21: True

QUESTION 22
   D. Tyre

QUESTION 23: False

QUESTION 24
   C. Commemorative

QUESTION 25: True

Unit 4: Post-Exilic Books

Unit Introduction

The Three Returns from Exile

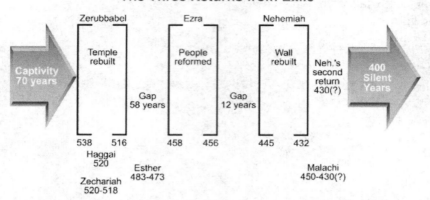

Much of this unit centers on events of the restoration that revolved around the three separate returns to the land from Babylon.

The first return, under Zerubbabel (538 BC), involved about 50,000 Jews who came back to the land to rebuild the temple as a result of Cyrus's decree (see Ezra 1–6). They quickly rebuilt the altar and re-instituted sacrifices, and then began rebuilding the temple (536 BC). However, opposition from Tattenai and others halted the work for sixteen years. It resumed in 520 BC and was finally finished in 516 BC. The prophets Zechariah and Haggai ministered at this time. Their exhortations to rebuild the temple contributed significantly to its reconstruction.

The second return, under Ezra (458 BC), brought back about five thousand Jews during the reign of Artaxerxes (Ezra 7–8). Ezra restored the people by leading them to obey the Law, which required undoing their practice of intermarriage with foreign women (Ezra 9–10). He taught and preached the Law of Moses, which led to a national revival.

The third return, under Nehemiah to rebuild the walls of Jerusalem (444 BC), mainly revolved around Nehemiah himself, as the number of Jews with him is never mentioned. His return under Artaxerxes rallied the people to work together, despite opposition from Sanballat, Tobias, and Gershem the Arab, so that the entire wall of Jerusalem was rebuilt in a mere fifty-two days. Nehemiah then organized the defense of the city, led a recommitment to observing the Sabbath, and enacted a process by which Jerusalem would be repopulated to defend it and the temple from attack. He, too, had to deal with the problem of intermarriage that Ezra had addressed less than two decades earlier (Neh 13).

The book of Malachi also records the deplorable state of the temple at this time. Sacrificial ritual had replaced genuine heart commitment to Yahweh. So Nehemiah's selfless example was a rebuke to the people for exacting interest from their fellow Israelites in violation of the Law.

Unit Outline

Lesson 10: Ezra 1–6, Haggai, and Zechariah

Lesson 11: Esther and Ezra 7–10

Lesson 12: Nehemiah and Malachi

Unit Objectives

By the end of this unit you will be able to do the following:

- Discuss the key word for each book in this unit and tell how it relates to the kingdom theme.

- Review the historical background, timeline and characteristics of the books in this unit.

- Explore how God's program and promises are advanced even through a disobedient people and external opposition.

- Discuss how the books purpose to encourage the Jewish people that God remembers His covenant with them.

- Examine the return of the faithful exiles to rebuild Jerusalem and the temple.

Returns from Exile

RETURN	FIRST	SECOND	THIRD
Reference	Ezra 1–6	Ezra 7–10	Nehemiah 1–13
Date	538 BC	458 BC	444 BC
Leaders	Sheshbazzar Zerubbabel Jeshua	Ezra	Nehemiah
Persian King	Cyrus	Artaxerxes	Artaxerxes
Elements of the Decree	As many as wished to could return. Temple could be rebuilt, partially financed by royal treasury. Vessels returned.	As many as wished to could return. Finances provided by royal treasury. Allowed to have own civil magistrates.	Allowed to rebuild the wall
Number Returning	42,360 7,337 (servants) 49,697	1,500 men 38 Levites 220 helpers 1,758+women+children =5,000?	Unknown
Events, Accomplishments, and Problems	Temple begun; sacrifices made and Feast of Tabernacles celebrated. Samaritans made trouble, and work ceased until 520. Temple completed in 516.	Problems with inter-marriage	Wall rebuilt in 52 days, despite opposition from Sanballat, Tobiah, and Geshem. Walls dedicated and Law read.

Lesson 10: Ezra 1–6, Haggai, and Zechariah

Lesson Introduction

After Judah's divinely ordained seventy-year exile in Babylon, God brought the people back to their land. The post-exilic books of Ezra and Nehemiah reveal that this return occurred in three waves with three distinct purposes. The first return under Zerubbabel had the rebuilding of the temple as its chief aim and is recorded in Ezra 1–6, Haggai and Zechariah. This lesson addresses these writings, which exhort the new community to proper priorities in light of their future reign. Since the returns described in Ezra 7–10 and Nehemiah occurred later, we will study these in subsequent lessons.

Lesson Outline

Topic 1: Introduction to Ezra

Topic 2: Return and Rebuilding

Topic 3: Introduction to Haggai

Topic 4: Drought Because of the Neglected Temple

Topic 5: Introduction to Zechariah

Topic 6: Visions of the Covenant

Topic 7: Visions of the Future

Topic 8: Knowing, Being, Doing

Lesson Objectives

By the end of this lesson you will be able to do the following:

- Evaluate the distinctions and timelines of Ezra, Haggai and Zechariah.

- Discuss how the books encourage the exiles to return to Jerusalem and to rebuild the temple.

- Explain the meanings of the messages and visions in Haggai and Zechariah.

- Discuss how God's program and promises are advanced even through a disobedient people and external opposition.

- Discuss God's predictions of political victory, cleansing, and rule through the future Messiah.

Topic 1: Introduction to Ezra

Ezra			
Restoring the Temple and People			
Temple		People	
Zerubbabel		Ezra	
1-6		7-10	
50,000 Return		5,000 Return	
Survival		Revival	
Working		Worshipping	
538-516 BC (22 years)		458-457 BC (1 year)	
External Opposition: Samaritans		Internal Opposition: Intermarriage	
Return 1-2	Rebuilding 3-6	Return 7-8	Restoration 9-10

(Book of Esther (58 year gap) spans the center of the chart)

Decree 1	Returnees 2	Begins 3	Opposed 4:1-6:12	Ends 6:13-22	Qualifications & Provisions 7	Returnees & Protection 8	Inter-marriage & Lament 9	Divorces carried out 10

Ezra continues the account of the Jewish history recorded in 2 Chronicles. The Chronicles record how God was faithful in fulfilling His promise of *judgment* for Judah's sin; Ezra records how God was faithful to His promise of *restoration* after seventy years as prophesied by Jeremiah (Jer 25:11-12; 29:10). Ezra's account of this restoration served to exhort the returnees to follow the Lord wholeheartedly—especially in true temple worship and covenant obedience. This emphasis was much needed, as the book of Malachi sadly reports deplorable conditions at this same time (e.g., intermarriage, ritualism, etc.).

- **Key Word:** Temple
- **Key Verse:** "But now briefly we have received mercy from the Lord our God, in that he has left us a remnant and has given us a secure position in his holy place. Thus our God has enlightened our eyes and has given us a little relief in our time of servitude" (Ezr 9:8).
- **Summary Statement:** The restorations of the temple and people to the land under Zerubbabel and Ezra show God's faithfulness and mercy in fulfilling His promise of restoration, to encourage the remnant in true temple worship and covenant obedience.
- **Application:** Restoration to God for the repentant believer requires action. What are some good examples of actions you can take to restore yourself to God?

Assignment

- Please read Ezra 1–3.
- Please read "Introduction to Ezra."

Introduction to Ezra

Title

Ezra and Nehemiah originally comprised a single book, according to the Jewish historian Josephus (*Against Apion* 1.8), Jerome, an early Christian priest and apologist (AD 347-420), and the Talmud (*Baba Bathra* 15a). The Hebrew Bible also has the two books together, under the title "Ezra Nehemiah." However, the repetition of Ezra 2 in Nehemiah 7 may indicate that the two were originally separate works. Ezra means "help, succor, assistance," and Nehemiah means "Yahweh comforts." Once again, the names are significant: Ezra's ministry enabled the Jews to return to the land and re-consecrate themselves, while Nehemiah functioned as God's comfort by building Jerusalem's protective wall.

Authorship

External Evidence: The Jewish Talmudic tradition has long held that Ezra authored this book that bears his name.

Internal Evidence: In Ezra 7:27–9:15, the author refers to himself in the first person. What makes this significant is the fact that, in all likelihood, Ezra was not even born when the events of chapters 1–6 took place (538-516 BC) and he is first introduced in 7:1 (458 BC). Like Chronicles, the book has a strong priestly emphasis, and Ezra was a direct descendant of Aaron through Eleazer, Phineas, and Zadok (Ezra 7:1-5). It is possible that Ezra had access to a library of documents gathered by Nehemiah, which then furnished him with the material to write Ezra 1–6 as well as the book of Chronicles (*Talk Thru The Bible*, 117). However, Nehemiah lived in Babylon until his arrival in Jerusalem in 444 BC, so if Ezra used Nehemiah's documents, it would have been after that date.

Circumstances

Date: The events of Ezra 7–10, in which Ezra participated, occurred in 458-457 BC. Ezra was a contemporary of Nehemiah (Neh 8:1-9; 12:36), who arrived in Jerusalem in 444 BC, which would place a likely date of composition between these dates, at approximately 450 BC (Walvoord, 1:651).

However, the book of Ezra itself covers two distinct time periods, separated by 58 years. Ezra 1–6 relates the story of Zerubbabel (538-516 BC) while Ezra 7–10 is mostly an autobiographical account of Ezra, beginning six decades later (458-457 BC). During the period covered by the book of Ezra, three other prominent non-biblical leaders lived: Gautama Buddha in India (ca. 560-480 BC), Confucius in China (551-479 BC), and Socrates in Greece (470-399 BC) (Wilkinson, 117).

Recipients: Ezra's first readers were Jews who had recently returned to Israel from Persia, as well as the grandchildren and great-grandchildren of those who had returned from Babylon a century earlier.

Characteristics

Ezra records the first events following the Babylonian exile in a selective sense; a 58-year gap separates chapters 1–6 and 7–10. (The events of the book of Esther occurred during this gap.) Ezra is one of only two books of Scripture that were originally written in two languages (the book of Daniel is the other). Almost one quarter (67 of 280 verses) is written in Aramaic, and the remaining three quarters is in Hebrew. The Aramaic material (Ezra 4:8–6:18; 7:12-26) mainly comprises official correspondence, for which Aramaic was the standard language of the day (Walvoord, 1:652).

Relationship to the Abrahamic Covenant: The restoration of Israel under Ezra and Nehemiah relates directly to God's purposes for Israel as stated in the promise to Abraham (Gen 12:1-3). The restoration era is important in that, without a return to the land, the Abrahamic Covenant could never be fulfilled.

   a) God promised Abraham that his descendants would **occupy the land** from the River of Egypt to the Euphrates (Gen 15:18), yet Israel was living in Babylon, outside of these specified boundaries. The nation needed to return to the land in order for the land promises to be fulfilled. Jeremiah 25:11-12 also promised a restoration to the land.

b) The **Messiah** had already been prophesied to be born in Bethlehem (Mic 5:2). In God's own prophetic timetable, as seen in Daniel 9:25-26, the nation needed to return to the land in order for this "seed" aspect of the Abrahamic Covenant to be fulfilled at the prophesied time of Christ's birth. Also, Jesus offered the kingdom to Israel during His earthly ministry, which would not have been possible apart from the nation's return to the Promised Land.

c) The books of Ezra and Nehemiah also relate the problem of intermarriage. It was vital to put away this sin so that Israel might keep the **purity of the Davidic line** to fulfill the seed promises originally given to Abraham. Had Ezra and Nehemiah not taken such drastic measures to stop intermarriage, it would have been difficult to ensure that the Messianic king was from the lineage of David (see Mt 1; Lk 3).

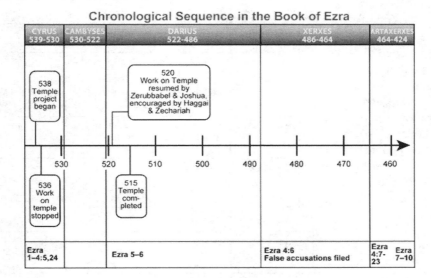

Chronological Sequence in the Book of Ezra

QUESTION 1

The key word for Ezra is _____.

QUESTION 2

Which of the following are true of the book of Ezra? *(Select all that apply.)*

    A. Its author was probably not even born when the events of Ezra 1–6 took place.

    B. In contrast to Chronicles, Ezra emphasizes judgment.

    C. It has a strong priestly emphasis.

    D. It was originally written in two languages.

QUESTION 3

Please briefly explain how the events of the restoration of Israel under Ezra and Nehemiah related directly to God's purposes for Israel as stated in the promise to Abraham (Gen 12:1-3).

Topic 1 Key Points

- The key word for Ezra is "temple"; he writes about the restorations of the temple and of the people to the land, to encourage the remnant in true temple worship and covenant obedience.

- Characteristics of Ezra include emphases on (1) restoration over judgment, and (2) the priesthood. The book was originally written in two languages.

- The events in the restoration of Israel to the land are directly related to God's purposes for Israel that were promised to Abraham (Gen 12:1-3).

Topic 2: Return and Rebuilding (Ezra 1–6)

The book of Ezra evidences a keen interest in the temple as it continues the account where the end of 2 Chronicles left off. Unfortunately, the remnant who returned did not exhibit as strong a commitment to the covenant and temple as one might expect. Therefore, Ezra records the restoration of the temple under Zerubbabel (Ezra 1–6), and the restoration of the people to their covenant obligations under his own leadership (Ezra 7–10), to encourage the remnant in true temple worship and covenant obedience.

Assignment

- Please read Ezra 4–6.
- Please read "Return and Rebuilding."

Temples in Scripture

	SOLOMON	ZERUBBABEL/HEROD	TRIBULATION	MILLENNIAL
Temple Period	First	Second	Third	Fourth
Description	1 Kings 6–7	Ezra 3–6	Dan 9:27	Ezk 40–43
Haggai Texts	Hag 2:3, 9	Hag 1:4, 8-9; 2:3	—	Hag 2:7, 9
Construction	966-959 BC	536-516 BC	Materials being gathered now	Still future
Desecrated by	Israelites and pagan kings	Antiochus, money changers, Pompey, Titus	Antichrist	No one (Zech 14:20-21)
Destruction	586 BC	AD 70	End of Great Tribulation?	Before new heavens and new earth (Rev 21:22)
Longevity	380 years	606 years	Under 7 years?	1000 years
Sacrifices	Before Christ	Before (approved) and after Christ (unapproved)	After Christ (unapproved)	After Christ (approved)
God's Glory	Filled it (1 Kings 8:10-11)	Didn't fill it	Won't fill it	Will fill it (Ezk 43:1-5)
Sanctuary	27.43m x 9.14m= 250.84 sq. m	?	?	26.67m x 53.3m = 1422.53 sq. m
Inner Court	45.7m x 121.9m= 5574.18 sq. m	?	?	53.3m x 130.3m = 6950.31 sq. m
Outer Court	?	?	?	266.7 x 266.7 = 71128.89 sq. m

Return and Rebuilding

Summary Statement for the Book

The restorations of the temple and people to the land under Zerubbabel and Ezra show God's faithfulness and mercy in fulfilling His promise of restoration, to encourage the remnant in true temple worship and covenant obedience.

The rebuilding of the temple, in the first return under Zerubbabel with 50,000 Jews, encourages the remnant to worship only at the temple because of God's faithfulness in fulfilling His promise of restoration (538 BC, Ezra 1–6).

The first return under Zerubbabel shows God's faithfulness to fulfill His promise of restoration (Ezra 1–2; Isa 45:1-6). In accordance with God's predictive decree, Cyrus of Persia proclaims that all Jews in Babylon may return to Jerusalem to rebuild the temple. He also provides financially for the returnees, just as Egypt provided for Israel during the exodus (Ezra 1). Exodus 12:36 says, "The Lord gave the people favor in the sight of the Egyptians, and they gave them whatever they wanted, and so they plundered Egypt." This verifies God's ability to fulfill His promise of restoration—even through a pagan king! As further verification, the list of returning exiles reveals that 50,000 Jews returned and gave freewill offerings to reconstruct the temple (Ezra 2).

Opposition to temple rebuilding (around 536 BC during the reign of Cyrus) interrupted the work for sixteen years (536-520 BC) (Ezra 4:1-5). A parenthetical summary of later opposition to rebuilding the walls (around 484 under Xerxes and 444 BC under Artaxerxes) shows the remnant that while their enemies continually opposed them, God did eventually give them success (Ezra 4:6-23). The sixteen-year interruption (536-520 BC) is due to the opposition of Jews who intermarried with pagans and are worshipping other gods (Ezra 4:24). Zechariah and Haggai successfully encourage the people to continue rebuilding the temple despite opposition (520 BC; Ezra 5:1-2). The opposition of Tattenai toward the temple rebuilding backfires, as Darius appoints him to make sure the work is funded and completed (Ezra 5:3–6:12).

In all of this, God's workings to provide a house in which He is to be properly worshiped are displayed (Ezra 5:3–6:12).

The completion of the temple rebuilding in 516 BC (twenty years after its beginning) is commemorated with a special dedication and Passover observance (Ezra 6:13-22).

QUESTION 4

In fulfillment of God's decree in Isaiah 45:1-6, the Gentile leader who proclaimed that all Jews in Babylon could return to Jerusalem to rebuild the temple was named _____.

QUESTION 5

What does the exodus from Egypt in Exodus 12 have in common with the Jews' return from Babylon to Jerusalem in Ezra 1?

    A. They carried supplies with them from their former captives.

    B. The leaders of the countries that held them captive gave them a written release.

    C. Both left in haste.

    D. Both times they returned from the east.

QUESTION 6

Please match the reference with the corresponding teaching.

Reference	Teaching
Ezra 4:1-5	A parenthetical summary of later opposition to rebuilding the walls shows the remnant that while their enemies continually opposed them, God did eventually give them success.
Ezra 4:6-23	The sixteen-year interruption was due to the opposition of Jews who intermarried with pagans and were worshipping other gods.
Ezra 4:24	The opposition of Tattenai towards the temple rebuilding backfired as Darius appointed him to make sure the work was funded and completed.
Ezra 5:1-2	Zechariah and Haggai successfully encouraged the people to continue rebuilding the temple despite opposition.
Ezra 5:3-6:12	Opposition to temple rebuilding interrupted the work for sixteen years.

Topic 2 Key Points

- Fulfilling God's decree in Isaiah 45:1-6, the Gentile leader who proclaimed that all Jews in Babylon could return to Jerusalem to rebuild the temple was named Cyrus.

- Cyrus provided financially for the returnees, just as Egypt provided for Israel during the exodus (Ezra 1; Exo 12:36).

- Though opposition to rebuilding the temple interrupted the work for sixteen years, God, through Zechariah and Haggai, successfully encouraged the people to continue rebuilding the temple.

Topic 3: Introduction to Haggai

In 538 BC, near the end of the seventy-year captivity, Cyrus of Persia decreed that the Jews living in Babylon could return to their homeland (Ezra 1:1-4). However, after living away from Jerusalem for nearly fifty years or even longer (since 605, 597, or 586 BC), most considered *Babylon* their home and were not thrilled about returning to the "homeland" they had never even visited. Following Jeremiah's advice, the exiles had built houses, planted gardens, married, and raised families (see Jer 29:4-7). Some had done well in business, and some, who had been born in exile fifty

Haggai — Drought for Neglected Temple Rebuilding			
Temple		**Blessings**	
Wrong Priorities	Greater Glory	Drought Judgment	Zerubbabel's Authority
1	2:1-9	2:10-19	2:20-23
Rebuke #1	Promise #1	Rebuke #2	Promise #2
"Is it a time for you yourselves to be living in your paneled houses, while this house remains in ruins?...Go...and build the house" (1:4, 8a)	"I will fill this house with glory...The glory of this present house will be greater than the glory of the former house" (2:7b, 9a)	"Whatever [my people] do and whatever they offer is defiled... [yet] from this day on I will bless you" (2:14b, 19b)	"I will shake the heavens and the earth. I will overturn royal thrones and shatter the power of the foreign kingdoms" (2:21-22)
Present	Kingdom	Present	Kingdom
Drought	Sadness	Food Shortage	Leadership
August 29, 520 BC	October 17, 520 BC	December 18, 520 BC	December 18, 520 BC
Jerusalem			

years earlier, undoubtedly had children and grandchildren of their own. Why move to a devastated "foreign" land that didn't even have a city wall?

As a result, the initial group that returned a few months later with Zerubbabel numbered only fifty thousand (September 538 BC; see Ezra 2:64-65). They quickly began work on the temple foundation, rebuilt the altar, and resumed the sacrifices (537 BC; see Ezra 3), but opposition by Samaritans caused the project to cease (536 BC; see Ezra 4).

The story picks up in the book of Haggai, which shows how the returnees adopted a lifestyle of comfort similar to that of their brethren who remained in Babylon. They lived in paneled houses—paneling is associated with royal buildings (1 Kgs 7:3) and the temple (Ezek 41:16)—while God's own house lay in ruins (1:4). Therefore, God raised up Haggai and Zechariah, and the temple work resumed on September 21, 520 at their encouragement (1:15). Not only did Haggai write to encourage the rebuilding of the temple, he also explained why the returnees experienced crop failure: the drought was sent by God to cause them to correct their priorities (1:11).

- **Key Word:** Priorities

- **Key Verse:** (God to Judah) "'You expected a large harvest, but instead there was little, and when you brought it home it disappeared right away. Why?' asks the Lord who rules over all. 'Because my temple remains in ruins, thanks to each of you favoring his own house!'" (Haggai 1:9).

- **Summary Statement:** Haggai rebukes the remnant to correct its wrong priorities. The returning Jews are judged with a drought to encourage them to rebuild the temple, so that God might bless the nation with crops and Zerubbabel with authority, foreshadowing Messiah's authority in the kingdom.

- **Application:** Don't pursue personal prosperity more than you pursue God's work. Ask yourself honestly: Which is more important to me—God or money?

Assignment

- Please read Haggai 1.
- Please read "Introduction to Haggai."

Introduction to Haggai

Title

The name Haggai (*haggay*) has uncertain origins but may be from *hag*, which means "festival-gathering, feast, pilgrim-feast." Thus, his name may mean "festal" or "feast," possibly because he was born on the day of a major feast, perhaps Tabernacles (LaSor, 482). Haggai's second message took place on that feast day (Hag 2:1; Wilkinson 283).

Authorship

External Evidence: Haggai is known only from this book and from two references to him by Ezra (Ezra 5:1; 6:14).

Internal Evidence: Some have supposed that the book was composed from several sources, especially since it is written in the third person. However, authors often used the third person in ancient writings (e.g., Moses, Jonah, etc.). Since Haggai's name appears nine times (Hag 1:1, 3, 12-13; 2:1, 10, 13-14, 20) few challenge his authorship of the book.

Circumstances

Date: Haggai is the most precisely dated book in the Bible, so it is virtually uncontested. The prophecy divides itself up into four sections, with three different dates ranging from

August 29, 520 BC to December 18 that same year. The reign of King Darius I Hystaspes establishes the basis for such an accurate accounting (Hag 1:1).

Recipients: The original readers of Haggai were the returning Jewish exiles who had begun to settle in Jerusalem.

Characteristics

As already noted, Haggai is the most precisely dated book in the Scripture, as well as the only scriptural writing organized by dates of prophetic revelations. Haggai is the first of the three post-exilic prophets (the others are Zechariah and Malachi).

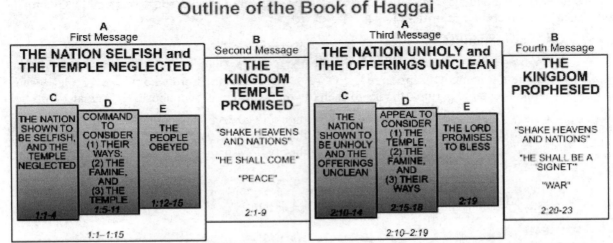

Outline of the Book of Haggai

LOCAL SETTING– At Jerusalem after the return from the exile. About four months during the second year of the reign of Darius.
SUBJECT (Dispensational)– The Temple and the Kingdom.
KEY THOUGHT– The Second Coming of the Lord "The desire of all nations shall come."
APPLICATION (Individual)– The Blessing of God is upon the obedient.
KEY VERSES– 1:1; 2:1; 2:10; 2:20. The dates of the four messages.

QUESTION 7

The key word for Haggai is _____.

QUESTION 8

Although God accuses the people of building paneled houses for themselves, paneled houses weren't considered anything special in the Old Testament. *True or False?*

Topic 3 Key Points

- Haggai rebuked the remnant to correct its wrong *priorities* and encouraged them to rebuild the temple so that God might bless the nation.

- God accused the people of building themselves houses fit for a king while ignoring the condition of His temple.

Topic 4: Drought Because of the Neglected Temple (Haggai 1–2)

Haggai's purpose in writing to the returned exiles was to explain that the drought they experienced was due to their neglect of the Lord's temple. His aim was to encourage them to resume the rebuilding of the temple so they could once again know God's blessing. He accomplished this by first rebuking them for having more concern for their own homes than for God's house (Ezra 1). Next, Haggai promised God's presence with glory even greater in the new temple than in Solomon's (Hag 2:1-9). Then he explained that neglect of the temple resulted in judgment by drought, but resuming the task would bring God's blessing in renewed crops (Hag 2:10-19). Finally Haggai promised Zerubbabel divinely bestowed authority, foreshadowing the authority of Messiah in the future messianic kingdom (Hag 2:20-23).

Temples in Scripture

	SOLOMON	ZERUBBABEL/ HEROD	TRIBULATION	MILLENNIAL
Temple Period	First	Second	Third	Fourth
Description	1 Kings 6–7	Ezra 3–6	Dan 9:27	Ezk 40–43
Haggai Texts	Hag 2:3, 9	Hag 1:4, 8-9; 2:3	—	Hag 2:7, 9
Construction	966-959 BC	536-516 BC	Materials being gathered now	Still future
Desecrated by	Israelites and pagan kings	Antiochus, money changers, Pompey, Titus	Antichrist	No one (Zech 14:20-21)
Destruction	586 BC	AD 70	End of Great Tribulation?	Before new heavens and new earth (Rev 21:22)
Longevity	380 years	606 years	Under 7 years?	1000 years
Sacrifices	Before Christ	Before (approved) and after Christ (unapproved)	After Christ (unapproved)	After Christ (approved)
God's Glory	Filled it (1 Kings 8:10-11)	Didn't fill it	Won't fill it	Will fill it (Ezk 43:1-5)
Sanctuary	27.43m x 9.14m= 250.84 sq. m	?	?	26.67m x 53.3m = 1422.53 sq. m
Inner Court	45.7m x 121.9m= 5574.18 sq. m	?	?	53.3m x 130.3m 6950.31 sq. m
Outer Court	?	?	?	266.7 x 266.7 = 71128.89 sq. m

Assignment

- Please read Haggai 2.
- Please read "Drought Because of the Neglected Temple."

Drought Because of the Neglected Temple

Summary Statement for the Book

Haggai rebukes the remnant to correct its wrong priorities. The returning Jews are judged with a drought, to encourage them to rebuild the temple so that God might bless the nation with crops and Zerubbabel with authority, foreshadowing Messiah's authority in the kingdom.

Haggai's first message (August 29, 520 BC) rebukes the people for their wrong priorities in order to convict them of the need to finish rebuilding the temple (Ezra 1).

On August 29, 520 BC, Haggai prophesied to Zerubbabel and Joshua, the high priest, his first message from the Lord (Hag 1:1). He rebuked the remnant for being more concerned for their own houses than for rebuilding the temple (Hag 1:2-6). He reminded the remnant that their economic poverty had resulted from postponing the temple rebuilding (Hag 1:7-11). They needed to know that resuming the task would please God and end the drought. Haggai recorded that the remnant responded by resuming the work on the temple, and he gave God's promise to be present for the remainder of the task (Hag 1:12-15).

The second message of Haggai (October 17, 520 BC) promises the remnant that God's presence and glory will be greater in the new temple than in Solomon's, to encourage them in the rebuilding (Hag 2:1-9).

On October 17, 520 BC, Haggai prophesied to Zerubbabel, Joshua, and the remnant his second message from the Lord, two months after the first (Hag 2:1-2). He promised that God would be present with the temple reconstruction, even though the new temple might appear inferior to Solomon's (Hag 2:3-5). God promised that a glory greater than that of Solomon's temple will rest in the Millennial temple; it will include the wealth of the nations and bring His peace (Hag 2:6-9).

Note: Some understand the glory in Haggai 2:7, 9 to be Christ's presence in Zerubbabel's temple during His first advent (see Mt 12:6; Lk 2:32; Jn 2:13-22). However, verse 6 seems to indicate that Christ's second advent, followed by treasures in the Millennial temple, is in view (see vv. 21-22; Isa 2:12-21; 13:13; Ezk 38:20; Amos 8:8; Joel 3:16; Mt 24:29-30).

The third message of Haggai (December 18, 520 BC) reveals that neglecting the temple has resulted in drought, but resuming the task will bring renewed crops; this encourages the remnant that their efforts will be rewarded (Hag 2:10-19).

Two months after the second message, on December 18, 520 BC, Haggai prophesied to the priests his third message from the Lord (Hag 2:10-11). The priests admitted that consecration could not be transferred, but defilement could. The nation's service and worship were defiled due to sin (Hag 2:12-14). Haggai revealed that the drought had resulted from the nation's neglect in rebuilding the temple (Hag 2:15-19). But with the return to the task, God's blessing would follow with renewed crops. If the people obeyed, their efforts would be rewarded.

The fourth message of Haggai, later that day (December 18, 520 BC), promises Zerubbabel divinely bestowed authority, foreshadowing the authority of Messiah in the future messianic kingdom (Hag 2:20-23).

Later on the same day, on December 18, 520 BC, Haggai prophesied to Zerubbabel alone his fourth message from the Lord (Hag 2:20-21). God promised to demonstrate His power by overthrowing the nations at the coming of the Millennial kingdom (Hag 2:21-22). God promised Zerubbabel divinely given authority, foreshadowing the authority of the Messiah in the future messianic kingdom (Hag 2:23).

Haggai and Zechariah Contrasted	
Haggai	Zechariah
Rebuke	Encouragement
Priorities	Messiah
More concrete	More abstract
Concise (2 chapters)	Expanded (14 chapters)
Present concern	Future concern
Four visions	Many visions
Take part	Take heart
Older Activist	Younger visionary
(adapted from Wilkinson, 291)	

From Wilkinson, 291, adapted

QUESTION 9

What does God send as judgment on the Jews in Haggai's time?

    A. Defeat by their enemies

    B. Drought

    C. Locusts

    D. Plague

QUESTION 10

Please summarize the teaching on the transfer of cleanliness in Haggai 2:10-14.

QUESTION 11

Please open your Life Notebook and record your thoughts on the following: The Old Testament priesthood was unable to transfer holiness but could transfer defilement (see previous question). Since this is true, how was Jesus able to touch a leper and heal him?

QUESTION 12

Please match the reference with the corresponding message.

Reference	*Message*
Haggai 1:2-6	Rebuke for being more concerned with their houses than with the temple.
Haggai 2:3-5	God promises to overthrow the nations and gives authority to Zerubbabel.
Haggai 2:10-19	Return to task and you will be blessed instead of cursed.
Haggai 2:20-23	God promises His presence while the people are rebuilding the temple.

Topic 4 Key Points

- Haggai wrote to the returned exiles to explain that the drought they were experiencing was due to their neglect of the Lord's temple, and that they could return to a state of blessing.

- Because God considered the people unclean, all of their offerings were also unclean Hosea 2:10-14.

- Though the above point was true for the Old Testament priesthood, Jesus did not become unclean by contact with defilement; rather, He transferred cleanliness to the defiled.

- God's promises to Zerubbabel are the eventual overthrow of the nations and the gift of divine authority, as a type of the future Messiah.

Topic 5: Introduction to Zechariah

Zechariah					
Rebuild the Temple for the Messiah					
God's Covenant Faithfulness			Future Messianic Rule		
1-6			7-14		
"The word of the LORD came to Zechariah..." (1:1)			"The word of the LORD came to Zechariah..." (7:1)		
Visions of the Covenant			Visions of the Messiah		
Command to Repent 1:1-6	Eight Covenantal Visions 1:7-6:8	Joshua's Symbolic Coronation 6:9-15	Four Restoration Messages 7-8	Two Burdens	
				Rejected at His First Advent 9-11	Received at His Second Advent 12-14
"The word of the Lord came to Zechariah"	"Then I looked up— and there before me"	"The word of the LORD came to me"	"The word of the LORD came to me"	"The burden of the word of the LORD"	"The burden of the word of the LORD"
Pictures			Problems	Predictions	
Israel's Fortune			Israel's Fasting	Israel's Future	
While building the temple 520-518 BC (1:1; 7:1)			After building the temple 480-470 BC (9:13)		
Jerusalem					

Zechariah can be divided into two halves. "Visions of the Covenant" are given in the first six chapters (Zech 1-6). Here Zechariah expands on the Abrahamic covenant (Gen 12:1-3).

"Visions of the Future" are given in the last eight chapters (Zech 7–14). In Zechariah 9–14, Zechariah's prophecies give two different pictures of the future Messiah. One picture is of a rejected Messiah, whose rejection will in turn lead to another scattering of Israel (Zech 9–11). In fact, Israel faces a future danger of following a false messiah, the Antichrist, who will lead them to destruction (Zech 11:4-17). Though it wasn't obvious or revealed at the time the prophecy was written, this vision of the Messiah's rejection would happen during the time of His First Advent.

The vision given in Zechariah 12–14 deals with Israel accepting a delivering Messiah (Zech 12:10–13:9). Just when their situation looks the bleakest, when they are besieged on all sides by the nations around them, their Deliverer appears for temporal deliverance (Zech 12:1-9). This temporal deliverance results in their spiritual salvation (Zech 12:10–13:9). This in turn leads to Israel enjoying a holy environment in their long-awaited millennial kingdom (Zech 14). This kingdom is the fulfillment of the promises given to Abraham in Genesis 12:1-3.

- **Key Word:** Messiah
- **Key Verse:** I have returned to Zion and will live within Jerusalem. Now Jerusalem will be called "truthful city," "mountain of the Lord who rules over all," "holy mountain" (Zech 8:3).
- **Summary Statement:** Zechariah prepares Judah for the Messiah by encouraging the nation to respond to its privileged covenantal position among the nations. The people should rebuild the temple in light of future blessings that will come when the Messiah rules in the kingdom.
- **Application:** Does the knowledge of your future reign with Christ affect how you make decisions today?

Assignment

- Please read Zechariah 1–2.
- Please read "Introduction to Zechariah."

Introduction to Zechariah

Title

The name Zechariah (*zekaryahu*) in Hebrew means "Yahweh remembers" (BDB 272b 1f). The title is fitting, as this book records how God remembers the covenant He made with the people of Israel, and will complete it through the Messiah's rule.

Authorship

External Evidence: The universal testimony of Jewish and Christian tradition affirms Zechariah as the author of the entire book (Wilkinson, 289). For exceptions, see "Date" below.

Internal Evidence: The name Zechariah is shared by about thirty men in the Old Testament, but this book specifically designates Zechariah, son of Berekiah, the son of Iddo as author (1:1). The same verse calls him a prophet, and his grandfather served as head of the priestly families that returned from the exile (Neh 12:4, 16). This makes Zechariah both prophet and priest, which accounts for his emphasis on the temple. Zechariah was born in Babylon and called to prophesy at a young age (2:4). He died at the hands of a murderer "between the temple and the altar" (Mt 23:35), in the same way that another Zechariah was murdered years earlier (see 2 Chron 24:20-21).

Circumstances

Date: The date of his writing is pinpointed to October-November 520 BC, during the reign of Darius I Hystaspes, King of Persia (1:1). The beginning of Zechariah's ministry occurred just two months after Haggai began his ministry. Chapters 1–8 include dated prophecies (1:7; 7:1) which occur over a two years period, while the remainder of the book is undated. The reference to Greek influence (9:13; around 490-470 BC) may indicate that Zechariah prophesied the latter chapters (Ezra 9–14) about forty years later, which would explain some of the differences in style, content, and vocabulary.

The dates in Zechariah and Haggai can be summarized as follows (*NIV Study Bible*, 1405, adapted):

Dates (BC) in Zachariah and Haggai	
1. Haggai's first message (Hag 1:1-11; Ezra 5:1)	Aug 29, 520
2. Rebuilding of the temple resumes (Hag 1:12-15; Ezra 5:2)	Sept 21, 520
3. Haggai's second message (Hag 2:1-9)	Oct 17, 520
4. Beginning of Zechariah's preaching (Zech 1:1-6)	Oct/Nov 520
5. Haggai's third message (Hag 2:10-19)	Dec 18, 520
6. Haggai's fourth message (Hag 2:20-23)	Dec 18, 520
7. Tattenai's letter to King Darius seeking to stop the temple building (Ezra 5:3-6:14)	519-518
8. Zechariah's eight night visions (Zech 1:7-6:8)	Feb 15, 519
9. Joshua crowned as high priest (Ezra 6:9-15)	Feb 15(?), 519
10. Repentance urged, blessings promised (Ezra 7-8)	Dec 7, 518
11. Dedication of the temple (Ezra 6:15-18)	March 12, 516
12. Zechariah's final prophecy (Ezra 9-14)	After 480 (?)

However, recent attacks from critical scholars advocate that chapters 9–14 come from either pre-exilic (before 586 BC) or late Maccabean (about 100 BC) authorship. But these arguments assume that predictive prophecy cannot occur, overemphasize differences in the two sections, and neglect to attribute differences in style and purpose to a change in topic or time. There is no reason to believe that the book of Zechariah was not actually recorded while the prophet himself preached.

Recipients: The post-exilic Jews who had returned to their homeland 18 years previously were the original recipients of this prophecy.

Characteristics

Zechariah is the "major Minor Prophet"—the longest of the Minor Prophets (Wilkinson, 290). This book is nine chapters longer than Lamentations, which is one of the Major Prophets. Zechariah is second only to Isaiah in number of messianic passages it contains.

There is considerable variety in style in the book's visions, messages, and apocalyptic oracles. While Zechariah and Daniel both tell about the age of Gentile domination, Daniel emphasizes the role of Gentiles, whereas Zechariah provides greater insight into Israel during this period. Zechariah is the most positive OT prophetic book, with little about judgment and much about blessings.

QUESTION 13

The key word for Zechariah is _____.

QUESTION 14

Which of the following is true of Zechariah?

    A. His ministry overlapped that of Nehemiah

    B. His book has more messianic passages than any other Old Testament book

    C. He emphasized Israel more than the Gentiles

    D. He emphasized judgment over blessing

Topic 5 Key Points

- Zechariah prepared Judah for the Messiah by encouraging them to rebuild the temple in light of future blessings that will come when the Messiah rules in the kingdom.

- Zechariah, like Daniel, told about Gentile domination, but Zechariah gave more insight into Israel, while Daniel emphasized the Gentiles.

Topic 6: Visions of the Covenant (Zech 1–6)

Zechariah's Eight Night Visions	
Vision	**Meaning**
The red-horse rider among the myrtles (Zech 1:7-17)	God's anger against the nations and blessing on restored Israel
The four horns and the four craftsmen (Zech 1:18-21)	God's judgment on the nations that afflict Israel
The surveyor with a measuring line (Zech 2)	God's future blessing on restored Israel
The cleansing and crowning of Joshua the high priest (Zech 3)	Israel's future cleansing from sin and reinstatement as a priestly nation
The golden lampstand and the two olive trees (Zech 4)	Israel as the light to the nations under the Messiah, the King-Priest
The flying scroll (Zech 5:1-4)	The severity and totality of divine judgment on the individual Israelites
The woman in the basket (Zech 5:5-11)	The removal of Israel's national sin of rebellion against God
The four chariots (Zech 6)	Divine judgment on Gentile nations

(From Bible Knowledge Commentary *p 1549)*

Zechariah's prophecy aimed to prepare the people of God for the coming Messiah. The first half (Zech 1–6) reminded Judah of God's faithfulness to His covenant, both in the past and in the present, to motivate the people to complete the temple construction because of their unique position before God. The second half (Zech 7–14) looked to the future messianic rule. Chapters 7–8 reminded the people that while God punished sin through the exile, restoration will come after the nation's obedience. Finally, chapters 9–14 encouraged obedience because, although the Messiah would be rejected at His first advent (Zech 9–11), redemption of the nation will result at His second advent (Zech 12–14). Therefore, since the Messiah is indeed coming, the nation should obey now, especially by rebuilding the temple, since the Messiah's glory will inhabit it.

Assignment

- Please read Zechariah 3–6.
- Please read "Visions of the Covenant."

Visions of the Covenant

Summary Statement for the Book

Zechariah prepares Judah for the Messiah by encouraging the nation to respond to its privileged covenantal position among the nations. The people should rebuild the temple in light of future blessings that will come when the Messiah rules in the kingdom.

The introductory oracle, eight visions, and symbolic coronation of Joshua show God's commitment to the Abrahamic covenant and encourage the remnant to see its privileged position as a motivation to complete the temple (Zech 1–6).

The introductory oracle commanded the remnant to repent *before* judgment—so that God could bless the people—rather than repenting *after* judgment as their forefathers had done (Zech 1:1-6).

The eight visions preached by Zechariah demonstrated God's commitment to the Abrahamic covenant (Zech 1:7–6:8). These visions were meant to stir Israel to see its privileged position among the nations as a motivation to complete the temple.

1. The vision of the man among the myrtle trees demonstrated God's anger toward the nations but favor toward Israel (Zech 1:7-17).

2. The vision of the four horns and four craftsmen demonstrated God's jealous care for Israel, as seen in His judgment upon nations that afflicted Israel from the four corners of the earth (Zech 1:18-21).

3. The vision of the man with the measuring line demonstrated God's protection of Israel through the rebuilding and re-inhabiting of Jerusalem (Zech 2). Meanwhile, the nations that destroyed Israel would fall for afflicting His special people.

4. The vision of the new garments for Joshua the high priest demonstrated God's gracious cleansing of Israel's sin through the future Messiah, who will restore Israel as a priestly nation (Zech 3).

5. The vision of the golden lampstand and two olive trees demonstrated that only through God's empowerment could Israel, Joshua, and Zerubbabel be a light to the nations (Zech 4).

6. The vision of the flying scroll demonstrated God's warning that the sins of individual Israelites would not go unpunished (Zech 5:1-4).

7. The vision of the woman in a basket demonstrated God's removing the nation's sins of wickedness and idolatry and sending them to Babylon (Zech 5:5-11).

8. The vision of the four chariots demonstrated God's judgment upon Gentile nations opposing Him and His people (Zech 6:1-8).

Joshua's symbolic coronation represented the coming Messiah, who will rebuild the future temple and serve as both Priest and King (Zech 6:9-15).

QUESTION 15

Please match the vision with the corresponding message it conveyed.

Vision	Message
The man among the myrtle trees	God's anger toward the nations but favor toward Israel
The four horns and four craftsmen	God's jealous care for Israel, as seen in His judgment upon nations
The man with the measuring line	God's gracious cleansing of Israel's sin through the future Messiah
The new garments for Joshua the high priest	God's protection of Israel through the rebuilding and re-inhabiting of Jerusalem

QUESTION 16

Please match the vision with the corresponding message it conveyed.

Vision	Message
The golden lampstand and two olive trees	God was removing the nation's sins of wickedness and idolatry and sending the people to Babylon
The flying scroll	The sins of individual Israelites would not go unpunished
The woman in a basket	Only through God's empowerment could Israel, Joshua, and Zerubbabel be a light to the nations
The four chariots	God would judge the Gentile nations opposing Him and His people

Topic 6 Key Points

- The first four visions, in Zechariah 1–3, emphasized God's favor and consequent protection and cleansing of Israel through the future Messiah.

- The next four visions, in Zechariah 4–6, emphasized Israel's responsibility for its sin as well as God's judgment and removal of that sin so that Israel could be a light to the nations.

Topic 7: Visions of the Future (Zech 7–14)

Zechariah was privileged here to get a preview, in vision form, of the Messiah's first and second advents. Looking at Zechariah's visions from our side of the Messiah's first advent is a big advantage. Even with Zechariah's visions, it had to be difficult for the Jews of that time to understand how their Messiah could be rejected—and betrayed for the price of a slave! Matthew records the fulfillment of Zechariah's prophecy, as this is the exact price Judas asked from the Jewish leaders to betray Christ into their hands (Zech 11:12-13; see also Mt 26:15; 27:3-5). Though warned ahead of time of this very mistake, Israel nationally rejected their true Shepherd and consequently followed the false one (Zech 11).

Assignment

- Please read Zechariah 7–14.
- Please read "Visions of the Future."

Visions of the Future

The two oracles about the first and second advents of the Messiah promise His rejection and Israel's judgment, but these are followed by salvation for Israel in the messianic kingdom, when the nation repents at the Second Advent (Zech 7–14).

Four messages of rebuke for sin and restoration for obedience remind Israel that the reason for the exile was national sin (Zech 7–8). These visions should encourage them to obey in light of future blessings.

A delegation from Bethel asked whether to stop their self-imposed religious fast commemorating Jerusalem's destruction (Zech 7:1-3). God responded with four messages that rebuked Israel's hypocritical fasting and disobedience (Zech 7:4–8:23). This disobedience would again result in exile, but restoration in Jerusalem was promised at the return of the Lord after the nation obeys.

1. The first message rebuked Israel's hypocritical fasting and feasting, revealing the nation's disobedience to the prophets (Zech 7:4-7).

2. The second message reminded the remnant that God requires justice and mercy (not fasting) because God's judgment in the exile resulted only from disobedience (Zech 7:8-14).

3. The third message promised restoration in response to the nation's faithfulness to God's commands (Zech 8:1-17).

4. The fourth message promised that the return of the Lord will be accompanied by joyful obedience rather than fasting (Zech 8:18-23). At that time Israel will be re-gathered in Jerusalem as a testimony to the Gentile nations.

The first oracle recorded how, despite God's judgments on the nations and the promise of a peaceful Messianic rule, the Messiah will be rejected at His first coming, resulting in the scattering of Israel (Zech 9-11). Before Israel experienced the blessings of the Messiah, Alexander the Great would be God's means of judgment on the nations surrounding Israel, but he won't destroy the temple (Zech 9:1-8).

- Israel could rejoice at the appearance of the Messiah as a peaceful deliverer (Zech 9:9-10). The Messiah's kingdom will bring deliverance for Israel (Zech 9:11-17), destruction of false shepherds (Zech 10:1-5), and the re-gathering of Israel (Zech 10:6-12).

The coming wrath after the Messiah's rejection will devastate the entire land of Palestine (fulfilled by the Roman generals Vespasian and Titus in AD 66-70; Zech 11:1-3).

Contrasts between the Messiah as the true Shepherd and the Antichrist as the false shepherd were given, to warn against following the wrong leader (Zech 11:4-17).

- Israel's true Shepherd would lead the nation, which was destined for slaughter by the Romans (Zech 11:4-14). But the nation will lose its favor and national unity in dispersion, due to the unbelief shown when they attached the price of a slave to the Messiah (Ex 21:32)

- Israel's false and wicked shepherd, the Antichrist, will be condemned for his selfish leading of the nation (Zech 11:15-17).

The second oracle declared that Jerusalem's redemption at the Second Advent will occur when the Messiah is worshipped and enthroned as King, following the destruction of Gentile oppressors (Zech 12–14; Mt 23:37-39). These events will allow holiness to characterize the age.

Israel will experience physical redemption from the Lord when other nations seek to lay siege to Jerusalem (Zech 12:1-9). The Jews will also experience spiritual redemption from the Lord when they realize they have been rejecting the Messiah and turn to Him for cleansing at the Second Advent (Zech 12:10–13:9).

- There will be an outpouring of the Holy Spirit after the Gentile nations are destroyed (Zech 12:10).

- The nation will mourn clan by clan over its murder of Jesus and rejection of Him as the Messiah (Zech 12:10-14).

- Israel will experience cleansing from sin (Zech 13:1-6).

- The nation's rejection of the Messiah as the true Shepherd at His first Advent, and the resulting judgment under the Romans, means that it will undergo the cleansing of God's discipline at the Messiah's Second Advent (Zech 13:7-9).

- After the destruction of Gentile oppressors, the Messiah will be worshipped and enthroned as King over the long-awaited messianic kingdom, so that holiness may characterize the age (Zech 14).

- Jerusalem will be delivered from Gentile oppressors by the Lord Himself at the Second Advent, when His coming will split the Mount of Olives (Zech 14:1-5).

- The Messiah's kingdom will be set up in Jerusalem in an amazing set of circumstances (Zech 14:6-11).

- Israel's enemies will be destroyed (Zech 14:12-15).

- The Messiah will be worshiped annually at the Feast of Tabernacles (Zech 14:16-19).

- Holiness will characterize Jerusalem and Judah during the messianic kingdom (Zech 14:20-21).

Fasts in Zechariah

ZECHARIAH	TIME	FAST COMMEMORATES	SCRIPTURE
8:19	10th Month 10th Day	Nebuchadnezzar Began Siege of Jerusalem (15 January 588)	Jer. 39:1; 52:4; 2 Kings 25:1
8:19	4th Month 9th Day	Jerusalem Destroyed (18 July 586)	Jer. 39:2; 52:6; 2 Kings 25:3
7:3, 5 8:19	5th Month 10th Day	Jerusalem & Temple Burned (15-18 August 586)	Jer. 52:12-13; 2 Kings 25:8
7:5 8:19	7th Month 3rd Day	Gedaliah Slain (9 October 586)	Jer. 41:1-3 2 Kings 25:25-26

QUESTION 17

Please match the reference with the corresponding message.

Reference	Message
Zechariah 7:4-7	A promise that the return of the Lord will be accompanied by joyful obedience rather than fasting
Zechariah 7:8-14	A rebuke for Israel's hypocritical fasting and feasting
Zechariah 8:1-17	A reminder to the remnant that God requires justice and mercy (not fasting)
Zechariah 8:18-23	A promise of restoration in response to the nation's faithfulness to God's commands

QUESTION 18

Please open your Life Notebook and record your thoughts on the following: Zechariah shows that God was not pleased with the fasting Israel observed over Jerusalem's destruction. What exactly about this fasting displeased Him? Is there anything in your life that reflects the same problem?

QUESTION 19

Zechariah's first oracle in Zechariah 9–11 predicted that the nation would attach the price of a slave to the Messiah. *True or False?*

QUESTION 20

According to Zechariah 14:16-19, during the Millennium the Messiah will be worshipped at which annual feast?

    A. Day of Atonement

    B. First Fruits

    C. Passover

    D. Tabernacles

Topic 7 Key Points

- The four messages in Zechariah 7 and 8 center on the question of Israel's self-imposed fasts that did not achieve the spiritual result of joyful obedience that God expected from the nation.

- Israel's true Shepherd would lead the nation, which was destined for slaughter by the Romans (Zech 11:4-14). But due to the unbelief shown when they attached the price of a slave to the Messiah, the nation would lose its favor and national unity in dispersion (Zech 11:4-14; see Ex 21:32; Mt 27:9).

- After the destruction of Gentile oppressors, the Messiah will be worshiped and enthroned as king over the long-awaited messianic kingdom, so that holiness may characterize the age (Zech 14).

Topic 8: Knowing, Being, and Doing

QUESTION 21

Match the event with the corresponding passage of Ezra.

Events in Ezra 1–6

Instructions

	Ezra 1	Ezra 2	Ezra 3	Ezra 4:1–6:12	Ezra 6:13–22
Decree to Rebuild					
Building Begins					
Building Ends					
Building Opposed					
List of Returnees					

QUESTION 22

Match the event with the corresponding passage of Haggai.

Outline of Haggai

Instructions

	Haggai 1	Haggai 2:1-9	Haggai 2:10-19	Haggai 2:20-23
Wrong Priorities				
Zerubbabel's Authority				
Drought Judgment				
Greater Glory				

QUESTION 23

Match the event with the corresponding passage of Zechariah.

Outline of Zechariah

	Zechariah 1:1-6	Zechariah 1:7–6:8	Zechariah 6:9-15	Zechariah 7–8	Zechariah 9–11	Zechariah 12–14
						Instructions
Four Restoration Messages						
Joshua's Symbolic Coronation						
Command to Repent						
Rejected at First Advent						
Eight Covenantal Visions						
Received at Second Advent						

QUESTION 24

Please open your Life Notebook and record anything new you have learned from this lesson, including any applications you should make to your life.

Lesson 10 Self Check

QUESTION 1

The key word for Haggai is _____.

    A. Glory

    B. Messiah

    C. Priorities

    D. Temple

QUESTION 2

The book of Ezra has a strong priestly emphasis. *True or False?*

QUESTION 3

The return of the exiles from Babylon was similar to the exodus from Egypt in that both left in haste. *True or False?*

QUESTION 4

When God accuses the Israelites of building "paneled" houses, He means luxurious houses fit for a king. *True or False?*

QUESTION 5

What did God use to judge the Jews in Haggai's time?

    A. Plague

    B. Pestilence

    C. Locusts

    D. Drought

QUESTION 6

The rules of the Old Testament priesthood regarding the transfer of defilement by touch, explained in Hosea 2:10-14, applied to Jesus during His earthly ministry. *True or False?*

QUESTION 7

Which of the following is true of Zechariah?

    A. His ministry overlapped that of Nehemiah

    B. His book has more Messianic passages than any other Old Testament book

    C. He emphasizes Gentiles more than the Jews

    D. He emphasizes blessing over judgment

QUESTION 8

In Zechariah 1–3, what did the vision of the man with the measuring line represent?

    A. God's anger toward the nations but favor towards Israel

    B. God's jealous care for Israel seen in His judgment upon nations

    C. God's protection of Israel through the rebuilding and re-inhabiting of Jerusalem

    D. God's gracious cleansing of Israel's sin through the future Messiah

QUESTION 9

In Zechariah 7–8, what does God require instead of fasting?

    A. Completion of His temple

    B. Justice and mercy

    C. Sacrifice

    D. Tithes brought into the storehouse

QUESTION 10

Zechariah predicted that Israel would attach the price of a slave to the Messiah at His first advent. *True or False?*

Lesson 10 Answers to Questions

QUESTION 1: Temple [The restorations of the temple and people to the land encourage the remnant in true temple worship and covenant obedience.]

QUESTION 2

A. Its author was probably not even born when the events of Ezra 1–6 took place.
C. It has a strong priestly emphasis.
D. It was originally written in two languages.
[In contrast to Chronicles, Ezra emphasizes restoration.]

QUESTION 3: *Your answer should be similar to the following:*
The nation needed to return to the land in order for the land promises to be fulfilled, and for the "seed" aspect of the Abrahamic Covenant to be fulfilled at the prophesied time of Christ's birth. The purity of marriage to other Israelites was necessary to ensure that the Messianic King was from the lineage of David (see Mt 1; Lk 3).

QUESTION 4: Cyrus [In accordance with God's foretelling, Cyrus of Persia proclaimed that all Jews in Babylon could return to Jerusalem to rebuild the temple (Ezra 1–2; Isa 45:1-6).]

QUESTION 5

A. They carried supplies with them from their former captives. [Cyrus provided financially for the returnees, just as Egypt provided for Israel during the exodus (Ezra 1; Ex 12:36). This verified God's ability to fulfill His promise of restoration—even through a pagan king.]

QUESTION 6

Reference	Teaching
Ezra 4:1-5	Opposition to temple rebuilding interrupted the work for sixteen years.
Ezra 4:6-23	A parenthetical summary of later opposition to rebuilding the walls shows the remnant that while their enemies continually opposed them, God did eventually give them success.
Ezra 4:24	The sixteen-year interruption was due to the opposition of Jews who intermarried with pagans and were worshipping other gods.
Ezra 5:1-2	Zechariah and Haggai successfully encouraged the people to continue rebuilding the temple despite opposition.
Ezra 5:3-6:12	The opposition of Tattenai towards the temple rebuilding backfired as Darius appointed him to make sure the work was funded and completed.

QUESTION 7: Priorities [Haggai rebuked the remnant to correct its wrong priorities and encouraged them to rebuild the temple so that God might bless the nation.]

QUESTION 8: False [Paneling is associated with royal buildings (1 Kgs 7:3) and the temple (Ezk 41:16). God's own house lay in ruins (1:4) while the Jews ignored it, making their own houses luxurious.]

QUESTION 9

B. Drought [Haggai's purpose in writing to the returned exiles is to explain that the drought they are experiencing is due to their neglect of the Lord's temple. His aim is to encourage them to resume rebuilding the temple so they can once again know God's blessing.]

QUESTION 10: *Your answer should be similar to the following:*
Holiness is not transferred by touch, but defilement is. The point is in Haggai 2:14: "The people of this nation are unclean in my sight,' says the Lord. (Consequently) everything they offer is also unclean."

QUESTION 11: *Your answer*

QUESTION 12

Reference	Message
Haggai 1:2-6	Rebuke for being more concerned with their houses than with the temple.
Haggai 2:3-5	God promises His presence while the people are rebuilding the temple.

| Haggai 2:10-19 | Return to task and you will be blessed instead of cursed. |
| Haggai 2:20-23 | God promises to overthrow the nations and gives authority to Zerubbabel. |

QUESTION 13: Messiah [Zechariah prepares Judah for the Messiah by encouraging the nation to respond to its privileged covenantal position among the nations. The people should rebuild the temple in light of future blessings that will come when the Messiah rules in the kingdom.]

QUESTION 14

    C. He emphasized Israel more than the Gentiles [While Zechariah and Daniel both told about the age of Gentile domination, Daniel emphasized the role of Gentiles, whereas Zechariah provided greater insight into Israel during this period.]

QUESTION 15

Vision	Message
The man among the myrtle trees	God's anger toward the nations but favor toward Israel
The four horns and four craftsmen	God's jealous care for Israel, as seen in His judgment upon nations
The man with the measuring line	God's protection of Israel through the rebuilding and re-inhabiting of Jerusalem
The new garments for Joshua the high priest	God's gracious cleansing of Israel's sin through the future Messiah

QUESTION 16

Vision	Message
The golden lampstand and two olive trees	Only through God's empowerment could Israel, Joshua, and Zerubbabel be a light to the nations
The flying scroll	The sins of individual Israelites would not go unpunished
The woman in a basket	God was removing the nation's sins of wickedness and idolatry and sending the people to Babylon
The four chariots	God would judge the Gentile nations opposing Him and His people

QUESTION 17

Reference	Message
Zechariah 7:4-7	A rebuke for Israel's hypocritical fasting and feasting
Zechariah 7:8-14	A reminder to the remnant that God requires justice and mercy (not fasting)
Zechariah 8:1-17	A promise of restoration in response to the nation's faithfulness to God's commands
Zechariah 8:18-23	A promise that the return of the Lord will be accompanied by joyful obedience rather than fasting

QUESTION 18: *Your answer*

QUESTION 19: True [Israel's true Shepherd would lead the nation, which was destined for slaughter by the Romans (Zech 11:4-14). But due to the unbelief shown when they attached the price of a slave to the Messiah, the nation would lose its favor and national unity in dispersion (Mt 27:9; Ex 21:32).]

QUESTION 20

    D. Tabernacles [After the destruction of Gentile oppressors, the Messiah will be worshipped and enthroned as king over the long-awaited messianic kingdom, so that holiness may characterize the age (Zech 14).]

QUESTION 21

Events in Ezra 1–6

				Instructions
Decree to Rebuild	List of Returnees	Building Begins	Building Opposed	Building Ends
Ezra 1	**Ezra 2**	**Ezra 3**	**Ezra 4:1–6:12**	**Ezra 6:13–22**

QUESTION 22

Outline of Haggai

			Instructions
Wrong Priorities	Greater Glory	Drought Judgment	Zerubbabel's Authority
Haggai 1	**Haggai 2:1-9**	**Haggai 2:10-19**	**Haggai 2:20-23**

QUESTION 23

Outline of Zechariah

	Command to Repent	Eight Covenantal Visions	Joshua's Symbolic Coronation	Four Restoration Messages	Rejected at First Advent	Received at Second Advent
						Instructions
	Zechariah 1:1-6	Zechariah 1:7–6:8	Zechariah 6:9-15	Zechariah 7–8	Zechariah 9–11	Zechariah 12–14

QUESTION 24: *Your answer*

Lesson 10 Self Check Answers

QUESTION 1
   C. Priorities
QUESTION 2: True
QUESTION 3: False
QUESTION 4: True
QUESTION 5
   D. Drought
QUESTION 6: False
QUESTION 7
   D. He emphasizes blessing over judgment
QUESTION 8
   C. God's protection of Israel through the rebuilding and re-inhabiting of Jerusalem
QUESTION 9
   B. Justice and mercy
QUESTION 10: True

Lesson 11: Esther and Ezra 7–10

Lesson Introduction

While Lesson 10 focused on the rebuilding of the temple, Lesson 11, on the post-exilic book of Esther and the latter part of Ezra, picks up the history fifty-eight years later and focus on the Jewish people themselves. Despite a wicked plan to exterminate all Jews throughout Persia, God providentially raised up Esther to save her people. Then, two decades later, Ezra the priest arrived in Jerusalem to lead the spiritual renewal of the returnees. Even though the former exiles had trusted God to return to the land, they still needed to abolish practices such as intermarriage to preserve the purity of their faith.

Chronology of the Persian Period

PERSIAN KING	DATES	BIBLICAL CORRELATION	GREEK CORRELATION
CYRUS	539-530	Return of Zerubbabel and Jeshua (Ezra 1-3)	
CAMBYSES	530-522	Rebuilding at Jerusalem stopped (Ezra 4)	
DARIUS I	522-486	Haggai and Zechariah prophesy (520) Temple completed (516) (Ezra 5–6)	Greeks defeat Persians at Marathon (490)
XERXES	486-464	Story of Esther (Esther 1–9)	Greeks defeat Persians at Thermopolae (480) and Salamis (479) Herodotus 485-425
ARTAXERXES I	464-423	Return of Ezra (458) (Ezra 7-10) Return of Nehemiah (445) (Nehemiah 1-2) Prophecy of Malachi (433)	Golden Age (461-431) Pericles (460-429) Athens rules
DARIUS II	423-404	BIBLICAL SILENCE	Peloponnesian Wars (431-404) Athens falls (404) Sparta rules
ARTAXERXES II	404-359		Socrates (470-339) Plato (428-348) Aristotle (384-322)
ARTAXERXES III	359-338		Philip II of Macedon defeats Greeks at Chaeronea in 338
ARSES	338-335		
DARIUS III	335-331		Alexander the Great overthrows Persian Empire
ALEXANDER	336-323		Establishment of Greek Empire

Lesson Outline

Topic 1: Introduction to Esther

Topic 2: Esther Exalted While Haman Plots

Topic 3: Connections with Daniel and Saul

    Connection With Daniel

    Connection With Saul

Topic 4: Mordecai and Israel Exalted

Topic 5: Ezra: Return and Restoration

Topic 6: Knowing, Being, and Doing

Lesson Objectives

By the end of this lesson you will be able to do the following:

- Examine the distinctions and timelines of Esther and Ezra.
- Discuss the books' purpose to encourage the Jewish people with God's faithfulness to His covenant with them.
- Evaluate the parallels between Esther and other Bible books and people.
- Explore how God's program and promises are advanced even through a disobedient people and external opposition.
- Internalize the key verses, Esther 4:14 and Ezra 7:10.

Topic 1: Introduction to Esther

The events of Esther chronicle ten years of the fifty-eight-year gap between Ezra 6 (516 BC) and Ezra 7 (458 BC). The story takes place from 483 to 473 BC, between the time of the first return under Zerubbabel (538 BC) and the second under Ezra (458 BC). Without Esther, Scripture would remain silent as to the state of the majority of post-exilic Jews, who chose to remain in Babylon when a small remnant of their brothers returned to the land. Why did they remain? They were prospering materially and saw nothing but hard work by returning to Jerusalem, a city that lacked even walls (see the book of Nehemiah). The books of Ezra and

Esther Extermination Plot Foiled				
Persia				
10 years (483–473 BC)				
Plot Planned		Plot Foiled		
Chapters 1–4		Chapters 5–10		
Threat		Triumph		
Providence Prepared		Providence Enacted		
Persecution		Preservation		
Grave Danger		Great Deliverance		
Feasts of Xerxes		Feasts of Esther and Purim		
Esther Exalted 1:1-21-18	Haman Plots 2:19–4:17	Mordecai over Haman 5:1–8:2	Israel over Enemies 8:3–9:32	Mordecai over Persia 10

Nehemiah assert God's providential care over the small remnant that returned. Esther reveals that God even graciously cared for the spiritually indifferent Jews whose priorities needed rearranging.

- **Key Word:** Providence
- **Key Verse:** (Mordecai to Esther) "Don't imagine that because you are part of the king's household you will be the one Jew who will escape. If you keep quiet at this time, liberation and protection for the Jews will appear from another source, while you and your father's household perish. It may very well be that you have achieved royal status for such a time as this" (Est 4:14).
- **Summary Statement:** The extermination of the Jewish nation plotted by Haman falls on his own head by God's providence through Mordecai and Esther, to encourage postexilic Israel that God remains committed to the Abrahamic covenant.
- **Application:** Use your providentially placed position to help God's people.

Assignment

- Please read Esther 1.
- Please read "Introduction to Esther."

Introduction to Esther

Title

The name Esther (*'ester*) is likely derived from the Persian word for "star." It was the Persian name given to the heroine of this tale, a Jewish girl named Hadassah (meaning "myrtle tree"; see Est 2:7), perhaps because of her star-like beauty.

Authorship

External Evidence: Authorship of Esther remains anonymous.

Internal Evidence: The book provides no clues as to the individual who wrote it; the only prospects are educated guesses. The account shows such detail of Persian and Jewish life that it is difficult to suppose the author was not both Jewish and well-acquainted with Persian ways. Some suggest Ezra or Nehemiah as author, but the vocabulary and style of Esther do not match that of either of the other books. Others maintain that Mordecai penned the work, since he was in fact a scribe (Wilkinson, 131). There is no conclusive indicator of the author of the book.

Circumstances

Date: Although critical scholars have claimed that differences in language and style indicate that the book of Esther was written much later than the events it relates, their arguments are unconvincing. Since the book's narrative closes at 473 BC, it is reasonable to presume a date shortly after this—perhaps after Xerxes' reign, which ended in 464 BC, but no later than 435 BC, when the palace at Susa was destroyed by fire, a significant event not mentioned in Esther.

Recipients: Esther's first readers were likely the post-exilic communities during the time of Nehemiah, Malachi, and the Intertestamental Period—probably initially in Persia, but soon in Israel when the book was copied and distributed. The account of God's providential dealings on their behalf would have been a tremendous source of encouragement to Jews both in Persia and in Israel.

Characteristics

Historicity: Esther contains much eyewitness information about the Persian Empire, but little has been verified from outside sources. Only relatively recently has the King Ahasuerus named in Esther been identified with the King Xerxes who reigned over Persia from 485-465 BC.

Canonicity: The usefulness of Esther has long been debated. Maimonides, a twelfth-century Jewish scholar, taught that when the Messiah comes, every book of the Jewish Scriptures will pass away except the Law and Esther, which would remain forever. However, Martin Luther wished the book had never been written because of its many problems (Donald K. Campbell, "Esther," DTS Class Notes, 1984, 1).

The reasons for differing opinions on the book stem from many unique characteristics:

- The name of God is never mentioned in the book (although His hand is very evident).

- Esther is never quoted in the New Testament; nor was it found among the Dead Sea Scrolls.

- It never mentions the Law or Jewish sacrifices or offerings.

- It never refers to prayer (although fasting is mentioned).

- The book contains no mention at all of anything spiritual.

- Its unique literary type (almost a drama) has given it placement within several different sections in various collections of Old Testament books.

Placement: Esther is the only biblical book that contains a history of the Jews outside of the land during the time of the Gentiles (586 BC until the return of Christ). This may explain why it appears as the last historical book in English Bibles. Even though it precedes Nehemiah chronologically, the same conditions described in the book continue throughout the time of the Gentiles, and will continue until the deliverance of the Jews at the return of Christ (Campbell, 2).

Lessons: The book of Esther teaches several principles such as (Campbell, 2):

- Satan's purpose is to destroy the Jews by use of the nations.

- God's purpose is to preserve the Jews by use of the nations.

- God works in the affairs of nations to accomplish His will to preserve His people.

- God works in the affairs of individuals to accomplish His will to preserve His people.

Interpretation: At least four different hermeneutical methods have been employed in seeking to understand the message of Esther:

1. **Prophetical**–Esther is a prediction that the Jews will be preserved while they are outside of the land during the times of the Gentiles. **Response:** Nothing is mentioned of the "times of the Gentiles," and the account is presented in a straightforward manner as history.

2. **Allegorical**–Esther is an allegorical presentation of the story of mankind. **Response:** This is ambiguous; the account is presented in a straightforward manner as history.

3. **Typical**–Esther is God's illustration of the Christian experience in the Church Age, or a type of the Millennium. For instance, the replacing of Vashti (a Gentile) by Esther (a Jew) typifies the setting aside of Christendom and the taking up of Israel. Haaman, the Jews' enemy, is a type of the anti-Christ who will be destroyed at the second coming. The numerical value of the Hebrew letters of "Haaman" is 666. Mordecai's exaltation is representative of Jesus' exaltation. The Jews' triumph, therefore, would resemble their future victory in the Millennium. **Response:** While this view is ingenious, it fails in that it reads the NT back into the OT, which means that its original readers would not have understood the meaning. Also, a non-traditional spelling of "Haaman," with a double "a," must be used, seemingly rather conveniently, to fit this numerological scenario.

4. **Historical**–Esther records God's providential care of His chosen people as evidence of His commitment to the Abrahamic covenant.

QUESTION 1

The key word for Esther is
_____.

QUESTION 2

Both Ezra and Esther fill in what happened to the majority of post-exilic Jews who chose to remain in Babylon when the small remnant of their brothers returned to the land. *True or False?*

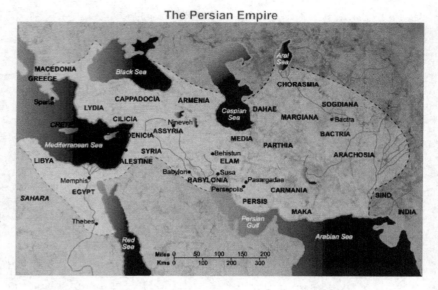
The Persian Empire

QUESTION 3

Which of the following is a characteristic of the book of Esther?

    A. God's name appears in the book

    B. It is quoted in the New Testament

    C. It often refers back to the Law

    D. Fasting is mentioned

QUESTION 4

Please briefly explain how the historical hermeneutical method views the message of Esther.

Topic 1 Key Points

- The extermination of the Jewish nation plotted by Haman falls on his own head by God's faithful providence through Mordecai and Esther.

- Esther fills in what happened to the majority of post-exilic Jews who chose to remain in Babylon when a small remnant of their brothers returned to the land.

- God's name and prayer are not mentioned in Esther, but His hand is very evident; the book contains no mention of anything spiritual and is a unique literary type (almost a drama).

- The historical hermeneutical method views the book of Esther as a record of God's providential care of His chosen people; evidence of His commitment to the Abrahamic covenant.

Topic 2: Esther Exalted While Haman Plots (Est 1:1–4:17)

Esther is a historical narrative about a plot to exterminate the entire Jewish population that was averted by God's providential workings through the godly Jewess, Queen Esther. The account cites the threat to the Jews (Est 1–4) and the triumph of the Jews over those who threatened their existence (Est 5–10). Chapter 9 celebrates the preservation of the nation during the Feast of Purim–an annual reminder of God's faithfulness on their behalf.

Assignment

- Please read Esther 2–4.
- Please read "Esther Exalted While Haman Plots."
- Please memorize Esther 4:14.

Key Dates Related to the Book of Esther

REFERENCE	DATE	EVENT
—	486	*Xerxes' reign began.*
1:3	483 (3rd year of Xerxes)	*Xerxes threw a 7-day banquet for his nobles and officials, during which Queen Vashti was deposed.*
—	482-479	*Xerxes led disastrous campaigns against Greece as recorded by the Greek historian Herodotus (7.8)*
2:16	December 479 or January 478	*Esther became queen after four years of beauty treatments.*
3:7	Early April 474	*During the fifth year of Esther's reign, Haman and the astrologers (5:10, 14; 6:12-13) cast the purim (lots) to decide the day of the planned extermination of the Jews: eleven months later (7 March 473).*
3:12	April 17, 474 (13th of Nisan)	*Xerxes' first edict (to destroy the Jews) informed everyone of the fateful day, royal secretaries wrote it out in the various languages of the empire and sent it out.*
8:9	June 25, 474 (23rd of Sivan)	*Xerxes' second edict (to protect the Jews) was sent out two months and ten days after the first one on April 17.*
3:13 8:12 9:1, 17	March 7, 473 (13th of Adar)	*Rather than being destroyed on this day, Jews protected themselves by killing at least 75, 810 enemies eight months and twenty days after the counter-edict was signed.*
9:17-18	March 8, 473 (14th of Adar)	*Jews feasted in celebration of their victory throughout the empire, except in Susa where they killed their enemies an additional day (today Jews everywhere except Jerusalem celebrate Purim on this day, the 14th of Adar).*
9:18	March 9, 473 (15th of Adar)	*Jews feasted in celebration of their victory in Susa (today Jews in Jerusalem celebrate Purim on this day, the 15th of Adar).*
—	464	*The palace at Susa was destroyed by fire and Xerxes reign ended.*

Esther Exalted While Haman Plots

Summary Statement for the Book

The extermination of the Jewish nation plotted by Haman falls on his own head by God's providence through Mordecai and Esther, to encourage postexilic Israel that God remains committed to the Abrahamic covenant.

Haman's plot to exterminate the Jewish people becomes known to Mordecai and Esther, whom God has strategically placed; this shows Israel that, apart from God's intervention, it could not exist as a nation (Est 1–4).

In the third year of his reign, King Xerxes (called Ahasuerus in the Hebrew text) held a lavish, 180-day banquet for all his officials, servants, nobles, and army (Est 1:3-4). When that banquet was finished, he then held another for seven days for all the people in the citadel of Susa (Est 1:5). At this banquet, he displayed the lavishness of his riches, supplying unlimited royal wine (Est 1:6-8).

Under the influence of the wine, the king sent for his wife, Queen Vashti, asking her to appear before him, presumably so that he could display her beauty to his guests. Proudly, Vashti refused to do as he asked (Est 1:10-15). However, both King Xerxes and his advisers saw her refusal as an issue that would affect how all wives responded to their husbands' requests (Est 1:16-20). The king's advisers counseled him to deal with Vashti publicly. So Xerxes sent out an order that every man should rule his family (Est 1:20-22). He also divorced, deposed, and exiled the disobedient Queen Vashti, unaware that through him, God was preparing the way for Esther to replace her (483 BC) (Est 1:18-19).

The kingdom did need a queen. Women of the kingdom were brought to the king's harem, to be looked after by Hegai, the king's eunuch, as they underwent a year of beauty treatments in preparation to be considered by the king. Esther, a young Jewish girl, was also brought to the harem. In obedience to the warnings of her relative Mordecai, she hid her nationality from those around her, using the name Esther instead of her Hebrew given name, Hadassah.

God ordained that Esther would find Hegai's special favor as she prepared (Est 2:1-18). And in much the same way, He sovereignly ordained that Esther would catch the eye of the king. Four years after he had deposed Vashti, Xerxes chose Esther and married her, unknowingly making a Jewess the queen of all of Persia. God was sovereignly and preemptively working to intervene in the disaster that would soon threaten to annihilate His chosen people.

After Esther became queen, God allowed Mordecai, who regularly sat at the king's gate, to uncover an assassination plot and save Xerxes' life (Est 2:19-23). But nothing was done for Mordecai after his good deed for the king; records were kept, but apparently the event was forgotten. These events were also in God's hand as He planned to provide for His people.

But Mordecai was not so popular with all of the king's officials. Xerxes had exalted Haman, an Agagite, making him a chief official and ordering that all should bow before him when he approached. Mordecai refused on the basis of being a Jew, which infuriated Haman and his tender pride (Est 3; compare with Dan 3). Extending that fury to Mordecai's people, Haman convinced Xerxes to decree the genocide of all God's people from Egypt to India (see Est 1:1; Est 3:6) on one day, which by lot fell to a date about eleven months distant.

Realizing the inevitability of the king's edict, Mordecai began to see the fullness of God's plan of protection for His people. Mordecai convinced Esther to risk her life for the Jews by suggesting that God had made her queen for this purpose (Est 4). Even if she refused, Mordecai told her, God's people would be delivered because of His faithfulness to the Abrahamic covenant, but Mordecai assured her that she herself, the hidden Jewess, would perish (Est 4:14).

QUESTION 5

When Queen Vashti refused the king's request, the king's advisors saw that it could influence the dynamics of every family unit in the kingdom. *True or False?*

QUESTION 6

What orders did the king give to counter the possible damaging effects of Queen Vashti's disobedience (Est 1:20-22)?

- A. That every man should rule his family
- B. That every woman must walk behind her husband
- C. That no woman could appear at a banquet.
- D. That no woman could work outside her house

QUESTION 7

Please match each person from the book of Esther with his or her corresponding description.

Person	Description
Vashti	The Jewish protector of Esther
Xerxes	The queen of Persia at the beginning of the story
Esther	The reigning king of Persia
Mordecai	The king's eunuch, the appointed overseer of the women
Hegai	A Jewess who became queen
Haman	An Agagite promoted above the king's other officials

QUESTION 8

Please read Esther 4:14. Have you ever applied this verse to a situation in your life? If you haven't yet, as a Christian leader you will almost surely have the chance. Please open your Life Notebook and write out how you will respond when the opportunity comes. Why do you think this is so difficult to apply?

QUESTION 9

Write Esther 4:14 from memory below.

Topic 2 Key Points

- When Queen Vashti refused the king's request, the king's advisors saw it as an issue that would determine how all wives would respond to their husbands' requests (Est 1:16-20).
- To counter the possible damage of the queen's disobedience, the king ordered that every man should rule his family.
- The following are the main characters of the book of Esther: Vashti, Xerxes, Esther, Mordecai, Hegai, and Haman.
- Esther 4:14 says that Esther achieved her position for the purpose of delivering the Jews, but if she did not fulfill this purpose, she would suffer their fate and God would raise up another deliverer.

Topic 3: Connections With Daniel and Saul

Sometimes Bible authors communicated their messages by drawing comparisons with previous Scripture or spiritually significant historical events. For example, when Jesus was tempted in the wilderness, He was tempted for forty days (Mt 4:1-11). For a Jew, that brought to mind other periods of testing involving the number forty: Israel wandered in the wilderness for forty years, and the rain fell during Noah's flood for forty days and nights (Gen 7:4, 17; Num 14:33-34). In another example, the author of Hebrews compared the situation of his readers with the Israelites' trial of faith at Kadesh-Barnea (Heb 3:7-19).

In the present case, it seems that as Daniel is a book that shows God's sovereignty over the Jews in Babylon, so Esther shows that God's sovereign presence was also with the Jews in Persia. He was with them and preserved them even though they had not returned to the land as the obedient remnant had. Though they didn't have the level of blessing from Him that the exiles who returned to the land did, He still protected and blessed them.

In this topic we will also look back at Saul and explore the long-term consequences of incomplete obedience, as illustrated by Haman in the story of Esther.

Banquets in the Book of Esther

	PASSAGE	HOSTS	GUESTS	EVENTS
1	1:3-4	Xerxes	Nobles and Officials	Wealth of the kingdom displayed over 180 days
2	1:5-8	Xerxes	All the people	Wine flowed for everyone for 7 days
3	1:9	Vashti	Palace women	Vashti deposed for declining to attend Xerxes' banquet
4	2:18	Xerxes	Nobles and Officials	Esther introduced as the new queen
5	3:15	Xerxes	Haman	Annihilation of the Jews decreed by the king
6	5:1-8	Esther	Xerxes and Haman	Xerxes kept in suspense as to Esther's request
7	7:1-10	Esther	Xerxes and Haman	Esther exposes Haman's plot
8	8:17	Jews	Jews	Rejoicing over the king's edict on the Jews behalf and many Gentiles became Jews
9	9:17	Jews	Jews	Rejoicing over slaughter of 75,810 or more enemies of the Jews
10	9:18-32	Jews	Jews	Feast of Purim established to be an annual event through Mordecai's decree

Connection With Daniel

Assignment

- Please read "Connection with Daniel."

> ## Connection with Daniel
>
> There are some interesting parallels between the stories in the books of Daniel and Esther. For example, there are similarities between Daniel 1 and Esther 2.
>
> - The stories of Daniel and Esther start similarly; each participated in a type of contest judging their physical attributes (Dan 1:3-4; Est 2:2). Daniel was chosen because he was a young man "in whom there was no physical defect and who [was] handsome," while in Esther's case there was "a search conducted in the king's behalf for attractive young women" (Dan 1:4; Est 2:2).
>
> - Both had the king's court official or eunuch help them prepare for this contest. In Daniel's case, the king commanded Ashpenaz, whom God made sympathetic to Daniel, to care for him (Dan 1:3, 9). In Esther's case, she was placed under the authority of Hegai, with whom she found favor (Est 2:8-9). Daniel was prepared for three years, while Esther's preparations lasted one year (Est 2:12; Dan 1:5).
>
> - Like Daniel , Esther had a foreign name as well as a Jewish name (Est 2:7; Dan

1:7). Both of these foreign names could be associated with pagan gods—Belteshazzar, Daniel's assigned name, means "Bel save the king," and Esther may be associated with "Ishtar," one of the gods of Persia.

- Both found favor when brought before the king: "He did not find among the entire group anyone like Daniel" (Dan 1:19) and "The king loved Esther more than all the other women" (Est 2:17).

- Other similarities are that both were given supplies, such as cosmetics or food, both were exiles, and neither had parents with them (Dan 1; Est 2).

The parallels continue in other chapters:

- Daniel, Mordecai, and Esther were all promoted for various reasons: Daniel for faithfulness and interpreting dreams, Mordecai for revealing the plot against the king, and Esther for her beauty (Dan 2:46-49; 5:29; Est 2:17; 10:1-3).

- In Esther 3:2 the issue was that bowing and homage were denied to Haman by Mordecai, and in Daniel 3:8-12 the issue was that the Jewish friends of Daniel would not bow down and pay homage to the golden statue. In both cases, God protected the ones who did not bow down to man.

- In the book of Daniel, his friends were preserved from the fires of a furnace; in Esther, Mordecai was protected from being hung on a gallows (Dan 3:24-27; Est 7).

- In both books, the persecution came from the highest government officials (Dan 6:5; Est 3:1).

- In both Daniel and Esther, the king of the land celebrated with a banquet while the city he ruled was in an uproar or being defeated in war (Dan 5:1, 30-31; Est 3:15).

- The persecution that came on both Daniel and Mordecai was solely because they were faithful Jews (Dan 6:6; Est 3:3-4).

- In both books, the ruling king issued a written edict that could not be changed (Dan 6:12; Est 3:8-15).

- In Daniel 6, the king struggled to find a way to rescue Daniel, but by law could not rescind his order. In Esther also, the king's order could not be rescinded, but he allowed Esther to write a new order so the Jews could defend themselves (Dan 6:15; Est 8:1-13).

- Daniel's persecutors lost their lives instead of him, just as Haman did instead of Mordecai (Est 9:5; Dan 6:25).

- As God gave Daniel protection in the lion's den, He also protected the Jews in Persia (Dan 6:23).

QUESTION 10

Please match the teaching and reference from Esther with the corresponding reference from Daniel.

Esther	Daniel
The contest of their attributes (Est 2:2)	Daniel 1:3, 9
The king's official or eunuch assigned to them (Est 2:8-9)	Daniel 1:3-4
Most favored by the king (Est 2:17)	Daniel 2:46-49; 5:29
Esther and Mordecai promoted (Est 2:17; 10:1-3)	Daniel 1:19
Not bowing and paying homage (Est 3:2)	Daniel 3:8-12

QUESTION 11

Please match the teaching and reference from Esther with the corresponding reference from Daniel.

Esther	Daniel
Jews preserved from death (Est 7)	Daniel 5:1
Persecution from high government officials (Est 3:1)	Daniel 3:24-27
King celebrating with a banquet (Est 3:15)	Daniel 6:13
King issues an unchangeable edict (Est 8:1-13)	Daniel 6:5
The conspiracy is turned against the persecutors (Est 9:5)	Daniel 6:25

QUESTION 12

The book of Daniel tells of the Jewish exiles in Babylon; similarly, the book of Esther tells of the Jewish exiles in _____.

QUESTION 13

These Jews for whom God provided in Persia were not the obedient Jews who had returned to the land. Are there examples in your life of times God has provided for you, even when you were not in perfect obedience to Him? What does this concept mean to you? Please open your Life Notebook and record your thoughts.

Connection With Saul

Assignment

- Please read "Connection with Saul."

Connection with Saul

There is also a possible connection between Saul's disobedience in 1 Samuel 15 and the presence in Esther of Haman the Agagite (Agag may have been a general term for a king of the Amalekites). In 1 Samuel 15, King Saul only partially obeyed God's order to fight against the Amalekites until they were completely destroyed (1 Sam 15:18-19). (Ever since the exodus from Egypt, God had intended to wipe out the remembrance of Amalek from under heaven, Ex 17:14). Because Saul had not obeyed and exterminated that nation, the Jews were now facing Amalek again six hundred years later as it threatened to exterminate them!

This shows the consequences (in this case of Saul's disobedience) even to future generations, of not carrying out God's instructions.

Also in 1 Samuel 15, Saul was ordered to not take plunder from the Amalekites, but instead to totally destroy all that belonged to them (1 Sam 15:13-19). Again he disobeyed God's command, considering his own judgment more valid, and took the Amalekites' best possessions, presumably to sacrifice to the Lord (1 Sam 15:7-9). The Jews in Esther's time struck all their enemies with the sword and did as they pleased with them (Est 9:5). However, unlike the exodus, when the Israelites took plunder from Egypt, and the more recent return from Babylon, during which they also took spoils, the Jews did not confiscate their enemies' property in Persia (Est 9:10).

We should rest in the fact that even when we don't know why, and even if God's orders seem harsh, He knows best. If Saul had been obedient, the threat of national destruction in Esther might never have come about! It also helps illustrate Esther's key verse: God raised her up as queen so He could deliver His people through her (Est 4:14). He had raised Saul previously to deliver His people permanently from the Amalekite threat, but Saul failed by obeying incompletely. Thus, the task fell to Queen Esther, six hundred years later, to eliminate the last of this threatening enemy nation.

The application is obvious for us: If we fail, through disobedience, to complete the tasks God has chosen for us, it may trouble other people of God, and He will raise up someone else who will fulfill that mission. Then we lose our reward; there is much to lose. Sometimes God's Old Testament commands to exterminate people or nations seem harsh to modern sensibilities, but this incident helps show that He was just and was taking appropriate actions to protect His people and His holiness.

QUESTION 14

In whose lifetime did God first announce His intention to fully exterminate the Amalekites?

    A. Abraham

    B. Moses

    C. Saul

    D. Esther

QUESTION 15

The Jews of Persia took spoils when they avenged themselves on their enemies in the time of Esther. *True or False?*

Topic 3 Key Points

- The stories in the books of Esther and Daniel have many parallels: a contest of attributes, officials assigned to both, both obtain the king's favor, problems with Jews not bowing or paying homage, Jews preserved, the tables turned on the persecutors, unchangeable edicts, and banquets.

- The book of Daniel tells of the Jewish exiles in Babylon; similarly, the book of Esther tells of the Jewish exiles in Persia.

- God provides for His people even when they aren't in perfect obedience to Him.

- God first announced His intention to fully exterminate the Amalekites in the time of Moses (Ex 17); in disobedience, Saul failed to exterminate them in his time (1 Sam 15).

- When the Jews avenged themselves on their enemies in the Persian Empire at the time of Esther, they refused to take plunder from them (Est 9:10).

Topic 4: Mordecai and Israel Exalted (Esther 5–10)

Shadow and Fulfillment	
Shadow	**Substance**
Esther's three-day period of fasting began during the daylight hours of Nisan 14, the first day of Passover.	Jesus' three-day period of death began sometime around three o'clock during the daylight hours of Nisan 14, the first day of Passover.
Fasting in general, and thus the fast undertaken by Esther, is identified in Scripture with "humiliation" or "affliction." Since mourning (represented by a change into mourning garments) was involved, the fast may also represent Esther's temporary "state of death."	Jesus' three-day period of physical death is identified in Scripture as the period of His "humiliation" or "affliction."
Esther's period of humiliation ended on the third day, Nisan 16 (Est 5:1)	Jesus' period of humiliation ended on the third day, Nisan 16 (Acts 10:40)
On concluding her fast (i.e., after arising from her symbolic state of death) but before her self-presentation to the king, Esther was robed in royal splendor (Est 5:1)	At the end of his three-day period of death, but before His self-presentation to God the Father in heaven, Jesus was resurrected "in glory" (1 Cor 15:20, 43)
Esther presented herself, on the basis of her fast, before the king, who then accepted her into his presence (Est 4:16; 5:2)	Jesus, on the basis of His atoning sacrifice and death (Heb 2:9-10, 14), entered into the Father's presence in the true holy of holies in heaven (Heb 9:12, 24) and was accepted into His presence to sit at "the right hand of God" (Heb 10:12; 12:2)
The result of Esther's acceptance by the king was the salvation of her people, which also involved the Gentiles who had been initiated by physical circumcision into the community of faith (Est 8:17)	The result of Jesus' acceptance by the Father is the salvation of His people—Jews and Gentiles alike who have been inducted into the remnant community of faith by spiritual circumcision (Rom 2:28-29; Col 2:11; Acts 11:18; Gal 3:8)

God's people and the messianic line were often in jeopardy of extermination. Because of Esther's connections and parallels with the stories in Daniel as well as with the work of Christ, her story seems typical of many throughout the Bible. Yet again God provided a substitute, a savior, like Esther; and His people were delivered, proving that He watches over them: "The eyes of the Lord are in every place, keeping watch on those who are evil and those who are good (Prov 15:3).

Assignment

- Please read Esther 5–10.
- Please read "Mordecai and Israel Exalted."

Mordecai and Israel Exalted

Haman's extermination plot reverts on his own head through God's providential workings in Mordecai and Esther, to encourage postexilic Israel that God remains committed to the Abrahamic covenant (Est 5–10).

Esther went to the king on behalf of her people, even though it endangered her life. Her boldness before the king was enthusiastically accepted, but instead of immediately begging him to spare her people, she merely invited him and Haman to a banquet, postponing her request in order to sway him to grant it (Est 5:1-8). Proving her remarkable wisdom and self-restraint yet again, even after that first banquet, she merely invited the king and Haman to attend a second banquet on the following night.

Feeling the blessing of royal favor, Haman went home from that first banquet in very high spirits—which were quashed immediately when he passed Mordecai, who still refused to grovel before him. But that night, the very night Haman arrogantly decided to have Mordecai hung from seventy-five-foot-high gallows, King Xerxes also decided to lift Mordecai up—by honoring Mordecai for saving his life (Est 5:9-14). Haman came to the king's chambers to ask permission to hang Mordecai, and left with the commission to lead his Jewish enemy through the streets, declaring his honor (Est 6)! Perhaps Haman should have realized the significance of this initial humiliation and taken warning that his entire plan of genocide was about to go horribly wrong.

At the banquet the following evening, Esther revealed her true identity and her real request. Infuriated, Xerxes decreed that Haman should die on the gallows he had prepared for Mordecai, showing God's protection for those who fear Him and punishment for those who oppose Him (Est 7). And Mordecai was elevated to Haman's position and appointed over Haman's estate, demonstrating that those who plot evil will only prepare the way for the righteous to prosper (Est 8:1-2).

Xerxes commanded Esther and Mordecai to write a counter-decree that would allow the Jews to defend themselves against their enemies on the day that had been scheduled for their demise. And so, when the time came, the Jews slaughtered at least 75,810 enemies in two days of vengeance, with the help of the royal officials. This turn of events caused many Gentiles to become converts (Est 8:3-17). Both the triumph and delivery showed God's faithfulness to the Abrahamic covenant by not allowing His people to be annihilated (Est 9:1-16). To commemorate this deliverance, Mordecai and Esther authorized an annual celebration of the Jews' victory over their enemies: the Feast of Purim (Est 9:17-32). This celebration would help Israel remember God's gracious workings on its behalf.

The Lord exalted Mordecai to the position of second-in-command, next to Xerxes, because of his selfless concern for the Jews (Est 10). God's hand of blessing comes on those who seek to selflessly serve the Lord and His people.

QUESTION 16

Who was hung on the gallows Haman built?

    A. Hegai

    B. Haman

    C. Mordecai

    D. No one

QUESTION 17

The feast that was celebrated to commemorate God's deliverance of the Jews in Esther is called the Feast of _____.

    A. Booths

    B. Lights

    C. Purim

    D. Tabernacles

Topic 4 Key Points

- Haman died on the gallows he had prepared for Mordecai, evidence that God protects those who fear Him and punishes those who oppose Him and His people (Est 7).

- The feast that Esther and Mordecai instituted to commemorate God's deliverance of the Jews is called the Feast of Purim.

Topic 5: Return and Restoration

Chronology: Ezra-Nehemiah

YEAR	MONTH	DAY	EVENT	REFERENCE
539 B.C.	Oct.	12	Capture of Babylon	Dan 5:30
538-537	Mar. to Mar.	24 11	Cyrus's first year	Ezr 1:1-4
537(?)			Return under Sheshbazzar	Ezr 1:1-4
537			Building of altar	Ezr 3:1
536			Work on temple begun	Ezr 3:8
536-530			Opposition during Cyrus's reign	Ezr 4:1-5
530-520			Work on temple ceased	Ezr 4:24
520	Sept.	24 21	Work on temple renewed under Darius	Ezr 5:2; Hag 1:14
516	Mar.	3 12	Temple completed	Ezr 6:15
458	Apr.	1 8	Ezra departs from Babylon	Ezr 7:6-9
	Aug.	1 4	Ezra arrives in Jerusalem	Ezr 7:8-9
	Dec.	20 19	People assemble	Ezr 10:9
	Dec.	1 29	Committee begins investigation	Ezr 10:16
457	Mar.	1 27	Committee ends investigation	Ezr 10:17
445-444	Apr. to Apr.	13 2	20th year of Artaxerxes I	Ne 1:1
445	Mar. - Apr.		Nehemiah approaches king	Neh 2:1
	Aug.(?)		Nehemiah arrives in Jerusalem	Neh 2:11
	Oct.	25 2	Completion of wall	Neh 6:15
	Oct. to Nov.	8 5	Public assembly	Neh 7:73-8:1
	Oct.	15-22 22-28	Feast of Tabernacles	Neh 8:14
	Oct.	24 30	Fast	Neh 9:1
433-432	Apr. to Apr.	1 19	32nd year of Artaxerxes; Nehemiah's recall and return	Neh 5:14; 13:6

Once more it seems that, at least from a human perspective, the Israelites' testimony as a nation separated unto God was in jeopardy. The people's disobedience, which likely spanned many issues, is represented by one of the foremost sins: The Israelites were disobeying the Mosaic covenant by marrying foreigners.

We all deal with sin issues every day—both in our own lives and, as Christian leaders, in the lives of other Christians. How did Ezra handle this sin issue?

Zerubbabel's Temple

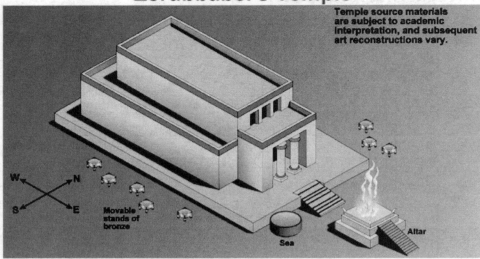

Temple source materials are subject to academic interpretation, and subsequent art reconstructions vary.

Assignment

- Please read Ezra 7–10.
- Please read "Return and Restoration."

Return and Restoration

The reformation of the people in the second return under Ezra is recorded to encourage the remnant to fulfill its covenant obligations on the basis of God's mercy (458 BC; Ezra 7–10).

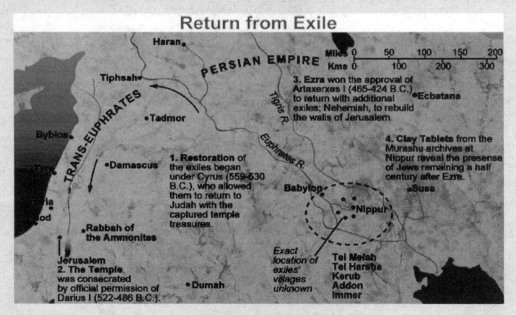

Return from Exile

1. Restoration of the exiles began under Cyrus (559-530 B.C.), who allowed them to return to Judah with the captured temple treasures.

2. The Temple was consecrated by official permission of Darius I (522-486 B.C.).

3. Ezra won the approval of Artaxerxes I (465-424 B.C.) to return with additional exiles; Nehemiah, to rebuild the walls of Jerusalem.

4. Clay Tablets from the Murashu archives at Nippur reveal the presence of Jews remaining a half century after Ezra.

Exact location of exiles' villages unknown

Tel Melah
Tel Harsha
Kerub
Addon
Immer

The second return, of 5,000 Jews under Ezra the priest, is recorded as evidence of God's merciful protection on all who trust Him (Ezra 7–8). Ezra's qualifications to lead more returnees back to Jerusalem are cited, showing how God led him in his life as priest for the spiritual restoration of the remnant (Ezra 7:1-10).

- Ezra was a priest (Ezra 7:1-5).

- Ezra was a teacher (Ezra 7:6).

- Ezra experienced the hand of God on his life (Ezra 7:6-9).

- Ezra made it his priority to study, obey, and teach the law (Ezra 7:10).

Ezra records how God provided for the return through King Artaxerxes, who supplied money, authorized Ezra to teach and govern, and exempted the temple workers from taxes. This reminded the exiles of God's blessing on their obedience (Ezra 7:11-28). Returnees included 18 family heads and 1,496 other men, plus women and children, totaling about 5,000—a much smaller group than the 50,000 who had returned with Zerubbabel eighty years earlier (Ezra 8:1-14). God protected the returnees because they prepared spiritually for the return, adding 258 Levites for temple leadership and celebrating a fast (Ezra 8:15-36).

Ezra learned that many leaders of the community had enticed the nation to sin by intermarrying with pagan women, in direct violation of the Law (Gen 24:3; 26:34-35; 28:1, 2, 8; Ex 34:16; Deut 7:1-2; 20:17-18; see Judg. 3:5; 1 Kgs 11) (Ezra 9:1-2). He lamented the intermarriage and confessed God's faithfulness, in contrast to Israel's unfaithfulness, to model for the people the proper response to sins which were serious enough to threaten the covenant community (Ezra 9:3-15).

- Intermarriage led Ezra to pull out his **own** hair (Ezra 9:3).

- Intermarriage led Nehemiah to pull out **others'** hair (Neh 13:25)!

Were Ezra and Nehemiah functioning primarily to teach us proper leadership style? Then whom should you follow?

The leaders' instruction to divorce foreign wives was carried out faithfully by 113 men. This exhorted Israel to live according to the covenant (Ezra 10). After all of Israel lamented the sin of intermarriage, the leaders who initiated the idea to divorce all foreign wives fulfilled their vow to do so (Ezra 10:1-17). The list of men required to divorce pagan foreign wives included priests, Levites, and common people; this shows the great extent to which this sin had pervaded the holy nation and shows the need for such a drastic action as divorce (Ezra 10:18-44).

- Please memorize Ezra 7:10. Every church leader and every aspiring church leader should take this verse to heart.

QUESTION 18

Please write Ezra 7:10 from memory.

QUESTION 19

Of the following, who participated in the sin of intermarriage with foreign wives? *(Select all that apply.)*

    A. Ezra

    B. Levites

    C. Priests

    D. Common people

Topic 5 Key Points

- Ezra 7:10 tells us that Ezra dedicated himself to the study of the law of the Lord, to its observance, and to teaching its statutes and judgments in Israel—a good creed for every Christian leader.

- The list of men required to divorce pagan foreign wives includes priests, Levites, and common people; this shows the great extent to which this sin had pervaded the holy nation and shows the need for such a drastic action as divorce (Ezra 10:18-44).

Topic 6: Knowing, Being, and Doing

QUESTION 20

Match the event from Esther with the corresponding passage.

Outline of Esther

	Instructions			
Israel over Enemies				
Mordecai over Haman				
Esther Exalted				
Mordecai over Persia				
Haman Plots				
Esther 1:1–2:18	**Esther 2:19**	**Esther 5:1–8:2**	**Esther 8:3–9:32**	**Esther 10**

QUESTION 21

Match the event from Ezra with the corresponding chapter.

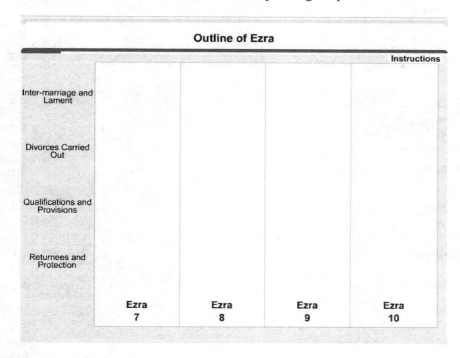

Outline of Ezra

Instructions

Inter-marriage and Lament

Divorces Carried Out

Qualifications and Provisions

Returnees and Protection

| Ezra 7 | Ezra 8 | Ezra 9 | Ezra 10 |

QUESTION 22

Please open your Life Notebook and record anything new you have learned from this lesson, including any applications you should make to your life.

Lesson 11 Self Check

QUESTION 1

The key word for Esther is _____.

QUESTION 2

Which of the following is a characteristic of the book of Esther?

    A. God's name is mentioned often

    B. Several short prayers are quoted

    C. It often refers back to the Law

    D. God's providence is evident

QUESTION 3

To counter the effects of the queen's disobedience to his orders, the Persian king ordered all men to rule in their own households. *True or False?*

QUESTION 4

Who was Hegai?

    A. The reigning king of Persia

    B. The Jewish protector of Esther

    C. The king's eunuch appointed overseer of the women

    D. An Agagite promoted above the king's other officials

QUESTION 5

Which of the following did **not** occur in the stories of both Daniel and Esther?

    A. Refusal to bow and pay homage

    B. A king changing his decree to save the Jews

    C. Persecution from high government officials

    D. A king celebrating with a banquet

QUESTION 6

God first announced His intention to fully exterminate the Amalekites during the time of which of the following men?

    A. Noah

    B. Moses

    C. Joshua

    D. Saul

QUESTION 7

The Jews plundered their enemies when they avenged themselves at the time of Esther. *True or False?*

QUESTION 8

Who was hung on the gallows Haman built?

    A. Haman

    B. Mordecai

    C. Vashti

    D. No one

QUESTION 9

Which of the following best reflects the message of Ezra 7:10?

    A. Purify your hands, you sinners

    B. Read God's Word, apply it to your life, and teach it to others

    C. If God doesn't deliver His people through you, He will use someone else

    D. Each of you must divorce his foreign wife

QUESTION 10

Even Ezra participated in the sin of intermarriage with foreign wives. *True or False?*

Lesson 11 Answers to Questions

QUESTION 1: Providence [The extermination of the Jewish nation plotted by Haman falls on his own head by God's providence through Mordecai and Esther, to encourage postexilic Israel that God remains committed to the Abrahamic covenant.]

QUESTION 2: False [The events of Esther chronicle ten years of the fifty-eight-year gap between Ezra 6 (516 BC) and Ezra 7 (458 BC). The story takes place from 483 to 473 BC, between the time of the first return under Zerubbabel (538 BC) and the second under Ezra (458 BC).]

QUESTION 3

    D. Fasting is mentioned [Neither God's name nor prayer are mentioned, but His hand is very evident. This book is not quoted in the New Testament. It also is a unique literary type (almost a drama).]

QUESTION 4: *Your answer should be similar to the following:*

Esther records God's providential care of His chosen people as evidence of His commitment to the Abrahamic covenant.

QUESTION 5: True [When the king asked for counsel on how to respond to the queen's refusal, his advisers said to deal with it as an issue that would determine how all wives would respond to their husbands' requests (Est 1:16-20).]

QUESTION 6

    A. That every man should rule his family

QUESTION 7

Person	Description
Vashti	The queen of Persia at the beginning of the story
Xerxes	The reigning king of Persia
Esther	A Jewess who became queen
Mordecai	The Jewish protector of Esther
Hegai	The king's eunuch, the appointed overseer of the women
Haman	An Agagite promoted above the king's other officials

QUESTION 8: *Your answer*

QUESTION 9: *Your answer should be similar to the following:*

"Don't imagine that because you are part of the king's household you will be the one Jew who will escape. If you keep quiet at this time, liberation and protection for the Jews will appear from another source, while you and your father's household perish. It may very well be that you have achieved royal status for such a time as this!"

QUESTION 10

Esther	Daniel
The contest of their attributes (Est 2:2)	Daniel 1:3-4
The king's official or eunuch assigned to them (Est 2:8-9)	Daniel 1:3, 9
Most favored by the king (Est 2:17)	Daniel 1:19
Esther and Mordecai promoted (Est 2:17; 10:1-3)	Daniel 2:46-49; 5:29
Not bowing and paying homage (Est 3:2)	Daniel 3:8-12

QUESTION 11

Esther	Daniel
Jews preserved from death (Est 7)	Daniel 3:24-27
Persecution from high government officials (Est 3:1)	Daniel 6:5
King celebrating with a banquet (Est 3:15)	Daniel 5:1
King issues an unchangeable edict (Est 8:1-13)	Daniel 6:13
The conspiracy is turned against the persecutors (Est 9:5)	Daniel 6:25

QUESTION 12: Persia [As Daniel shows God's sovereignty over the Jews in Babylon, so Esther shows that God's sovereign presence was also with the Jews in Persia. He was with them and preserved them, even though they had not returned to the land as the obedient remnant had, as detailed by Ezra and Nehemiah and the post-exilic prophets.]

QUESTION 13: *Your answer*

QUESTION 14

    B. Moses [Ever since the exodus from Egypt, God had intended to wipe out the remembrance of Amalek from under heaven (Ex 17:14).]

QUESTION 15: False [The Jews in Esther's time struck all their enemies with the sword and did as they pleased with them (Est 9:5.) However, unlike both the exodus from Egypt and Israel's more recent return from Babylon, when they took spoils from those who opposed them, the Jews did not confiscate their enemies' property in Persia (Est 9:10). They did not act like disobedient Saul, who took plunder from the Amalekites instead of destroying it as God commanded (1 Sam 15:13-19).]

QUESTION 16

    B. Haman [Haman died on the gallows he had prepared for Mordecai, as evidence that God protects those who fear Him and punishes those who oppose Him and His people (Est 7).]

QUESTION 17

    C. Purim [To commemorate this deliverance Mordecai and Esther authorized an annual celebration of the Jews' victory over their enemies in the Feast of Purim—plural for "pur," the lot that was cast by Haman (Est 9:17-32). This celebration would help Israel remember God's gracious workings on its behalf.]

QUESTION 18: *Your answer should be similar to the following:*
"Now Ezra had given himself to the study of the law of the Lord, to its observance, and to teaching its statutes and judgments in Israel."

QUESTION 19

    B. Levites

    C. Priests

    D. Common people

[The list of men required to divorce pagan foreign wives includes priests, Levites, and common people; this shows the great extent to which this sin had pervaded the holy nation and shows the need for such a drastic action as divorce (Ezra 10:18-44).]

QUESTION 20

Outline of Esther				
				Instructions
Esther Exalted	Haman Plots	Mordecai over Haman	Israel over Enemies	Mordecai over Persia
Esther 1:1–2:18	Esther 2:19	Esther 5:1–8:2	Esther 8:3–9:32	Esther 10

QUESTION 21

Outline of Ezra

Instructions

Qualifications and Provisions	Returnees and Protection	Inter-marriage and Lament	Divorces Carried Out
Ezra 7	Ezra 8	Ezra 9	Ezra 10

QUESTION 22: *Your answer*

Lesson 11 Self Check Answers

QUESTION 1: Providence

QUESTION 2
    D. God's providence is evident

QUESTION 3: True

QUESTION 4
    C. The king's eunuch appointed overseer of the women

QUESTION 5
    B. A king changing his decree to save the Jews

QUESTION 6
    B. Moses

QUESTION 7: False

QUESTION 8
    A. Haman

QUESTION 9
    B. Read God's Word, apply it to your life, and teach it to others

QUESTION 10: False

Lesson 12: Nehemiah and Malachi

Lesson Introduction

Although the post-exilic books we have studied so far have related to restoring the temple and people, thirteen years after the revival under Ezra, problems still persisted. Nehemiah had to restore the walls of Jerusalem, and Malachi needed to address hypocrisy within the community.

Proverbs 25:28 says, "Like a city that is broken down and without a wall, so is a person who cannot control his temper." Jerusalem had been without walls since 586 BC when Babylon destroyed them. Until Nehemiah rebuilt the walls, it was a city without defense and an easy target for an invading army.

The apostle John has the final word in the New Testament, where he records Jesus saying,

> "Yes, I am coming soon!" Amen! Come, Lord Jesus! The grace of the Lord Jesus be with all. (Rev 22:20-21)

Malachi is in the privileged position of having the final word in the Old Testament, and his last words are a similar message of looking forward to the next advent of the Messiah—but with a definite Old Testament flavor. In Malachi 4:5-6 God says,

> Look, I will send you Elijah the prophet before the great and terrible day of the Lord comes. He will encourage fathers and their children to return to me, so that I will not come and strike the earth with judgment.

And this would be God's final Word to His people until the birth of the Messiah 420 years later.

Jerusalem of the Returning Exiles

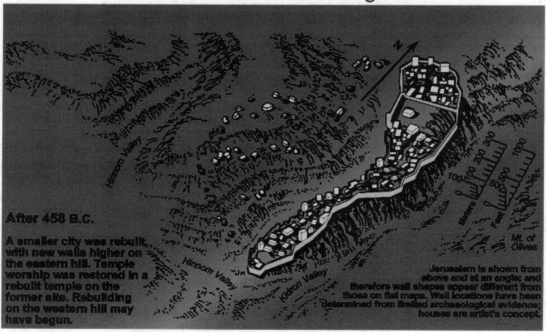

After 458 B.C.

A smaller city was rebuilt, with new walls higher on the eastern hill. Temple worship was restored in a rebuilt temple on the former site. Rebuilding on the western hill may have begun.

Jerusalem is shown from above and at an angle; and therefore wall shapes appear different from those on flat maps. Wall locations have been determined from limited archaeological evidence; houses are artist's concept.

Lesson Outline

> Topic 1: Introduction to Nehemiah
>
> Topic 2: Return
>
> Topic 3: Rebuilding
>
> Topic 4: Renewal
>
> Topic 5: Reforms
>
> Topic 6: Introduction to Malachi
>
> Topic 7: Rebuke of Seven Sins
>
> Topic 8: Blessing by Heeding Elijah
>
> Topic 9: Knowing, Being, Doing

Lesson Objectives

By the end of this lesson you will be able to do the following:

- Examine the distinctions and timelines of Nehemiah and Malachi

- Discuss the books' purpose to encourage the returned exiles to rebuild Jerusalem's walls and cleanse themselves spiritually

- Explore the spiritual struggle in Nehemiah, how he accomplished his purpose and how this applies to us

- Evaluate the seven questions Israel asked God in Malachi 1–3

- Discuss God's predictions of judgment and blessing through the future Messiah

Topic 1: Introduction to Nehemiah

Nehemiah Restoring the Walls and People									
445-433 BC									
Walls					People				
Chapters 1–7					Chapters 8–13				
Construction					Instruction				
Political					Spiritual				
Return 1–2		Rebuilding 3–7			Renewal 8–10			Reforms 11–13	
Persia Prayer 1	Jerusalem Inspection 2	Delegation 3	Opposed/ Finished 4–6	Organized 7	Conviction 8	Con- fession 9	Covenant 10	Resettlement & Dedication 11	Sabbath & Inter- marriage Reforms 12–13

The book of Nehemiah continues the account of Ezra and, as they originally formed a single work, has the same theme: the record of the restoration of God's people in the land. This theme would encourage the remnant toward covenant obedience, especially in true temple worship. Ezra indicates how the returns of

Zerubbabel and Ezra contributed to the establishment of the new covenant community. Nehemiah completes the restoration, with the third and final return under Nehemiah to rebuild the walls (Neh 1–7), followed by the restoration of the people (Neh 8–13). The book also includes some very insightful teaching on leadership principles (Neh 1–7), spiritual principles (Neh 8–10), and moral and social principles (Neh 11–13; see Wilkinson, 126).

Zerubbabel

(Easton's Bible Dictionary)

The seed of Babylon, the son of Salathiel or Shealtiel (Hag 1:1; Zorobabel, Mt 1:12); called also the son of Pedaiah (1 Chr 3:17-19), i.e., according to a frequent usage of the word "son;" the grandson or the nephew of Salathiel. He is also known by the Persian name of Sheshbazzar (Ezra 1:8, 11). In the first year of Cyrus, king of Persia, he led the first band of Jews, numbering 42,360 (Ezra 2:64), exclusive of a large number of servants, who returned from captivity at the close of the seventy years. In the second year after the Return, he erected an altar and laid the foundation of the temple on the ruins of that which had been destroyed by Nebuchadnezzar (Ezra 3:8-13; 4–6). All through the work he occupied a prominent place, inasmuch as he was a descendant of the royal line of David.

- **Key Word:** Walls
- **Key Verse:** "So the wall was completed on the twenty-fifth day of Elul, in just fifty-two days. When all our enemies heard and all the nations who were around us saw this, they were greatly disheartened. They knew that this work had been accomplished with the help of our God" (Neh 6:15-16).
- **Summary Statement:** The restoration of the walls of Jerusalem and the people in the land under Nehemiah records God's faithfulness to His promise of restoration, to encourage the remnant in covenant obedience rooted in temple worship at Jerusalem.
- **Application:** Completing God's projects should lead us to further obedience.

Assignment

- Please read Nehemiah 1.
- Please read "Introduction to Nehemiah."

Introduction to Nehemiah

Title

Ezra and Nehemiah originally formed a single book, according to the ancient sources Josephus (*Against Apion* 1.8), Jerome (*Preface to the Commentary on Galatians*), and the Talmud (Baba Bathra 15a). The Hebrew Bible also has the two books together under the title Ezra Nehemiah. However, the repetition of Ezra 2 in Nehemiah 7 may indicate that the two were originally separate works. Ezra means "help, succor, assistance," and Nehemiah means "Yahweh comforts." Significantly, Ezra's ministry enabled the Jews to return to the land and re-consecrate themselves, while Nehemiah functioned as God's comfort through building Jerusalem's protective wall.

Authorship

External Evidence: No significant external evidence about Nehemiah's authorship is known.

Internal Evidence: The inspired title of the book reads, "The Words of Nehemiah, Son of Hacaliah" (Neh 1:1), and much of the content appears in the first person (Neh 1:1–7:5; 12:27-43; 13:2-31). This makes it clear that Nehemiah recorded this book. Some believe the third-person sections (Neh 7:6–12:26; 12:44–13:2) were written by Ezra, since Nehemiah was in Babylon during these events (Neh 13:6). Nehemiah 7:5-73 is nearly identical to Ezra 2:1-70, but both lists probably were derived from another record of the same period (Wilkinson, 124).

Nothing is known of Nehemiah's childhood, youth, or family background since the account opens with him as an adult serving King Artaxerxes of Persia. The text does reveal that his father's name was Hacaliah (Neh 1:1) and he had a brother named Hanani (Neh 1:2). This is of little help, as neither these men nor Nehemiah are mentioned elsewhere in Scripture. The Nehemiah mentioned in Ezra 2:2 and Nehemiah 7:7 (in 538 BC) must have been another man of the same name, since he came to Judah 90 years before this Nehemiah, who arrived in 445 BC. What is known of this Nehemiah is his prayerfulness, diligence, intellectual capabilities, emotional maturity, spiritual status, and wisdom, evidenced by the high position he held as cupbearer to the king of Persia.

Circumstances

Date: Nehemiah left Persia in the twentieth year of Artaxerxes (Neh 2:1; 445 BC) and returned in the king's thirty-second year (Neh 13:6; 433 BC). "Some time later" he came again to Jerusalem (Neh 13:6). Perhaps it was 425 BC (Wilkinson, 125) or even 420. This chronology places the writing after 425 BC, perhaps even as late as 400 BC (LaSor, 647). Arguments for dates later than 400 BC, based on stylistic affinities to later Aramaic, are unconvincing, since the Aramaic of Ezra is clearly earlier than that at second century Qumran (LaSor, 648). Dating the writing at approximately 425 BC makes Nehemiah a contemporary of Malachi, which is supported by their common descriptions of post-exilic Judaism.

Recipients: Those who first read Nehemiah comprised Jews who had returned from Persia with Ezra three or four decades before, as well as the grandchildren and great-grandchildren of those who had returned with Zerubbabel about 125 years earlier.

Characteristics

Although Esther follows Nehemiah in English Bibles, the events of Nehemiah actually come later chronologically. Thus, the book concludes the account of the historical books of the English Old Testament. (Nehemiah's book is followed by Chronicles in the Hebrew Bible.)

Perhaps no other book of Scripture provides a better depiction of the balance between dependence on God and self-discipline, as well as between prayer and planning. Nehemiah's prayers are generally short but fervent (see Neh 1:5-11; 2:1-4, 19-20; 4:1-6, 7-10, 11-14; 6:9, 14).

One difficulty in reconciling Nehemiah with Ezra concerns the walls themselves. At the beginning of the account, Nehemiah seems surprised to learn that the walls were broken down. Why would this be news to him in 445 BC, since the Babylonians had destroyed them much earlier, in 586 BC (2 Kgs 25:10)? Perhaps Ezra had begun to rebuild the walls during the reign of Artaxerxes, but had been stopped (Ezra 4:12, 21-23). Nehemiah had probably thought the project was completed (Walvoord, 1:674).

Nehemiah is the only Old Testament book written mostly in the first person (see Authorship above).

QUESTION 1

The key word for Nehemiah is _____.

QUESTION 2

Which of the following are characteristics of the book of Nehemiah? *(Select all that apply.)*

A. Mostly a first-person account

B. Long prayers

C. Fervent prayer

D. Dependence on God

E. Human discipline

Topic 1 Key Points

- The restoration of the walls of Jerusalem and the people in the land under Nehemiah records God's faithfulness to His promise of restoration.

- Nehemiah wrote in the first person, prayed briefly but fervently, and depended on God but served Him with self-discipline.

Topic 2: Return (Neh 1–2)

This story continues from Ezra, about eleven years after Ezra's spiritual reforms among the remnant in Jerusalem. Whereas Ezra helped lead the spiritual establishment of the new community, Nehemiah gave it physical, geographical, and political stability (LaSor, 655). Before Nehemiah came on the scene in 445 BC, the restored remnant had been back in Judea more than ninety years (since 538 BC), the temple had been rebuilt (516 BC), and Ezra's reforms had been instituted (458 BC). However, Nehemiah found the walls and gates still in ruins and took it on himself to see that the city was not left unprotected. Nehemiah's faith in God saw Him accomplish in fifty-two days what had not been done in the ninety-three years since the return under Zerubbabel. Afterwards, he wrote this account of how the Lord used him to rebuild the walls, to encourage the people with God's obvious hand in reestablishing His people in their homeland. This account undoubtedly helped the original readers see that obedient faith can accomplish God's will despite what appears impossible.

Assignment

- Please read Nehemiah 2.
- Please read "Return."

Return

Summary Statement for the Book

The restoration of the walls of Jerusalem and the people in the land under Nehemiah records God's faithfulness to His promise of restoration, to encourage the remnant in covenant obedience rooted in temple worship at Jerusalem.

God enabled Nehemiah in both Persia and Jerusalem to prepare for reconstructing the wall, by addressing spiritual, economic, planning, enlistment, and defensive procedures (Neh 1–2). Once the wall was rebuilt, Jerusalem would be repopulated and would once again be a center for worship at the temple.

But while he was in Persia, Nehemiah learned of the broken wall in Jerusalem. He interceded with God and Artaxerxes on behalf of his people, fulfilling the prophecy of Daniel 9:25 and starting the seventy sevens timeline in 444 BC (Neh 1:1–2:8). This set in motion the spiritual and economic preparation needed to reconstruct the wall. After arriving in Jerusalem, Nehemiah prepared to reconstruct the wall by inspecting the project, exhorting the people, and rebuffing his opponents (Neh 2:9-20).

QUESTION 3

Please match the dates with the corresponding event it marks.

Date	Event
538 BC	Nehemiah arrives in Jerusalem
516 BC	Most likely date for writing of Nehemiah
458 BC	The restored remnant returns to Judah under Zerubbabel.
445 BC	The temple rebuilding is completed.
425 BC	Ezra's reforms are instituted

QUESTION 4

Artaxerxes' command to rebuild Jerusalem in 445 BC fulfills the prediction in Daniel 9:25. *True or False?*

Topic 2 Key Points

- Ezra's reforms were instituted in 458 BC and Nehemiah arrived in Jerusalem in 445 BC.
- Artaxerxes' command to rebuild Jerusalem in 444 BC fulfills the prediction in Daniel 9:25 and provides the spiritual and economic preparation needed to reconstruct the wall.

Topic 3: Rebuilding (Neh 3–7)

Historical background: About 1,500 years earlier, God had promised Abraham that He would make his descendants into a great nation possessing the entire land from the River of Egypt to the Euphrates River (Gen 12:1-3; 15:18). Hundreds of years later, God further promised, through Isaiah and many other prophets, that a Davidic king called the Messiah would rule Israel in this geographic domain. However, the nation rebelled against the Lord and went into exile as the Law had warned (Deut 28). The key question looming in the minds of the exiled Jews was whether God would still fulfill His promise of a new nation in Palestine under the Messiah as ruler. Was He still sovereign even though His people were in such distress?

Assignment

- Please read Nehemiah 3–7.
- Please read "Rebuilding."

Rebuilding

Nehemiah reconstructed the wall so that former exiles would feel safe to repopulate Jerusalem. He accomplished this project in an amazing fifty-two days.

He wisely delegated each section of the rebuilding project to workers who would construct the portion of the wall nearest their homes, giving them incentive to do quality work (Neh 3).

As they worked, Nehemiah effectively handled both internal and external opposition by appealing to the Lord as well as standing guard against the enemies (Neh 4:1–6:14).

External opposition to the building came from Sanballat and Tobiah, who tried to stop the work on the wall by ridiculing the builders, threatening to attack, and being constantly discouraging (Neh 4).

Internal opposition to the building came from Jews who would seize fellow Jews' property and exact a 12 percent interest rate on debts, in contrast to Nehemiah's selfless service as governor (Neh 5). Since the people had been working on the wall for only a few weeks, "the hundredth part of the money, grain, new wine and oil" (Neh 5:11) likely refers to interest charged on a monthly basis, yielding an actual interest rate of 12 percent annually. Charging any interest of fellow Israelites was a clear violation of the Law (Ex 22:25; Lev 25:35-37; Deut 23:19-20), even though this law was rarely enforced. Perhaps the actual interest even exceeded 12 percent, since commodities were included as well.

External opposition to the building came again from Sanballat, Tobiah, Geshem the Arab, and other enemies who sought to stop the work through compromise, blackmail, treachery, and intimidation by false prophets (Neh 6:1-14).

Despite opposition from Tobiah's relatives, Nehemiah and the people finished the wall in an amazing fifty-two days. This displayed to all of Israel's enemies the fact that God alone must have enabled the small remnant to complete such a task (Neh 6:15-19).

Nehemiah organized Jerusalem by posting guards at the gates and using the list of exiles who returned a century earlier to encourage people to feel safe as they repopulated the large but almost uninhabited city with proven Jews (Neh 7).

QUESTION 5

The key question looming in the minds of the exiled Jews was whether God would still fulfill His promise of a new nation in Palestine ruled by the Messiah. *True or False?*

QUESTION 6

Which of the following did Nehemiah do to encourage the workers to quality work while rebuilding the walls?

    A. He allowed them to bypass required fasts while working on the wall.

    B. He gave them no-interest loans.

    C. He had the priest offer continual prayer during the rebuilding.

    D. He had them construct the portion of the wall closest to their homes.

QUESTION 7

Please match the reference with the corresponding plan.

Reference	Plan
Nehemiah 6:1-4	Sanballat sends a letter saying the Jews are attempting to revolt, to scare them into stopping work.
Nehemiah 6:5-9	Shemaiah tells Nehemiah to hide in the temple to save his life, trying to scare Nehemiah.
Nehemiah 6:10-14	Four times Sanballat and Geshem attempt to meet with Nehemiah to bring the work to a halt.
Nehemiah 6:15-16	The work on the walls is completed in just fifty-two days with God's blessing; this discourages the enemies.
Nehemiah 6:17-19	The aristocrats in Judah support Tobiah, to whom they are related by marriage, in an attempt to scare Nehemiah.

QUESTION 8

In Nehemiah 6, Nehemiah faced many plots to slow down his work for the Lord. Have you experienced opposition intended to slow down or halt your work for the Lord? Please open your Life Notebook. Identify those plots and explain how you can apply the teachings in Nehemiah to these situations.

Topic 3 Key Points

- The key question looming in the minds of the exiled Jews was whether God would still fulfill His promise of a new nation in Palestine, ruled by the Messiah, despite the current distress.

- Political enemies of Nehemiah tried several times to derail the work on the walls through intimidation.

- These same tactics of intimidation are used by the enemies of God's people today to distract us from our work for the Lord.

Topic 4: Renewal (Neh 8–10)

Nehemiah's Responses to Problems	
(Gene Getz, Bible Knowledge Commentary 1:681)	
Problem	**Response**
Walls broken and gates burned	Grief, prayer, motivating people to rebuild (Neh 1:4, 2:17-18)
False accusation of the workers (Neh 2:19)	Confidence that God would grant success (Neh 2:20)
Ridicule of the workers (Neh 4:1-3)	Prayer (Neh 4:4-5) and action (greater diligence, Neh 4:6)
Threat to attack the workers (Neh 4:7-8)	Prayer and action (posting a guard in Neh 4:9)
Physical exhaustion and threat of murder (Neh 4:10-20)	Positioning the people by families and arming them, encouraging them
Economic crisis; greed (Neh 5:1-11)	Anger, reflection, rebuke, and action (having the people return debtors' interest)
Plot to assassinate or harm Nehemiah (Neh 6:1-3)	Refusal to cooperate (Neh 6:3)
Slander against Nehemiah (Neh 6:5-7)	Denial and prayer (Neh 6:8-9)
Tobiah moved into a temple storeroom (Neh 13:4-8)	Tobiah's furniture tossed out
Neglect of temple tithes and offerings (Neh 13:10-14)	Rebuke, stationing the Levites at their posts, and prayer
Violation of the Sabbath (Neh 13:15-22)	Rebuke, posting of guards, and prayer
Mixed marriages (Neh 13:23-29)	Rebuke, removal of a guilty priest, and prayer

Historical background:

No doubt people wondered how a Messiah could be offered to the nation if Israel was still in exile. For example, one of the messianic prophecies stated that He would be born in Bethlehem (see Mic 5:2, written nearly two hundred years earlier). Surely the nation would have to return to its homeland at some point for the Messiah to offer the kingdom there—an offer which indeed did occur under Christ (Mt 10:7) but was rejected. Furthermore, Daniel had recorded only a few years earlier Artaxerxes' command to rebuild Jerusalem under Nehemiah (444 BC) would begin "seventy sevens" (490) of prophetic years in the nation's history (Dan 9:25). The sixty-ninth prophetic year (483rd year) would culminate in the death of Messiah in AD 33 (Dan 9:26).

The postexilic era testifies to the gracious hand of a sovereign God who had not forgotten His promises, for under Zerubbabel and Ezra a small remnant had returned from Babylon, rebuilt the temple and begun reforms. The building under Nehemiah completes this record with a direct fulfillment of Daniel 9:25. Thus, the account of Ezra-Nehemiah shows that God is indeed the God over all gods (Ezra 1:2)—a covenant-keeping God. Likewise, His people need to keep the covenant as well (*Easton's Bible Commentary*, 4:590).

Assignment

- Please read Nehemiah 8–10.
- Please read "Renewal."

Renewal

The restoration of the people, through Nehemiah's leading Israel to renew and obey the covenant, encourages the remnant in covenant obedience and commitment to the temple (Neh 8–13).

The covenant was renewed and put into writing after the people responded to the Word of God in two days of reading and exposition. This encouraged the remnant in covenant obedience (Neh 8–10).

Conviction: Ezra's reading of the Pentateuch, along with the Levites' exposition, urged the nation to celebrate the Feast of Tabernacles and began a revival based on the Word of God (Neh 8).

Confession: Everyone gathered again twenty-four days later to fast, listen to the Law of Moses, worship, confess sin, and renew themselves to obey a written covenant (Neh 9).

Covenant: Nehemiah provided a list of the priests, Levites, and leaders who publicly agreed to follow the covenant (Neh 10:1-27). He also recorded the stipulations of the covenant: submission to the Word, separation by avoiding intermarriage, observance of the Sabbath, and responsible stewardship. His writing served as a written record of the people's agreement (Neh 10:28-39).

QUESTION 9

Which feast was the nation convicted to observe after Ezra's reading of the Pentateuch (Neh 8)?

    A. Passover

    B. Unleavened Bread

    C. Tabernacles

    D. First Fruits

QUESTION 10

Please briefly describe the spiritual steps the people took in Nehemiah 9, when they gathered again twenty-four days after Ezra's reading of the Pentateuch in Nehemiah 8.

Topic 4 Key Points

- Ezra's reading of the Pentateuch, with the Levites' exposition, urges the nation to celebrate the Feast of Tabernacles and begins a revival based on the Word of God (Neh 8).

- In Nehemiah 9, the people fasted, listened to the Law, worshipped, confessed their sin and renewed themselves to obey a written covenant in response to Ezra's reading in Nehemiah 8.

Topic 5: Reforms (Neh 11–13)

Even though the people were now restored to the land and once again practicing the temple rituals, they were still falling short of God's standards. In these chapters, Nehemiah points them in the right direction. If Nehemiah's level of patience reflects God's, and it probably does, it shows His patience is running short with His people. In some ways, Nehemiah parallels what the Apostle Paul does in Romans 1:18-3:20; he convicts his audience of sin. Nehemiah takes stern measures to get the people to realize they fall short of God's standards. But unlike Paul, who is on the other side of the timeline of the Messiah's first advent, Nehemiah can offer these sinners only the provisions of the old covenant. So, he moves them to obey the old covenant, which includes the Law of Moses and the temple ritual. But, even if they follow the Law and temple rituals faithfully, their hearts could still be far from God!

It will be left to Malachi to offer the blessings that will come through the message of the "Elijah" who comes before the day of the Lord (Mal 4).

Assignment

- Please read Nehemiah 11–13.
- Please read "Reforms."

Nehemiah's Leadership

While leadership is not the main purpose of the book, neverless, the man Nehemiah exemplifies many principles for good leadership. Some of these include the following:

1. He established a reasonable and attainable goal.
2. He had a sense of mission.
3. He was willing to get involved.
4. He rearranged his priorities in order to accomplish his goal.
5. He patiently waited for God's timing.
6. He showed respect to his superior.
7. He prayed at crucial times.
8. He made his request with tact and graciousness.
9. He was well prepared and thought of his needs in advance.
10. He went through proper channels.
11. He took time (three times) to rest, pray, and plan.
12. He investigated the situation firsthand.
13. He informed others only after he knew the size of the problem.
14. He identified himself as one with the people.
15. He set before them a reasonable and attainable goal.
16. He assured them God was in the project.
17. He displayed self-confidence in facing obstacles.
18. He displayed God's confidence in facing obstacles.
19. He did not argue with opponents.
20. He was not discouraged by opposition.
21. He courageously used the authority of his position.

Reforms

The people agreed to a plan for 10 percent of the nation (leaders, draftees, volunteers, priests, and Levites) to resettle in Jerusalem to protect the city and temple from attack, thus demonstrating their commitment to the house of the Lord (Neh 11:1–12:26).

The Jerusalem wall was dedicated, with participation by Levites, two choirs, and men who collected contributions for the temple service. This again demonstrated the people's commitment to the house of the Lord (Neh 12:27-47).

Nehemiah's final reforms (432 BC) forbade foreigners from entering the temple, supplied support for temple workers who had returned to farming, corrected Sabbath abuses, and prohibited future mixed marriages; these reforms forced Israel to obey the covenant stipulations (Neh 13).

QUESTION 11

What percentage of the nation resettles in Jerusalem to help protect the city from attack (Neh 11:1–12:26)?

    A. 5 percent

    B. 10 percent

    C. 15 percent

    D. 20 percent

QUESTION 12

Which of the following were included in Nehemiah's final reforms in Nehemiah 13? *(Select all that apply.)*

    A. Foreigners would now be allowed in the temple

    B. Support for temple workers forced to take up farming

    C. Correction of Sabbath abuses

    D. Israelites would now be allowed to marry foreigners

Topic 5 Key Points

- The people obey a plan for 10 percent of the nation (leaders, draftees, volunteers, priests, and Levites) to resettle Jerusalem to protect the city and temple from attack (Neh 11:1–12:26).

- Nehemiah took four steps to cleanse the nation in his final reforms in Nehemiah 13: He forbade foreigners in the temple; he directed support for temple workers forced to take up farming; he corrected abuses of the Sabbath; and he prohibited marriages with foreigners.

Topic 6: Introduction to Malachi

Malachi **Warning of Judgment for Hypocrisy**					
Jerusalem in 425 BC					
Rebuke of Seven Sins			Blessing by Heeding Elijah		
Chapter 1–3			Chapter 4		
Present			Future		
Pollution of the Nation			Promise to the Nation		
1:1-3:18	Israel's 7 Questions	God's 7 Responses	Day of Judgment	Obey Law	Heed Elijah
1:1-5	How have you loved us?	Election	4:1-3	4:4	4:5-6
1:6-2:9	How have we despised your name?	Unacceptable Sacrifices			
2:10-16	Why do you despise our offerings?	Divorce			
2:17-3:7	Why aren't you just?	The Messiah will judge			
3:7-8	How can we repent?	Stop robbing Me			
3:8-12	How have we robbed you?	Withholding tithes			
3:13-18	How have we blasphemed you?	Materialistic motives			

Given the deplorable conditions in post-exilic Israel, the average Jew probably doubted whether God would indeed fulfill His covenant promise of a new, messianic kingdom. Malachi prophesies that God will indeed bring in this time of future blessing, but it must be preceded by a repentant nation. The author accomplishes this by introducing the book as God's "burden" (Mal 1:1 NASB; translated as "oracle" in the NIV), thus indicating that God would rebuke them. First, however, God opens with a statement of His love for Israel (Mal 1:2), beginning an interchange between the nation and Himself. Israel responds with seven questions posed to the Lord, and God answers in seven responses backed by His evidence that Israel has sinned (Mal 1:2–3:18). The final section (Mal 4) shows that while the day of the Lord is coming for punishment, those who revere God and heed the ministry of an "Elijah" will find this "day" a time of blessing (Malachi 4:2-3). Therefore, Malachi's purpose is to rebuke Israel's sin, exhorting the people to leave their sinful lifestyle in exchange for blessing in the kingdom.

- **Key Word:** Hypocrites

- **Key Verse:** "You have wearied the Lord with your words. But you say, 'How have we wearied Him?' Because you say, 'Everyone who does evil is good in the Lord's opinion, and He delights in them,' or 'Where is the God of justice?' I am about to send my messenger, who will clear the way before me. Indeed, the Lord you are seeking will suddenly come to His temple, and the messenger of the covenant whom you long for, is certainly coming,' says the Lord" (Mal 2:17-3:1).

- **Summary Statement:** The Lord rebukes His backslidden people for their hypocrisy — answering their defensive questions, in order to encourage them to leave their sinful lifestyle and return to Him in preparation for the coming day of judgment and blessing.

- **Application:** Fear God by repenting of superficial religion so you won't need to be disciplined. Are you prepared for Christ's imminent return? Do you pray for it?

Assignment

- Please read Malachi 1.
- Please read "Introduction to Malachi."

Introduction to Malachi

Title

The name Malachi literally means "my messenger."

Authorship

External Evidence: No significant external evidence about Malachi's authorship is known.

Internal Evidence: The only mention of the name Malachi is in the first verse of the prophecy (Mal 1:1), and nothing is known of his family background (not even his father's name), although a Jewish tradition says that he was a member of the Great Synagogue, a group of Jewish leaders who began to meet in Persia during the time of the exile (Wilkinson, 295). However, most scholars do not believe that Malachi is the historical name of an author (LaSor, 501). The Targum, an Aramaic translation of the Bible, adds a phrase to make the statement in Malachi 1:1 read: "by the hand of my messenger whose name is called Ezra the scribe" (see Mal 3:1), but scholarship in general does not identify Malachi with Ezra. Some suppose that "my messenger" in Malachi 3:1 is an anonymous designation, so the same ought to be true of Malachi 1:1. The Septuagint complicates the matter further with the translation "his messenger."

However, no legitimate reason exists for considering this author the "anonymous prophet." All of the other prophetic writings that state the same or similar formula "the word of the LORD…through…" give proper names, and no legitimate reason exists to interpret otherwise for Malachi.

Circumstances

Date: Scholarly consensus dates the book at approximately 450 BC, supported by the first two points below. However, a later date of 433-420 BC may have merit as well (point #3).

1. The mention of the Persian term for governor, *pechah* (Mal 1:8; see Neh 5:14; Hag 1:1, 14; 2:21), indicates that the book was likely written during the Persian domination of Israel (539-333 BC).

2. Sacrifices are offered in the temple (Mal 1:7-10; 3:8), which was rebuilt in 516 BC. It appears that the temple had been in operation long enough for the people to grow complacent (Mal 2:13).

3. The conditions in Israel may point to a date between 433 and 420 BC (Wilkinson, 295; see Walvoord, 1:1573). The situation surrounding the book is very similar to the one Ezra (458 BC) and Nehemiah (444 BC) encountered when they returned to the land: intermarriage with Gentiles (Mal 2:10-11; see Ezra 9:1-2; Neh 13:1-3, 23-28), neglect of tithes and offerings for the Levites (Mal 3:7-12; Neh 13:10-13), corrupt priests (Mal 1:6–2:9; Neh 13:1-9), and oppression of the poor (Mal 3:5; see Neh 5:4-5).

Nehemiah returned to Persia in 433 BC, but he came back to Palestine about 420 BC and dealt with the sins described in Malachi (Neh 13). It could be that Malachi prophetically addressed these vices in this interim, just before Nehemiah returned and set the people right.

Recipients: Those addressed by Malachi are the second to fourth generations of the Jews who returned from Babylon about 110 years earlier as well as those who returned later under Ezra and Nehemiah.

Characteristics

Malachi marks the end of Old Testament prophecy, closing the divine utterances until the time of John the Baptist, four hundred years later.

Malachi is one of only two books in Scripture that employ a question-and-answer style in their entirety (the other book is Habakkuk).

Malachi and Isaiah are the only prophets who end their books with a judgment section (Isa 66:22-24).

QUESTION 13

The key word for Malachi is _____.

QUESTION 14

Malachi may have been written about 420 BC because he addressed some of the same sin issues that Nehemiah did. *True or False?*

QUESTION 15

Please match the sin and verse from Nehemiah with the corresponding verse from Malachi that teaches about that same sin.

Nehemiah	Malachi
Intermarriage with Gentiles in Nehemiah 13:1-3, 23-28	Malachi 2:10-11
Neglect of tithes and offerings in Nehemiah 13:10-13	Malachi 3:5
Corrupt priests in Nehemiah 13:1-9	Malachi 3:7-12
Oppression of the poor in Nehemiah 5:4-5	Malachi 1:6–2:9

QUESTION 16

Which of the following are characteristic of Malachi? *(Select all that apply.)*

  A. He speaks the last words of the Old Testament prophets.

  B. He employs a question-and-answer style throughout his entire book.

  C. He preaches a baptism of repentance.

  D. He ends his book by promising the Messiah's future blessing.

Topic 6 Key Points

- The Lord rebukes His backslidden people for their hypocrisy by answering their defensive questions, in order to encourage them to leave their sinful lifestyle and return to Him.

- Malachi may have been written about 420 BC because he addressed some of the same sin issues that Nehemiah did.

- Malachi and Nehemiah both dealt with four sin issues:

  1. Intermarriage with Gentiles (Neh 13:1-3, 23-28; Mal 2:10-11)

  2. Neglect of tithes and offerings (Neh 13:10-13; Mal 3:7-12)

  3. Corrupt priests (Neh 13:1-9; Mal 1:6–2:9)

  4. Oppression of the poor (Neh 5:4-5; Mal 3:5)

- Malachi is rare among prophetic books because it ends in judgment, not blessing (Mal 4:4-6).

Topic 7: Rebuke of Seven Sins (Mal 1–3)

FROM MALACHI TO CHRIST

Malachi c. 430 B.C.

THE PERSIAN PERIOD
450-330 B.C.

For about 200 years after Nehemiah's time the Persians controlled Judah, but the Jews were allowed to carry on their religious observances and were not interfered with. During this time Judah was ruled by high priests who were responsible to the Jewish government.

410	
400B.C.	
390	
380	
370	
360	
350	
340	

Rule of Alexander the Great—

THE HELLENISTIC PERIOD
330-166 B.C.

In 333 B.C. the Persian armies stationed in Macedonia were defeated by Alexander the Great. He was convinced that Greek culture was the one force that could unify the world. Alexander permitted the Jews to observe their laws and even granted them exemption from tribute or tax during their sabbath years. When he built Alexandria in Egypt, he encouraged Jews to live there and gave them some of the same privileges he gave his Greek subjects. The Greek conquest prepared the way for the translation of the OT into Greek (Septuagint version) c.250 B.C.

THE HASMONEAN PERIOD
166-63 B.C.

When this historical period began, the Jews were being greatly oppressed. The Ptolemies had been tolerant of the Jews and their religious practices, but the Seleucid rulers were determined to force Hellenism on the. Copies of the Scriptures were ordered destroyed and laws were enforced with extreme cruelty. The oppressed Jews revolted, led by Judas the Maccabee.

THE ROMAN PERIOD
63 B.C.

In the year 63 B.C. Pompey, the Roman general, captured Jerusalem, and the provinces of Palestine became subject to Rome. The local government was entrusted part of the time to procurators who were appointed by the emperors. Herod the Great was ruler of all Palestine at the time of Christ's birth.

Rule of the Ptolemies of Egypt

Rule of the Seleucids of Syria

Hasmonean Dynasty

Herod the Great rules as king; subject to Rome

330	334-323 Alexander the Great conquers the East
320	330-328 Alexander's years of power
310	320 Ptolemy (I) Soter conquers Jerusalem
300	311 Seleucus conquers Babylon; Seleucid dynasty begins
290	
280	
270	
260	
250	
240	
230	226 Antiochus III (the Great) of Syria overpowers Palestine
220	223-187 Antiochus becomes Seleucid ruler of Syria
210	
200	
190	198 Antiochus defeats Egypt and gains control of Palestine
180	175-164 Antiochus (IV) Epiphanes rules Syria; Judaism is prohibited
170	167 Mattathias and his sons rebel against Antiochus Maccabean revolt begins
160	166-160 Judas Maccabeus's leadership
150	160-143 Jonathan is high priest
140	142 Tower of Jerusalem cleansed
130	142-134 Simon becomes high priest; establishes Hasmonean dynasty
120	134-104 John Hyrcanus enlarges the independent Jewish state
110	103 Aristobulus's rule
100	102-76 Alexander Janneus's rule
90	
80	
70	75-67 Rule of Salome Alexandra with Hyrcanus II as high priest
60	66-63 Battle between Aristobulus II and Hyrcanus II
50	63 Pompey invades Palestine; Roman rule begins
40	63-40 Hyrcanus II rules but is subject to Rome
30	40-37 Parthians conquer Jerusalem
20	37 Jerusalem besieged for six months
10	32 Herod defeated
	19 Herod's temple begun
	16 Herod visits Agrippa
10	4 Herod dies; Archelaus succeeds
20	
A.D. 30	

After more than a century of living in the land again, it was obvious that what the people were experiencing was anything but the messianic age. The temple and houses had been rebuilt, but Persia still had political domination over the people (Mal 1:8). Harvests were poor and locusts had eaten what was left (Mal 3:11). Little respect for the Law existed among the people and even the priests (Mal 1:6-14). Intermarriage and divorce were commonplace (Mal 2:10-16), and the loss of heart was evident, both in the people's tears (Mal 2:13) and their skepticism (Mal 1:2; 2:17; 3:1, 10). Malachi therefore writes in an attempt to alleviate this sense of hopelessness among the people that the kingdom would not be restored to Israel.

Assignment

- Please read Malachi 2–3.
- Please read "Rebuke of Seven Sins."

Rebuke of Seven Sins

Summary Statement for the Book

The Lord rebukes His backslidden people for their hypocrisy—answering their defensive questions, encouraging them to leave their sinful lifestyle and return to Him in preparation for the coming day of judgment and blessing.

The title of the book (a "burden," "oracle," or "revelation") indicates that the Lord was rebuking His people Israel through Malachi (Mal 1:1). God answered Israel's seven self-defensive questions to encourage the nation to leave its lifestyle of sin and return to Him (Mal 1:2–3:18):

1. When Israel questioned God's love, God affirmed that He had chosen Israel over its neighbor Edom, even while the people were living in rebellion, so that they would respond to His love despite His rebuke (Mal 1:2-5).

2. When Israel questioned how it had despised God, He proved it by presenting as evidence the priests who offered unacceptable Levitical offerings in disregard for the Law (Mal 1:6–2:9).

3. When Israel questioned why God rejected its offerings, God said it was because the people had divorced their fellow Israelites to intermarry with pagans. He exhorted His people to be faithful to their own marriage covenants (Mal 2:10-16).

4. When Israel questioned God's justice, God promised to send His messianic Messenger to judge the nation justly (Mal 2:17–3:7).

5. When Israel asked how it could repent, God said that they should quit robbing Him; this encouraged the people to think about *how* they might be doing just that (Mal 3:7-8).

6. When Israel questioned how it was robbing God, He explained that the people had withheld their tithes and offerings. He encouraged them to give again so that He could bless them (Mal 3:8-12).

7. When Israel questioned how it had blasphemed God, He revealed the nation's materialistic motives. He then promised security to the obedient who signed a scroll of remembrance, so that the nation would know that God distinguishes between the righteous and wicked (Mal 3:13-18).
